Global Issues 12/13
Twenty-Eighth Edition

EDITOR

Robert M. Jackson
California State University, Chico

Robert M. Jackson is a professor emeritus of political science and past dean of the School of Graduate, International and Sponsored Programs at California State University, Chico. In addition to teaching courses on third-world politics and globalization, he has published articles on the international political economy, international relations simulations, and political behavior. Dr. Jackson has been responsible for numerous international training programs for professionals from throughout the world. International educational exchanges and study-abroad programs also have been an area of special interest. His research and professional travels include China, Japan, Hong Kong, Taiwan, Singapore, Malaysia, Spain, Portugal, Morocco, Belgium, Germany, the Czech Republic, the Netherlands, Italy, Russia, Mexico, Guatemala, Honduras, Costa Rica, El Salvador, Brazil, Chile, and Argentina.

ANNUAL EDITIONS: GLOBAL ISSUES, TWENTY-EIGHTH EDITION

Published by McGraw-Hill, a business unit of The McGraw-Hill Companies, Inc., 1221 Avenue of the Americas, New York, NY 10020. Copyright © 2013 by The McGraw-Hill Companies, Inc. All rights reserved. Printed in the United States of America. Previous edition(s) © 2012, 2011, 2010, and 2009. No part of this publication may be reproduced or distributed in any form or by any means, or stored in a database or retrieval system, without the prior written consent of The McGraw-Hill Companies, Inc., including, but not limited to, in any network or other electronic storage or transmission, or broadcast for distance learning.

Some ancillaries, including electronic and print components, may not be available to customers outside the United States.

This book is printed on acid-free paper.

Annual Editions® is a registered trademark of The McGraw-Hill Companies, Inc.

Annual Editions is published by the **Contemporary Learning Series** group within the McGraw-Hill Higher Education division.

1 2 3 4 5 6 7 8 9 0 QDB/QDB 1 0 9 8 7 6 5 4 3 2

ISBN: 978-0-07-805118-0
MHID: 0-07-805118-5
ISSN: 1093-278X (print)
ISSN: 2158-4060 (online)

Managing Editor: *Larry Loeppke*
Developmental Editor: *Debra A. Henricks*
Permissions Coordinator: *Shirley Lanners*
Senior Marketing Communications Specialist: *Mary Klein*
Senior Project Manager: *Joyce Watters*
Design Coordinator: *Margarite Reynolds*
Cover Designer: *Studio Montage, St. Louis, Missouri*
Buyer: *Susan K. Culbertson*
Media Project Manager: *Sridevi Palani*

Compositor: Laserwords Private Limited
Cover Image Credits: Staff Sgt. Samuel Morse/US Air Force/DoD (inset); MC3 Alexander Tidd/US Navy (background)

Editors/Academic Advisory Board

Members of the Academic Advisory Board are instrumental in the final selection of articles for each edition of ANNUAL EDITIONS. Their review of articles for content, level, and appropriateness provides critical direction to the editors and staff. We think that you will find their careful consideration well reflected in this volume.

ANNUAL EDITIONS: Global Issues 12/13
28th Edition

EDITOR

Robert M. Jackson
California State University, Chico

ACADEMIC ADVISORY BOARD MEMBERS

Preface

The beginning of the new millennium was celebrated with considerable fanfare. The prevailing opinion in much of the world was that there was a great deal for which we could congratulate ourselves. The very act of sequentially watching on television live celebrations from one time zone to the next was proclaimed as a testimonial to globalization and the benefits of modern technology. The tragic events of September 11, 2001, however, were a stark reminder of the methods of destruction available to those determined to challenge the status quo. The subsequent wars in Afghanistan and Iraq, along with continuing acts of terror, have dampened the optimism that was expressed at the outset of the twenty-first century.

In the second decade of the twenty-first century, new challenges have risen to the top of the political agenda. Global climate change, growing pressure on the supply of oil, and the problem of nuclear weapons proliferation are among those most frequently discussed.

Although the mass media may focus on the latest crisis for a few weeks or months, the broad forces that are shaping the world are seldom given the in-depth analysis that they warrant. Scholarly research about these historic forces of change can be found in a wide variety of publications, but these are not readily accessible. In addition, students just beginning to study global issues can be discouraged by the terminology and abstract concepts that characterize much of the scholarly literature. In selecting and organizing the materials for this book, we have been mindful of the needs of beginning students and have, thus, selected articles that invite the student into the subject matter.

Each unit begins with an introductory article(s) providing a broad overview of the subject area to be studied. The following articles examine in more detail specific case studies that often identify the positive steps being taken to remedy problems. Recent events are a continual reminder that the world faces many serious challenges, the magnitude of which would discourage even the most stout-hearted individual. Although identifying problems is easier than solving them, it is encouraging to know that many are being addressed.

Perhaps the most striking feature of the study of contemporary global issues is the absence of any single, widely held theory that explains what is taking place. As a result, we have made a conscious effort to present a wide variety of points of view. The most important consideration has been to present global issues from an international perspective, rather than from a purely American or Western point of view. By encompassing materials originally published in different countries and written by authors of various nationalities, the anthology represents the great diversity of opinions that people hold. Two writers examining the same phenomenon may reach very different conclusions. It is not just a question of who is right or wrong, but rather understanding that people from different vantage points can have differing perspectives on an issue.

Another major consideration when organizing these materials is to explore the complex interrelationship of factors that produces social problems such as poverty. Too often, discussions of this problem (and others like it) are reduced to arguments about the fallacies of not following the correct economic policy or not having the correct form of government. As a result, many people overlook the interplay of historic, cultural, environmental, economic, and political factors that form complex webs that bring about many different problems. Every effort has been made to select materials that illustrate this complex interaction of factors, stimulating the beginning student to consider realistic rather than overly simplistic approaches to the pressing problems that threaten the existence of civilization.

In addition to an annotated *Table of Contents* and a *Topic Guide,* a list of *Internet References* that can be used to further explore topics addressed in the articles is provided.

Learning Outcomes for each unit are organized around two principles. The first: all the articles have a central point of view (usually identified in the opening paragraphs), which is supported by specific reasons and illustrated with examples. The articles typically conclude by reconsidering the point of view in terms of counterarguments, policy implications, and/or forecasts of the future. Basic comprehension of each article requires an understanding of the author's point of view and supporting reasons. In a number of cases, articles are paired to illustrate contending points of view so that the reader is aware of ongoing policy debates. The process of comparing and contrasting, therefore, requires a higher level of understanding beyond the comprehension of each article's content of and by itself.

The second principle is the interconnectedness of the units of the book. As identified in the introduction to Unit 1, the Allegory of the Balloon portrays the interconnectedness of the book's four organizing concepts. An ability to identify and articulate these connections is the second focus of the *Learning Outcomes.*

At the conclusion of each article, is a Critical Thinking section. This is comprised of a series of questions linked to the Learning Outcomes of each unit.

This is the twenty-eighth edition of *Annual Editions: Global Issues.* When looking back over more than a quarter century of work, a great deal has taken place in world affairs, and the contents and organization of the book reflect these changes. Nonetheless, there is one underlying constant. It is my continuing goal to work with the editors and staff at McGraw-Hill Contemporary Learning Series to provide materials that encourage the readers of this book to develop a lifelong appreciation of the complex and rapidly changing world in which we live. This collection of articles is an invitation to further explore the global issues of the twenty-first century and become personally involved in the great issues of our time.

Finally, materials in this book were selected for both their intellectual insights and readability. Timely and well-written materials should stimulate good classroom lectures and discussions. I hope that students and teachers will enjoy using this book.

Robert M. Jackson
Editor

The Annual Editions Series

VOLUMES AVAILABLE

Adolescent Psychology

Aging

American Foreign Policy

American Government

Anthropology

Archaeology

Assessment and Evaluation

Business Ethics

Child Growth and Development

Comparative Politics

Criminal Justice

Developing World

Drugs, Society, and Behavior

Dying, Death, and Bereavement

Early Childhood Education

Economics

Educating Children with Exceptionalities

Education

Educational Psychology

Entrepreneurship

Environment

The Family

Gender

Geography

Global Issues

Health

Homeland Security

Human Development

Human Resources

Human Sexualities

International Business

Management

Marketing

Mass Media

Microbiology

Multicultural Education

Nursing

Nutrition

Physical Anthropology

Psychology

Race and Ethnic Relations

Social Problems

Sociology

State and Local Government

Sustainability

Technologies, Social Media, and Society

United States History, Volume 1

United States History, Volume 2

Urban Society

Violence and Terrorism

Western Civilization, Volume 1

World History, Volume 1

World History, Volume 2

World Politics

Contents

UNIT 1
Global Issues in the Twenty-First Century: An Overview

1. **Global Trends 2025: A Transformed World: Executive Summary,** *U.S. National Intelligence Council,* November 2008

   This widely quoted report examines important **change factors** transforming the **international political system** from the structure established following WWII. The executive summary of the report is presented here.

2. **The New Geopolitics of Food,** Lester R. Brown, *Foreign Policy,* May/June 2011

   Lester Brown argues that both farmers and foreign ministers need to get ready for a new era of **world food scarcity**. He describes the reasons why the era of abundant food supplies has ended.

3. **Navigating the Energy Transition,** Michael T. Klare, *Current History,* January 2009

   The transition from the current **fossil fuel** energy system to one based largely on **renewables** will be **technically** difficult and filled with **political dangers.** The reasons for these difficulties are described.

4. **Asia's Rise: Rise and Fall,** Paul Kennedy, *The World Today,* August 2010

   The shift of **international power** toward Asia is analyzed in the context of the broader historical question of why nations gain and lose power. Kennedy argues that **economic growth** is the primary factor that provides the means to extend and defend power.

5. **China's Search for a Grand Strategy,** Wang Jisi, *Foreign Affairs,* March/April 2011

   The author, who is dean of the School of International Studies at Peking University, discusses China's growing influence in global affairs. Devising an effective **foreign policy** will not be easy for China as it simultaneously protects its core interests while pursuing rapid **economic development.**

The concepts in bold italics are developed in the article. For further expansion, please refer to the Topic Guide.

UNIT 2
Population and Food Production

UNIT 3
The Global Environment and Natural Resources Utilization

The concepts in bold italics are developed in the article. For further expansion, please refer to the Topic Guide.

UNIT 4
Political Economy

The concepts in bold italics are developed in the article. For further expansion, please refer to the Topic Guide.

The concepts in bold italics are developed in the article. For further expansion, please refer to the Topic Guide.

UNIT 5
Conflict

The concepts in bold italics are developed in the article. For further expansion, please refer to the Topic Guide.

UNIT 6
Cooperation

UNIT 7
Values and Visions

The concepts in bold italics are developed in the article. For further expansion, please refer to the Topic Guide.

The concepts in bold italics are developed in the article. For further expansion, please refer to the Topic Guide.

Correlation Guide

The *Annual Editions* series provides students with convenient, inexpensive access to current, carefully selected articles from the public press. **Annual Editions: Global Issues 12/13** is an easy-to-use reader that presents articles on important topics such as *population, environment, political economy,* and many more. For more information on *Annual Editions* and other *McGraw-Hill Contemporary Learning Series* titles, visit www.mhhe.com/cls.

This convenient guide matches the units in **Annual Editions: Global Issues 12/13** with the corresponding chapters in one of our best-selling McGraw-Hill Political Science textbooks by Rourke/Boyer.

Annual Editions: Global Issues 12/13	International Politics on the World Stage, Brief, 8/e by Rourke/Boyer
Unit 1: Global Issues in the Twenty-First Century: An Overview	**Chapter 1:** Thinking and Caring about World Politics **Chapter 2:** The Evolution of World Politics **Chapter 5:** Globalization: The Alternative Orientation
Unit 2: Population and Food Production	**Chapter 8:** International Law and Human Rights
Unit 3: The Global Environment and Natural Resources Utilization	**Chapter 12:** Preserving and Enhancing the Biosphere
Unit 4: Political Economy	**Chapter 6:** Power, Statecraft, and the National State: The Traditional Structure **Chapter 7:** Intergovernmental Organizations: Alternative Governance **Chapter 10:** National Economic Competition: The Traditional Road **Chapter 11:** International Economics: The Alternative Road
Unit 5: Conflict	**Chapter 6:** Power, Statecraft, and the National States: The Traditional Structure **Chapter 9:** Pursuing Security
Unit 6: Cooperation	**Chapter 8:** International Law and Human Rights **Chapter 11:** International Economics: The Alternative Road
Unit 7: Values and Visions	**Chapter 3:** Levels of Analysis and Foreign Policy **Chapter 8:** International Law and Human Rights

Topic Guide

This topic guide suggests how the selections in this book relate to the subjects covered in your course. You may want to use the topics listed on these pages to search the Web more easily.

On the following pages a number of websites have been gathered specifically for this book. They are arranged to reflect the units of this Annual Editions reader. You can link to these sites by going to www.mhhe.com/cls

All the articles that relate to each topic are listed below the bold-faced term.

Agriculture
1. Global Trends 2025: A Transformed World: Executive Summary
2. The New Geopolitics of Food
9. The Blue Food Revolution
12. The Big Melt
18. Can Extreme Poverty Be Eliminated?

Communication
16. It's a Flat World, After All
17. Why the World Isn't Flat
36. War in the Fifth Domain
42. Humanitarian Workers: Comprehensive Response

Conservation
2. The New Geopolitics of Food
3. Navigating the Energy Transition
9. The Blue Food Revolution
12. The Big Melt
13. Troubled Waters
14. Asian Carp, Other Invasive Species Make a Splash

Cultural Customs and Values
4. Asia's Rise: Rise and Fall
6. The New Population Bomb: The Four Megatrends That Will Change the World
7. Population and Sustainability
8. Why Migration Matters
15. Globalization and Its Contents
16. It's a Flat World, After All
17. Why the World Isn't Flat
18. Can Extreme Poverty Be Eliminated?
21. The Case against the West: America and Europe in the Asian Century
23. Supply and Demand: Human Trafficking in the Global Economy
34. Demystifying the Arab Spring: Parsing the Differences between Tunisia, Egypt, and Libya
38. Geneva Conventions
41. Is Bigger Better?
43. Humanity's Common Values: Seeking a Positive Future
45. UN Women's Head Michelle Bachelet: A New Superhero?
46. The End of Men

Demographics
1. Global Trends 2025: A Transformed World: Executive Summary
6. The New Population Bomb: The Four Megatrends That Will Change the World
7. Population and Sustainability
8. Why Migration Matters
40. The 30 Years War

Dependencies, International
4. Asia's Rise: Rise and Fall
8. Why Migration Matters
15. Globalization and Its Contents
16. It's a Flat World, After All
17. Why the World Isn't Flat
21. The Case against the West: America and Europe in the Asian Century
22. Bolivia and Its Lithium
23. Supply and Demand: Human Trafficking in the Global Economy

24. More Aid Is Not the Answer
25. It's Still the One

Development, Economic
1. Global Trends 2025: A Transformed World: Executive Summary
2. The New Geopolitics of Food
4. Asia's Rise: Rise and Fall
5. China's Search for a Grand Strategy
9. The Blue Food Revolution
15. Globalization and Its Contents
16. It's a Flat World, After All
17. Why the World Isn't Flat
18. Can Extreme Poverty Be Eliminated?
21. The Case against the West: America and Europe in the Asian Century
22. Bolivia and its Lithium
23. Supply and Demand: Human Trafficking in the Global Economy
24. More Aid Is Not the Answer
41. Is Bigger Better?

Development, Social
18. Can Extreme Poverty Be Eliminated?
21. The Case against the West: America and Europe in the Asian Century
33. Drug Violence Isn't Mexico's Only Problem
38. Geneva Conventions
40. The 30 Years War
41. Is Bigger Better?
42. Humanitarian Workers: Comprehensive Response
43. Humanity's Common Values: Seeking a Positive Future
44. Visible Man: Ethics in a World without Secrets
45. UN's Women's Head Michelle Bachelet: A New Superhero?
46. End of Men

Ecology
2. The New Geopolitics of Food
3. Navigating the Energy Transition
7. Population and Sustainability
9. The Blue Food Revolution
10. Climate Change
11. The Other Climate Changers
12. The Big Melt
13. Troubled Waters
14. Asian Carp, Other Invasive Species Make a Splash
16. It's a Flat World, After All
18. Can Extreme Poverty Be Eliminated?
27. The End of Easy Oil
29. Nuclear Power after Fukushima
37. Climate Change after Copenhagen: Beyond the Doom and Gloom

Economics
1. Global Trends 2025: A Transformed World: Executive Summary
2. The New Geopolitics of Food
3. Navigating the Energy Transition
4. Asia's Rise: Rise and Fall
9. The Blue Food Revolution
15. Globalization and Its Contents
16. It's a Flat World, After All
17. Why the World Isn't Flat
18. Can Extreme Poverty Be Eliminated?
19. Gazing Across the Divides

Internet References

The following Internet sites have been selected to support the articles found in this reader. These sites were available at the time of publication. However, because websites often change their structure and content, the information listed may no longer be available. We invite you to visit www.mhhe.com/cls for easy access to these sites.

Annual Editions: Global Issues 12/13

General Sources

U.S. Information Agency (USIA)
www.america.gov

USIA's home page provides definitions, related documentation, and discussions of topics of concern to students of global issues. The site addresses today's Hot Topics as well as ongoing issues that form the foundation of the field.

World Wide Web Virtual Library: International Affairs Resources
www.etown.edu/vl

Surf this site and its extensive links to learn about specific countries and regions, to research various think tanks and international organizations, and to study such vital topics as international law, development, the international economy, human rights, and peacekeeping.

UNIT 1: Global Issues in the Twenty-First Century: An Overview

The Henry L. Stimson Center
www.stimson.org

The Stimson Center, a nonpartisan organization, focuses on issues where policy, technology, and politics intersect. Use this site to find varying assessments of U.S. foreign policy in the post–Cold War world and to research other topics.

The Heritage Foundation
www.heritage.org

This page offers discussion about and links to many sites having to do with foreign policy and foreign affairs, including news and commentary, policy review, events, and a resource bank.

The North-South Institute
www.nsi-ins.ca/ensi/index.htm

Searching this site of the North-South Institute, which works to strengthen international development cooperation and enhance gender and social equity, will help you find information and debates on a variety of global issues.

UNIT 2: Population and Food Production

The Hunger Project
www.thp.org

Browse through this nonprofit organization's site, whose goal is the sustainable end to global hunger through leadership at all levels of society. The Hunger Project contends that the persistence of hunger is at the heart of the major security issues threatening our planet.

Penn Library: Resources by Subject
www.library.upenn.edu/cgi-bin/res/sr.cgi

This vast site is rich in links to information about subjects of interest to students of global issues. Its extensive population and demography resources address such concerns as migration, family planning, and health and nutrition in various world regions.

World Health Organization
www.who.int

This home page of the World Health Organization will provide you with links to a wealth of statistical and analytical information about health and the environment in the developing world.

WWW Virtual Library: Demography & Population Studies
http://demography.anu.edu.au/VirtualLibrary

A definitive guide to demography and population studies can be found at this site. It contains a multitude of important links to information about global poverty and hunger.

UNIT 3: The Global Environment and Natural Resources Utilization

National Geographic Society
www.nationalgeographic.com

This site provides links to material related to the atmosphere, the oceans, and other environmental topics.

National Oceanic and Atmospheric Administration (NOAA)
www.noaa.gov

Through this home page of NOAA, part of the U.S. Department of Commerce, you can find information about coastal issues, fisheries, climate, and more. The site provides many links to research materials and to other Web resources.

SocioSite: Sociological Subject Areas
www.pscw.uva.nl/sociosite/TOPICS

This huge site provides many references of interest to those interested in global issues, such as links to information on ecology and the impact of consumerism.

United Nations Environment Programme (UNEP)
www.unep.ch

Consult this home page of UNEP for links to critical topics of concern to students of global issues, including desertification, migratory species, and the impact of trade on the environment.

UNIT 4: Political Economy

Belfer Center for Science and International Affairs (BCSIA)
http://belfercenter.ksg.harvard.edu

BCSIA is the hub of Harvard University's John F. Kennedy School of Government's research, teaching, and training in international affairs related to security, environment, and technology.

U.S. Agency for International Development
www.usaid.gov

Broad and overlapping issues such as democracy, population and health, economic growth, and development are covered on this website. It provides specific information about different regions and countries.

Internet References

The World Bank Group
www.worldbank.org

News, press releases, summaries of new projects, speeches, publications, and coverage of numerous topics regarding development, countries, and regions are provided at this World Bank site. It also contains links to other important global financial organizations.

UNIT 5: Conflict

DefenseLINK
www.defenselink.mil

Learn about security news and research-related publications at this U.S. Department of Defense site. Links to related sites of interest are provided. The information systems BosniaLINK and GulfLINK can also be found here. Use the search function to investigate such issues as land mines.

Federation of American Scientists (FAS)
www.fas.org

FAS, a nonprofit policy organization, maintains this site to provide coverage of and links to such topics as global security, peace, and governance in the post–Cold War world. It notes a variety of resources of value to students of global issues.

ISN International Relations and Security Network
www.isn.ethz.ch

This site, maintained by the Center for Security Studies and Conflict Research, is a clearinghouse for information on international relations and security policy. Topics are listed by category (Traditional Dimensions of Security, New Dimensions of Security, and Related Fields) and by major world region.

The NATO Integrated Data Service (NIDS)
www.nato.int/structur/nids/nids.htm

NIDS was created to bring information on security-related matters to within easy reach of the widest possible audience. Check out this website to review North Atlantic Treaty Organization documentation of all kinds, to read *NATO Review,* and to explore key issues in the field of European security and transatlantic cooperation.

UNIT 6: Cooperation

Carnegie Endowment for International Peace
www.ceip.org

An important goal of this organization is to stimulate discussion and learning among both experts and the public at large on a wide range of international issues. The site provides links to *Foreign Policy,* to the Moscow Center, to descriptions of various programs, and much more.

OECD/FDI Statistics
www.oecd.org/statistics

Explore world trade and investment trends and statistics on this site from the Organization for Economic Cooperation and Development. It provides links to many related topics and addresses the issues on a country-by-country basis.

U.S. Institute of Peace
www.usip.org

USIP, which was created by the U.S. Congress to promote peaceful resolution of international conflicts, seeks to educate people and to disseminate information on how to achieve peace. Click on Highlights, Publications, Events, Research Areas, and Library and Links.

UNIT 7: Values and Visions

Human Rights Web
www.hrweb.org

The history of the human rights movement, text on seminal figures, landmark legal and political documents, and ideas on how individuals can get involved in helping to protect human rights around the world can be found at this valuable site.

InterAction
www.interaction.org

InterAction encourages grassroots action and engages government policymakers on advocacy issues. The organization's Advocacy Committee provides this site to inform people on its initiatives to expand international humanitarian relief, refugee, and development-assistance programs.

World Map

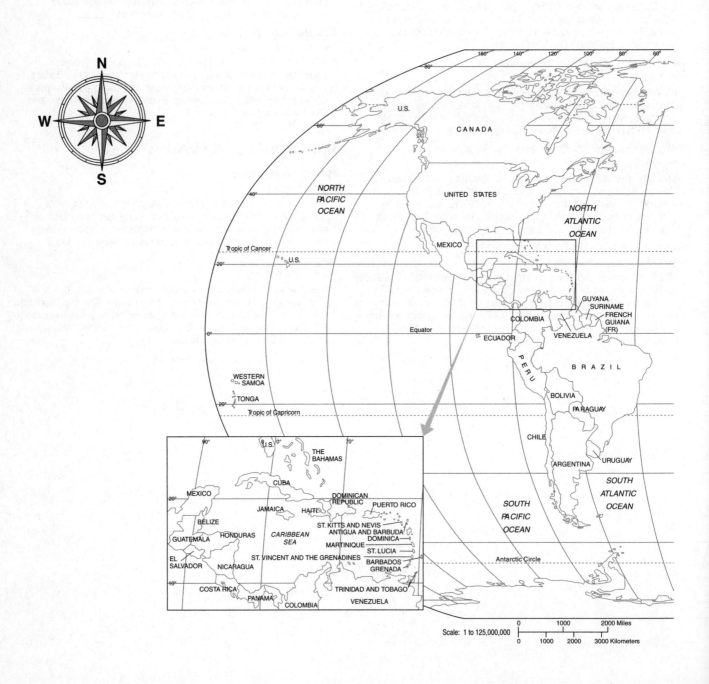

N

W   E

S

80°

160° 140° 120° 100° 80° 60°

U.S.

CANADA

60°

40°

NORTH
PACIFIC
OCEAN

UNITED STATES

NORTH
ATLANTIC
OCEAN

Tropic of Cancer

MEXICO

20°

U.S.

GUYANA
SURINAME
FRENCH
GUIANA
(FR)

COLOMBIA

Equator

0°

ECUADOR

VENEZUELA

P
E
R
U

B R A Z I L

WESTERN
SAMOA

BOLIVIA

TONGA

20°

PARAGUAY

Tropic of Capricorn

CHILE

URUGUAY

ARGENTINA

SOUTH
ATLANTIC
OCEAN

SOUTH
PACIFIC
OCEAN

Antarctic Circle

90°

0°

70°

U.S.

THE
BAHAMAS

CUBA

MEXICO

20°

DOMINICAN
REPUBLIC

PUERTO RICO

JAMAICA

HAITI

BELIZE

ST. KITTS AND NEVIS
ANTIGUA AND BARBUDA
DOMINICA

GUATEMALA

HONDURAS

CARIBBEAN
SEA

MARTINIQUE

ST. LUCIA

EL
SALVADOR

NICARAGUA

ST. VINCENT AND THE GRENADINES

BARBADOS
GRENADA

10°

COSTA RICA

TRINIDAD AND TOBAGO

PANAMA

COLOMBIA

VENEZUELA

Scale: 1 to 125,000,000

0   1000   2000 Miles

0   1000   2000   3000 Kilometers

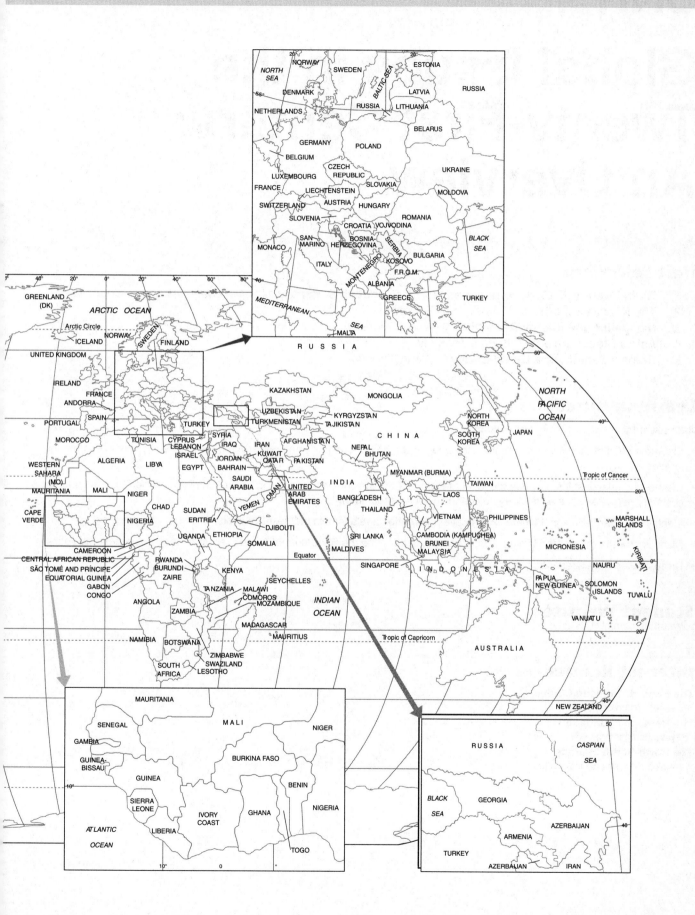

UNIT 1

Global Issues in the Twenty-First Century: An Overview

Unit Selections

Learning Outcomes

After reading this Unit, you will be able to:

- Elaborate each of the four components of the Allegory of the Balloon (e.g., natural resources) with specific examples from the articles.

- Discuss the relationships between the four categories of the allegory with examples from each of the articles (e.g., the increasing costs of energy resource extraction and changing social structures).

- Identify key change factors that are likely to alter international relations in the next fifty years.

- Discuss how the roles of the United States, Europe, Japan, and the BRIC countries are likely to change in the next fifty years.

- Discuss alternative scenarios of the future.

Student Website
www.mhhe.com/cls

Internet References

The Henry L. Stimson Center
www.stimson.org
The Heritage Foundation
www.heritage.org
The North-South Institute
www.nsi-ins.ca/ensi/index.htm

Imagine yellow paint being brushed onto an inflated, clear balloon. The yellow color, for purposes of this allegory, represents "people." In many ways the study of global issues is first and foremost the study of people. Today, there are more human beings occupying Earth than ever before. In addition, we are in the midst of a period of unprecedented population growth. Not only are there many countries where the majority of people are under age 16, but also due to improved health care, there are a greater number of older people alive today than ever before. The effect of a growing global population, however, goes beyond sheer numbers, for this trend has unprecedented impacts on natural resources and social services. An examination of population trends and the related topic of food production is a good place to begin an in-depth study of global issues.

Imagine that our fictional artist next dips the brush into a container of blue paint to represent "nature." The natural world plays an important role in setting the international agenda. Shortages of raw materials, climate change, regional droughts, and pollution of waterways are just a few examples of how natural resources can have global implications.

Adding blue paint to the balloon reveals one of the most important underlying concepts found in this book. Although the balloon originally was covered by both yellow and blue paint (people and nature as separate conceptual entities), the two combined produce an entirely different color: green. Talking about nature as a separate entity or people as though they were somehow removed from the forces of the natural world is a serious intellectual error. The people–nature relationship is one of the keys to understanding many of today's most important global issues.

The third color to be added to the balloon is red. This color represents social structures. Factors falling into this category include whether a society is urban or rural, industrial or agrarian, and consumer oriented or dedicated to the needs of the state. The relationship between this component and the others is extremely important. The impact of political decisions on the environment, for example, is one of the most significant features of the contemporary world. Will the whales or bald eagles survive? Historically, the forces of nature determined which species survived or perished. Today, survival depends on political decisions or indecision. Understanding the complex relationship between social structure and nature (known as ecopolitics) is central to the study of global issues.

Added to the three primary colors is the fourth and final color of white. It represents the "meta" component (i.e., those qualities that make human beings different from other life forms). These include new ideas and inventions, culture and values, religion and spirituality, and art and literature. The addition of the white paint immediately changes the intensity and shade of the mixture of colors, again emphasizing the relationship among all four factors.

If the painter continues to ply the paintbrush over the miniature globe, a marbling effect becomes evident. From one area to the next, the shading varies because one element is more dominant than another. Further, the miniature system appears dynamic.

© Digital Vision/PunchStock

Nothing is static; relationships are continually changing. This leads to a number of important insights: (1) There are no such things as separate elements, only connections or relationships; (2) changes in one area (such as the climate) will result in changes in all other areas; and (3) complex and dynamic relationships make it difficult to predict events accurately, so observers and policy makers are often surprised by unexpected events.

This book is organized along the basic lines of the balloon allegory. The first unit provides a broad overview of a variety of perspectives on the major forces that are shaping the world of the twenty-first century. From this "big picture" perspective, more in-depth analyses follow. Unit 2, for example, focuses on population and food production. Unit 3 examines the environment and related natural resource issues. The next three units look at different aspects of the world's social structures. They explore issues of economics, national security, conflict, and international cooperation. In the final unit, a number of "meta" factors are presented.

The reader should keep in mind that, just as it was impossible to keep the individual colors from blending into new colors on the balloon, it is also impossible to separate global issues into discrete chapters in a book. Any discussion of agriculture, for example, must take into account the impact of a growing population on soil and water resources, as well as new scientific breakthroughs in food production. Therefore, the organization of this book focuses attention on issue areas; it does not mean to imply that these factors are somehow separate.

With the collapse of the Soviet empire and the end of the Cold War, the outlines of a new global agenda have emerged. Rather than being based on the ideology and interests of the two superpowers, new political, economic, environmental, cultural, and security issues are interacting in an unprecedented fashion. Rapid population growth, environmental decline, uneven economic progress, and global terrorist networks are all parts of a complex state of affairs for which there is no historic parallel. In the second decade of the twenty-first century, signs abound that we are entering a new era. In the words of Abraham Lincoln, "As our case is new, so we must think anew." Compounding this situation, however, is a whole series of old problems such as ethnic and religious rivalries.

The authors in this first unit provide a variety of perspectives on the trends that they believe are the most important in understanding the historic changes at work. This discussion is then pursued in greater detail in the following units.

Global Trends 2025: A Transformed World

Executive Summary

U.S. NATIONAL INTELLIGENCE COUNCIL

The **international system**—as constructed following the Second World War—will be almost unrecognizable by 2025 owing to the rise of emerging powers, a globalizing economy, a historic transfer of relative wealth and economic power from West to East, and the growing influence of nonstate actors. By 2025, the international system will be a **global multipolar one** with gaps in national power[1] continuing to narrow between developed and developing countries. Concurrent with the shift in power among nation-states, the relative power of various nonstate actors—including businesses, tribes, religious organizations, and criminal networks—is increasing. The players are changing, but so too are the scope and breadth of transnational issues important for continued global prosperity. Aging populations in the developed world; growing energy, food, and water constraints; and worries about climate change will limit and diminish what will still be an historically unprecedented age of prosperity.

Historically, emerging multipolar systems have been more unstable than bipolar or unipolar ones. Despite the recent financial volatility—which could end up accelerating many ongoing trends—we do not believe that we are headed toward a complete breakdown of the international system, as occurred in 1914–1918 when an earlier phase of globalization came to a halt. However, the next 20 years of transition to a new system are fraught with risks. Strategic rivalries are most likely to revolve around trade, investments, and technological innovation and acquisition, but we cannot rule out a 19th century-like scenario of arms races, territorial expansion, and military rivalries.

This is a story with **no clear outcome,** as illustrated by a series of vignettes we use to map out divergent futures. Although the United States is likely to remain the single most powerful actor, the United States' relative strength—even in the military realm—will decline and U.S. leverage will become more constrained. At the same time, the extent to which other actors—both state and nonstate—will be willing or able to shoulder increased burdens is unclear. Policymakers and publics will have to cope with a growing demand for multilateral cooperation when the international system will be stressed by the incomplete transition from the old to a still-forming new order.

Economic Growth Fueling Rise of Emerging Players

In terms of size, speed, and directional flow, the transfer of **global wealth and economic power** now under way—roughly from West to East—is without precedent in modern history. This shift derives from two sources. First, increases in oil and commodity prices have generated windfall profits for the Gulf states and Russia. Second, lower costs combined with government policies have shifted the locus of manufacturing and some service industries to Asia.

Growth projections for Brazil, Russia, India, and China (the BRICs) indicate they will collectively match the original G-7's share of global GDP by 2040–2050. **China** is poised to have more impact on the world over the next 20 years than any other country. If current trends persist, by 2025 China will have the world's second largest economy and will be a leading military power. It also could be the largest importer of natural resources and the biggest polluter. **India** probably will continue to enjoy relatively rapid economic growth and will strive for a multipolar world in which New Delhi is one of the poles. China and India must decide the extent to which they are willing and capable of playing increasing global roles and how each will relate to the other. **Russia** has the potential to be richer, more powerful, and more self-assured in 2025 if it invests in human capital, expands and diversifies its economy, and integrates with global markets. On the other hand, Russia could experience a significant decline if it fails to take these steps and oil and gas prices remain in the $50–70 per barrel range. No other countries are projected to rise to the level of China, India, or Russia, and none is likely to match their individual global clout. We expect, however, to see the political and economic power of other countries—such as Indonesia, Iran, and Turkey—increase.

For the most part, China, India, and Russia are not following the Western liberal model for self-development but instead are using a different model, "**state capitalism.**" State capitalism is a loose term used to describe a system of economic management that gives a prominent role to the state. Other rising powers—South Korea, Taiwan, and Singapore—also used state capitalism to develop their economies. However, the impact of Russia, and particularly China, following this path is potentially much greater owing to their size and approach to "democratization." We remain optimistic about the *long-term* prospects for **greater democratization,** even though advances are likely to be slow and globalization is subjecting many recently democratized countries to increasing social and economic pressures with the potential to undermine liberal institutions.

Many other countries will fall further behind economically. **Sub-Saharan Africa** will remain the region most vulnerable to economic disruption, population stresses, civil conflict, and political instability. Despite increased global demand for commodities for which Sub-Saharan Africa will be a major supplier, local populations are unlikely to experience significant economic gain. Windfall profits arising from sustained increases in commodity prices might further entrench corrupt or otherwise ill-equipped governments in several regions, diminishing the prospects for democratic and market-based reforms. Although many of **Latin America's** major countries will have become middle income powers by 2025, others, particularly those such as Venezuela and Bolivia that have embraced populist policies for a protracted period, will lag behind—and some, such as Haiti, will have become even poorer and less governable. Overall, Latin America will continue to lag behind Asia and other fast-growing areas in terms of economic competitiveness.

Asia, Africa, and Latin America will account for virtually all **population growth** over the next 20 years; less than 3 percent of the growth will occur in the West. Europe and Japan will continue to far outdistance the emerging powers of China and India in per capita wealth, but they will struggle to maintain robust growth rates because the size of their working-age populations will decrease. The US will be a partial exception to the aging of populations in the developed world because it will experience higher birth rates and more immigration. The number of migrants seeking to move from disadvantaged to relatively privileged countries is likely to increase.

The number of countries with youthful age structures in the current "arc of instability" is projected to decline by as much as 40 percent. Three of every four youth-bulge countries that remain will be located in Sub-Saharan Africa; nearly all of the remainder will be located in the core of the Middle East, scattered through southern and central Asia, and in the Pacific Islands.

New Transnational Agenda

Resource issues will gain prominence on the international agenda. Unprecedented global economic growth—positive in so many other regards—will continue to put pressure on a number of **highly strategic resources,** including energy, food, and water, and demand is projected to outstrip easily available supplies over the next decade or so. For example, non-OPEC liquid hydrocarbon production—crude oil, natural gas liquids, and unconventionals such as tar sands—will not grow commensurate with demand. Oil and gas production of many traditional energy producers already is declining. Elsewhere—in China, India, and Mexico—production has flattened. Countries capable of significantly expanding production will dwindle; oil and gas production will be concentrated in unstable areas. As a result of this and other factors, the world will be in the midst of a fundamental energy transition away from oil toward natural gas, coal and other alternatives.

The World Bank estimates that **demand for food** will rise by 50 percent by 2030, as a result of growing world population, rising affluence, and the shift to Western dietary preferences by a larger middle class. Lack of access to stable supplies of water is reaching critical proportions, particularly for agricultural purposes, and the problem will worsen because of rapid urbanization worldwide and the roughly 1.2 billion persons to be added over the next 20 years. Today, experts consider 21 countries, with a combined population of about 600 million, to be either cropland or freshwater scarce. Owing to continuing population growth, 36 countries, with about 1.4 billion people, are projected to fall into this category by 2025.

Climate change is expected to exacerbate resource scarcities. Although the impact of climate change will vary by region, a number of regions will begin to suffer harmful effects, particularly water scarcity and loss of agricultural production. Regional differences in agricultural production are likely to become more pronounced over time with declines disproportionately concentrated in developing countries, particularly those in Sub-Saharan Africa. Agricultural losses are expected to mount with substantial impacts forecast by most economists by late this century. For many developing countries, decreased agricultural output will be devastating because agriculture accounts for a large share of their economies and many of their citizens live close to subsistence levels.

New technologies could again provide solutions, such as viable alternatives to fossil fuels or means to overcome food and water constraints. However, all current technologies are inadequate for replacing the traditional energy architecture on the scale needed, and new energy technologies probably will not be commercially viable and widespread by 2025. The pace of technological innovation will be key. Even with a favorable policy and funding environment for biofuels, clean coal, or hydrogen, the transition to new fuels will be slow. Major technologies historically have had an "adoption lag." In the energy sector, a recent study found that it takes an average of 25 years for a new production technology to become widely adopted.

Despite what are seen as long odds now, we cannot rule out the possibility of an **energy transition** by 2025 that would avoid the costs of an energy infrastructure overhaul. The greatest possibility for a relatively quick and inexpensive transition during the period comes from better renewable generation sources (photovoltaic and wind) and improvements in battery technology. With many of these technologies, the infrastructure cost hurdle for individual projects would be lower, enabling many small economic actors to develop their own energy transformation projects that directly serve their interests—e.g., stationary fuel cells powering homes and offices, recharging plug-in hybrid autos, and selling energy back to the grid. Also, energy conversion schemes—such as plans to generate hydrogen for automotive fuel cells from electricity in the homeowner's garage—could avoid the need to develop complex hydrogen transportation infrastructure.

Prospects for Terrorism, Conflict, and Proliferation

Terrorism, proliferation, and conflict will remain key concerns even as resource issues move up on the international agenda. Terrorism is unlikely to disappear by 2025, but its appeal could diminish if economic growth continues and youth unemployment is mitigated in the Middle East. Economic opportunities for youth and greater political pluralism probably would dissuade some from joining terrorists' ranks, but others—motivated by a variety of factors, such as a desire for revenge or to become "martyrs"—will continue to turn to violence to pursue their objectives.

In the absence of employment opportunities and legal means for political expression, conditions will be ripe for disaffection, growing radicalism, and possible recruitment of youths into **terrorist groups.** Terrorist groups in 2025 will likely be a combination of descendants of long-established groups—that inherit organizational structures, command and control processes, and training procedures necessary to conduct sophisticated attacks—and newly emergent collections of the angry and disenfranchised that become self-radicalized. For those terrorist groups that are active in 2025, the diffusion of technologies and scientific knowledge will place some of the world's most dangerous capabilities within their reach. One of our greatest concerns continues to be that terrorist or other malevolent groups might acquire and employ biological agents, or less likely, a nuclear device, to create mass casualties.

Although **Iran's** acquisition of nuclear weapons is not inevitable, other countries' worries about a nuclear-armed Iran could lead states in the region to develop new security arrangements with external powers, acquire additional weapons, and consider pursuing their own nuclear ambitions. It is not clear that the type of stable deterrent relationship that existed between the great powers for most of the Cold War would emerge naturally in the Middle East with a nuclear-weapons capable Iran. Episodes of low-intensity conflict taking place under a nuclear umbrella could lead to an unintended escalation and broader conflict if clear red lines between those states involved are not well established.

We believe **ideological conflicts** akin to the Cold War are unlikely to take root in a world in which most states will be preoccupied with the pragmatic challenges of globalization and shifting global power alignments. The force of ideology is likely to be strongest in the Muslim world—particularly the Arab core. In those countries that are likely to struggle with youth bulges and weak economic underpinnings—such as Pakistan, Afghanistan, Nigeria, and Yemen—the radical Salafi trend of Islam is likely to gain traction.

Types of **conflict** we have not seen for awhile—such as over resources—could reemerge. Perceptions of energy scarcity will drive countries to take actions to assure their future access to energy supplies. In the worst case, this could result in interstate conflicts if government leaders deem assured access to energy resources, for example, to be essential for maintaining domestic stability and the survival of their regimes. However, even actions short of war will have important geopolitical consequences. Maritime security concerns are providing a rationale for naval buildups and modernization efforts, such as China's and India's development of blue-water naval capabilities. The buildup of regional naval capabilities could lead to increased tensions, rivalries, and counterbalancing moves but it also will create opportunities for multinational cooperation in protecting critical sea lanes. With water becoming more scarce in Asia and the Middle East, cooperation to manage changing water resources is likely to become more difficult within and between states.

The risk of **nuclear weapon use** over the next 20 years, although remaining very low, is likely to be greater than it is today as a result of several converging trends. The spread of nuclear technologies and expertise is generating concerns about the potential emergence of new nuclear weapon states and the acquisition of nuclear materials by terrorist groups. Ongoing low-intensity clashes between India and Pakistan continue to raise the specter that such events could escalate to a broader conflict between those nuclear powers. The possibility of a future disruptive regime change or collapse occurring in a nuclear weapon state such as North Korea also continues to raise questions regarding the ability of weak states to control and secure their nuclear arsenals.

If nuclear weapons are used in the next 15–20 years, the international system will be shocked as it experiences immediate humanitarian, economic, and political-military repercussions. A future use of nuclear weapons probably would bring about significant geopolitical changes as some states would seek to establish or reinforce security alliances with existing nuclear powers and others would push for global nuclear disarmament.

A More Complex International System

The trend toward greater diffusion of authority and power that has been occurring for a couple decades is likely to accelerate because of the emergence of new global players, the worsening institutional deficit, potential expansion of regional blocs, and enhanced strength of nonstate actors and networks. The **multiplicity of actors** on the international scene could add strength—in terms of filling gaps left by aging post-World War II institutions—or further fragment the international system and incapacitate international cooperation. The diversity in type of actor raises the likelihood of fragmentation occurring over the next two decades, particularly given the wide array of transnational challenges facing the international community.

The rising BRIC powers are unlikely to challenge the international system as did Germany and Japan in the 19th and 20th centuries, but because of their growing geopolitical and economic clout, they will have a high degree of freedom to customize their political and economic policies rather than fully adopting Western norms. They also are likely to want to preserve their policy freedom to maneuver, allowing others to carry the primary burden for dealing with such issues as terrorism, climate change, proliferation, and energy security.

Existing multilateral institutions—which are large and cumbersome and were designed for a different geopolitical order—will have difficulty adapting quickly to undertake new missions, accommodate changing memberships, and augment their resources.

Nongovernmental organizations (NGOs)—concentrating on specific issues—increasingly will be a part of the landscape, but NGO networks are likely to be limited in their ability to effect change in the absence of concerted efforts by multilateral institutions or governments. Efforts at greater inclusiveness—to reflect the emergence of the newer powers—may make it harder for international organizations to tackle transnational challenges. Respect for the dissenting views of member nations will continue to shape the agenda of organizations and limit the kinds of solutions that can be attempted.

Greater **Asian regionalism**—possible by 2025—would have global implications, sparking or reinforcing a trend toward three trade and financial clusters that could become quasi-blocs: North America, Europe, and East Asia. Establishment of such quasi-blocs would have implications for the ability to achieve future global World Trade Organization (WTO) agreements. Regional clusters could compete in setting trans-regional product standards for information technology, biotechnology, nanotechnology, intellectual property rights, and other aspects of the "new economy." On the other hand, an absence of regional cooperation in Asia could help spur competition among China, India, and Japan over resources such as energy.

Intrinsic to the growing complexity of the overlapping roles of states, institutions, and nonstate actors is the **proliferation of political identities,** which is leading to establishment of new networks and rediscovered communities. No one political identity is likely to be dominant in most societies by 2025. Religion-based networks may be quintessential issue networks and overall may play a more powerful role on many transnational issues such as the environment and inequalities than secular groupings.

The United States: Less Dominant Power

By 2025 the US will find itself as one of a number of important actors on the world stage, albeit still the most powerful one. Even in the military realm, where the US will continue to possess considerable advantages in 2025, advances by others in science and technology, expanded adoption of irregular warfare tactics by both state and nonstate actors, proliferation of long-range precision weapons, and growing use of cyber warfare attacks increasingly will constrict US freedom of action. A more constrained US role has implications for others and the likelihood of new agenda issues being tackled effectively. Despite the recent rise in anti-Americanism, the US probably will continue to be seen as a much-needed regional balancer in the Middle East and Asia. The US will continue to be expected to play a significant role in using its military power to counter global terrorism. On newer security issues like climate change, US leadership will be widely perceived as critical to leveraging competing and divisive views to find solutions. At the same time, the multiplicity of influential actors and distrust of vast power means less room for the US to call the shots without the support of strong partnerships. Developments in the rest of the world, including internal developments in a number of key states—particularly China and Russia—are also likely to be crucial determinants of US policy.

2025—What Kind of Future?

The above trends suggest major **discontinuities,** shocks, and surprises, which we highlight throughout the text. Examples include nuclear weapons use or a pandemic. In some cases, the surprise element is only a matter of **timing:** an energy transition, for example, is inevitable; the only questions are when and how abruptly or smoothly such a transition occurs. An energy transition from one type of fuel (fossil fuels) to another (alternative) is an event that historically has only happened once a century at most with momentous consequences. The transition from wood to coal helped trigger industrialization. In this case, a transition—particularly an abrupt one—out of fossil fuels would have major repercussions for energy producers in the Middle East and Eurasia, potentially causing permanent decline of some states as global and regional powers.

Other discontinuities are less predictable. They are likely to result from an interaction of several trends and depend on the quality of leadership. We put uncertainties such as whether China or Russia becomes a democracy in this category. China's growing middle class increases the chances but does not make such a development inevitable. Political pluralism seems less likely in Russia in the absence of economic diversification. Pressure from below may force the issue, or a leader might begin or enhance the democratization process to sustain the economy or spur economic growth. A sustained plunge in the price of oil and gas would alter the outlook and increase prospects for greater political and economic liberalization in Russia. If either country were to democratize, it would represent another wave of democratization with wide significance for many other developing states.

Also **uncertain** are the outcomes of demographic challenges facing Europe, Japan, and even Russia. In none of these cases does demography have to spell destiny with less regional and global power an inevitable outcome. Technology, the role of immigration, public health improvements, and laws encouraging greater female participation in the economy are some of the measures that could change the trajectory of current trends pointing toward less economic growth, increased social tensions, and possible decline.

Whether global institutions adapt and revive—another key uncertainty—also is a function of leadership. Current trends suggest a dispersion of power and authority will create a global governance deficit. Reversing those trend lines would require strong leadership in the international community by a number of powers, including the emerging ones.

Some uncertainties would have greater consequences—should they occur—than would others. In this work, we emphasize the overall potential for greater conflict—some forms of which could threaten globalization. We put WMD terrorism and a Middle East nuclear arms race in this category. In the four fictionalized scenarios, we have highlighted new challenges that could emerge as a result of the ongoing global transformation. They present new situations, dilemmas, or predicaments that represent departures from recent developments. As a set, they do not cover all possible futures. *None of these is inevitable or even necessarily likely;* but, as with many other uncertainties, the scenarios are potential game-changers.

- In *A World Without the West,* the new powers supplant the West as the leaders on the world stage.
- *October Surprise* illustrates the impact of inattention to global climate change; unexpected major impacts narrow the world's range of options.
- In *BRICs' Bust-Up,* disputes over vital resources emerge as a source of conflict between major powers—in this case two emerging heavyweights—India and China.
- In *Politics Is Not Always Local,* nonstate networks emerge to set the international agenda on the environment, eclipsing governments.

Note

1. National power scores, computed by the International Futures computer model, are the product of an index combining the weighted factors of GDP, defense spending, population, and technology.

Critical Thinking

1. What is the authors' point of view, which is the basis of this article?
2. What reasons are given to support this point of view?
3. Who are the so-called BRIC countries?
4. What is meant by state capitalism?
5. What is the new transnational agenda?
6. In addition to nation-states (i.e., countries), who are some of the new international actors?
7. Are there plausible scenarios of the future that have been left out?
8. In the "note" at the end of the article, the variables are identified that comprise the National Power Score. Assess the centrality of these variables to predicting the future and identify other variables that may have been omitted. Note: this assessment reveals a general outline of your international relations theory. Is it similar or different from the theory underlying the analysis presented in this article?

From *Atlantic Council,* November 2008, pp. vi–xiii.

The New Geopolitics of Food

From the Middle East to Madagascar, high prices are spawning land grabs and ousting dictators. Welcome to the 21st-century food wars.

LESTER R. BROWN

In the United States, when world wheat prices rise by 75 percent, as they have over the last year, it means the difference between a $2 loaf of bread and a loaf costing maybe $2.10. If, however, you live in New Delhi, those skyrocketing costs really matter: A doubling in the world price of wheat actually means that the wheat you carry home from the market to hand-grind into flour for chapatis costs twice as much. And the same is true with rice. If the world price of rice doubles, so does the price of rice in your neighborhood market in Jakarta. And so does the cost of the bowl of boiled rice on an Indonesian family's dinner table.

Welcome to the new food economics of 2011: Prices are climbing, but the impact is not at all being felt equally. For Americans, who spend less than one-tenth of their income in the supermarket, the soaring food prices we've seen so far this year are an annoyance, not a calamity. But for the planet's poorest 2 billion people, who spend 50 to 70 percent of their income on food, these soaring prices may mean going from two meals a day to one. Those who are barely hanging on to the lower rungs of the global economic ladder risk losing their grip entirely. This can contribute—and it has—to revolutions and upheaval.

Already in 2011, the U.N. Food Price Index has eclipsed its previous all-time global high; as of March it had climbed for eight consecutive months. With this year's harvest predicted to fall short, with governments in the Middle East and Africa teetering as a result of the price spikes, and with anxious markets sustaining one shock after another, food has quickly become the hidden driver of world politics. And crises like these are going to become increasingly common. The new geopolitics of food looks a whole lot more volatile—and a whole lot more contentious—than it used to. Scarcity is the new norm.

Until recently, sudden price surges just didn't matter as much, as they were quickly followed by a return to the relatively low food prices that helped shape the political stability of the late 20th century across much of the globe. But now both the causes and consequences are ominously different.

In many ways, this is a resumption of the 2007–2008 food crisis, which subsided not because the world somehow came together to solve its grain crunch once and for all, but because the Great Recession tempered growth in demand even as favorable weather helped farmers produce the largest grain harvest on record. Historically, price spikes tended to be almost exclusively driven by unusual weather—a monsoon failure in India, a drought in the former Soviet Union, a heat wave in the U.S. Midwest. Such events were always disruptive, but thankfully infrequent. Unfortunately, today's price hikes are driven by trends that are both elevating demand and making it more difficult to increase production: among them, a rapidly expanding population, crop-withering temperature increases, and irrigation wells running dry. Each night, there are 219,000 additional people to feed at the global dinner table.

More alarming still, the world is losing its ability to soften the effect of shortages. In response to previous price surges, the United States, the world's largest grain producer, was effectively able to steer the world away from potential catastrophe. From the mid-20th century until 1995, the United States had either grain surpluses or idle cropland that could be planted to rescue countries in trouble. When the Indian monsoon failed in 1965, for example, President Lyndon Johnson's administration shipped one-fifth of the U.S. wheat crop to India, successfully staving off famine. We can't do that anymore; the safety cushion is gone.

That's why the food crisis of 2011 is for real, and why it may bring with it yet more bread riots cum political revolutions. What if the upheavals that greeted dictators Zine el-Abidine Ben Ali in Tunisia, Hosni Mubarak in Egypt, and Muammar al-Qaddafi in Libya (a country that imports 90 percent of its grain) are not the end of the story, but the beginning of it? Get ready, farmers and foreign ministers alike, for a new era in which world food scarcity increasingly shapes global politics.

The doubling of world grain prices since early 2007 has been driven primarily by two factors: accelerating growth in demand and the increasing difficulty of rapidly expanding production. The result is a world that looks strikingly different from the bountiful global grain economy of the last century. What will the geopolitics of food look like in a new era dominated by scarcity? Even at this early stage, we can see at least the broad outlines of the emerging food economy.

On the demand side, farmers now face clear sources of increasing pressure. The first is population growth. Each year the world's farmers must feed 80 million additional people, nearly all of them in developing countries. The world's population has nearly doubled since 1970 and is headed toward 9 billion by midcentury. Some 3 billion people, meanwhile, are also trying to move up the food chain, consuming more meat, milk, and eggs. As more families in China and elsewhere enter the middle class, they expect to eat better. But as global consumption of grain-intensive livestock products climbs, so does the demand for the extra corn and soybeans needed to feed all that livestock. (Grain consumption per person in the United States, for example, is four times that in India, where little grain is converted into animal protein. For now.)

At the same time, the United States, which once was able to act as a global buffer of sorts against poor harvests elsewhere, is now converting massive quantities of grain into fuel for cars, even as world grain consumption, which is already up to roughly 2.2 billion metric tons per year, is growing at an accelerating rate. A decade ago, the growth in consumption was 20 million tons per year. More recently it has risen by 40 million tons every year. But the rate at which the United States is converting grain into ethanol has grown even faster. In 2010, the United States harvested nearly 400 million tons of grain, of which 126 million tons went to ethanol fuel distilleries (up from 16 million tons in 2000). This massive capacity to convert grain into fuel means that the price of grain is now tied to the price of oil. So if oil goes to $150 per barrel or more, the price of grain will follow it upward as it becomes ever more profitable to convert grain into oil substitutes. And it's not just a U.S. phenomenon: Brazil, which distills ethanol from sugar cane, ranks second in production after the United States, while the European Union's goal of getting 10 percent of its transport energy from renewables, mostly biofuels, by 2020 is also diverting land from food crops.

This is not merely a story about the booming demand for food. Everything from falling water tables to eroding soils and the consequences of global warming means that the world's food supply is unlikely to keep up with our collectively growing appetites. Take climate change: The rule of thumb among crop ecologists is that for every 1 degree Celsius rise in temperature above the growing season optimum, farmers can expect a 10 percent decline in grain yields. This relationship was borne out all too dramatically during the 2010 heat wave in Russia, which reduced the country's grain harvest by nearly 40 percent.

While temperatures are rising, water tables are falling as farmers overpump for irrigation. This artificially inflates food production in the short run, creating a food bubble that bursts when aquifers are depleted and pumping is necessarily reduced to the rate of recharge. In arid Saudi Arabia, irrigation had surprisingly enabled the country to be self-sufficient in wheat for more than 20 years; now, wheat production is collapsing because the non-replenishable aquifer the country uses for irrigation is largely depleted. The Saudis soon will be importing all their grain.

Saudi Arabia is only one of some 18 countries with water-based food bubbles. All together, more than half the world's people live in countries where water tables are falling. The politically troubled Arab Middle East is the first geographic region where grain production has peaked and begun to decline because of water shortages, even as populations continue to grow. Grain production is already going down in Syria and Iraq and may soon decline in Yemen. But the largest food bubbles are in India and China. In India, where farmers have drilled some 20 million irrigation wells, water tables are falling and the wells are starting to go dry. The World Bank reports that 175 million Indians are being fed with grain produced by overpumping. In China, overpumping is concentrated in the North China Plain, which produces half of China's wheat and a third of its corn. An estimated 130 million Chinese are currently fed by overpumping. How will these countries make up for the inevitable shortfalls when the aquifers are depleted?

Even as we are running our wells dry, we are also mismanaging our soils, creating new deserts. Soil erosion as a result of overplowing and land mismanagement is undermining the productivity of one-third of the world's cropland. How severe is it? Look at satellite images showing two huge new dust bowls: one stretching across northern and western China and western Mongolia; the other across central Africa. Wang Tao, a leading Chinese desert scholar, reports that each year some 1,400 square miles of land in northern China turn to desert. In Mongolia and Lesotho, grain harvests have shrunk by half or more over the last few decades. North Korea and Haiti are also suffering from heavy soil losses; both countries face famine if they lose international food aid. Civilization can survive the loss of its oil reserves, but it cannot survive the loss of its soil reserves.

Beyond the changes in the environment that make it ever harder to meet human demand, there's an important intangible factor to consider: Over the last half-century or so, we have come to take agricultural progress for granted. Decade after decade, advancing technology underpinned steady gains in raising land productivity. Indeed, world grain yield per acre has tripled since 1950. But now that era is coming to an end in some of the more agriculturally advanced countries, where farmers are already using all available technologies to raise yields. In effect, the farmers have caught up with the scientists. After climbing for a century, rice yield per acre in Japan has not risen at all for 16 years. In China, yields may level off soon. Just those two countries alone account for one-third of the world's rice harvest. Meanwhile, wheat yields have plateaued in Britain, France, and Germany—Western Europe's three largest wheat producers.

I n this era of tightening world food supplies, the ability to grow food is fast becoming a new form of geopolitical leverage, and countries are scrambling to secure their own parochial interests at the expense of the common good.

The first signs of trouble came in 2007, when farmers began having difficulty keeping up with the growth in global demand for grain. Grain and soybean prices started to climb, tripling by mid-2008. In response, many exporting countries tried to control the rise of domestic food prices by restricting exports. Among them were Russia and Argentina, two leading wheat exporters. Vietnam, the No. 2 rice exporter, banned exports entirely for several months in early 2008. So did several other smaller exporters of grain.

With exporting countries restricting exports in 2007 and 2008, importing countries panicked. No longer able to rely on the market to supply the grain they needed, several countries took the novel step of trying to negotiate long-term grain-supply agreements with exporting countries. The Philippines, for instance, negotiated a three-year agreement with Vietnam for 1.5 million tons of rice per year. A delegation of Yemenis traveled to Australia with a similar goal in mind, but had no luck. In a seller's market, exporters were reluctant to make long-term commitments.

Fearing they might not be able to buy needed grain from the market, some of the more affluent countries, led by Saudi Arabia, South Korea, and China, took the unusual step in 2008 of buying or leasing land in other countries on which to grow grain for themselves. Most of these land acquisitions are in Africa, where some governments lease cropland for less than $1 per acre per year. Among the principal destinations were Ethiopia and Sudan, countries where millions of people are being sustained with food from the U.N. World Food Program. That the governments of these two countries are willing to sell land to foreign interests when their own people are hungry is a sad commentary on their leadership.

By the end of 2009, hundreds of land acquisition deals had been negotiated, some of them exceeding a million acres. A 2010 World Bank analysis of these "land grabs" reported that a total of nearly 140 million acres were involved—an area that exceeds the cropland devoted to corn and wheat combined in the United States. Such acquisitions also typically involve water rights, meaning that land grabs potentially affect all downstream countries as well. Any water extracted from the upper Nile River basin to irrigate crops in Ethiopia or Sudan, for instance, will now not reach Egypt, upending the delicate water politics of the Nile by adding new countries with which Egypt must negotiate.

The potential for conflict—and not just over water—is high. Many of the land deals have been made in secret, and in most cases, the land involved was already in use by villagers when it was sold or leased. Often those already farming the land were neither consulted about nor even informed of the new arrangements. And because there typically are no formal land titles in many developing-country villages, the farmers who lost their land have had little backing to bring their cases to court. Reporter John Vidal, writing in Britain's *Observer,* quotes Nyikaw Ochalla from Ethiopia's Gambella region: "The foreign companies are arriving in large numbers, depriving people of land they have used for centuries. There is no consultation with the indigenous population. The deals are done secretly. The only thing the local people see is people coming with lots of tractors to invade their lands."

Local hostility toward such land grabs is the rule, not the exception. In 2007, as food prices were starting to rise, China signed an agreement with the Philippines to lease 2.5 million acres of land slated for food crops that would be shipped home. Once word leaked, the public outcry—much of it from Filipino farmers—forced Manila to suspend the agreement. A similar uproar rocked Madagascar, where a South Korean firm, Daewoo Logistics, had pursued rights to more than 3 million acres of land. Word of the deal helped stoke a political furor that toppled the government and forced cancellation of the agreement. Indeed, few things are more likely to fuel insurgencies than taking land from people. Agricultural equipment is easily sabotaged. If ripe fields of grain are torched, they burn quickly.

Not only are these deals risky, but foreign investors producing food in a country full of hungry people face another political question of how to get the grain out. Will villagers permit trucks laden with grain headed for port cities to proceed when they themselves may be on the verge of starvation? The potential for political instability in countries where villagers have lost their land and their livelihoods is high. Conflicts could easily develop between investor and host countries.

These acquisitions represent a potential investment in agriculture in developing countries of an estimated $50 billion. But it could take many years to realize any substantial production gains. The public infrastructure for modern market-oriented agriculture does not yet exist in most of Africa. In some countries it will take years just to build the roads and ports needed to bring in agricultural inputs such as fertilizer and to export farm products. Beyond that, modern agriculture requires its own infrastructure: machine sheds, grain-drying equipment, silos, fertilizer storage sheds, fuel storage facilities, equipment repair and maintenance services, well-drilling equipment, irrigation pumps, and energy to power the pumps. Overall, development of the land acquired to date appears to be moving very slowly.

So how much will all this expand world food output? We don't know, but the World Bank analysis indicates that only 37 percent of the projects will be devoted to food crops. Most of the land bought up so far will be used to produce biofuels and other industrial crops.

Even if some of these projects do eventually boost land productivity, who will benefit? If virtually all the inputs—the farm equipment, the fertilizer, the pesticides, the seeds—are brought in from abroad and if all the output is shipped out of the country, it will contribute little to the host country's economy. At best, locals may find work as farm laborers, but in highly mechanized operations, the jobs will be few. At worst, impoverished countries like Mozambique and Sudan will be left with less land and water with which to feed their already hungry populations. Thus far the land grabs have contributed more to stirring unrest than to expanding food production.

And this rich country-poor country divide could grow even more pronounced—and soon. This January, a new stage in the scramble among importing countries to secure food began to unfold when South Korea, which imports 70 percent of its grain, announced that it was creating a new public-private entity that will be responsible for acquiring part of this grain. With an initial office in Chicago, the plan is to bypass the large international trading firms by buying grain directly from U.S. farmers. As the Koreans acquire their own grain elevators, they may well sign multiyear delivery contracts with farmers, agreeing to buy specified quantities of wheat, corn, or soybeans at a fixed price.

Other importers will not stand idly by as South Korea tries to tie up a portion of the U.S. grain harvest even before it gets to market. The enterprising Koreans may soon be joined by China, Japan, Saudi Arabia, and other leading importers. Although South Korea's initial focus is the United States, far and away the world's largest grain exporter, it may later consider brokering deals with Canada, Australia, Argentina, and other major exporters. This is happening just as China may be on the verge of entering the U.S. market as a potentially massive importer of grain. With China's 1.4 billion increasingly affluent consumers starting to compete with U.S. consumers for the U.S. grain harvest, cheap food, seen by many as an American birthright, may be coming to an end.

No one knows where this intensifying competition for food supplies will go, but the world seems to be moving away from the international cooperation that evolved over several decades following World War II to an every-country-for-itself philosophy. Food nationalism may help secure food supplies for individual affluent countries, but it does little to enhance world food security. Indeed, the low-income countries that host land grabs or import grain will likely see their food situation deteriorate.

After the carnage of two world wars and the economic missteps that led to the Great Depression, countries joined together in 1945 to create the United Nations, finally realizing that in the modern world we cannot live in isolation, tempting though that might be. The International Monetary Fund was created to help manage the monetary system and promote economic stability

and progress. Within the U.N. system, specialized agencies from the World Health Organization to the Food and Agriculture Organization (FAO) play major roles in the world today. All this has fostered international cooperation.

But while the FAO collects and analyzes global agricultural data and provides technical assistance, there is no organized effort to ensure the adequacy of world food supplies. Indeed, most international negotiations on agricultural trade until recently focused on access to markets, with the United States, Canada, Australia, and Argentina persistently pressing Europe and Japan to open their highly protected agricultural markets. But in the first decade of this century, access to supplies has emerged as the overriding issue as the world transitions from an era of food surpluses to a new politics of food scarcity. At the same time, the U.S. food aid program that once worked to fend off famine wherever it threatened has largely been replaced by the U.N. World Food Program (WFP), where the United States is the leading donor. The WFP now has food-assistance operations in some 70 countries and an annual budget of $4 billion. There is little international coordination otherwise. French President Nicolas Sarkozy—the reigning president of the G-20—is proposing to deal with rising food prices by curbing speculation in commodity markets. Useful though this may be, it treats the symptoms of growing food insecurity, not the causes, such as population growth and climate change. The world now needs to focus not only on agricultural policy, but on a structure that integrates it with energy, population, and water policies, each of which directly affects food security.

But that is not happening. Instead, as land and water become scarcer, as the Earth's temperature rises, and as world food security deteriorates, a dangerous geopolitics of food scarcity is emerging. Land grabbing, water grabbing, and buying grain directly from farmers in exporting countries are now integral parts of a global power struggle for food security.

With grain stocks low and climate volatility increasing, the risks are also increasing. We are now so close to the edge that a breakdown in the food system could come at any time. Consider, for example, what would have happened if the 2010 heat wave that was centered in Moscow had instead been centered in Chicago. In round numbers, the 40 percent drop in Russia's hoped-for harvest of roughly 100 million tons cost the world 40 million tons of grain, but a 40 percent drop in the far larger U.S. grain harvest of 400 million tons would have cost 160 million tons. The world's carryover stocks of grain (the amount in the bin when the new harvest begins) would have dropped to just 52 days of consumption. This level would have been not only the lowest on record, but also well below the 62-day carryover that set the stage for the 2007–2008 tripling of world grain prices.

Then what? There would have been chaos in world grain markets. Grain prices would have climbed off the charts. Some grain-exporting countries, trying to hold down domestic food prices, would have restricted or even banned exports, as they did in 2007 and 2008. The TV news would have been dominated not by the hundreds of fires in the Russian countryside, but by footage of food riots in low-income grain-importing countries and reports of governments falling as hunger spread out of control. Oil-exporting countries that import grain would have been trying to barter oil for grain, and low-income grain importers would have lost out. With governments toppling and confidence in the world grain market shattered, the global economy could have started to unravel.

We may not always be so lucky. At issue now is whether the world can go beyond focusing on the symptoms of the deteriorating food situation and instead attack the underlying causes. If we cannot produce higher crop yields with less water and conserve fertile soils, many agricultural areas will cease to be viable. And this goes far beyond farmers. If we cannot move at wartime speed to stabilize the climate, we may not be able to avoid runaway food prices. If we cannot accelerate the shift to smaller families and stabilize the world population sooner rather than later, the ranks of the hungry will almost certainly continue to expand. The time to act is now—before the food crisis of 2011 becomes the new normal.

Critical Thinking

1. Identify Lester Brown's point of view, which is the basis for this article.
2. What are the primary reasons he offers to support his point of view?
3. What are the reasons for grain prices doubling since 2007?
4. What impact on food prices does the demand for crop-based fuels have?
5. What three environmental trends are making it more difficult to expand grain supply?
6. How does this article illustrate the relationship between natural resources and social structures?
7. How is the concept of sustainability illustrated in this article?
8. What alternatives to current practices does Brown propose?
9. Do the authors of Article 1 give the same priority to threats to the food supply that Brown does?

LESTER R. BROWN, president of the Earth Policy Institute, is author of *World on the Edge: How to Prevent Environmental and Economic Collapse.*

Reprinted in entirety by McGraw-Hill with permission from *Foreign Policy,* May/June 2011, pp. 56–58, 61–62. www.foreignpolicy.com. © 2011 Washingtonpost.Newsweek Interactive, LLC.

Navigating the Energy Transition

M<small>ICHAEL</small> T. K<small>LARE</small>

B etween now and 2050 or so, the world will undergo a great social, economic, and technological transition. In place of the fossil fuels—oil, coal, and natural gas—that now satisfy most of our energy needs and define key aspects of contemporary civilization, a new class of renewable energy sources will come to dominate the industrial landscape. Huge arrays of wind turbines and solar panels will replace the smoke-stacks and refineries that now surround major cities. In place of gasoline, filling stations will provide advanced biofuels or hydrogen to supply fuel cells. High-speed rail lines will connect major cities, while light rail will snake through large and small cities and their suburbs. Our homes, schools, factories, and offices will be designed to use as little energy as possible for heating, cooling, and illumination.

From our vantage point today, we can readily envision the world of 2050, and picture how the development of alternative sources of energy will alter our lives and those of our descendants. What is *less* clear is how we will get from here to there. At the conclusion of the process, the global economy and its myriad transportation systems will have been reconstructed along new lines, and the human population will have learned to live in new and more environmentally sensitive ways. But the transition from our current energy system to one based largely on renewables will be fraught with danger and crisis, as the supply of existing fuels dwindles and that of alternative fuels proves inadequate to make up the difference. Navigating this great transition could well prove the most difficult challenge facing the human community in the twenty-first century—and it is a challenge that has already forced itself upon us.

Why will this prove such a great challenge, and why is it upon us now? Let us begin with the obvious: An abundant supply of affordable energy is essential for the effective functioning of the world economy. Without such a supply, the global economy slows and suffers all sorts of disorders and trauma. We saw ample evidence of this in the spring and summer of 2008, when oil prices reached record levels, causing intense misery for the automotive, airline, and tourism industries, as well as for farmers, truckers, and commuters. High oil prices were not the direct cause of the financial meltdown of late 2008, but they were a significant factor in the subprime mortgage crisis that ultimately triggered the meltdown, in that they boosted the monthly costs faced by hard-pressed homebuyers in remote exurbs (the epicenter of the subprime pandemic). The price of gasoline only dropped when the economic crisis suppressed international demand, and it will stay low only so long as the crisis persists. As soon as economic activity rebounds, oil prices will climb again.

Energy is tied to another critical concern of the emerging era: global climate change. The largest single constituent of the greenhouse gases that are deemed responsible for planetary warming is carbon dioxide (CO_2), and the principal source of the CO_2 now accumulating in the outer atmosphere is the burning of fossil fuels to generate electricity or power motor vehicles. The more we rely on fossil fuels for these purposes, the greater will be the emissions of CO_2 and the faster the warming of the planet. The obvious solution to this peril is to reduce consumption of oil, coal, and natural gas. But this will require accelerating the development of climate-friendly alternatives, and this will take time and a great infusion of capital. Meanwhile, we still need abundant supplies of energy—affordable energy—and this puts a premium on the increased output of fossil fuels.

The intensified pursuit of fossil fuels to satisfy vital economic requirements will also bear on yet another key aspect of the current epoch: growing geopolitical rivalry among the major powers. In a world in which every nation must endeavor to satisfy its requirement for an adequate supply of energy, the competition for access to the world's remaining reserves of oil and natural gas is destined to become increasingly fierce. This has led the major consuming nations to employ every means at their disposal—including military means—to gain advantage in the competitive struggle over diminishing stocks of energy. In some cases, this has led to an influx of arms into areas of instability, as in Africa and Central Asia; in others, to the permanent deployment of military forces, as in the Persian Gulf and Caspian Sea basin. As the competition for fossil fuels increases, these geopolitical rivalries are likely to gain further momentum.

So the three greatest concerns of the moment—the global economy, the environment, and geopolitical competition—are directly tied to the nature of the world's existing energy mix. And this is where the problem lies. The types of energy on which we currently rely to satisfy most of our needs are not likely to prove adequate to meet future requirements—yet the harder we work to increase their availability, the more we doom the planet to catastrophic climate disorder and recurring geopolitical crisis.

Things as They Are

To grasp better these underlying realities, it is essential to examine the world's existing energy balance. At present, most of the world's energy is derived from fossil fuels. According to the US Department of Energy (DOE), fully 86 percent of total world energy consumption was satisfied in 2005, the most recent year for which comprehensive figures are available, by such fuels—36.7 percent by oil, 26.5 percent by coal, and 23.2 percent by natural gas. An additional 7.7 percent was provided by hydropower and renewable sources of energy, and 5.9 percent by nuclear power (see the table World Energy Consumption by Source).

It is the relative abundance of fossil fuels that has largely propelled the great economic expansion of the past 65 years, enabling not only the reconstruction of Europe and Japan after World War II but also the industrialization of Brazil, China, India, South Korea, Taiwan, and other rapidly growing economies. Over the course of this remarkable epoch, the industrialized nations erected a global civilization based on easy access to affordable fuels and electricity to power a vast array of motor vehicles, aircraft, computers, and other power-hungry devices. All this has been made possible because the international energy industry has—until now—largely succeeded in continually expanding the global output of oil, coal, and natural gas. Clearly, if this civilization is to continue to thrive in the years ahead and be extended to even more countries in the developing world, this extraordinary feat of energy-supply expansion will have to be repeated again and again.

Indeed, the DOE projected in the summer of 2008 that worldwide energy demand would grow by 50 percent between 2005 and 2030, from 462 to 695 quadrillion British thermal units (BTUs). This represents an enormous increase—the 233 quadrillion BTUs that must be added over the next quarter century is the equivalent of current energy consumption by the United States, Europe, and Japan combined. Most of this added energy, the DOE assumes, will have to be supplied by the most common and well-developed fuels: oil, coal, and natural gas. According to DOE projections, these three fuels will provide approximately the same share of world energy in 2030—85.8 percent—as they did in 2005.

Only a radical increase in the tempo of change can ensure that alternative sources of energy will be available in 2025.

If the energy industry were capable of supplying all this added fossil-fuel energy in 2030, that would be good news for the global economy, in that the older industrialized nations could maintain their high levels of consumption while the developing world experienced fast consumption growth. But it is extremely unlikely that the industry will be capable of meeting this objective. Although the net supply of fossil fuels may continue to increase, the global availability of oil will probably go into decline well before the end of this period. Natural gas supplies are likely to remain stagnant. This leaves only coal—the most CO_2-intensive of the three fossil fuels—as a rising source of energy. The bottom line: insufficient energy supplies combined with rising greenhouse-gas emissions.

The most troubling aspect of this equation involves oil. Although the DOE and many oil industry officials claim that global petroleum supplies will be sufficient to satisfy international requirements between now and 2030, many experts doubt that this will prove to be the case. In its *World Energy Outlook* released on November 12, 2008, the International Energy Agency (IEA), a Paris-based organization affiliated with the Organization for Economic Cooperation and Development, warned that global oil supplies may not be adequate to meet global needs in the years ahead. The agency gave three reasons that this might be so. First, existing fields are running out of oil at a faster rate than previously thought. Second, most newly developed oil fields are smaller and less productive than those currently in operation. And third, investors are shying away from costly and complex projects in "frontier" oil regions like the deep waters of the Gulf of Mexico, the Gulf of Guinea, Siberia, and the Caspian Sea.

Of the three reasons, perhaps the most startling was the revelation concerning the rapid depletion of existing fields. Although the world possesses tens of thousands of operating wells, most of our oil is drawn from several hundred giant reservoirs that

World Energy Consumption by Source—2005 (Actual) and 2030 (Projected)

Energy Source	2005 (Actual)		2030 (Projected)	
	Consumption Quad BTUs	Percent of World Total	Consumption Quad BTUs	Percent of World Total
Oil and biofuels	169.4	36.7	229.3	33.0
Natural gas	107.4	23.2	164.7	23.7
Coal	122.5	26.5	202.2	29.1
Nuclear	27.5	5.9	39.4	5.7
Hydropower, Renewables, others	35.5	7.7	59.0	8.5
Total, world	462.2	100.0	694.7	100.0

Source: US Department of Energy, *International Energy Outlook 2008* (Washington, DC: 2008), Table A2, p. 97.

produce hundreds of thousands of barrels per day. Almost all of these fields were discovered a quarter of a century or more ago, and many have already passed their peak level of daily output and are now experiencing a steady rate of decline. Previously, energy analysts assumed that this rate of decline was, on average, about 4 to 5 percent per year across the board—a conceivably manageable rate assuming sufficient investment in new oil field development by the major oil companies. But after conducting a survey of the world's 800 top-producing oil fields, the IEA concluded that the natural decline rate of these reservoirs is closer to 9 percent per year, a wholly unexpected and troubling outcome that tells us we are moving far more rapidly toward the end of the Petroleum Age than was previously assumed.

Replacing 4 percent of the world's oil supply every year is one thing; replacing 9 percent is a vastly greater challenge, given the huge cost and difficulty of developing new fields. Although the oil companies are spending greater amounts every year to locate and develop promising deposits, they are finding fewer and smaller fields. And the reservoirs they do manage to bring on line tend to empty out much faster than the giants discovered earlier, in the golden years of discovery following World War II. For example, the two major discoveries of the 1960s, the North Slope of Alaska and the North Sea, are already experiencing rapid rates of output decline. Only two large discoveries have been made since then—the Kashagan field in the Caspian Sea and the Tupi field in Atlantic waters off Rio de Janeiro—and both pose extraordinary technical challenges to the companies hoping to bring them into production.

The only way to ensure adequate supplies of oil in the years ahead is for the world's oil companies to make mammoth investments in drilling rigs, pipelines, and other infrastructure to bring new reservoirs into production. According to the IEA, satisfying anticipated world demand in 2030 will require a minimum of $350 billion per year (in 2007 dollars) in such investments *every year* between now and then. But much of this money will have to be spent on facilities in the hurricane-prone waters of the Gulf of Mexico and the Atlantic, or in conflict-prone areas of Africa, the Middle East, and Central Asia—which gives pause to investors.

Even before the onset of the world's current economic crisis, many investors were deterred by the rising cost of such ventures and, in the case of projects in Africa, the Middle East, and the former Soviet Union, by the potential for big losses as a result of conflict, sabotage, corruption, or governmental intervention. Since the economic crisis erupted, investors have become even more skittish, proving extremely reluctant to commit large sums to any projects that entail risks of this sort. Thus, even though oil resources could prove abundant in some of these areas, it is questionable whether they will be brought on line in time to satisfy global needs. As noted by the IEA in its November 12 report: "It cannot be taken for granted" that the major private oil companies and government-owned oil firms like Saudi Aramco will allocate sufficient funds "to keep up the necessary pace of investment."

What this means, in sum, is that the worldwide supply of petroleum is likely to fall short of projected global requirements in the decades to come. To put this in further perspective, the most recent edition of the DOE's *International Energy Outlook* projects that world oil supply will rise from 83.6 million barrels per day in 2005 to 95.7 million barrels in 2015, 101.3 million in 2020, and 112.5 million in 2030. (This includes conventional oil plus "nonconventional" supplies such as shale oil, Canadian tar sands, and biofuels.) But many experts, drawing on the sort of analysis presented above, now believe that world production will reach a peak in output well before 2030, probably between 2010 and 2015, at a level of about 95 million barrels per day. They believe output will remain at about that level for several years and then commence an irreversible decline—dropping far below the DOE's estimate of 112 million barrels for 2030. This means that, by 2030 or so, the world could be looking at a shortfall of anywhere from 25 to 30 million barrels of oil per day—a huge plunge in the global supply of energy.

More Carbon Needed

Clearly, any effort to satisfy world fuel requirements in the years after 2015 will require a significant increase in the production of *other* sources of energy. In the first instance, this will lead to greater dependence on the two other fossil fuels, natural gas and coal. Many experts believe that the output of gas and coal can be substantially augmented to compensate for the declining availability of oil. But this, too, could prove problematic.

Without going into great detail, any increase in the global output of natural gas will confront many of the same sorts of hurdles encountered in the case of petroleum. Like petroleum, gas is a finite substance produced by natural phenomena over many millions of years and is often found in similar geological formations. Just as the global output of oil is expected to reach a maximum or peak level in the not-too-distant future, so too will natural gas attain a peak in the third or fourth decade of the century.

Competition for access to the world's remaining reserves of oil and natural gas is destined to become increasingly fierce.

Also as in the case of oil, many of the world's largest reservoirs of gas have already been located and exploited, suggesting that less-attractive fields—those in remote locations like northern Alaska, eastern Siberia, and the Arctic Ocean—are all that remain for future development. Some additional gas is trapped in coal beds, shale rock, and other distinctive geological formations that can be mined with appropriate technologies. Industry experts believe it will be possible to exploit all these remote and "nonconventional" sources of gas. However, the cost will be high, and it is doubtful that these sources will ever prove sufficient to replace more than a tiny share of the energy now provided by oil.

Any increase in the consumption of natural gas will also entail significant geopolitical risks. No less than 56 percent of the world's known gas reserves are held by just three countries—Russia, Iran, and Qatar—and these three have recently taken steps to solidify their control over the fuel's future utilization by creating the nucleus of a "natural gas OPEC." Several other leading gas producers, including Algeria, Libya, Saudi Arabia, and the Central Asian states, have also expressed interest in forming such a cartel, suggesting the likelihood of future constraints on natural gas's global availability. This is precisely the sort of environment in which conflict could arise over access to sources of natural gas, much as has been the case in past years over access to sources of petroleum.

Coal presents a rather different set of problems. Coal is expected to remain relatively abundant well into the middle of the century (after which it, too, will reach a peak in production and go into decline). Moreover, large deposits of it are located in major energy-consuming nations like China, India, Russia, and the United States. With existing technology, coal is the cheapest fuel available for producing electricity, so its use is growing in many developing countries as well as in the United States. According to the DOE, China's coal consumption will grow by 120 percent between 2005 and 2030; in India it will grow by 80 percent, and in the United States by 31 percent. Coal can also be used as a feedstock for synthetic gas and diesel fuel, making it an attractive substitute for natural gas and oil as these materials become increasingly scarce.

However, any increase in coal consumption using existing combustion technologies will result in a speed-up of global warming and an onslaught of climatic disasters. This is so because coal releases more carbon dioxide per unit of energy generated than do the other two fossil fuels. Scientists and engineers are working on a technique to separate the carbon from the coal and bury it before combustion occurs—so-called carbon capture and storage (CCS) technology. But plants using this technique are expected to be far more costly than existing ones, and at this point no commercial facility employs this method. As the impacts of global warming grow more severe, power companies will come under greater pressure to use this technology, but it is unlikely that it will have achieved widespread adoption by 2030. What is more likely, at that point, is an increase in conventional coal technology, producing a heightened risk of catastrophic climate change.

Alternating Current

Obviously, the best hope for all of us on the planet (and for our descendents) is for the energy industry—and the world's major governments—to invest in a massive, rapid expansion of alternative sources of energy, especially renewables like solar, wind, geothermal, and advanced (non-edible) biofuels. These sources are not derived from finite materials like oil, natural gas, and coal but are infinitely replaceable, and release very little or no carbon in their operation. Eventually, when the great energy transition is completed, most of the world's energy supply is likely to be derived from these sources. But increasing the amount of energy supplied by these sources will prove an uphill and expensive struggle—and until that process is completed, we could be in for very difficult times.

At present, renewables and hydropower supply only 7.7 percent of the world's energy. According to the latest projections

from the DOE, this figure will only rise to 8.5 percent by 2030, not including biofuels; with the addition of bio-fuels, it would rise by another percentage point or two. (Nuclear power provides another 5.9 percent of world supply currently. Although nuclear power is likely to continue playing a small but significant role in satisfying world energy needs, it poses so many safety, non-proliferation, and waste disposal challenges, as well as legal and financial challenges to investors, that it is unlikely to exceed single digits in its net contribution to the global supply.) Even if we assume these figures are overly pessimistic, this is hardly enough to compensate for the decline in oil or our perilous reliance on coal. Only a tripling or quadrupling in the share of energy provided by renewables and advanced biofuels by 2030 can put us far along the path of a successful transition.

Several factors account for the slow pace of renewable energy's development. To begin with, major utilities and their government backers have long been accustomed to relying on oil, coal, gas, and nuclear power, so they have been reluctant to make major investments in alternative sources of power. According to the IEA, three-quarters of the world's projected output of electricity in 2020 (and more than half in 2030) will come from generation facilities that are already in operation today—almost all of them powered by fossil fuels or nuclear energy. Furthermore, most of the new plants under construction—especially in China and India, where the demand for added electricity is greatest—are of this type. It will be very hard, under these circumstances, to increase the share of energy provided by alternative sources.

In addition, wind, solar, biofuels, and other, more advanced sources of energy face many obstacles that must be overcome before they can replace fossil fuels on a very large scale. Wind and solar power pose a common set of problems. Both collect energy intermittently, and so are off line for considerable periods of time. Also, both achieve their maximum effectiveness in remote areas like the American Southwest (in the case of solar power) or high plains (for wind) that are far removed from areas of greatest demand, and so lack adequate connectivity to the electrical grid. Biofuels pose different problems. Most ethanol in the United States is manufactured from corn ears, a valuable source of food for humans and animals; the very process of making it, moreover, entails a large and wasteful input of energy.

To overcome these various obstacles, huge sums must be spent—on developing new storage batteries so that energy collected from wind and the sun can be harvested when the supply is great and later dispersed when it is not; on an expanded (and more efficient) electrical grid connecting vast solar arrays and wind farms to major population centers; and on advanced biofuels using nonfood plant matter as a feedstock, and chemical rather than thermal means of manufacturing ethanol. Additional investment is also needed to develop other promising but as-yet unproven technologies, including hydrogen fuel cells, wave energy, and fusion reactors.

But even with a huge increase in spending on energy alternatives, such as President-elect Barack Obama and his supporters in Congress have proposed, it is highly unlikely that renewables, advanced biofuels, and climate-safe (that is, CCS) coal will be available on a large enough scale in 2030 to make up for what is likely to be an inadequate supply of oil and natural gas. Increased efforts at conservation will help, as will greater reliance on public transportation. But it is hard to escape the conclusion that in the middle stages of the great transition, from roughly 2020 to 2040, global energy supplies—except for climate-threatening coal—will be insufficient to meet global needs.

Competition Heats Up

In a world constrained by inadequate stockpiles of energy, we can expect intense geopolitical competition for whatever supplies *are* available at any given time. As the US National Intelligence Council (NIC) suggested in its November 2008 assessment of the likely strategic environment in 2025: "The rising energy demands of growing populations and economies may bring into question the availability, reliability, and affordability of energy supplies. Such a situation would heighten tensions between states competing for limited resources, especially if accompanied by increased political turbulence in the Middle East and a general loss of confidence in the ability of the marketplace to satisfy rising demands."

The NIC report, *Global Trends 2025: A Transformed World,* is particularly illuminating because it focuses on the same period discussed in this article: the midpoint in the great transition from fossil fuels to a post-petroleum economy. The report suggests, as well, that the world of 2025 will be well on its way toward the adoption of alternative forms of energy, yet will still be highly dependent on fossil fuels to satisfy most day-to-day requirements. At the same time, according to the report, significant problems will have arisen in boosting output of oil and gas to match rising worldwide demand. The result, it predicts, is an environment of perceived scarcity. In such an environment, political leaders will see no option but to employ any means at their disposal to maximize their own country's supplies—even at the risk of conflict with equally desperate competitors.

Most of our oil is drawn from several hundred giant reservoirs and many have already passed their peak.

"In the worst case," observes the NIC report, "this could lead to interstate conflicts if government leaders deem assured access to energy resources to be essential to maintaining domestic stability and the survival of their regime." Even in the absence of war, competition for energy will have important geopolitical implications as states undertake strategies to hedge against the possibility that existing energy supplies will not meet rising demands. For example, "energy-deficient states may employ transfers of arms and sensitive technologies and the promise of a political and military alliance as inducements to establish strategic relationships with energy-producing states."

Read deeper into the NIC report, and you find numerous portrayals of a world torn apart by relentless struggle over precarious supplies of oil and natural gas. Central Asia comes in for particular attention as a site of potential conflict among the United States, Russia, and China for control over that region's hydrocarbon reserves. Africa, a growing source of oil for the United States and China, is also seen as a potential site of geopolitical rivalry. Even the Arctic—increasingly open to oil and gas drilling as a result of global warming—is deemed a possible locale for conflict.

These kinds of rivalries are doubly dangerous. Not only do they risk full-scale war among the major powers, with all the destructive effects that would entail, but they would also consume mammoth sums of money that could otherwise be devoted to the development of energy alternatives, thereby slowing the transition to a post-petroleum industrial system. In fact, a world of recurring energy wars could make a successful transition impossible, or delay it until such time as the world economy had contracted substantially and global warming had advanced much further than it might have otherwise.

It is painfully evident, then, that the current pace of transition is far too slow to achieve the intended results in time to avert global catastrophe. Only a radical increase in the tempo of change can ensure that alternative sources of energy will be available in 2025 and beyond to compensate for the decline in oil and prevent increased dependence on unsafe coal. This will require vastly greater expenditures on efforts to realize the full potential of wind power, solar, geothermal, advanced biofuels, hydrogen, and climate-safe coal, along with increased investment in public transportation. The world of 2050 can be a bright, livable environment in which renewable energy sources power prosperity—but only if we take steps now to accelerate the transition from our current energy system to its unavoidable replacement.

Critical Thinking

1. What is Michael Klare's point of view?
2. What are the primary reasons he offers to support this point of view?
3. What are some of the implications of the projected patterns of world energy consumption in 2030?
4. How is the consumption of oil, coal and natural gas likely to change in the next 30 years?
5. What are some of the political and technical obstacles to developing alternative energy sources? How do these obstacles illustrate the relationships between the four components of the Allegory of the Balloon?
6. Do the authors of Article 1 give the same priority to the challenges of the energy transition that Klare does?

Michael T. Klare, a *Current History* contributing editor, is a professor at Hampshire College and author of *Rising Powers, Shrinking Planet: The New Geopolitics of Energy* (Metropolitan Books, 2008).

From *Current History*, January 2009, pp. 26–32. Copyright © 2009 by Current History, Inc. Reprinted by permission.

Asia's Rise: Rise and Fall

How are we to understand the shift of power towards Asia and what does it mean for those 'old' power centres in Europe and the United States? The most important historical question is probably why nations gain and lose power. Growth provides the most elegant answer and the means to defend that power.

Paul Kennedy

The first time I visited Japan, it was in the still-powerful after glow of the appearance of Ezra Vogel's bestseller, *Japan as Number One,* originally published by Harvard University Press in 1979, but continually re-published in Japan. To a person, Japanese intellectuals and politicians were excited by that prognostication, although also anxious to avoid giving a neuralgic late Ronald Reagan presidential administration any hint that they were looking forward to America's future relative decline.

I therefore found myself being asked coyly, time and again, what I thought about the ever-moving-westwards theory of international politics. When I asked my interlocutors to explain, the reply was always identical: for thousands of years East Asia had been the centre of the world, the most advanced and productive civilisation, etc. . .; then that centre began to shift westwards, through the Indian Ocean, and up to the Mediterranean; but Braudel's famous 'Mediterranean world' of the sixteenth century was eclipsed by nation-states north of the Alps, France, the Netherlands, eventually Britain.

This British predominance was impressively long-lasting, but by around 1900 it was losing out to the massive industrial states of the eastern half of the United States; and yet, after 1945 and as if by force of nature, the world's weight shifted steadily to the western side of the US.

So all that was happening, you see, was that the caravan of world wealth and civilisation was moving westwards again, to Japan. And that was why Professor Vogel's book was so impressive and convincing. And it was not Japan's fault it was overtaking America; it is just that it was now its turn to be Number One. No hard feelings.

When I pointed out, politely, that there was no reason why the westwards shift would not continue—in fact, the logic of the argument made that shift inevitable—and thus see China in future replacing Japan as Number One in the world, the conversations tended to dry up. As we parted company, both sides agreed to think about this matter a bit more.

Growth Counts

I have been thinking about it ever since. Without needing a complicated Toynbeean explanation of changes in world history—'action-response', the saving grace of religion, and all that—there is something fascinating—and important—to all of us about this shifting dynamic of power and influence over the course of time.

It is a story that has captured the attention of the great writers and thinkers of the past—Ibn Khaldun, Raleigh, Vico, Gibbon, Brooks Adams, Ranke, Wells, Weber, Spengler, Mackinder, Braudel, McNeill—and with good reason. Why does one organised human unit—a nation, an empire, a civilization, call it what you will—rise to occupy a greater share of power and influence than the others and then, again, begin to lose that pre-eminence? Is this not the most important historical question of all?

It is at this point that the horde of answers charge in, like cavalry-horses answering the bugle: the answer can be culture, or science, or germs and disease, or a breakdown of morals, or the coming of the steam-engine, or a Roman-like capacity for organisation.

To my mind still, and at the risk of sounding like an out-of-date Marxist don, I feel that Lenin himself probably came closest when he pointed to the 'uneven rate of development' as the key. Could anyone believe, he asks his readers again and again, that the unification of Germany and the entry of Japan into the ranks of the Great Powers could have occurred without their successful long-term growth? Of course not.

The beauty about Lenin's approach is that he does not get himself embroiled in debates about some cultures and civilisations being superior to others, or Protestantism and capitalism, or relative resistance to disease, or democracy versus autocracy, or any of the other long-winded stuff, to explain the relative rise and decline of particular economies and their influence in the world. He simply points out—as any natural scientist observing a run of data would—that if the record shows one country's productivity and economy growing faster than others, then there will be a steady shift in the balances of power towards it. The antecedent causes are mere intellectualism. It is what is happening that counts.

And this, it seems to me, is the only sensible way we can discuss the most significant political phenomenon of our new century: the relative rise of Asia, perhaps China especially, and its natural concomitant, the relative decline of the west as a whole and more particularly of both of its two greatest components, Europe and the US.

At some stage, somewhere, those two parts need to be treated separately, since their responses to Asia's rise are so different. In Europe—at least according to some recent conferences I have attended—the mood is one of resigned acquiescence, mingled with a weird panglossian assumption that it will all work out well in the end. In the US, the 'declinist' or 'exceptionalist' debate is much more intense, presumably because—as Henry Kissinger might say—the stakes are so high.

It is difficult to judge which of these two debates are the more depressing to watch, or the less intelligible. Probably the European fatalism—occasionally interrupted by Sarkovian calls for the continent to unite or perish—possesses the superior logic.

By contrast, the debate in the US on Asia's rise now borders on the fatuous, but with three quarrelling variants. Either [a] it is not really happening, and the twenty-first century will still be America's century, despite all the statistical evidence and forecasts to the contrary; or [b] it is indeed happening, but there is nothing to worry about since America and Asia are natural and complementary trading partners so they will all get richer at the same time, as if members of some gigantic trans-Pacific Hanseatic League. This displaying a naivete about power-politics that is breathtaking; or [c] the most puzzling variation of all, though trumpeted by dozens of respectable political scientists and economists—not historians—which goes like this. Yes, the global dynamic proceeds apace; and yes, Asia and China are rising fast, so America's share on virtually all indices is shrinking, relatively; but, notwithstanding all that, the US will continue to occupy a special place in world affairs, over and above all the rest, the indispensable nation.

Calling the Tune

Just how one part of the globe can be relatively rising without other parts relatively falling is neither explained nor admitted. Truly, the first generations of a nation grappling with signs of long-term relative decline have an awfully hard time in being reconciled to that idea.

Yet, once one casts those emotions aside, the facts are clear; the accumulating evidence points to a conclusion which realists from Lenin going back to Thucydides—'it was the rising power of Athens'—would completely understand. Year on year, decade over decade, Asia is growing at a significantly faster pace than the mature economies of the US and Europe.

This is so well known that there is no need to throw in a lot of statistics—per capita gross domestic product, annualised growth-rates, Goldman Sachs projections—at this stage. But two changes are worth pointing to, apart from this massive shift in the relative productive outputs of each nation's goods and services.

The first is the stunning transformation of the world's capital balances over the past twenty years. This is not the place to discuss in detail whether the gigantic Asian capital surpluses—China, Japan, South Korea—will last forever, probably not; but no historian can resist pointing out that surplus bank savings

have usually accompanied the alterations in the military-political balances of power, either running ahead of them or following them: from the Lombard cities to Antwerp and Amsterdam; from there to London; from London, after a long time, to New York; and from New York . . . to where? Shanghai? Does it not matter when, as a Great Power, you owe an awful lot of money to someone else? He who pays the piper will, sooner or later, call the tune.

Sea Denial

The second accompanying shift is in military balances, especially at sea. In brief, we see a triangular situation which looks like this: Europe's maritime capacities are evaporating fast, and without there being a single substantive debate on what that means; Asia's maritime capacities are exploding in both power and reach, but no-one wants to talk about it; and the US Navy is worried.

The first of these deserves a far lengthier examination, but in essence the roster of European warships is shrinking so steadily, decade by decade, that it is fair to conclude that the five hundred-year-old Vasco da Gama era in world affairs is now well and truly over; an occasional run-in with Somali pirates by a French frigate makes for little.

Contrast their collective shrinkage, then, with the soaring naval expenditures of all the navies of East Asia, the Pacific, and South Asia, the frenzied attention to gaining naval-base rights, the drumbeat of propaganda on protecting one's vital sea-lines of communication.

Admiral Mahan has gone east. The Japanese Navy, for example, eclipses any European navy, and is in turn eclipsed by the Chinese Navy. What do those Asian governments know about the future of global power-politics that European governments do not? No politician will say.

Then there is the US, frantically trying to figure out what this rise of Asian sea-power means for its own overstretched world position. The bug-a-boo is of course China. Why is Beijing spending so much on defence; though probably about one-eighth of the Pentagon's budget? Why this heavy investment into cyber-warfare?; into military satellites?; into commercial espionage? What about those medium-range sea-skimming missiles that fly below the radar screens of US warships, and those ultra-long-range rockets that can cross the wide Pacific? Or the super-quiet diesel submarines, now wrapped in an anti-detection 'stealth' coating? How valid are all these rumours about the first Chinese aircraft-carrier?

Overall, then, are we not watching an older-fashioned American blue-water surface navy being pushed ever further away from the Asian coasts, and facing the problem of 'sea denial'? The Chinese navy is not planning to anchor off the entrance to Long Beach, California; but it does not imagine that Nimitz's navy will be in the western Pacific for much longer, either.

Strategy Light

Since it is the US which is much more exercised about Asia's rise than the limp but hopeful Europeans, one might expect to glean some idea of Washington's thinking by perusing the two most important documents so far issued on this topic in the present year: namely, [a] the February Quadrennial Defense Review Report, a Pentagon document requested by the Congress, and [b] the May National Security Strategy, emanating from the White House and signed off by President Barack Obama himself. But if one reads and attempts to de-construct those documents, one will have looked in vain; talk about the hunting of the Snark!

The presidential document is especially vacuous. One must wait until pages 43–45—of a 52-page document—to discover a section called Build Cooperation with Other 21st Century Centers of Influence, and indeed there is a paragraph on China and another on India. But they are followed in rapid succession by paragraphs on Russia, Indonesia, Brazil, the Middle East, Africa; interestingly, no reference to Japan, so much for the round-the-world movement of history! And there are a lot more pages on 'our most cherished values . . .' than there are on hard strategic issues.

The Quadrennial Defense Review seems at first to be a bit more relevant, in part because each of the services is putting in a bid for a large slice of the total Pentagon budget, and therefore has to say something about threats and capacities, or lack thereof. Even so, it looks like a bulky, multi-page menu in an expensive Manhattan restaurant; there is something in there for everyone, carriers, air wings, army groups, the Marines. But, in essence, there is little there. Charming sections on 'Supporting Families' and on 'Strengthening Interagency Partnerships' lead to nothing.

For understandable diplomatic reasons, no doubt, there is no discussion on what are the best ways to intimidate China's military growth; or how best to reach out to India to be your largest global ally, like reaching out to Britain after 1941; or how much it might take to get the shifty Russian Prime Minister Vladimir Putin onto your side, a sublimely Bismarckian stroke that the

Joint Chiefs simply dare not suggest. It is all very sad. Since Kissinger, or perhaps since the Bush-Baker-Scowcroft team, nobody in Washington thinks strategically.

So the shift in the world's power balances will go on. Asia will rise, though not without a stumble here and there, and China in particular seems likely to encounter some environmental or social difficulty before resuming its forward path, difficulties which will give hope to all those who hate the idea of the return of the Middle Kingdom. And the rest of Asia—India, Indonesia, Vietnam, Korea—will also advance, in a ragged though obvious direction.

And Europe will sit back, feeling quite exhausted by all these transformations, getting ever more obsessed about immigrants, high taxes and hedge funds. Meanwhile the US will, I fear, not have a clue where it is going, and what to do. Ninety years ago, Mackinder wrote that democracies, unless they are forced into war, simply cannot think strategically. Is that true? I hope it is not. But the evidence increasingly suggests he is right.

And so the centre of the world rolls, always to the west, to Asia and China. If we wait long enough, it might end up again in Lombardy; but that could take quite a while. Today, most roads seem to be leading to Beijing. Truly, as the Chinese curse puts it, we live in interesting times.

Critical Thinking

1. What is Paul Kennedy's point of view?
2. How does he contrast his point of view with other historians?
3. How does sea power figure into Kennedy's argument?
4. How does this article complement or contradict the analysis offered in Article 1? Or to state this differently: What is Kennedy's theory of international relations?

China's Search for a Grand Strategy

Wang Jisi

A Rising Great Power Finds Its Way

Any country's grand strategy must answer at least three questions: What are the nation's core interests? What external forces threaten them? And what can the national leadership do to safeguard them? Whether China has any such strategy today is open to debate. On the one hand, over the last three decades or so, its foreign and defense policies have been remarkably consistent and reasonably well coordinated with the country's domestic priorities. On the other hand, the Chinese government has yet to disclose any document that comprehensively expounds the country's strategic goals and the ways to achieve them. For both policy analysts in China and China watchers abroad, China's grand strategy is a field still to be plowed.

In recent years, China's power and influence relative to those of other great states have outgrown the expectations of even its own leaders. Based on the country's enhanced position, China's international behavior has become increasingly assertive, as was shown by its strong reactions to a chain of events in 2010: for example, Washington's decision to sell arms to Taiwan, U.S.–South Korean military exercises in the Yellow Sea, and Japan's detention of a Chinese sailor found in disputed waters. It has become imperative for the international community to understand China's strategic thinking and try to forecast how it might evolve according to China's interests and its leaders' vision.

The Enemy Within and Without

A unique feature of Chinese leaders' understanding of their country's history is their persistent sensitivity to domestic disorder caused by foreign threats. From ancient times, the ruling regime of the day has often been brought down by a combination of internal uprising and external invasion. The Ming dynasty collapsed in 1644 after rebelling peasants took the capital city of Beijing and the Manchu, with the collusion of Ming generals, invaded from the north. Some three centuries later, the Manchu's own Qing dynasty collapsed after a series of internal revolts coincided with invasions by Western and Japanese forces. The end of the Kuomintang's rule and the founding of the People's Republic in 1949 was caused by an indigenous revolution inspired and then bolstered by the Soviet Union and the international communist movement.

Since then, apprehensions about internal turbulences have lingered. Under Mao Zedong's leadership, from 1949 to 1976, the Chinese government never formally applied the concept of "national interest" to delineate its strategic aims, but its international strategies were clearly dominated by political and military security interests—themselves often framed by ideological principles such as "proletarian internationalism."

Strategic thinking at the time followed the Leninist tradition of dividing the world into political camps: archenemies, secondary enemies, potential allies, revolutionary forces. Mao's "three worlds theory" pointed to the Soviet Union and the United States as China's main external threats, with corresponding internal threats coming from pro-Soviet "revisionists" and pro-American "class enemies." China's political life in those years was characterized by recurrent struggles against international and domestic schemes to topple the Chinese Communist Party (CCP) leadership or change its political coloring. Still, since Mao's foreign policy supposedly represented the interests of the "international proletariat" rather than China's own, and since China was economically and socially isolated from much of the world, Beijing had no comprehensive grand strategy to speak of.

Then came the 1980s and Deng Xiaoping. As China embarked on reform and opened up, the CCP made economic development its top priority. Deng's foreign policy thinking departed appreciably from that of Mao. A major war with either the Soviet Union or the United States was no longer deemed inevitable. China made great efforts to develop friendly and cooperative relations with countries all over the world, regardless of their political or ideological orientation; it reasoned that a nonconfrontational posture would attract foreign investment to China and boost trade. A peaceful international environment, an enhanced position for China in the global arena, and China's steady integration into the existing economic order would also help consolidate the CCP's power at home.

But even as economic interests became a major driver of China's behavior on the international scene, traditional security concerns and the need to guard against Western political interference remained important. Most saliently, the Tiananmen Square incident of 1989 and, in its wake, the West's sanctions against Beijing served as an alarming reminder to China's leaders that internal and external troubles could easily intertwine. Over the next decade, Beijing responded to Western censure by contending that the state's sovereign rights trumped human rights. It resolutely refused to consider adopting Western-type democratic institutions. And it insisted that it would never give up the option of using force if Taiwan tried to secede.

Despite those concerns, however, by the beginning of the twenty-first century, China's strategic thinkers were depicting a generally favorable international situation. In his 2002 report to the CCP National Congress, General Secretary Jiang Zemin foresaw a "20 years' period of strategic opportunity," during which China could continue to concentrate on domestic tasks. Unrest has erupted at times—such as the violent riots in Tibet in March 2008 and in Xinjiang in July 2009, which the central government blamed on "foreign hostile forces" and responded to with harsh reprisals. And Beijing claims that the awarding of the 2010 Nobel Peace Prize to Liu Xiaobo, a political activist it deems to be a "criminal trying to sabotage the socialist system," has proved once again Westerners' "ill intentions." Still, the Chinese government has been perturbed by such episodes only occasionally, which has allowed it to focus on redressing domestic imbalances and the unsustainability of its development.

Under President Hu Jintao, Beijing has in recent years formulated a new development and social policy geared toward continuing to promote fast economic growth while emphasizing good governance, improving the social safety net, protecting the environment, encouraging independent innovation, lessening social tensions, perfecting the financial system, and stimulating domestic consumption. As Chinese exports have suffered from the global economic crisis since 2008, the need for such economic and social transformations has become more urgent.

With that in mind, the Chinese leadership has redefined the purpose of China's foreign policy. As Hu announced in July 2009, China's diplomacy must "safeguard the interests of sovereignty, security, and development." Dai Bingguo, the state councilor for external relations, further defined those core interests in an article last December: first, China's political stability, namely, the stability of the CCP leadership and of the socialist system; second, sovereign security, territorial integrity, and national unification; and third, China's sustainable economic and social development.

Apart from the issue of Taiwan, which Beijing considers to be an integral part of China's territory, the Chinese government has never officially identified any single foreign policy issue as one of the country's core interests. Last year, some Chinese commentators reportedly referred to the South China Sea and North Korea as such, but these reckless statements, made with no official authorization, created a great deal of confusion. In fact, for the central government, sovereignty, security, and development all continue to be China's main goals. As long as no grave danger—for example, Taiwan's formal secession—threatens the CCP leadership or China's unity, Beijing will remain preoccupied with the country's economic and social development, including its foreign policy.

The Principle's Principle

The need to identify an organizing principle to guide Chinese foreign policy is widely recognized today in China's policy circles and scholarly community, as well as among international analysts. However, defining China's core interests according to the three prongs of sovereignty, security, and development, which sometimes are in tension, means that it is almost impossible to devise a straightforward organizing principle. And the variety of views among Chinese political elites complicates efforts to devise any such grand strategy based on political consensus.

One popular proposal has been to focus on the United States as a major threat to China. Proponents of this view cite the ancient Chinese philosopher Mencius, who said, "A state without an enemy or external peril is absolutely doomed." Or they reverse the political scientist Samuel Huntington's argument that "the ideal enemy for America would be ideologically hostile, racially and culturally different, and militarily strong enough to pose a credible threat to American security" and cast the United States as an ideal enemy for China. This notion is based on the long-held conviction that the United States, along with other Western powers and Japan, is hostile to China's political values and wants to contain its rise by supporting Taiwan's separation from the mainland. Its proponents also point to U.S. politicians' sympathy for the Dalai Lama and Uighur separatists, continued U.S. arms sales to Taiwan, U.S. military alliances and arrangements supposedly designed to encircle the Chinese mainland, the currency and trade wars waged by U.S. businesses and the U.S. Congress, and the West's argument that China should slow down its economic growth in order to help stem climate change.

This view is reflected in many newspapers and on many Web sites in China (particularly those about military affairs and political security). Its proponents argue that China's current approach to foreign relations is far too soft; Mao's tit-for-tat manner is touted as a better model. As a corollary, it is said that China should try to find strategic allies among countries that seem defiant toward the West, such as Iran, North Korea, and Russia. Some also recommend that Beijing use its holdings of U.S. Treasury bonds as a policy instrument, standing ready to sell them if U.S. government actions undermine China's interests.

This proposal is essentially misguided, for even though the United States does pose some strategic and security challenges to China, it would be impractical and risky to construct a grand strategy based on the view that the United States is China's main adversary. Few countries, if any, would want to join China in an anti-U.S. alliance. And it would seriously hold back China's economic development to antagonize the country's largest trading partner and the world's strongest economic and military power. Fortunately, the Chinese leadership is not about to carry out such a strategy. Premier Wen Jiabao was not just being diplomatic last year when he said of China and the United States that "our common interests far outweigh our differences."

Well aware of this, an alternative school of thought favors Deng's teaching of tao guang yang hui, or keeping a low profile in international affairs. Members of this group, including prominent political figures, such as Tang Jiaxuan, former foreign minister, and General Xiong Guangkai, former deputy chief of staff of the People's Liberation Army, argue that since China remains a developing country, it should concentrate on economic development. Without necessarily rebuffing the notion that the West, particularly the United States, is a long-term threat to China, they contend that China is not capable of challenging Western primacy for the time being—and some even caution against hastily concluding that the West is in decline. Meanwhile, they argue, keeping a low profile in the coming decades will allow China to concentrate on domestic priorities.

Although this view appears to be better received internationally than the other, it, too, elicits some concerns. Its adherents have had to take great pains to explain that tao guang yang hui, which is sometimes mistranslated as "hiding one's capabilities and biding one's time," is not a calculated call for temporary moderation until China has enough material power and confidence to promote its hidden agenda. Domestically, the low-profile approach is vulnerable to the charge that it is too soft, especially when security issues become acute. As nationalist feelings surge in China, some Chinese are pressing for a more can-do foreign policy. Opponents also contend that this notion, which Deng put forward more than 20 years ago, may no longer be appropriate now that China is far more powerful.

Some thoughtful strategists appreciate that even if keeping a low profile could serve China's political and security relations with the United States well, it might not apply to China's relations with many other countries or to economic issues and those nontraditional security issues that have become essential in recent years, such as climate change, public health, and energy security. (Beijing can hardly keep a low profile when it actively participates in mechanisms such as BRIC, the informal group formed by Brazil, Russia, India, China, and the new member South Africa.) A foreign policy that insists merely on keeping China's profile low cannot cope effectively with the multi-faceted challenges facing the country today.

Home Is Where the Heart Is

A more sophisticated grand strategy is needed to serve China's domestic priorities. The government has issued no official written statement outlining such a vision, but some direction can be gleaned from the concepts of a "scientific outlook on development" and "building a harmonious society," which have been enunciated by Hu and have been recorded in all important CCP documents since 2003. In 2006, the Central Committee of the CCP announced that China's foreign policy "must maintain economic construction as its centerpiece, be closely integrated into domestic work, and be advanced by coordinating domestic and international situations." Moreover, four ongoing changes in China's strategic thinking may suggest the foundations for a new grand strategy.

The first transformation is the Chinese government's adoption of a comprehensive understanding of security, which incorporates economic and nontraditional concerns with traditional military and political interests. Chinese military planners have begun to take into consideration transnational problems such as terrorism and piracy, as well as cooperative activities such as participation in UN peacekeeping operations. Similarly, it is now clear that China must join other countries in stabilizing the global financial market in order to protect its own economic security. All this means that it is virtually impossible to distinguish China's friends from its foes. The United States might pose political and military threats, and Japan, a staunch U.S. ally, could be a geopolitical competitor of China's, but these two countries also happen to be two of China's greatest economic partners. Even though political difficulties appear to be on the rise with the European Union, it remains China's top economic partner. Russia, which some Chinese see as a potential security ally, is far less important economically and socially to China than is South Korea, another U.S. military ally. It will take painstaking efforts on Beijing's part to limit tensions between China's traditional political–military perspectives and its broadening socioeconomic interests—efforts that effectively amount to reconciling the diverging legacies of Mao and Deng. The best Beijing can do is to strengthen its economic ties with great powers while minimizing the likelihood of a military and political confrontation with them.

A second transformation is unfolding in Chinese diplomacy: it is becoming less country-oriented and more multilateral and issue-oriented. This shift toward functional focuses—counterterrorism, nuclear nonproliferation, environmental protection, energy security, food safety, post-disaster reconstruction—has complicated China's bilateral relationships, regardless of how friendly other states are toward it. For example, diverging geostrategic interests and territorial disputes have long come between China and India, but the two countries' common interest in fending off the West's pressure to reduce carbon emissions has drawn them closer. And now that Iran has become a key supplier of oil to China, its problems with the West over its nuclear program are testing China's stated commitment to the nuclear non-proliferation regime.

Changes in the mode of China's economic development account for a third transformation in the country's strategic thinking. Beijing's preoccupation with GDP growth is slowly giving way to concerns about economic efficiency, product quality, environmental protection, the creation of a social safety net, and technological innovation. Beijing's understanding of the core interest of development is expanding to include social dimensions. Correspondingly, China's leaders have decided to try to sustain the country's high growth rate by propping up domestic consumption and reducing over the long term the country's dependence on exports and foreign investment. They are now more concerned with global economic imbalances and financial fluctuations, even as international economic frictions are becoming more intense because of the global financial crisis. China's long-term interests will require some incremental appreciation of the yuan, but its desire to increase its exports in the short term will prevent its decision-makers from taking the quick measures urged by the United States and many other countries. Only the enhancement of China's domestic consumption and a steady opening of its capital markets will help it shake off these international pressures.

The fourth transformation has to do with China's values. So far, China's officials have said that although China has a distinctive political system and ideology, it can cooperate with other countries based on shared interests—although not, the suggestion seems to be, on shared values. But now that they strongly wish to enhance what they call the "cultural soft power of the nation" and improve China's international image, it appears necessary to also seek common values in the global arena, such as good governance and transparency. Continuing trials and tribulations at home, such as pervasive corruption and ethnic and social unrest in some regions, could also reinforce a shift in values among China's political elite by demonstrating that their hold on power and the country's continued resurgence depend on greater transparency and accountability, as well as on a firmer commitment to the rule of law, democracy, and human rights, all values that are widely shared throughout the world today.

All four of these developments are unfolding haltingly and are by no means irreversible. Nonetheless, they do reveal fundamental trends that will likely shape China's grand strategy in the foreseeable future. When Hu and other leaders call for "coordinating domestic and international situations," they mean that efforts to meet international challenges must not undermine domestic reforms. And with external challenges now coming not only from foreign powers—especially the United States and Japan—but also, and increasingly, from functional issues, coping with them effectively will require engaging foreign countries cooperatively and emphasizing compatible values.

Thus, it would be imprudent of Beijing to identify any one country as a major threat and invoke the need to keep it at bay as an organizing principle of Chinese foreign policy—unless the United States, or another great power, truly did regard China as its main adversary and so forced China to respond in kind. On the other hand, if keeping a low profile is a necessary component of Beijing's foreign policy, it is also insufficient. A grand strategy needs to consider other long-term objectives as well. One that appeals to some Chinese is the notion of building China into the most powerful state in the world: Liu Mingfu, a senior colonel who teaches at the People's Liberation Army's National Defense University, has declared that replacing the United States as the world's top military power should be China's goal. Another idea is to cast China as an alternative model of development (the "Beijing consensus") that can challenge Western systems, values, and leadership. But the Chinese leadership does not dream of turning China into a hegemon or a standard-bearer. Faced with mounting pressures on both the domestic and the international fronts, it is sober in its objectives, be they short- or long-term ones. Its main concern is how best to protect China's core interests—sovereignty, security, and development—against the messy cluster of threats that the country faces today. If an organizing principle must be established to guide China's grand strategy, it should be the improvement of the Chinese people's living standards, welfare, and happiness through social justice.

The Birth of a Great Nation

Having identified China's core interests and the external pressures that threaten them, the remaining question is, how can China's leadership safeguard the country's interests against those threats? China's continued success in modernizing its economy and lifting its people's standards of living depends heavily on global stability. Thus, it is in China's interest to contribute to a peaceful international environment. China should seek peaceful solutions to residual sovereignty and security issues, including the thorny territorial disputes between it and its neighbors. With the current leadership in Taiwan refraining from seeking formal independence from the mainland, Beijing is more confident that peace can be maintained across the Taiwan Strait. But it has yet to reach a political agreement with Taipei that would prevent renewed tensions in the future. The Chinese government also needs to find effective means to pacify Tibet and Xinjiang, as more unrest in those regions would likely elicit reactions from other countries.

Although the vast majority of people in China support a stronger Chinese military to defend the country's major interests, they should also recognize the dilemma that poses. As China builds its defense capabilities, especially its navy, it will have to convince others, including the United States and China's neighbors in Asia, that it is taking their concerns into consideration. It will have to make the plans of the People's Liberation Army more transparent and show a willingness to join efforts to establish security structures in the Asia-Pacific region and safeguard existing global security regimes, especially the nuclear nonproliferation regime. It must also continue to work with other states to prevent Iran and North Korea from obtaining nuclear weapons. China's national security will be well served if it makes more contributions to other countries' efforts to strengthen security in cyberspace and outer space. Of course, none of this excludes the possibility that China might have to use force to protect its sovereignty or its security in some special circumstances, such as in the event of a terrorist attack.

China has been committed to almost all existing global economic regimes. But it will have to do much more before it is recognized as a full-fledged market economy. It has already gained an increasingly larger say in global economic mechanisms, such as the G-20, the World Bank, and the International Monetary Fund. Now, it needs to make specific policy proposals and adjustments to help rebalance the global economy and facilitate its plans to change its development pattern at home. Setting a good example by building a low-carbon economy is one major step that would benefit both China and the world.

A grand strategy requires defining a geostrategic focus, and China's geostrategic focus is Asia. When communication lines in Central Asia and South Asia were poor, China's development strategy and economic interests tilted toward its east coast and the Pacific Ocean. Today, East Asia is still of vital importance, but China should and will begin to pay more strategic attention to the west. The central government has been conducting the Grand Western Development Program in many western provinces and regions, notably Tibet and Xinjiang, for more than a decade. It is now more actively initiating and participating in new development projects in Afghanistan, India, Pakistan, Central Asia, and throughout the Caspian Sea region, all the way to Europe. This new western outlook may reshape China's geostrategic vision as well as the Eurasian landscape.

Still, relationships with great powers remain crucial to defending China's core interests. Notwithstanding the unprecedented economic interdependence of China, Japan, and the United States, strategic trust is still lacking between China and the United States and China and Japan. It is imperative that the Chinese–Japanese–U.S. trilateral interaction be stable and constructive, and a trilateral strategic dialogue is desirable. More generally, too, China will have to invest tremendous resources to promote a more benign image on the world stage. A China with good governance will be a likeable China. Even more important, it will have to learn that soft power cannot be artificially created: such influence originates more from a society than from a state.

Two daunting tasks lie ahead before a better-designed Chinese grand strategy can take shape and be implemented. The first is to improve policy coordination among Chinese government agencies. Almost all institutions in the central leadership and local governments are involved in foreign relations to varying degrees, and it is virtually impossible for them to see China's national interest the same way or to speak with one voice. These differences confuse outsiders as well as the Chinese people.

The second challenge will be to manage the diversity of views among China's political elite and the general public, at a time when the value system in China is changing rapidly. Mobilizing public support for government policies is expected to strengthen Beijing's diplomatic bargaining power while also helping consolidate its domestic popularity. But excessive nationalism could breed more public frustration and create more pressure on the government if its policies fail to deliver immediately, which could hurt China's political order, as well as its foreign relations. Even as it allows different voices to be heard on foreign affairs, the central leadership should more vigorously inform the population of its own view, which is consistently more moderate and prudent than the inflammatory remarks found in the media and on Web sites.

No major power's interests can conform exactly to those of the international community; China is no exception. And with one-fifth of the world's population, it is more like a continent than a country. Yet despite the complexity of developing a grand strategy for China, the effort is at once consistent with China's internal priorities and generally positive for the international community. China will serve its interests better if it can provide more common goods to the international community and share more values with other states.

How other countries respond to the emergence of China as a global power will also have a great impact on China's internal development and external behavior. If the international community appears not to understand China's aspirations, its anxieties, and its difficulties in feeding itself and modernizing, the Chinese people may ask themselves why China should be bound by rules that were essentially established by the Western powers. China can rightfully be expected to take on more international responsibilities. But then the international community should take on the responsibility of helping the world's largest member support itself.

Critical Thinking

1. What is Wang Jisi's point of view?
2. What are the main reasons he offers to support his point of view?
3. How do domestic concerns such as economic and social development influence China's foreign policy?
4. Why is an anti-United States strategy unlikely to be adopted?
5. What are two challenges that China must overcome before a grand strategy takes shape?
6. Do the authors of Article 1 view China in a similar or different perspective than Wang Jisi?

WANG JISI is Dean of the School of International Studies at Peking University, in Beijing.

UNIT 2

Population and Food Production

Unit Selections

Learning Outcomes

After reading this Unit, you will be able to:

- Describe major demographic trends and the variations in these trends between regions of the world.

- Describe patterns in international migration.

- Describe the Blue Food movement in comparison to traditional livestock production.

- Offer examples of how demographic changes affect natural resources and social structures.

- Assess your initial effort at identifying your theory of international relations and how this unit changes/complements it.

Student Website
www.mhhe.com/cls

Internet References

The Hunger Project
www.thp.org
Penn Library: Resources by Subject
www.library.upenn.edu/cgi-bin/res/sr.cgi
World Health Organization
www.who.int
WWW Virtual Library: Demography & Population Studies
http://demography.anu.edu.au/VirtualLibrary

After World War II, the world's population reached an estimated 2 billion people. It had taken 250 years to triple to that level. In the six decades following World War II, the population tripled again to 6 billion. When the typical reader of this book reaches the age of 50, demographers estimate that the global population will have reached 8.5 billion! By 2050, or about 100 years after World War II, some experts forecast that 10 to 12 billion people may populate the world. A person born in 1946 (a so-called baby boomer) who lives to be 100 could see a sixfold increase in population.

Nothing like this has ever occurred before. To state this in a different way: In the next 50 years there will have to be twice as much food grown, twice as many schools and hospitals available, and twice as much of everything else just to maintain the current and rather uneven standard of living. We live in an unprecedented time in human history.

One of the most interesting aspects of this population growth is that there is little agreement about whether this situation is good or bad. The government of China, for example, has a policy that encourages couples to have only one child. In contrast, a few governments use various financial incentives to promote large families.

In the second decade of the new millennium, many population issues transcend simple numeric or economic considerations. The disappearance of indigenous cultures is a good example of the pressures of population growth on people who live on the margins of modern society. Finally, although demographers develop various scenarios forecasting population growth, it is important to remember that there are circumstances that could lead not to growth but to a significant decline in global population. The spread of AIDS and other infectious diseases reveals that confidence in modern medicine's ability to control these scourges may be premature. Nature has its own checks and balances to the population dynamic. This factor is often overlooked in an age of technological optimism.

The lead article in this section provides an overview of general demographic trends, with a special focus on issues related to aging. In the second article, the often-overlooked issue of reversing the increase in human population as a strategy for achieving long-term balance with the environment is described. The third article examines the politically important issue of global patterns in migration.

There are, of course, no greater checks on population growth than the availability of an adequate food supply and control of the spread of infectious diseases. Some experts question whether current agricultural technologies are sustainable over the long run. How much food are we going to need, and how are farmers and fishermen going to provide it? Will markets deliver food to those in greatest need?

© Ingram Publishing

Making predictions about the future of the world's population is a complicated task, for a variety of forces are at work and considerable variation exists from region to region. The danger of oversimplification must be overcome if governments and international organizations are going to respond with meaningful policies. Perhaps one could say that there is not a global population problem but rather many population challenges that vary from country to country and region to region.

The New Population Bomb: The Four Megatrends That Will Change the World

JACK A. GOLDSTONE

Forty-two years ago, the biologist Paul Ehrlich warned in The Population Bomb that mass starvation would strike in the 1970s and 1980s, with the world's population growth outpacing the production of food and other critical resources. Thanks to innovations and efforts such as the "green revolution" in farming and the widespread adoption of family planning, Ehrlich's worst fears did not come to pass. In fact, since the 1970s, global economic output has increased and fertility has fallen dramatically, especially in developing countries.

The United Nations Population Division now projects that global population growth will nearly halt by 2050. By that date, the world's population will have stabilized at 9.15 billion people, according to the "medium growth" variant of the UN's authoritative population database World Population Prospects: The 2008 Revision. (Today's global population is 6.83 billion.) Barring a cataclysmic climate crisis or a complete failure to recover from the current economic malaise, global economic output is expected to increase by two to three percent per year, meaning that global income will increase far more than population over the next four decades.

But twenty-first-century international security will depend less on how many people inhabit the world than on how the global population is composed and distributed: where populations are declining and where they are growing, which countries are relatively older and which are more youthful, and how demographics will influence population movements across regions.

These elements are not well recognized or widely understood. A recent article in The Economist, for example, cheered the decline in global fertility without noting other vital demographic developments. Indeed, the same UN data cited by The Economist reveal four historic shifts that will fundamentally alter the world's population over the next four decades: the relative demographic weight of the world's developed countries will drop by nearly 25 percent, shifting economic power to the developing nations; the developed countries' labor forces will substantially age and decline, constraining economic growth in the developed world and raising the demand for immigrant workers; most of the world's expected population growth will increasingly be concentrated in today's poorest, youngest, and most heavily Muslim countries, which have a dangerous lack of quality education, capital, and employment opportunities; and, for the first time in history, most of the world's population will become urbanized, with the largest urban centers being in the world's poorest countries, where policing, sanitation, and health care are often scarce. Taken together, these trends will pose challenges every bit as alarming as those noted by Ehrlich. Coping with them will require nothing less than a major reconsideration of the world's basic global governance structures.

Europe's Reversal of Fortunes

At the beginning of the eighteenth century, approximately 20 percent of the world's inhabitants lived in Europe (including Russia). Then, with the Industrial Revolution, Europe's population boomed, and streams of European emigrants set off for the Americas. By the eve of World War I, Europe's population had more than quadrupled. In 1913, Europe had more people than China, and the proportion of the world's population living in Europe and the former European colonies of North America had risen to over 33 percent. But this trend reversed after World War I, as basic health care and sanitation began to spread to poorer countries. In Asia, Africa, and Latin America, people began to live longer, and birthrates remained high or fell only slowly. By 2003, the combined populations of Europe, the United States, and Canada accounted for just 17 percent of the global population. In 2050, this figure is expected to be just 12 percent—far less than it was in 1700. (These projections, moreover, might even understate the reality because they reflect the "medium growth" projection of the UN forecasts, which assumes that the fertility rates of developing countries will decline while those of developed countries will increase. In fact, many developed countries show no evidence of increasing fertility rates.) The West's relative decline is even more dramatic if one also considers changes in income. The Industrial Revolution made Europeans not only more numerous than they had been but also considerably richer per capita than others worldwide. According to the economic historian Angus Maddison, Europe, the United States, and Canada together produced about 32 percent of the world's GDP at the beginning of the nineteenth century. By 1950, that proportion had increased to a remarkable 68 percent of the world's total output (adjusted to reflect purchasing power parity).

This trend, too, is headed for a sharp reversal. The proportion of global GDP produced by Europe, the United States, and Canada fell from 68 percent in 1950 to 47 percent in 2003 and will decline even more steeply in the future. If the growth rate of per capita income (again, adjusted for purchasing power parity) between 2003 and 2050 remains as it was between 1973 and 2003—averaging 1.68 percent annually in Europe, the United States, and Canada and 2.47 percent annually in the rest of the world—then the combined GDP of Europe, the United States, and Canada will roughly double by 2050, whereas the GDP of the rest of the world will grow by a factor of five. The portion of global GDP produced by Europe, the United States, and Canada in 2050 will then be less than 30 percent—smaller than it was in 1820.

These figures also imply that an overwhelming proportion of the world's GDP growth between 2003 and 2050—nearly 80 percent—will occur outside of Europe, the United States, and Canada. By the middle of this century, the global middle class—those capable of purchasing durable consumer products, such as cars, appliances, and electronics—will increasingly be found in what is now considered the developing world. The World Bank has predicted that by 2030 the number of middle-class people in the developing world will be 1.2 billion—a rise of 200 percent since 2005. This means that the developing world's middle class alone will be larger than the total populations of Europe, Japan, and the United States combined. From now on, therefore, the main driver of global economic expansion will be the economic growth of newly industrialized countries, such as Brazil, China, India, Indonesia, Mexico, and Turkey.

Aging Pains

Part of the reason developed countries will be less economically dynamic in the coming decades is that their populations will become substantially older. The European countries, Canada, the United States, Japan, South Korea, and even China are aging at unprecedented rates. Today, the proportion of people aged 60 or older in China and South Korea is 12–15 percent. It is 15–22 percent in the European Union, Canada, and the United States and 30 percent in Japan. With baby boomers aging and life expectancy increasing, these numbers will increase dramatically. In 2050, approximately 30 percent of Americans, Canadians, Chinese, and Europeans will be over 60, as will more than 40 percent of Japanese and South Koreans.

Over the next decades, therefore, these countries will have increasingly large proportions of retirees and increasingly small proportions of workers. As workers born during the baby boom of 1945–65 are retiring, they are not being replaced by a new cohort of citizens of prime working age (15–59 years old).

Industrialized countries are experiencing a drop in their working-age populations that is even more severe than the overall slowdown in their population growth. South Korea represents the most extreme example. Even as its total population is projected to decline by almost 9 percent by 2050 (from 48.3

million to 44.1 million), the population of working-age South Koreans is expected to drop by 36 percent (from 32.9 million to 21.1 million), and the number of South Koreans aged 60 and older will increase by almost 150 percent (from 7.3 million to 18 million). By 2050, in other words, the entire working-age population will barely exceed the 60-and-older population. Although South Korea's case is extreme, it represents an increasingly common fate for developed countries. Europe is expected to lose 24 percent of its prime working-age population (about 120 million workers) by 2050, and its 60-and-older population is expected to increase by 47 percent. In the United States, where higher fertility and more immigration are expected than in Europe, the working-age population will grow by 15 percent over the next four decades—a steep decline from its growth of 62 percent between 1950 and 2010. And by 2050, the United States' 60-and-older population is expected to double.

All this will have a dramatic impact on economic growth, health care, and military strength in the developed world. The forces that fueled economic growth in industrialized countries during the second half of the twentieth century—increased productivity due to better education, the movement of women into the labor force, and innovations in technology—will all likely weaken in the coming decades. College enrollment boomed after World War II, a trend that is not likely to recur in the twenty-first century; the extensive movement of women into the labor force also was a one-time social change; and the technological change of the time resulted from innovators who created new products and leading-edge consumers who were willing to try them out—two groups that are thinning out as the industrialized world's population ages.

Overall economic growth will also be hampered by a decline in the number of new consumers and new households. When developed countries' labor forces were growing by 0.5–1.0 percent per year, as they did until 2005, even annual increases in real output per worker of just 1.7 percent meant that annual economic growth totaled 2.2–2.7 percent per year. But with the labor forces of many developed countries (such as Germany, Hungary, Japan, Russia, and the Baltic states) now shrinking by 0.2 percent per year and those of other countries (including Austria, the Czech Republic, Denmark, Greece, and Italy) growing by less than 0.2 percent per year, the same 1.7 percent increase in real output per worker yields only 1.5–1.9 percent annual overall growth. Moreover, developed countries will be lucky to keep productivity growth at even that level; in many developed countries, productivity is more likely to decline as the population ages.

A further strain on industrialized economies will be rising medical costs: as populations age, they will demand more health care for longer periods of time. Public pension schemes for aging populations are already being reformed in various industrialized countries—often prompting heated debate. In theory, at least, pensions might be kept solvent by increasing the retirement age, raising taxes modestly, and phasing out benefits for the wealthy. Regardless, the number of 80- and 90-year-olds—who are unlikely to work and highly likely to require nursing-home and other expensive care—will rise dramatically. And even if 60- and 70-year-olds remain active and employed, they will require procedures and medications—hip replacements, kidney transplants, blood-pressure treatments—to sustain their health in old age.

All this means that just as aging developed countries will have proportionally fewer workers, innovators, and consumerist young households, a large portion of those countries' remaining economic growth will have to be diverted to pay for the medical bills and pensions of their growing elderly populations. Basic services, meanwhile, will be increasingly costly because fewer young workers will be available for strenuous and labor-intensive jobs. Unfortunately, policymakers seldom reckon with these potentially disruptive effects of otherwise welcome developments, such as higher life expectancy.

Youth and Islam in the Developing World

Even as the industrialized countries of Europe, North America, and Northeast Asia will experience unprecedented aging this century, fast-growing countries in Africa, Latin America, the Middle East, and Southeast Asia will have exceptionally youthful populations. Today, roughly nine out of ten children under the age of 15 live in developing countries. And these are the countries that will continue to have the world's highest birthrates. Indeed, over 70 percent of the world's population growth between now and 2050 will occur in 24 countries, all of which are classified by the World Bank as low income or lower-middle income, with an average per capita income of under $3,855 in 2008.

Many developing countries have few ways of providing employment to their young, fast-growing populations. Would-be laborers, therefore, will be increasingly attracted to the labor markets of the aging developed countries of Europe, North America, and Northeast Asia. Youthful immigrants from nearby regions with high unemployment—Central America, North Africa, and Southeast Asia, for example—will be drawn to those vital entry-level and manual-labor jobs that sustain advanced economies: janitors, nursing-home aides, bus drivers, plumbers, security guards, farm workers, and the like. Current levels of immigration from developing to developed countries are paltry compared to those that the forces of supply and demand might soon create across the world.

These forces will act strongly on the Muslim world, where many economically weak countries will continue to experience dramatic population growth in the decades ahead. In 1950, Bangladesh, Egypt, Indonesia, Nigeria, Pakistan, and Turkey had a combined population of 242 million. By 2009, those six countries were the world's most populous Muslim-majority countries and had a combined population of 886 million. Their populations are continuing to grow and indeed are expected to increase by 475 million between now and 2050—during which time, by comparison, the six most populous developed countries are projected to gain only 44 million inhabitants. Worldwide, of the 48 fastest-growing countries today—those with annual population growth of two percent or more—28 are majority Muslim or have Muslim minorities of 33 percent or more.

It is therefore imperative to improve relations between Muslim and Western societies. This will be difficult given that many Muslims live in poor communities vulnerable to radical appeals and many see the West as antagonistic and militaristic. In the 2009 Pew Global Attitudes Project survey, for example, whereas 69 percent of those Indonesians and Nigerians surveyed reported viewing the United States favorably, just 18 percent of those polled in Egypt, Jordan, Pakistan, and Turkey (all U.S. allies) did. And in 2006, when the Pew survey last asked detailed questions about Muslim-Western relations, more than half of the respondents in Muslim countries characterized those relations as bad and blamed the West for this state of affairs.

But improving relations is all the more important because of the growing demographic weight of poor Muslim countries and the attendant increase in Muslim immigration, especially to Europe from North Africa and the Middle East. (To be sure, forecasts that Muslims will soon dominate Europe are outlandish: Muslims compose just three to ten percent of the population in the major European countries today, and this proportion will at most double by midcentury.) Strategists worldwide must consider that the world's young are becoming concentrated in those countries least prepared to educate and employ them, including some Muslim states. Any resulting poverty, social tension, or ideological radicalization could have disruptive effects in many corners of the world. But this need not be the case; the healthy immigration of workers to the developed world and the movement of capital to the developing world, among other things, could lead to better results.

Urban Sprawl

Exacerbating twenty-first-century risks will be the fact that the world is urbanizing to an unprecedented degree. The year 2010 will likely be the first time in history that a majority of the world's people live in cities rather than in the countryside. Whereas less than 30 percent of the world's population was urban in 1950, according to UN projections, more than 70 percent will be by 2050.

Lower-income countries in Asia and Africa are urbanizing especially rapidly, as agriculture becomes less labor intensive and as employment opportunities shift to the industrial and service sectors. Already, most of the world's urban agglomerations—Mumbai (population 20.1 million), Mexico City (19.5 million), New Delhi (17 million), Shanghai (15.8 million), Calcutta (15.6 million), Karachi (13.1 million), Cairo (12.5 million), Manila (11.7 million), Lagos (10.6 million), Jakarta (9.7 million)—are found in low-income countries. Many of these countries have multiple cities with over one million residents each: Pakistan has eight, Mexico 12, and China more than 100. The UN projects that the urbanized proportion of sub-Saharan Africa will nearly double between 2005 and 2050, from 35 percent (300 million people) to over 67 percent (1 billion). China, which is roughly 40 percent urbanized today, is expected to be 73 percent urbanized by 2050; India, which is less than 30 percent urbanized today, is expected to be 55 percent urbanized by 2050. Overall, the world's urban population is expected to grow by 3 billion people by 2050.

This urbanization may prove destabilizing. Developing countries that urbanize in the twenty-first century will have far lower per capita incomes than did many industrial countries when they first urbanized. The United States, for example, did not reach 65 percent urbanization until 1950, when per capita income was nearly $13,000 (in 2005 dollars). By contrast, Nigeria, Pakistan, and the Philippines, which are approaching similar levels of urbanization, currently have per capita incomes of just $1,800–$4,000 (in 2005 dollars).

According to the research of Richard Cincotta and other political demographers, countries with younger populations are especially prone to civil unrest and are less able to create or sustain democratic institutions. And the more heavily urbanized, the more such countries are likely to experience Dickensian poverty and anarchic violence. In good times, a thriving economy might keep urban residents employed and governments flush with sufficient resources to meet their needs. More often, however, sprawling and impoverished cities are vulnerable to crime lords, gangs, and petty rebellions. Thus, the rapid urbanization of the developing world in the decades ahead might bring, in exaggerated form, problems similar to those that urbanization brought to nineteenth-century Europe. Back then, cyclical employment, inadequate policing, and limited sanitation and education often spawned widespread labor strife, periodic violence, and sometimes—as in the 1820s, the 1830s, and 1848—even revolutions.

International terrorism might also originate in fast-urbanizing developing countries (even more than it already does). With their neighborhood networks, access to the Internet and digital communications technology, and concentration of valuable targets, sprawling cities offer excellent opportunities for recruiting, maintaining, and hiding terrorist networks.

Defusing the Bomb

Averting this century's potential dangers will require sweeping measures. Three major global efforts defused the population bomb of Ehrlich's day: a commitment by governments and nongovernmental organizations to control reproduction rates; agricultural advances, such as the green revolution and the spread of new technology; and a vast increase in international trade, which globalized markets and thus allowed developing countries to export foodstuffs in exchange for seeds, fertilizers, and machinery, which in turn helped them boost production. But today's population bomb is the product less of absolute growth in the world's population than of changes in its age and distribution. Policymakers must therefore adapt today's global governance institutions to the new realities of the aging of the industrialized world, the concentration of the world's economic and population growth in developing countries, and the increase in international immigration.

During the Cold War, Western strategists divided the world into a "First World," of democratic industrialized countries; a "Second World," of communist industrialized countries; and a "Third World," of developing countries. These strategists focused chiefly on deterring or managing conflict between the First and the Second Worlds and on launching proxy wars and diplomatic initiatives to attract Third World countries into

the First World's camp. Since the end of the Cold War, strategists have largely abandoned this three-group division and have tended to believe either that the United States, as the sole superpower, would maintain a Pax Americana or that the world would become multipolar, with the United States, Europe, and China playing major roles.

Unfortunately, because they ignore current global demographic trends, these views will be obsolete within a few decades. A better approach would be to consider a different three-world order, with a new First World of the aging industrialized nations of North America, Europe, and Asia's Pacific Rim (including Japan, Singapore, South Korea, and Taiwan, as well as China after 2030, by which point the one-child policy will have produced significant aging); a Second World comprising fast-growing and economically dynamic countries with a healthy mix of young and old inhabitants (such as Brazil, Iran, Mexico, Thailand, Turkey, and Vietnam, as well as China until 2030); and a Third World of fast-growing, very young, and increasingly urbanized countries with poorer economies and often weak governments. To cope with the instability that will likely arise from the new Third World's urbanization, economic strife, lawlessness, and potential terrorist activity, the aging industrialized nations of the new First World must build effective alliances with the growing powers of the new Second World and together reach out to Third World nations. Second World powers will be pivotal in the twenty-first century not just because they will drive economic growth and consume technologies and other products engineered in the First World; they will also be central to international security and cooperation. The realities of religion, culture, and geographic proximity mean that any peaceful and productive engagement by the First World of Third World countries will have to include the open cooperation of Second World countries.

Strategists, therefore, must fundamentally reconsider the structure of various current global institutions. The G-8, for example, will likely become obsolete as a body for making global economic policy. The G-20 is already becoming increasingly important, and this is less a short-term consequence of the ongoing global financial crisis than the beginning of the necessary recognition that Brazil, China, India, Indonesia, Mexico, Turkey, and others are becoming global economic powers. International institutions will not retain their legitimacy if they exclude the world's fastest-growing and most economically dynamic countries. It is essential, therefore, despite European concerns about the potential effects on immigration, to take steps such as admitting Turkey into the European Union. This would add youth and economic dynamism to the EU—and would prove that Muslims are welcome to join Europeans as equals in shaping a free and prosperous future. On the other hand, excluding Turkey from the EU could lead to hostility not only on the part of Turkish citizens, who are expected to number 100 million by 2050, but also on the part of Muslim populations worldwide.

NATO must also adapt. The alliance today is composed almost entirely of countries with aging, shrinking populations and relatively slow-growing economies. It is oriented toward the Northern Hemisphere and holds on to a Cold War structure that cannot adequately respond to contemporary threats. The young and increasingly populous countries of Africa, the Middle East, Central Asia, and South Asia could mobilize insurgents much more easily than NATO could mobilize the troops it would need if it were called on to stabilize those countries. Long-standing NATO members should, therefore—although it would require atypical creativity and flexibility—consider the logistical and demographic advantages of inviting into the alliance countries such as Brazil and Morocco, rather than countries such as Albania. That this seems far-fetched does not minimize the imperative that First World countries begin including large and strategic Second and Third World powers in formal international alliances.

The case of Afghanistan—a country whose population is growing fast and where NATO is currently engaged—illustrates the importance of building effective global institutions. Today, there are 28 million Afghans; by 2025, there will be 45 million; and by 2050, there will be close to 75 million. As nearly 20 million additional Afghans are born over the next 15 years, NATO will have an opportunity to help Afghanistan become reasonably stable, self-governing, and prosperous. If NATO's efforts fail and the Afghans judge that NATO intervention harmed their interests, tens of millions of young Afghans will become more hostile to the West. But if they come to think that NATO's involvement benefited their society, the West will have tens of millions of new friends. The example might then motivate the approximately one billion other young Muslims growing up in low-income countries over the next four decades to look more kindly on relations between their countries and the countries of the industrialized West.

Creative Reforms at Home

The aging industrialized countries can also take various steps at home to promote stability in light of the coming demographic trends. First, they should encourage families to have more children. France and Sweden have had success providing child care, generous leave time, and financial allowances to families with young children. Yet there is no consensus among policymakers—and certainly not among demographers—about what policies best encourage fertility.

More important than unproven tactics for increasing family size is immigration. Correctly managed, population movement can benefit developed and developing countries alike. Given the dangers of young, underemployed, and unstable populations in developing countries, immigration to developed countries can provide economic opportunities for the ambitious and serve as a safety valve for all. Countries that embrace immigrants, such as the United States, gain economically by having willing laborers and greater entrepreneurial spirit. And countries with high levels of emigration (but not so much that they experience so-called brain drains) also benefit because emigrants often send remittances home or return

to their native countries with valuable education and work experience.

One somewhat daring approach to immigration would be to encourage a reverse flow of older immigrants from developed to developing countries. If older residents of developed countries took their retirements along the southern coast of the Mediterranean or in Latin America or Africa, it would greatly reduce the strain on their home countries' public entitlement systems. The developing countries involved, meanwhile, would benefit because caring for the elderly and providing retirement and leisure services is highly labor intensive. Relocating a portion of these activities to developing countries would provide employment and valuable training to the young, growing populations of the Second and Third Worlds.

This would require developing residential and medical facilities of First World quality in Second and Third World countries. Yet even this difficult task would be preferable to the status quo, by which low wages and poor facilities lead to a steady drain of medical and nursing talent from developing to developed countries. Many residents of developed countries who desire cheaper medical procedures already practice medical tourism today, with India, Singapore, and Thailand being the most common destinations. (For example, the international consulting firm Deloitte estimated that 750,000 Americans traveled abroad for care in 2008.)

Never since 1800 has a majority of the world's economic growth occurred outside of Europe, the United States, and Canada. Never have so many people in those regions been over 60 years old. And never have low-income countries' populations been so young and so urbanized. But such will be the world's demography in the twenty-first century. The strategic and economic policies of the twentieth century are obsolete, and it is time to find new ones.

Reference

Goldstone, Jack A. "The new population bomb: the four megatrends that will change the world." *Foreign Affairs* 89.1 (2010): 31. *General OneFile*. Web. 23 Jan. 2010. http://0-find.galegroup.com.www.consuls.org/gps/start.do?proId=IPS&userGroupName=a30wc.

Critical Thinking

1. Identify the four demographic trends.
2. How does the author argue that international politics is changing due to these trends?
3. Summarize the Afghanistan case study.
4. How are these trends related to Kennedy's analysis in Article 4?
5. How does this discussion of demographic trends relate to the Allegory of the Balloon?

Population and Sustainability

Reversing the rise in human numbers is the most overlooked and essential strategy for achieving long-term balance with the environment. Contrary to widespread opinion, it does not require "population control."

ROBERT ENGELMAN

In an era of changing climate and sinking economies, Malthusian limits to growth are back—and squeezing us painfully. Whereas *more people* once meant more ingenuity, more talent, and more innovation, today it just seems to mean *less for each.* Less water for every cattle herder in the Horn of Africa. (The United Nations projects there will be more than four billion people living in nations defined as water-scarce or water-stressed by 2050, up from half a billion in 1995.) Less land for every farmer already tilling slopes so steep they risk killing themselves by falling off their fields. (At a bit less than six tenths of an acre, global per capita cropland today is little more than half of what it was in 1961, and more than 900 million people are hungry.) Less capacity in the atmosphere to accept the heat-trapping gases that could fry the planet for centuries to come. Scarcer and higher-priced energy and food. And if the world's economy does not bounce back to its glory days, less credit and fewer jobs.

It's not surprising that this kind of predicament brings back an old sore topic: human population and whether to do anything about it. Let's concede up front that nothing short of a catastrophic population crash (think of the film *Children of Men,* set in a world without children) would make much difference to climate change, water scarcity or land shortages over the next decade or so. There are 6.8 billion of us today, and more are on the way. To make a dent in these problems in the short term without throwing anyone overboard, we will need to radically reduce individuals' footprint on the environment through improvements in technology and possibly wrenching changes in lifestyle.

But until the world's population stops growing, there will be no end to the need to squeeze individuals' consumption of fossil fuels and other natural resources. A close look at this problem is sobering: short of catastrophic leaps in the death rate or unwanted crashes in fertility, the world's population is all but certain to grow by at least one billion to two billion people. The low-consuming billions of the developing world would love to consume as Americans do, with similar disregard for the environment—and they have as much of a right to do so. These facts suggest that the coming ecological impact will be of a scale that we will simply have to manage and adapt to as best we can.

Population growth constantly pushes the consequences of any level of individual consumption to a higher plateau, and reductions in individual consumption can always be overwhelmed by increases in population. The simple reality is that acting on both, consistently and simultaneously, is the key to long-term environmental sustainability. The sustainability benefits of level or falling human numbers are too powerful to ignore for long.

In the U.S., this discussion remains muted all the same. Population concerns may lurk within the public anger over illegal immigration or over the unwed California mother of octuplets earlier this year. But to the extent that the news media address domestic population growth at all, it is through euphemisms such as "sprawl" (the theoretical culprit in pollution of the Chesapeake Bay, for example) or the economy (the theoretical driver of increased greenhouse gas emissions). You are more likely to read about population growth in a letter to the editor than in a news story or editorial.

When President-elect Barack Obama pledged in late 2008 to bring U.S. carbon dioxide emissions to their 1990 levels by 2020, environmentalists struggled to swallow their dismay. The European Union, after all, had committed itself to 20 percent *reductions* from 1990 levels. But on a per capita basis, President Obama's pledge was somewhat *more* ambitious than the E.U.'s was. Because of much more rapid population growth than in the E.U., Americans would be cutting their individual emissions by 26 percent under his plan and Europeans by 25 percent under theirs. Any pledges to lower emissions by a uniform percentage among industrial countries will be much harder for the U.S. to achieve, simply because it is gaining people so fast through immigration and a birthrate that is higher than average for a developed nation.

The bitterness of the immigration debate has helped keep U.S. population growth off-limits in the national conversation. In industrial countries outside of North America, however, population is creeping back into public and even political consciousness. In the U.K., an all-party parliamentary panel issued a report called "Return of the Population Growth Factor" and called for stronger efforts to slow that growth. And the concern in the U.K.

is not just about the people "over there" in developing countries. In early 2009 Jonathon Porritt, chair of the government's Sustainable Development Commission, whacked a hornet's nest by calling parents of more than two children "irresponsible" and blasting mainstream environmental groups for "betraying" their members by fearing to call for small families. "It is the ghost at the table," Porritt said of population in an interview with the *Daily Telegraph,* a London broadsheet. Blog comments on his remarks, most of them supportive, soared into the thousands.

Meanwhile, in Australia, as summer temperatures hovered near 117 degrees Fahrenheit (47 degrees Celsius) and murderous flames converted forests into carbon dioxide, a new book entitled *Overloading Australia: How Governments and Media Dither and Deny on Population* issued an unusual ecological battle cry: ignore all admonitions to conserve the country's increasingly scarce water supplies until the government eliminates "baby bonuses" in the tax code and clamps down on immigration. A former premier of New South Wales spoke at the book's launch.

With comments such as these gaining attention—and in some circles, approval—are environmentalists and eventually policy makers likely to renew the decades-old call for "population control"? Would they be wise to do so?

A Number of Us

Two big questions present themselves as population reemerges from the shadows: Can any feasible downshift in population growth actually put the environment on a more sustainable path? And if so, are there measures that the public and policy makers would support that could actually bring about such a change?

Nature, of course, couldn't care less how many of us there are. What matters to the environment are the sums of human pulls and pushes, the extractions of resources and the injections of wastes. When these exceed key tipping points, nature and its systems can change quickly and dramatically. But the magnitudes of environmental impacts stem not just from our numbers but also from behaviors we learn from our parents and cultures. Broadly speaking, if population is the number of us, then consumption is the way each of us behaves. In this unequal world, the behavior of a dozen people in one place sometimes has more environmental impact than does that of a few hundred somewhere else.

Consider how these principles relate to global warming. The greenhouse gases already released into the atmosphere are likely to bring us quite close to the 3.6 degree F (two degree C) increase from the preindustrial global temperature average that many scientists see as the best-guess threshold of potential climate catastrophe. Already the earth is experiencing harsher droughts, fiercer storms and higher sea levels. If the scientists are right, these impacts will worsen for decades or centuries. Indeed, even if we ended all emissions tomorrow, additional warming is on the way thanks to the momentum built into the earth's intricate climate system. (The oceans, for example, have yet to come into equilibrium with the extra heat-trapping capacity of the atmosphere. As the oceans continue to warm, so will the land around them.)

Our species' demographic growth since its birth in Africa 200,000 years ago clearly contributed to this crisis. If world population had stayed stable at roughly 300 million people—a number that demographers believe characterized humanity from the birth of Christ to A.D. 1000 and that equals the population of just the U.S. today—there would not be enough of us to have the effect of relocating the coastlines even if we all drove Hummers. But instead we kept growing our numbers, which are projected to reach 9.1 billion by midcentury.

Humanity's consumption behaviors consequently did and do matter, and in this arena, all people have not been created equal. Greenhouse gas release has been linked overwhelmingly, at least up until recently, to the high-consumption habits of the industrial nations. As a result, in an ethical outrage as big as all outdoors, the coming shifts in climate and sea level will most harm the world's poor, who are least responsible for the atmosphere's composition, and will least harm the wealthy, who bear the biggest responsibility.

All-Consuming Passions

What part can the size of the human race play in finding a happy ending to this morality play? Population scenarios cannot directly address the inequity in emissions patterns—but they are far from unimportant.

Countries with the highest emissions per capita tend to have smaller families on average, whereas those with low emissions per capita tend to have larger ones. Americans, for example, consumed 8.6 tons of oil or its commercial energy equivalent per capita in 2007, according to data kept by British Petroleum; Indians consumed just 0.4 ton per capita. (These figures somewhat distort the gap because they exclude biomass and other noncommercial forms of energy, for which data are unreliable.)

So while India gained 17 million people in that year and the U.S. gained three million, by this simplified math the U.S. growth in population counted for the equivalent of an additional 25.6 million tons of oil consumed, whereas India's much greater growth counted for only 6.6 million additional tons. With such large disparities, the climate would be better served if the Americans emulated Indian consumption than if India emulated U.S. population.

End of story? For a variety of reasons, not quite. Population is not a contrasting force to consumption but something very close to its parent. Alone, each of us has no significant impact on the planet, even when our collective behavior overwhelms its natural processes. Historically, population has grown fastest when per capita consumption is modest. Later, consumption tends to explode on the base of a population that is large, but it is by then growing more slowly. Throughout the 19th century, the U.S. population grew at rates typical of Africa today. That century of rapid growth helped to make 21st-century America (with 307 million people now) a consumption behemoth.

The same one-two punch of population growth followed by consumption growth is now occurring in China (1.34 billion people) and India (1.2 billion). Per capita commercial energy use has been growing so rapidly in both countries (or at least it

Human Population Growth.

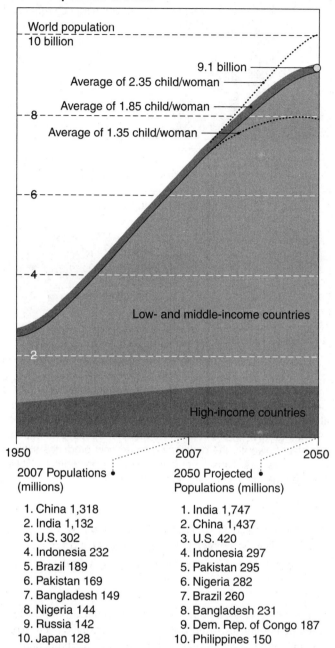

2007 Populations •
(millions)

1. China 1,318
2. India 1,132
3. U.S. 302
4. Indonesia 232
5. Brazil 189
6. Pakistan 169
7. Bangladesh 149
8. Nigeria 144
9. Russia 142
10. Japan 128

2050 Projected •
Populations (millions)

1. India 1,747
2. China 1,437
3. U.S. 420
4. Indonesia 297
5. Pakistan 295
6. Nigeria 282
7. Brazil 260
8. Bangladesh 231
9. Dem. Rep. of Congo 187
10. Philippines 150

The challenge to sustainability. For most of its history, the human race has numbered no more than several million and has expanded only slowly. As late as A.D. 1000, our species was smaller than the current population of the U.S. Only in the past few centuries have our numbers exploded, especially (during recent decades) in low- and middle-income nations, with increases in consumption habits following suit. Projections suggest that by 2050 or so, the population will probably stabilize around 9.1 billion. But very small changes in fertility could shift that figure up or down by about a billion—with a powerful impact on innumerable sustainability issues.

was through 2007 on the eve of the economic meltdown) that if the trends continue unabated the typical Chinese will out-consume the typical American before 2040, with Indians sur-

passing Americans by 2080. Population and consumption thus feed on each other's growth to expand humans' environmental footprint exponentially over time.

Moreover, because every human being consumes and disposes of multiple natural resources, a birth that does not occur averts consumption impacts in every direction. A person reducing her carbon footprint, conversely, does not automatically use less water. A wind turbine displaces coal-fired electricity but hardly prevents the depletion of forests (now disappearing in the tropics at the rate of one Kentucky-size swath a year) or fisheries (at current depletion rates facing exhaustion by the middle of the century). But unlike wind turbines, humans reproduce themselves. So every smaller generation means that the multipliers of consumption linked to population also shrink on into the future.

Because most environmental challenges emerge on scales of decades and centuries, population growth packs a long-term wallop. With respect to saving the planet, over a few short years it is hard for smaller families to beat sharp reductions in per capita consumption. Since the early 1990s, however, published calculations have demonstrated that slower population growth over decades yields significant reductions of greenhouse gas emissions even in countries where per capita fossil-fuel consumption is modest.

Slower population growth that leads to eight billion people in 2050 rather than to the currently projected 9.1 billion would save one billion to two billion tons of carbon annually by 2050, according to estimates by climate scientist Brian O'Neill of the National Center for Atmospheric Research and his colleagues. The subsequent savings in emissions would grow year by year ever afterward—while the billion-plus fewer people would need less land, forest products, water, fish and other foodstuffs.

Those improvements still would not be enough on their own to avert significant climate change. Other similar billion-ton savings in emissions (what Princeton University professors Stephen Pacala and Robert Socolow have dubbed "stabilization wedges") are desperately needed and can come only from reduction in fossil-fuel consumption through energy efficiency, low-carbon technologies and changes in way of life. If two billion automobiles getting 30 miles per gallon traveled only 5,000 miles a year instead of 10,000, that change would save another billion tons of carbon emissions. So would replacing coal-fired power plants that produce 1.4 trillion watts of electricity with equivalent plants burning natural gas. But without a population that stops growing, comparable technology improvements or lifestyle downshifts will be needed indefinitely to keep greenhouse gas emissions sustainable.

The complications that population growth poses to every environmental problem are not to be dismissed. In fact, they are accepted and understood best by the governments of poorer countries, where the impacts of dense and rapidly growing populations are most obvious. During the past few years, most of the reports that developing countries have filed with the U.N. on how they plan to adapt to climate change mention population growth as a complicating factor.

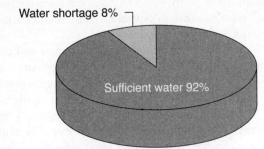

Water shortage 8%

Sufficient water 92%

1995 population: 5.7 billion

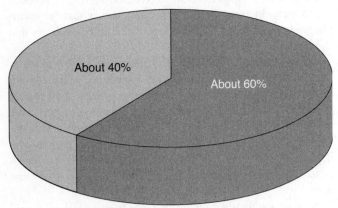

About 40%

About 60%

2050 population: 9.1 billion (projected)
More of the population will suffer water shortages.

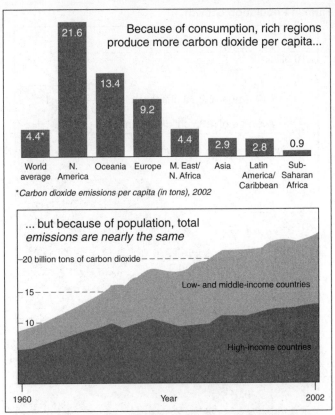

Because of consumption, rich regions produce more carbon dioxide per capita...

| 21.6 | 13.4 | 9.2 | 4.4* | 4.4 | 2.9 | 2.8 | 0.9 |

World average · N. America · Oceania · Europe · M. East/ N. Africa · Asia · Latin America/ Caribbean · Sub-Saharan Africa

Carbon dioxide emissions per capita (in tons), 2002

... but because of population, total *emissions are nearly the same*

—20 billion tons of carbon dioxide— — — — — — — —

Low- and middle-income countries

—15 — — — — —

—10 —

High-income countries

1960   Year   2002

Consumption and the greenhouse gap. Citizens of industrial nations produce far more climate-warming carbon dioxide per capita than their peers in poorer countries. Because of population size, however, the developing world now produces slightly more of the gas. Thus, population exerts a powerful multiplier effect on the toll of consumption on the earth.

Instruments of Policy

A commonsense strategy for dealing with rising environmental risk would be to probe every reasonable opportunity for shifting to sustainability as quickly, easily and inexpensively as possible. No single energy strategy—whether nuclear, efficiency, wind, solar or geothermal—shows much promise on its own for eliminating the release of carbon dioxide into the air. Obstacles such as high up-front costs hamper most of those energy strategies even as part of a collective fix for the climate problem. No single change in land use will turn soils and plants into net absorbers of heat-trapping gases. Without technological breakthroughs in energy or land use, only higher prices for fossil fuels show much potential for edging down per capita emissions—a "solution" that policy makers have yet to grapple with effectively.

Given the long-term contribution that a turnaround in population growth could make in easing our most recalcitrant challenges, why doesn't the idea get more respect and attention? Politicians' apathy toward long-term solutions is part of the answer. But the more obvious reason is the discomfort most of us feel in grappling with the topics of sex, contraception, abortion, immigration and family sizes that differ by ethnicity and income. What in the population mix is *not* a hot button? Especially when the word "control" is added, and when the world's biggest religions have fruitful multiplication embedded in their philosophical DNA. And so critics from left, right and the intellectual center gang up on the handful of environmentalists and other activists who try to get population into national and global discussions.

Population and consumption feed on each other's growth to expand humans' environmental footprint exponentially.

Yet newly released population data from the U.N. show that developed countries, from the U.S. to Spain, have been experiencing (at least up through the beginnings of the economic crisis in 2008), if not baby booms, at least reproductive "rat-a-tat-tats." For the first time since the 1970s, the average number of children born to U.S. women has topped 2.1—the number at which parents replace themselves in the populations of developed and many developing countries. Even if net immigration ended tomorrow, continuation of that fertility rate would guarantee further growth in U.S. population for decades to come.

Those who do consider population to be a key to the problem typically say little about which policies would spare the planet many more billions of people. Should we restructure tax rates to favor small families? Propagandize the benefits of small families for the planet? Reward family-planning workers for clients they have sterilized? Each of those steps alone or in combination might help bend birthrates downward for a time, but none has proved to affect demographic trends over the long term or, critically, to gain and keep public support. When the

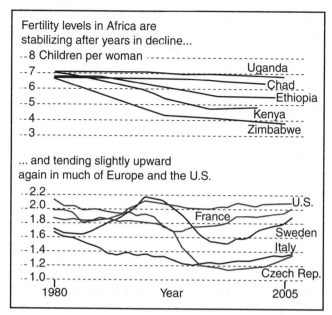

Fertility levels in Africa are stabilizing after years in decline...

... and tending slightly upward again in much of Europe and the U.S.

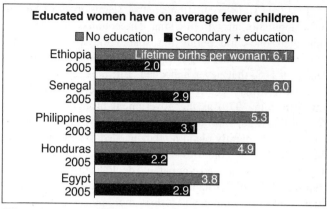

Educated women have on average fewer children

Education and fertility. Data from around the world testify to a robust trend: birthrates fall where women have more access to education. Improving women's access to schooling (and the opportunities it opens) may be one of the most powerful ways to reduce population growth.

Reason for concern. Declines in fertility rates cannot be taken for granted. In parts of Africa, the rates seem to be flattening out well above the replacement rate. Surprisingly, the U.S. and parts of Europe seem to be experiencing a small but significant increase in fertility, compounding the population increases from immigration.

government of India rewarded health workers for meeting sterilization quotas in 1976, the zeal of some of them for wielding scalpels regardless of their patients' wishes contributed to the downfall of Indira Gandhi's government in 1977.

And how can we reduce consumption? Ideas such as cap-and-trade plans for limiting greenhouse gas emissions and allowing companies to trade emission rights are based on the same principle: raise the price of what harms the environment to reduce consumption of it. Beyond the consumption cuts, however, such schemes don't have much to recommend them. Governments can also eliminate subsidies of polluting behavior, an approach that is more palatable—except to the often powerful interests that benefit from the subsidies. Or governments can subsidize low consumption through tax deductions and credits, but the funds to do so on the needed scale will likely be increasingly scarce.

The Zen of Population

Mostly ignored in the environmental debates about population and consumption is that nearly all the world's nations agreed to an altogether different approach to the problem of growth 15 years ago, one that bases positive demographic outcomes on decisions individuals make in their own self-interest. (If only something comparable could be imagined to shrink consumption.) The strategy that 179 nations signed onto at a U.N. conference in Cairo in 1994 was: forget population control and instead help every woman bear a child in good health when she wants one.

That approach, which powerfully supports reproductive liberty, might sound counterintuitive for shrinking population growth, like handing a teenager the keys to the family car without so much as a lecture. But the evidence suggests that what women want—and have always wanted—is not so much to have *more*

children as to have *more for* a smaller number of children they can reliably raise to healthy adulthood. Women left to their own devices, contraceptive or otherwise, would collectively "control" population while acting on their own intentions.

More than 200 million women in developing countries are sexually active without effective modern contraception even though they do not want to be pregnant anytime soon, according to the Guttmacher Institute, a reproductive health research group. By the best estimates, some 80 million pregnancies around the world are unintended. Although the numbers aren't strictly comparable—many unplanned pregnancies end in abortion—the unintended pregnancies exceed the 78 million by which world population grows every year.

In the U.S., which is well informed and spends nearly 20 cents per dollar of economic activity on health care, nearly one out of every two pregnancies is unintended. That proportion has not changed much for decades. In every nation, rich and poor, in which a choice of contraceptives is available and is backed up by reasonably accessible safe abortion for when contraception fails, women have two or fewer children. Furthermore, educating girls reduces birthrates. Worldwide, according to a calculation provided for this article by demographers at the International Institute for Applied Systems Analysis in Austria, women with no schooling have an average of 4.5 children, whereas those with a few years of primary school have just three. Women who complete one or two years of secondary school have an average of 1.9 children apiece—a figure that over time leads to a decreasing population. With one or two years of college, the average child-bearing rate falls even further, to 1.7. And when women enter the workforce, start businesses, inherit assets and otherwise interact with men on an equal footing, their desire for more than a couple of children fades even more dramatically.

Forget population control and instead help every woman bear a child in good health when she wants one.

True, old-style population control seems to have helped slow population growth in China. The country's leaders brag that their one-child policy has spared the world's climate 300 million greenhouse gas emitters, the population equivalent of a U.S. that never happened. But most of the drop in Chinese fertility occurred before that coercive policy went into effect in 1979, as the government brought women by the millions into farm and industry collectives and provided them with the family planning they needed to stay on the job. Many developing countries—from Thailand and Colombia to Iran—have experienced comparable declines in family size by getting better family-planning services and educational opportunities to more women and girls in more places.

With President Obama in the White House and Democrats dominant in Congress, the signs are good that the U.S. will support the kind of development abroad and reproductive health at home most likely to encourage slower population growth. Like almost all politicians, however, Obama never mentions population or the way it bridges problems from health and education all the way to food, energy security and climate change.

Bringing population back into the public conversation is risky, but the world has come a long way in understanding that the subject is only one part of most of today's problems and that "population control" can't really control population. Handing control of their lives and their bodies to women—the right thing to do for countless other reasons—can. There is no reason to fear the discussion.

Critical Thinking

1. Identify Robert Engelman's point of view.
2. What are some of the proposed policies to reduce the number of new babies?
3. Summarize his argument that a "downshift" in population will put the environment on a more sustainable path.

ROBERT ENGELMAN is vice president for programs at the Worldwatch Institute and author of *More: Population, Nature, and What Women Want* (Island Press).

Why Migration Matters

The world total of international migrants has more than doubled in just 25 years; about 25 million were added in just the first 5 years of the twenty-first century.

KHALID KOSER

Migration has always mattered—but today it matters more than ever before. The increasing importance of migration derives from its growing scale and its widening global reach, but also from a number of new dynamics. These include the feminization of migration, the growth of so-called irregular migration, and migration's inextricable linkages with globalization in terms of economic growth, development, and security. Climate change, moreover, is certain to raise migration still higher on nations' and international institutions' policy agendas.

The history of migration begins with humanity's very origins in the Rift Valley of Africa. It was from there that Homo sapiens emerged about 120,000 years ago, subsequently migrating across Africa, through the Middle East to Europe and Central and South Asia, and finally to the New World, reaching the Bering Straits about 20,000 years ago. Then, in the ancient world, Greek colonization and Roman expansion depended on migration; significant movements of people were also associated with the Mesopotamian, Incan, Indus, and Zhou empires. Later we see major migrations such as those involving the Vikings along the shorelines of the Atlantic and North Sea, and the Crusaders to the Holy Land.

In more recent history—in other words, in the past two or three centuries—it is possible to discern, according to migration historian Robin Cohen, a series of major migration periods or events. In the eighteenth and nineteenth centuries, one of the most prominent migration events was the forced transportation of slaves. About 12 million people were taken, mainly from West Africa, to the New World (and also, in lesser numbers, across the Indian Ocean and the Mediterranean Sea). One of the reasons this migration is considered so important, other than its scale, is that it still resonates for descendants of slaves and for African Americans in particular. After slavery's collapse, indentured laborers from China, India, and Japan moved overseas in significant numbers—1.5 million from India alone—to work the plantations of the European powers.

European expansion, especially during the nineteenth century, brought about large-scale voluntary migration away from Europe, particularly to the colonies of settlement, dominions, and the Americas. The great mercantile powers—Britain, the Netherlands, Spain, and France—all promoted settlement of their nationals abroad, not just workers but also peasants, dissident soldiers, convicts, and orphans. Migration associated with expansion largely came to an end with the rise of anticolonial movements toward the end of the nineteenth century, and indeed over the next decades some significant reverse flows back to Europe occurred, for example of the so-called *pieds noirs* to France.

The next period of migration was marked by the rise of the United States as an industrial power. Between the 1850s and the Great Depression of the 1930s, millions of workers fled the stagnant economies and repressive political regimes of northern, southern, and eastern Europe and moved to the United States. (Many fled the Irish famine as well.) Some 12 million of these migrants landed at Ellis Island in New York Harbor. Opportunities for work in the United States also attracted large numbers of Chinese migrants in the first wave of the so-called Chinese diaspora, during the last 50 years of the nineteenth century.

The next major period of migration came after World War II, when the booming postwar economies in Europe, North America, and Australia needed labor. This was the era when, for example, many Turkish migrants arrived to work in Germany and many North Africans went to France and Belgium. It was also the period when, between 1945 and 1972, about 1 million Britons migrated to Australia as so-called "Ten Pound Poms" under an assisted passage scheme. During the same era but in other parts of the world, decolonization continued to have an impact on migration, most significantly in the movement of millions of Hindus and Muslims after the partition of India in 1947 and of Jews and Palestinians after the creation of Israel.

By the late 1970s, and in part as a consequence of the 1973 oil crisis, the international migrant labor boom had ended in Europe, though in the United States it continued into the 1990s. Now, with the global economy's momentum shifting decisively to Asia, labor migration on that continent has grown heavily, and it is still growing. How much longer this will be true, given the current global financial crisis, is a matter open to debate.

More and More

As even this (inevitably selective) overview of international migration's history should make clear, large movements of people have always been associated with significant global events like revolutions, wars, and the rise and fall of empires; with epochal changes like economic expansion, nation building, and political transformations; and with enduring challenges like conflict, persecution, and dispossession.

Nevertheless, one reason to argue that migration matters more today than ever before is sheer numbers. If we define an international migrant as a person who stays outside his usual country of residence for at least one year, there are about 200 million such migrants worldwide. This is roughly equivalent to the population of the fifth-most populous country on earth, Brazil. In fact, 1 in every 35 people in the world today is an international migrant.

Of course, a less dramatic way to express this statistic is to say that only 3 percent of the world's population is composed of international migrants. (In migration, statistics are often used to alarm rather than to inform.) And it is also worth noting that internal migration is a far more significant phenomenon than is international migration (China alone has at least 130 million internal migrants). Still, the world total of international migrants has more than doubled in just 25 years; about 25 million were added in just the first 5 years of the twenty-first century.

And international migration affects many more people than just those who migrate. According to Stephen Castles and Mark Miller, authors of the influential volume *The Age of Migration*, "There can be few people in either industrialized or less developed countries today who do not have personal experience of migration and its effects; this universal experience has become the hallmark of the age of migration." In host countries, migrants' contributions are felt keenly in social, cultural, and economic spheres. Throughout the world, people of different national origins, who speak different languages and practice different customs and religions, are coming into unprecedented contact with each other. For some this is a threat, for others an opportunity.

Migration is also a far more global process than ever before, as migrants today travel both from and to all of the world's regions. In 2005 (the most recent year for which global data are available) there were about 60 million international migrants in Europe, 44 million in Asia, 41 million in North America, 16 million in Africa, and 6 million each in Latin America and Australia. A significant portion of the world's migrants—about 35 million—lived in the United States. The Russian Federation was the second-largest host country for migrants, with about 13 million living there. Following in the rankings were Germany, Ukraine, and India, each with between 6 million and 7 million migrants.

It is much harder to say which countries migrants come from, largely because origin countries tend not to keep count of how many of their nationals are living abroad. It has been estimated that at least 35 million Chinese currently live outside their country, along with 20 million Indians and 8 million Filipinos. But in fact the traditional distinctions among migrants' countries of origin, transit, and destination have become increasingly blurred. Today almost every country in the world fulfills all three roles—migrants leave them, pass through them, and head for them.

A World of Reasons

The reasons for the recent rise in international migration and its widening global reach are complex. The factors include growing global disparities in development, democracy, and demography; in some parts of the world, job shortages that will be exacerbated by the current economic downturn; the segmentation of labor markets in high-income economies, a situation that attracts migrant workers to so-called "3D" jobs (dirty, difficult, or dangerous); revolutions in communications and transportation, which result in more people than ever before knowing about life elsewhere and having the ability to travel there; migration networks that allow existing migrant and ethnic communities to act as magnets for further migration; and a robust migration industry, including migrant smugglers and human traffickers, that profits from international migration.

In addition to being bigger, international migration today is also a more complex phenomenon than it has been in the past, as people of all ages and types move for a wide variety of reasons. For example, child migration appears to be on the increase around the world. Migrants with few skills working "3D" jobs make important contributions to the global economy, but so do highly skilled migrants and students. Some people move away from their home countries permanently, but an increasing proportion moves only temporarily, or circulates between countries. And though an important legal distinction can be made between people who move for work purposes and those who flee conflict and persecution, in reality the two can be difficult to distinguish, as members of the two groups sometimes move together in so-called "mixed flows."

One trend of particular note is that women's representation among migrants has increased rapidly, starting in the 1960s and accelerating in the 1990s. Very nearly half the world's authorized migrants in 2005 were women, and more female than male authorized migrants resided in Europe, North America, Latin America and the Caribbean, the states of the former Soviet Union, and Oceania. What is more, whereas women have traditionally migrated to join their partners, an increasing proportion who migrate today do so independently. Indeed, they are often primary breadwinners for families that they leave behind.

A number of reasons help explain why women comprise an increasing proportion of the world's migrants. One is that global demand for foreign labor, especially in more developed countries, is becoming increasingly gender-selective. That is, more jobs are available in the fields typically staffed by women—services, health care, and entertainment. Second, an increasing number of countries have extended the right of family reunion to migrants, allowing them to be joined by their spouses and children. Third, in some countries of origin, changes in gender relations mean that women enjoy more freedom than previously to migrate independently. Finally, in trends especially evident in Asia, there has been growth in migration of women for domestic work (this is sometimes called the "maid trade"); in organized migration for marriage (with the women sometimes referred to as "mail-order brides"); and in the trafficking of women, above all into the sex industry.

Most Irregular

Another defining characteristic of the new global migration is the growth of irregular migration and the rapid rise of this phenomenon in policy agendas. Indeed, of all the categories of international migrants, none attracts as much attention or divides opinion as consistently as irregular migrants—people often described as "illegal," "undocumented," or "unauthorized."

Almost by definition, irregular migration defies enumeration (although most commentators believe that its scale is increasing).

A commonly cited estimate holds that there are around 40 million irregular migrants worldwide, of whom perhaps one-third are in the United States. There are between 3.5 million and 5 million irregular migrants in the Russian Federation, and perhaps 5 million in Europe. Each year, an estimated 2.5 million to 4 million migrants are thought to cross international borders without authorization.

One reason that it is difficult to count irregular migrants is that even this single category covers people in a range of different situations. It includes migrants who enter or remain in a country without authorization; those who are smuggled or trafficked across an international border; those who seek asylum, are not granted it, and then fail to observe a deportation order; and people who circumvent immigration controls, for example by arranging bogus marriages or fake adoptions.

What is more, an individual migrant's status can change—often rapidly. A migrant can enter a country in an irregular fashion but then regularize her status, for example by applying for asylum or entering a regularization program. Conversely, a migrant can enter regularly then become irregular by working without a permit or overstaying a visa. In Australia, for example, British citizens who have stayed beyond the expiration of their visas account for by far the largest number of irregular migrants.

The Rich Get Richer

International migration matters more today than ever because of its new dimensions and dynamics, but even more because of its increased impact—on the global economy, on international politics, and on society. Three impacts are particularly worth noting: international migration's contribution to the global economy; the significance of migration for development; and the linkages between migration and security.

Kodak, Atlantic Records, RCA, NBC, Google, Intel, Hotmail, Sun, Microsoft, Yahoo, eBay—all these US firms were founded or cofounded by migrants. It has been estimated that international migrants make a net contribution to the US economy of $60 billion, and that half of the scientists, engineers, and holders of PhD degrees in the United States were born overseas. It is often suggested (though this is hard to substantiate) that migrants are worth more to the British economy than is North Sea oil. Worldwide migrant labor is thought to earn at least $20 trillion. In some of the Gulf states, migrants comprise 90 percent of the labor force.

Such a selection of facts and figures can suggest a number of conclusions about international migration's significance for the global economy. First, migrants are often among the most dynamic and entrepreneurial members of society. This has always been the case. In many ways the history of US economic growth is the history of migrants: Andrew Carnegie (steel), Adolphus Busch (beer), Samuel Goldwyn (movies), and Helena Rubenstein (cosmetics) were all migrants. Second, migrants fill labor market gaps both at the top end and the bottom end—a notion commonly captured in the phrase "Migrants do the work that natives are either unable or unwilling to do." Third, the significance of migrant labor varies across countries but more importantly across economic sectors. In the majority of advanced economies, migrant workers are overrepresented in agriculture, construction, heavy industry, manufacturing, and services—especially food, hospitality, and domestic services. (It is precisely these sectors that the global financial crisis is currently hitting hardest.) Finally, migrant workers contribute significantly more to national economies than they take away (through, for example, pensions and welfare benefits). That is, migrants tend to be young and they tend to work.

This last conclusion explains why migration is increasingly considered one possible response to the demographic crisis that affects increasing numbers of advanced economies (though it does not affect the United States yet). In a number of wealthy countries, a diminishing workforce supports an expanding retired population, and a mismatch results between taxes that are paid into pension and related programs and the payments that those programs must make. Importing youthful workers in the form of migrants appears at first to be a solution—but for two reasons, it turns out to be only a short-term response. First, migrants themselves age and eventually retire. Second, recent research indicates that, within a generation, migrants adapt their fertility rates to those that prevail in the countries where they settle. In other words, it would not take long for migrants to exacerbate rather then relieve a demographic crisis.

The Poor Get Richer

International migration does not affect only the economies of countries to which migrants travel—it also strongly affects the economies of countries from which migrants depart, especially in the realm of development in poorer countries. The World Bank estimates that each year migrants worldwide send home about $300 billion. This amounts to triple the value of official development assistance, and is the second-largest source of external funding for developing countries after foreign direct investment. The most important recipient countries for remittances are India ($27 billion), China ($26 billion), Mexico ($25 billion), and the Philippines ($17 billion). The top countries from which remittances are dispatched are the United States ($42 billion), Saudi Arabia ($16 billion), Switzerland ($14 billion), and Germany ($12 billion).

The impact of remittances on development is hotly debated, and to an extent the impact depends on who receives the money and how it is spent. It is indisputable that remittances can lift individuals and families out of poverty: Annual household incomes in Somaliland are doubled by remittances. Where remittances are spent on community projects such as wells and schools, as is often the case in Mexico, they also have a wider benefit. And remittances make a significant contribution to gross domestic product (GDP) at the national level, comprising for example 37 percent of GDP in Tonga and 27 percent in both Jordan and Lesotho.

Most experts emphasize that remittances should not be viewed as a substitute for official development assistance. One reason is that remittances are private monies, and thus it is difficult to influence how they are spent or invested. Also, remittances fluctuate over time, as is now becoming apparent in the context of the global economic crisis. Finally, it has been suggested that remittances can generate a "culture of migration," encouraging further migration, and even provide a disincentive to work where families come to expect money from abroad. It has to be said, even so, that the net impact of remittances in developing countries is positive.

International migration, moreover, can contribute to development through other means than remittances. For example, it can relieve pressure on the labor markets in countries from which migrants originate, reducing competition and unemployment. Indonesia and the Philippines are examples of countries that deliberately export labor for this reason (as well as to obtain remittance income). In addition, migrants can contribute to their home countries when they return by using their savings and the new skills they have acquired—although the impact they can have really depends on the extent to which necessary infrastructure is in place for them to realize their potential.

At the same time, however, international migration can undermine development through so-called "brain drain." This term describes a situation in which skills that are already in short supply in a country depart that country through migration. Brain drain is a particular problem in sub-Saharan Africa's health sector, as significant numbers of African doctors and nurses work in the United Kingdom and elsewhere in Europe. Not only does brain drain deprive a country of skills that are in high demand—it undermines that country's investment in the education and training of its own nationals.

Safety First

A third impact of international migration—one that perhaps more than any other explains why it has risen toward the top of policy agendas—is the perception that migration constitutes a heightened security issue in the era after 9/11. Discussions of this issue often revolve around irregular migration—which, in public and policy discourses, is frequently associated with the risk of terrorism, the spread of infectious diseases, and criminality.

Such associations are certainly fair in some cases. A strong link, for example, has been established between irregular migrants from Morocco, Algeria, and Syria and the Madrid bombings of March 2004. For the vast majority of irregular migrants, however, the associations are not fair. Irregular migrants are often assigned bad intentions without any substantiation. Misrepresenting evidence can criminalize and demonize all irregular migrants, encourage them to remain underground—and divert attention from those irregular migrants who actually are criminals and should be prosecuted, as well as those who are suffering from disease and should receive treatment.

Irregular migration is indeed associated with risks, but not with the risks most commonly identified. One legitimate risk is irregular migration's threat to the exercise of sovereignty. States have a sovereign right to control who crosses their borders and remains on their territory, and irregular migration challenges this right. Where irregular migration involves corruption and organized crime, it can also become a threat to public security. This is particularly the case when illegal entry is facilitated by migrant smugglers and human traffickers, or when criminal gangs compete for control of migrants' labor after they have arrived.

Irregular migration is indeed associated with risks, but not with the risks most commonly identified.

When irregular migration results in competition for scarce jobs, this can generate xenophobic sentiments within host populations. Importantly, these sentiments are often directed not only at migrants with irregular status but also at established migrants, refugees, and ethnic minorities. When irregular migration receives

a great deal of media attention, it can also undermine public confidence in the integrity and effectiveness of a state's migration and asylum policies.

In addition, irregular migration can undermine the "human security" of migrants themselves. The harm done to migrants by irregular migration is often underestimated—in fact, irregular migration can be very dangerous. A large number of people die each year trying to cross land and sea borders while avoiding detection by the authorities. It has been estimated, for example, that as many as 2,000 migrants die each year trying to cross the Mediterranean from Africa to Europe, and that about 400 Mexicans die annually trying to cross the border into the United States.

People who enter a country or remain in it without authorization are often at risk of exploitation by employers and landlords. Female migrants with irregular status, because they are confronted with gender-based discrimination, are often obliged to accept the most menial jobs in the informal sector, and they may face specific health-related risks, including exposure to HIV/AIDS. Such can be the level of human rights abuses involved in contemporary human trafficking that some commentators have compared it to the slave trade.

Migrants with irregular status are often unwilling to seek redress from authorities because they fear arrest and deportation. For the same reason, they do not always make use of public services to which they are entitled, such as emergency health care. In most countries, they are also barred from using the full range of services available both to citizens and to migrants with regular status. In such situations, already hard-pressed nongovernmental organizations, religious bodies, and other civil society institutions are obliged to provide assistance, at times compromising their own legality.

In Hard Times

What might the future of international migration look like? Tentatively at least, the implications of the current global economic crisis for migration are beginning to emerge. Already a slowdown in the movement of people at a worldwide level has been reported, albeit with significant regional and national variations, and this appears to be largely a result of declining job opportunities in destination countries. The economic sectors in which migrants tend to be overrepresented have been hit first; as a consequence migrant workers around the world are being laid off in substantial numbers.

Migrant workers around the world are being laid off in substantial numbers.

Interestingly, it appears that most workers are nevertheless not returning home, choosing instead to stay and look for new jobs. Those entitled to draw on social welfare systems can be expected to do so, thus reducing their net positive impact on national economies. (It remains to be seen whether national economic stimulus packages, such as the one recently enacted in the United States, will help migrant workers get back to work.) Scattered cases of xenophobia have been reported around the world, as anxious natives increasingly fear labor competition from migrant workers.

In the last quarter of 2008 remittances slowed down. Some project that in 2009 remittances, for the first time in decades, may shrink. Moreover, changes in exchange rates mean that even if the volume of remittances remains stable, their net value to recipients may decrease. These looming trends hold worrying implications for households, communities, and even national economies in poor countries.

Our experience of previous economic downturns and financial crises—including the Great Depression, the oil crisis of the early 1970s, and the Asian, Russian, and Latin American financial crises between 1997 and 2000—tells us that such crises' impact on international migration is relatively short-lived and that migration trends soon rebound. Few experts are predicting that the current economic crisis will fundamentally alter overall trends toward increased international migration and its growing global reach.

Hot in Here

In the longer term, what will affect migration patterns and processes far more than any financial crisis is climate change. One commonly cited prediction holds that 200 million people will be forced to move as a result of climate change by 2050, although other projections range from 50 million to a startling 1 billion people moving during this century.

In the longer term, what will affect migration patterns and processes far more than any financial crisis is climate change.

The relationship that will develop between climate change and migration appears complex and unpredictable. One type of variable is in climate change events themselves—a distinction is usually made between slow-onset events like rising sea levels and rapid-onset events like hurricanes and tsunamis. In addition, migration is only one of a number of possible responses to most climate change events. Protective measures such as erecting sea walls may reduce the impact. Societies throughout history have adapted to climate change by altering their agricultural and settlement practices.

Global warming, moreover, will make some places better able to support larger populations, as growing seasons are extended, frost risks reduced, and new crops sustained. Where migration does take place, it is difficult to predict whether the movement will mainly be internal or cross-border, or temporary or permanent. And finally, the relationship between climate change and migration may turn out to be indirect. For example, people may flee conflicts that arise over scarce resources in arid areas, rather than flee desertification itself.

Notwithstanding the considerable uncertainty, a consensus has emerged that, within the next 10 years, climate-related international migration will become observably more frequent, and the scale of overall international migration will increase significantly. Such

migration will add still further complexity to the migration situation, as the new migrants will largely defy current classifications.

One immediately contentious issue is whether people who cross borders as a result of the effects of climate change should be defined as "climate refugees" or "climate migrants." The former conveys the fact that at least some people will literally need to seek refuge from the impacts of climate change, will find themselves in situations as desperate as those of other refugees, and will deserve international assistance and protection. But the current definition of a refugee in international law does not extend to people fleeing environmental pressures, and few states are willing to amend the law. Equally, the description "climate migrant" underestimates the involuntariness of the movement, and opens up the possibility for such people to be labeled and dealt with as irregular migrants.

Another legal challenge arises with the prospect of the total submergence by rising sea levels of low-lying island states such as the Maldives—namely, how to categorize people who no longer have a state. Will their national flags be lowered outside UN headquarters in New York, and will they be granted citizenship in another country?

The complexities of responding to climate-related movements of people illustrate a more general point, that new responses are required to international migration as it grows in scale and complexity. Most of the legal frameworks and international institutions established to govern migration were established at the end of World War II, in response to a migration reality very different from that existing today, and as a result new categories of migrants are falling into gaps in protection. New actors have also emerged in international migration, including most importantly the corporate sector, and they have very little representation in migration policy decisions at the moment.

Perhaps most fundamentally, a shift in attitude is required, away from the notion that migration can be controlled, focusing instead on trying to manage migration and maximize its benefits.

Critical Thinking

1. According to Khalid Koser, why does international migration matter more now than ever before?

2. What are the reasons for this?

3. What countries are the primary recipients of "irregular" migrants?

4. How do immigrants economically benefit their country of origin?

5. What might the future of international migration look like?

KHALID KOSER directs the New Issues in Security program at the Geneva Center for Security Policy. He is also a non-resident fellow at the Brookings Institution and author of *International Migration: A Very Short Introduction* (Oxford University Press, 2007).

The Blue Food Revolution

New fish farms out at sea, and cleaner operations along the shore, could provide the world with a rich supply of much needed protein.

SARAH SIMPSON

Neil Sims tends his rowdy stock like any devoted farmer. But rather than saddling a horse like the Australian sheep drovers he grew up with, Sims dons a snorkel and mask to wrangle his herd: 480,000 silver fish corralled half a mile off the Kona coast of Hawaii's Big Island.

Tucked discretely below the waves, Sims's farm is one of 20 operations worldwide that are trying to take advantage of the earth's last great agricultural frontier: the ocean. Their offshore locations offer a distinct advantage over the thousands of conventional fish farms—flotillas of pens that hug the coastline. Too often old-style coastal farms, scorned as eyesores and ocean polluters, exude enough fish excrement and food scraps to cloud the calm, shallow waters, triggering harmful algal blooms or snuffing out sea life underneath the pens. At offshore sites such as Kona Blue Water Farms, pollution is not an issue, Sims explains. The seven submerged paddocks, each one as big as a high school gymnasium, are anchored within rapid currents that sweep away the waste, which is quickly diluted to harmless levels in the open waters.

Rather than taking Sims's word for it, I put swim fins on my feet and a snorkel around my neck, high-step to the edge of his small service boat, and take the plunge. From the water, the double-cone-shape cage is aglow like a colossal Chinese lantern, with shimmering streams of sunlight and glinting forms of darting fish. To the touch, the material that stretches taut around the outside of the cage's frame feels more like a fence than a net. The solid, Kevlar-esque material would repel hungry sharks as effectively as it contains teeming masses of Seriola rivoliana, a local species of yellowtail that Kona Blue has domesticated as an alternative to wild tuna.

Why yellowtail? Many wild tuna fisheries are collapsing, and sushi-grade yellowtail fetches a high price. Sims and fellow marine biologist Dale Sarver founded Kona Blue in 2001 to raise popular fish sustainably. But the company's methods could just as well be applied to run-of-the-mill fish—and we may need them. The global population of 6.9 billion people is estimated to rise to 9.3 billion by 2050, and people with higher living standards also tend to eat more meat and seafood. Yet the global catch from wild fisheries has been stagnant or declining for a decade. Raising cows, pigs, chickens and other animals consumes vast amounts of land, freshwater, fossil fuels that pollute the air and fertilizers that run off and choke rivers and oceans.

Where will all the needed protein for people come from? The answer could well be new offshore farms, if they can function efficiently, and coastal farms, if they can be cleaned up.

Cleaner Is Better

To some scientists, feeding the world calls for transferring the production of our animal protein to the seas. If a blue food revolution is to fill such an exalted plate at the dinner table, however, it must operate in environmentally sound ways—and make its benefits better known both to a jaded public and to policy makers with the power to help or retard its spread.

In the past, condemnation might have been apt. When modern coastal fish farming began about 30 years ago, virtually no one was doing things right, either for the environment or for the industry's long-term sustainability. Fish sewage was just one of the issues. Shrimp farmers in Southeast Asia and Mexico clear-cut coastal mangrove forests to make ponds to grow their shrimp. In the salmon farms of Europe and the Americas, animals were often too densely packed, helping disease and parasites sweep through the populations. Fish that escaped farms sometimes spread their diseases to native species. Making matters worse, the aquaculture industry represented (and still does) a net drain on fish mass; wild forage fish—small, cheap species that humans do not prefer but that bigger, wild fish eat—are captured in large quantities and ground into feed for the bigger, tastier, more expensive farmed fish folks favor.

Clearly, such ills were not good for business, and the industry has devised innovative solutions. Kona Blue's strategy of situating the farm within rapid offshore currents is one example. Other farmers are beginning to raise seaweed and filter-feeding animals such as mollusks near the fish pens to gobble up waste. Throughout the industry, including freshwater pens, improvements in animal husbandry and feed formulations are reducing disease and helping fish grow faster, with less forage fish in their diets. It may still be a long time before environmental groups remove farmed fish from "don't buy" lists, however.

Some cutting-edge thinkers are experimenting with an even bolder move. Nations exercise sole rights to manage waters out to 200 nautical miles from their shores—a vast frontier untapped for domesticated food production. Around the U.S., that frontier measures 3.4 million square nautical miles. Submerged fish pens, steered by large propellers, could ride in stable ocean currents, returning months later to their starting points or a distant destination to deliver fresh fish for market.

Ocean engineer Clifford Goudey tested the world's first self-propelled, submersible fish pen off the coast of Puerto Rico in late 2008. A geodesic sphere 62 feet in diameter, the cage proved surprisingly maneuverable when outfitted with a pair of eight-foot propellers, says Goudey, former director of M.I.T. Sea Grant's Offshore Aquaculture Engineering Center. Goudey imagines launching dozens of mobile farms in a steady progression within a predictable current that traverses the Caribbean Sea every nine months.

Feeding Frenzy

The aspect of marine (saltwater) aquaculture that has been hardest to fix is the need to use small, wild fish as food for the large, farmed varieties. (The small fish are not farmed, because a mature industry already exists that catches and grinds them into fish meal and oil.) The feed issue comes into pungent focus for me when Sims and I climb aboard an old U.S. Navy transport ship cleverly transformed into a feeding barge. The sea swell pitches me sideways as I make my way to the bow, calling to mind a bumpy pickup truck ride I took long ago, across a semi-frozen Missouri pasture to deliver hay to my cousin's Herefords. The memory of sweet-smelling dried grass vanishes when I grab a handful of oily brown feed from a 2,000-pound sack propped open on the deck. The pellets look like kibble for a small terrier but reek of an empty anchovy tin.

The odor is no surprise; 30 percent of Kona Blue's feed is ground up Peruvian anchovy. Yellowtail could survive on a vegetarian diet, but they wouldn't taste as good, Sims explains. Nor would their flesh include all the fatty acids and amino acids that make them healthy to eat. Those ingredients come from fish meal and fish oil, and that is the issue. "We are often pilloried because we're killing fish to grow fish," Sims says. Salmon farming, done in coastal pens, draws the same ire.

Detractors worry that rising demand from fish farms will wipe out wild anchovies, sardines and other forage fish. Before modern fish farming began, most fish meal was fed to pigs and chickens, but today aquaculture consumes 68 percent of the fish meal. Consumption has lessened under advanced feed formulas, however. When Kona Blue started raising yellowtail in 2005, its feed pellets were 80 percent anchovy. By early 2008 the company had reduced the share to 30 percent—without sacrificing taste or health benefit, Sims says—by increasing the concentration of soybean meal and adding chicken oil, a byproduct of poultry processing. The compound feed pellets are a big improvement over the egregious practice of dumping whole sardines into the fish cages. Unfortunately, this wasteful habit remains the norm among less responsible farmers.

A goal for the more enlightened proprietors is a break-even ratio, in which the amount of fish in feed equals the weight of fish produced for market. Farmers of freshwater tilapia and catfish have attained this magic ratio, but marine farmers have not. Because 70 percent of Kona Blue's feed is agricultural protein and oil, it now needs only 1.6 to 2.0 pounds of anchovies to produce one pound of yellowtail. The average for the farmed salmon industry is around 3.0. To achieve no net loss of marine protein, the industry would have to reduce that ratio. Still, farmed fish take a far smaller bite than their wild equivalents do: over its lifetime, a wild tuna may consume as much as 100 pounds of food per pound of its own weight, all of it fish.

The pressure to reduce sardine and anchovy catches will increase as the number of fish farms grows. Aquaculture is the fastest-growing food production sector in the world, expanding at 7.5 percent a year since 1994. At that pace, fish meal and fish oil resources could be exhausted by 2040. An overarching goal, therefore, is to eliminate wild fish products from feed altogether, within a decade or so, asserts marine ecologist Carlos M. Duarte, who directs the International Laboratory for Global Change at the Spanish Council for Scientific Research in Majorca.

One breakthrough that could help is coaxing the coveted omega-3 fatty acid DHA out of microscopic algae, which could replace some of the forage fish content in feed. Advanced Bio-Nutrition in Columbia, Md., is testing feed that contains the same algae-derived DHA that enhances infant formula, milk and juice now sold in stores. Recently researchers at Australia's Commonwealth Scientific and Industrial Research Organization coaxed DHA out of land plants for the first time. Duarte suggests that fierce competition for agricultural land and freshwater means that fish farmers should eventually eliminate soy, chicken oil and other terrestrial products as well, instead feeding their flocks on zooplankton and seaweed, which is easy to grow. (Seaweed already accounts for nearly one quarter of all marine aquaculture value.)

Despite improvements in marine fish farming, prominent environmentalists and academics still shoot it down. Marine ecologist Jeremy Jackson of the Scripps Institution of Oceanography says he is "violently opposed" to aquaculture of predatory fish and shrimp—basically, any fish people like to eat sashimi-style. He calls the practice "environmentally catastrophic" in the pressure it puts on wild fish supplies and insists it should be "illegal."

Smarter than Beef

Jackson's point, echoed by other critics, is that the risk of collapsing forage fisheries, which are already overexploited, is too great to justify serving up a luxury food most of the world will never taste. Far better would be to eat the herbivorous sardines and anchovies directly instead of farmed, top-end predators.

Sims agrees that we should fish lower on the food web but says that does not mean we need to eat lower. "Let's get real. I eat anchovies on my pizza, but I can't get anyone else in my family to do it," he says. "If you can get a pound of farmed sushi for every pound of anchovy, why not give people the thing they want to eat?"

Certain people scoff at fish consumption—whether wild-caught or farm-raised—on the premise that the planet and its human inhabitants would be healthier if people ate more plants. But society is not rushing to become vegetarian. More people are eating more meat, particularly as populations in the developing world become wealthier, more urban and more Western. The World Health Organization predicts a 25 percent increase in per capita meat consumption by 2050. Even if consumption held steady, crop and grazing areas would have to increase by 50 to 70 percent, at current yields, to produce the food required in 2050.

That reality begs for a comparison rarely made: fish farming versus terrestrial farming. Done right, fish farming could provide much needed protein for the world while minimizing the expansion of land-based farming and the attendant environmental costs.

Land-based farmers have already transformed 40 percent of the earth's terrestrial surface. And after 10,000 years to work out the kinks, major problems still abound. Cattle eat tremendous amounts of heavily fertilized crops, and pig and chicken farms are notorious polluters. The dead zones underneath coastal fish farms pale in comparison to the huge dead zones that fertilizer run-off triggers in the Gulf of Mexico, Black Sea and elsewhere and to the harmful algal blooms that pig farm effluent has caused in Chesapeake Bay.

A growing number of scientists are beginning to compare the environmental impacts of all the various protein production systems, so that society can "focus its energies on efficiently solving the most demanding problems," writes Kenneth M. Brooks, an independent aquatic environmental consultant in Port Townsend, Wash. Brooks estimates that raising Angus beef requires 4,400 times more high-quality pasture land than sea-floor needed for the equivalent weight of farmed Atlantic salmon filets. What is more, the ecosystem below a salmon farm can recover in less than a decade, instead of the centuries it would take for a cattle pasture to revert to mature forest.

An even more compelling reason to raise protein in the sea may be to reduce humanity's drain on freshwater. As Duarte points out, animal meat products represent only 3.5 percent of food production but consume 45 percent of the water used in agriculture. By shifting most protein production to the ocean, he says, "land agriculture could grow considerably without exceeding current levels of water use."

Of course, collecting and transporting soybean meal and chicken oil and feeding fish flocks all consume energy and create emissions, too. Fuel consumption and emissions are greater for farms that are farther from shore, but both types of farming rate better than most fishing fleets. The only way offshore farmers can be profitable right now is to raise high-priced fish, but costs can come down: a few experimental farms are already raising cost-competitive mussels in the ocean.

Environmental Distinctions

If providing more fish to consumers is an answer to meeting global demands for protein, why not just catch more fish directly? Many wild fisheries are maxed out, right at a time when global population, as well as per capita demand for fish, is booming. North Americans, for example, are heeding health experts' advice to eat fish to help reduce the risk of heart attacks and improve brain function.

What is more, fishing fleets consume vast amounts of fuel and emit volumes of greenhouse gases and pollutants. Widely used, indiscriminate fishing methods, such as trawling and dredging, kill millions of animals; studies indicate that at least half the sea life fishers haul in this way is discarded as too small, overquota or the wrong species. All too often this so-called by-catch is dead by the time it is tossed overboard. Aquaculture eliminates this waste altogether: "Farmers only harvest the fish in their pens," Sims notes.

Goudey points out another often overlooked reality: you can grow fish more efficiently than you can catch them. Farmed fish convert food into flesh much more effectively than their wild brethren, which expend enormous amounts of energy as they hunt for food and evade predators, seek a mate and reproduce. Farmed fish have it easy by comparison, so most of their diet goes into growth.

Kona Blue's yellowtail and most farmed salmon are between one and three years old at harvest, one-third the age of the large, wild tuna targeted for sushi. The younger age also means farmed fish have less opportunity to accumulate mercury and other persistent pollutants that can make mature tuna and swordfish a potential health threat.

Indeed, fish farming already accounts for 47 percent of the seafood people consume worldwide, up from only 9 percent in 1980. Experts predict the share could rise to 62 percent of the total protein supply by 2050. "Clearly, aquaculture is big, and it is here to stay. People who are against it really aren't getting it," says Jose Villalon, aquaculture director at the World Wildlife Fund. Looking only at the ills of aquaculture is misleading if they are not compared with the ills of other forms of food production. Aquaculture affects the earth, and no number of improvements will eliminate all problems. But every food production system taxes the environment, and wild fish, beef, pork and poultry producers impose some of the greatest burdens.

To encourage good practices and help distinguish clean fish farms from the worst offenders, the World Wildlife Fund has co-founded the Aquaculture Stewardship Council to set global standards for responsible practices and to use independent auditors to certify compliant farms. The council's first set of standards is expected early this year. The council believes certification could have the greatest effect by motivating the world's 100 to 200 big seafood retailers to buy fish from certified farms, rather than trying to crack down directly on thousands of producers.

The Ocean Conservancy's aquaculture director George Leonard agrees that this kind of farm-to-plate certification program is an important way to encourage fish farmers to pursue better sustainability practices. As in any global industry, he says, cheap, unscrupulous providers will always exist. Setting a regulatory "floor" could require U.S. farmers to behave responsibly "without making it impossible for them to compete."

That point is key. Only five of the world's 20 offshore installations are in U.S. waters. Goudey thinks more aquaculture entrepreneurs would dive in if the U.S. put a licensing system into place for federal waters, from three nautical miles offshore to the 200-mile boundary. "No investor is going to back a U.S. operation when there are no statutes granting rights of tenancy to an operation," Goudey asserts. All U.S. farms exist inside the three-mile-wide strip of water that states control, and only a few states, such as Hawaii, allow them. California has yet to grant permits, despite government estimates that a sustainable offshore fish-farming industry in less than 1 percent of the state's waters could bring in up to $1 billion a year.

Protein Policy

To grow, and do so sustainably, the fish-farming industry will need appropriate policies and a fairer playing field. At the moment, robust government fuel subsidies keep trawling and dredging fleets alive, despite their well-known destruction of the sea-floor and the terrible volume of dead by-catch. Farm subsidies help to keep beef, pork and poultry production profitable. And powerful farm lobbies continue to block attempts to curtail the flow of nitrogen-rich fertilizer down the Mississippi River. "Almost none of these more traditional ways of producing food have received the scrutiny that aquaculture has," Brooks says. The public has accepted domestication of the land but maintains that the ocean is a wild frontier to be left alone, even though this imbalance may not be the most sustainable plan for feeding the world.

Policy shifts at the federal and regional levels may soon open up U.S. federal waters. In January 2009 the Gulf of Mexico Fishery Management Council voted in favor of an unprecedented plan for permitting offshore aquaculture within its jurisdiction, pending approval from higher levels within the U.S. National Oceanic and Atmospheric Administration. NOAA will evaluate the plan only after it finalizes its new national aquaculture policy, which addresses all forms of the industry and will probably include guidance for the development of a consistent, nationwide framework for regulating commercial activities. "We don't want the blue revolution to repeat the mistakes of the green revolution," says NOAA director Jane Lubchenco. "It's too important to get it wrong, and there are so many ways to get it wrong."

Given relentlessly rising demand, society has to make hard choices about where greater protein production should occur.

"One of my goals has been to get us to a position where, when people say food security, they don't just mean grains and livestock but also fisheries and aquaculture," Lubchenco says. Duarte suggests we take some pressure off the land and turn to the seas, where we have the opportunity to do aquaculture right, rather than looking back 40 years from now wishing we had done so.

As for Neil Sims's part of the blue food revolution, he is courting technology companies for upgrades. Tools such as robotic net cleaners, automated feeders and satellite-controlled video cameras to monitor fish health and cage damage would help Kona Blue's crew manage its offshore farms remotely. "Not just so we can grow more fish in the ocean," Sims says. "So we can grow more fish better."

In Brief

Meat consumption is rising worldwide, but production involves vast amounts of energy, water and emissions. At the same time, wild fisheries are declining. Aquaculture could become the most sustainable source of protein for humans.

Fish farming already accounts for half of global seafood production. Most of it is done along coastlines, which creates substantial water pollution.

Large, offshore pens that are anchored to the seafloor are often cleaner. Those farms, other new forms of aquaculture. and practices that clean up coastal operations could expand aquaculture significantly.

Questions remain about how sustainable and cost-effective the approaches can be.

Critical Thinking

1. What is the Blue Food Revolution?
2. What are some of the environmental challenges facing large-scale fish farming?
3. Can fish farming be more sustainable than raising livestock?
4. How does this article complement or contradict Article 2?

Sarah Simpson is a freelance writer and contributing editor for *Scientific American*. She lives in Riverside, Calif.

From *Scientific American*, February 2011, pp. 54–61. Copyright © 2011 by Scientific American, a division of Nature America, Inc. All rights reserved. Reprinted by permission.

UNIT 3

The Global Environment and Natural Resources Utilization

Unit Selections

Learning Outcomes

After reading this Unit, you will be able to

- Discuss the basic pro and con arguments regarding the causes of climate change.

- Describe the impact of human activities on glaciers, oceans, tropical forests, and other ecological systems.

- Identify some of the policy debates related to mitigating climate change impacts.

- Describe a case study of an invasive species.

- Assess your ongoing effort at identifying your theory of international relations and how this unit changes/complements it.

Student Website

www.mhhe.com/cls

Internet References

National Geographic Society
www.nationalgeographic.com
National Oceanic and Atmospheric Administration (NOAA)
www.noaa.gov
SocioSite: Sociological Subject Areas
www.pscw.uva.nl/sociosite/TOPICS
United Nations Environment Programme (UNEP)
www.unep.ch

In the eighteenth century, the modern nation–state emerged, and over many generations, it evolved to the point where it is difficult to imagine a world without national governments. These legal entities have been viewed as separate, self-contained units that independently pursue their "national interests." Scholars often describe the world as a political community of sovereign units that interact with each other (a concept described as a billiard ball model).

This perspective of the international community as comprised of self-contained and self-directed units has undergone major rethinking in the past 35 years. One of the reasons for this is the international consequences of the growing demands being placed on natural resources. The Middle East, for example, contains a majority of the world's known oil reserves. The United States, Western Europe, China, India, and Japan are dependent on this vital source of energy. The unbalanced oil supply and demand equation has created an unprecedented lack of self-sufficiency for the world's major economic powers.

The increased interdependence of countries is further illustrated by the fact that air and water pollution do not respect political boundaries. One country's smoke is often another country's acid rain. The concept that independent political units control their own destiny makes less sense than it might have 100 years ago. To more fully understand why this is so, one must first look at how natural resources are being utilized and how this may be affecting the climate.

The first two articles examine the debate surrounding global climate change and the challenges facing policy makers. Climate change directly or indirectly affects everyone, and if these changes are to be mitigated, international collaboration will be required. The consequences of basic human activities such as growing and cooking food are profound when multiplied billions of times every day. A single country or even a few countries working together cannot have a significant impact on redressing these problems. Solutions will have to be conceived that are truly global in scope. Just as there are shortages of natural resources, there are also shortages of new ideas for solving many of these problems.

© Lucidio Studio Inc./Corbis

Unit 3 continues by examining specific case studies. Implicit in these discussions is the challenge of moving from the perspective of the environment as primarily an economic resource to be consumed to a perspective that has been defined as "sustainable development." This change is easily called for, but in fact it goes to the core of social values and basic economic activities. Developing sustainable practices, therefore, is a challenge of unprecedented magnitude.

Nature is not some object "out there" to be visited at a national park. It is the food we eat and the energy we consume. Human beings are joined in the most intimate of relationships with the natural world to survive from one day to the next. It is ironic how little time is spent thinking about this relationship. This lack of attention, however, is not likely to continue, for rapidly growing numbers of people and the increased use of energy consuming technologies are placing unprecedented pressures on Earth's carrying capacity.

Climate Change

BILL MCKIBBEN

"Scientists Are Divided"

No, they're not. In the early years of the global warming debate, there was great controversy over whether the planet was warming, whether humans were the cause, and whether it would be a significant problem. That debate is long since over. Although the details of future forecasts remain unclear, there's no serious question about the general shape of what's to come.

Every national academy of science, long lists of Nobel laureates, and in recent years even the science advisors of President George W. Bush have agreed that we are heating the planet. Indeed, there is a more thorough scientific process here than on almost any other issue: Two decades ago, the United Nations formed the Intergovernmental Panel on Climate Change (IPCC) and charged its scientists with synthesizing the peer-reviewed science and developing broad-based conclusions. The reports have found since 1995 that warming is dangerous and caused by humans. The panel's most recent report, in November 2007, found it is "very likely" (defined as more than 90 percent certain, or about as certain as science gets) that heat-trapping emissions from human activities have caused "most of the observed increase in global average temperatures since the mid-20th century."

If anything, many scientists now think that the IPCC has been too conservative—both because member countries must sign off on the conclusions and because there's a time lag. Its last report synthesized data from the early part of the decade, not the latest scary results, such as what we're now seeing in the Arctic.

In the summer of 2007, ice in the Arctic Ocean melted. It melts a little every summer, of course, but this time was different—by late September, there was 25 percent less ice than ever measured before. And it wasn't a one-time accident. By the end of the summer season in 2008, so much ice had melted that both the Northwest and Northeast passages were open. In other words, you could circumnavigate the Arctic on open water. The computer models, which are just a few years old, said this shouldn't have happened until sometime late in the 21st century. Even skeptics can't dispute such alarming events.

"We Have Time"

Wrong. Time might be the toughest part of the equation. That melting Arctic ice is unsettling not only because it proves the planet is warming rapidly, but also because it will help speed up the warming. That old white ice reflected 80 percent of incoming solar radiation back to space; the new blue water left behind absorbs 80 percent of that sunshine. The process amps up. And there are many other such feedback loops. Another occurs as northern permafrost thaws. Huge amounts of methane long trapped below the ice begin to escape into the atmosphere; methane is an even more potent greenhouse gas than carbon dioxide.

Such examples are the biggest reason why many experts are now fast-forwarding their estimates of how quickly we must shift away from fossil fuel. Indian economist Rajendra Pachauri, who accepted the 2007 Nobel Peace Prize alongside Al Gore on behalf of the IPCC, said recently that we must begin to make fundamental reforms by 2012 or watch the climate system spin out of control; NASA scientist James Hansen, who was the first to blow the whistle on climate change in the late 1980s, has said that we must stop burning coal by 2030. Period.

All of which makes the Copenhagen climate change talks that are set to take place in December 2009 more urgent than they appeared a few years ago. At issue is a seemingly small number: the level of carbon dioxide in the air. Hansen argues that 350 parts per million is the highest level we can maintain "if humanity wishes to preserve a planet similar to that on which civilization developed and to which life on Earth is adapted." But because we're already past that mark—the air outside is currently about 387 parts per million and growing by about 2 parts annually—global warming suddenly feels less like a huge problem, and more like an Oh-My-God Emergency.

"Climate Change Will Help as Many Places as It Hurts"

Wishful thinking. For a long time, the winners-and-losers calculus was pretty standard: Though climate change will cause some parts of the planet to flood or shrivel up, other frigid, rainy regions would at least get some warmer days every year. Or so the thinking went. But more recently, models have begun to show that after a certain point almost everyone on the planet will suffer. Crops might be easier to grow in some places for a few decades as the danger of frost recedes, but over time the threat of heat stress and drought will almost certainly be stronger.

A 2003 report commissioned by the Pentagon forecasts the possibility of violent storms across Europe, megadroughts across the Southwest United States and Mexico, and unpredictable monsoons causing food shortages in China. "Envision Pakistan, India, and China—all armed with nuclear weapons—skirmishing at their borders over refugees, access to shared rivers, and arable land," the report warned. Or Spain and Portugal "fighting over fishing rights—leading to conflicts at sea."

Of course, there are a few places we used to think of as possible winners—mostly the far north, where Canada and Russia could theoretically produce more grain with longer growing seasons, or perhaps explore for oil beneath the newly melted Arctic ice cap. But even those places will have to deal with expensive consequences—a real military race across the high Arctic, for instance.

Want more bad news? Here's how that Pentagon report's scenario played out: As the planet's carrying capacity shrinks, an ancient pattern of desperate, all-out wars over food, water, and energy supplies would reemerge. The report refers to the work of Harvard archaeologist Steven LeBlanc, who notes that wars over resources were the norm until about three centuries ago. When such conflicts broke out, 25 percent of a population's adult males usually died. As abrupt climate change hits home, warfare may again come to define human life. Set against that bleak backdrop, the potential upside of a few longer growing seasons in Vladivostok doesn't seem like an even trade.

"It's China's Fault"

Not so much. China is an easy target to blame for the climate crisis. In the midst of its industrial revolution, China has overtaken the United States as the world's biggest carbon dioxide producer. And everyone has read about the one-a-week pace of power plant construction there. But those numbers are misleading, and not just because a lot of that carbon dioxide was emitted to build products for the West to consume. Rather, it's because China has four times the population of the United States, and per capita is really the only way to think about these emissions. And by that standard, each Chinese person now emits just over a quarter of the carbon dioxide that each American does. Not only that, but carbon dioxide lives in the atmosphere for more than a century. China has been at it in a big way less than 20 years, so it will be many, many years before the Chinese are as responsible for global warming as Americans.

What's more, unlike many of their counterparts in the United States, Chinese officials have begun a concerted effort to reduce emissions in the midst of their country's staggering growth. China now leads the world in the deployment of renewable energy, and there's barely a car made in the United States that can meet China's much tougher fuel-economy standards.

For its part, the United States must develop a plan to cut emissions—something that has eluded Americans for the entire two-decade history of the problem. Although the U.S. Senate voted down the last such attempt, Barack Obama has promised that it will be a priority in his administration. He favors some variation of a "cap and trade" plan that would limit the total amount of carbon dioxide the United States could release, thus putting a price on what has until now been free.

Despite the rapid industrialization of countries such as China and India, and the careless neglect of rich ones such as the United States, climate change is neither any one country's fault, nor any one country's responsibility. It will require sacrifice from everyone. Just as the Chinese might have to use somewhat more expensive power to protect the global environment, Americans will have to pay some of the difference in price, even if just in technology. Call it a Marshall Plan for the environment. Such a plan makes eminent moral and practical sense and could probably be structured so as to bolster emerging green energy industries in the West. But asking Americans to pay to put up windmills in China will be a hard political sell in a country that already thinks China is prospering at its expense. It could be the biggest test of the country's political maturity in many years.

"Climate Change Is an Environmental Problem"

Not really. Environmentalists were the first to sound the alarm. But carbon dioxide is not like traditional pollution. There's no Clean Air Act that can solve it. We must make a fundamental transformation in the most important part of our economies, shifting away from fossil fuels and on to something else. That means, for the United States, it's at least as much a problem for the Commerce and Treasury departments as it is for the Environmental Protection Agency.

And because every country on Earth will have to coordinate, it's far and away the biggest foreign-policy issue we face. (You were thinking terrorism? It's hard to figure out a scenario in which Osama bin Laden destroys Western civilization. It's easy to figure out how it happens with a rising sea level and a wrecked hydrological cycle.)

Expecting the environmental movement to lead this fight is like asking the USDA to wage the war in Iraq. It's not equipped for this kind of battle. It may be ready to save Alaska's Arctic National Wildlife Refuge, which is a noble undertaking but on a far smaller scale. Unless climate change is quickly deghettoized, the chances of making a real difference are small.

"Solving It Will Be Painful"

It depends. What's your definition of painful? On the one hand, you're talking about transforming the backbone of the world's industrial and consumer system. That's certainly expensive. On the other hand, say you manage to convert a lot of it to solar or wind power—think of the money you'd save on fuel.

And then there's the growing realization that we don't have many other possible sources for the economic growth we'll need to pull ourselves out of our current economic crisis. Luckily, green energy should be bigger than IT and biotech combined.

Almost from the moment scientists began studying the problem of climate change, people have been trying to estimate the costs of solving it. The real answer, though, is that it's such a huge transformation that no one really knows for sure. The bottom line is, the growth rate in energy use worldwide could be cut in half during the next 15 years and the steps would, net, save more money than they cost. The IPCC included a cost estimate in its latest five-year update on climate change and looked a little further into the future. It found that an attempt to keep carbon levels below about 500 parts per million would shave a little bit off the world's economic growth—but only a little. As in, the world would have to wait until Thanksgiving 2030 to be as rich as it would have been on January 1 of that year. And in return, it would have a much-transformed energy system.

Unfortunately though, those estimates are probably too optimistic. For one thing, in the years since they were published, the science has grown darker. Deeper and quicker cuts now seem mandatory.

But so far we've just been counting the costs of fixing the system. What about the cost of doing nothing? Nicholas Stern, a renowned economist commissioned by the British government to study the question, concluded that the costs of climate change could eventually reach the combined costs of both world wars and the Great Depression. In 2003, Swiss Re, the world's biggest reinsurance company, and Harvard Medical School explained why global warming would be so expensive. It's not just the infrastructure, such as sea walls against rising oceans, for example. It's also that the increased costs of natural disasters begin to compound. The diminishing time between monster storms in places such as the U.S. Gulf Coast could eventually mean that parts of "developed countries would experience developing nation conditions for prolonged periods." Quite simply, we've already done too much damage and waited too long to have any easy options left.

"We Can Reverse Climate Change"

If only. Solving this crisis is no longer an option. Human beings have already raised the temperature of the planet about a degree Fahrenheit. When people first began to focus on global warming (which is, remember, only 20 years ago), the general consensus was that at this point we'd just be standing on the threshold of realizing its consequences—that the big changes would be a degree or two and hence several decades down the road. But scientists seem to have systematically underestimated just how delicate the balance of the planet's physical systems really is.

The warming is happening faster than we expected, and the results are more widespread and more disturbing. Even that rise of 1 degree has seriously perturbed hydrological cycles: Because warm air holds more water vapor than cold air does, both droughts and floods are increasing dramatically. Just look at the record levels of insurance payouts, for instance. Mosquitoes, able to survive in new places, are spreading more malaria and dengue. Coral reefs are dying, and so are vast stretches of forest.

None of that is going to stop, even if we do everything right from here on out. Given the time lag between when we emit carbon and when the air heats up, we're already guaranteed at least another degree of warming.

The only question now is whether we're going to hold off catastrophe. It won't be easy, because the scientific consensus calls for roughly 5 degrees more warming this century unless we do just about everything right. And if our behavior up until now is any indication, we won't.

Critical Thinking

1. What is Bill McKibben's point of view?
2. What reasons does McKibben offer to support his point of view?
3. Identify some of the challenges to reversing climate change?

Reprinted in entirety by McGraw-Hill with permission from *Foreign Policy,* January/February 2009, pp. 32–38. www.foreignpolicy.com. © 2009 Washingtonpost.Newsweek Interactive, LLC.

The Other Climate Changers

JESSICA SEDDON WALLACK AND VEERABHADRAN RAMANATHAN

Why Black Carbon and Ozone Also Matter

At last, world leaders have recognized that climate change is a threat. And to slow or reverse it, they are launching initiatives to reduce greenhouse gases, especially carbon dioxide, the gas responsible for about half of global warming to date. Significantly reducing emissions of carbon dioxide is essential, as they will likely become an even greater cause of global warming by the end of this century. But it is a daunting task: carbon dioxide remains in the atmosphere for centuries, and it is difficult to get governments to agree on reducing emissions because whereas the benefits of doing so are shared globally, the costs are borne by individual countries. As a result, no government is moving fast enough to offset the impact of past and present emissions. Even if current emissions were cut in half by 2050—one of the targets discussed at the 2008 UN Climate Change Conference—by then, humans' total contribution to the level of carbon dioxide in the atmosphere would still have increased by a third since the beginning of this century.

Meanwhile, little attention has been given to a low-risk, cost-effective, and high-reward option: reducing emissions of light-absorbing carbon particles (known as "black carbon") and of the gases that form ozone. Together, these pollutants' warming effect is around 40-70 percent of that of carbon dioxide. Limiting their presence in the atmosphere is an easier, cheaper, and more politically feasible proposition than the most popular proposals for slowing climate change—and it would have a more immediate effect.

Time is running out. Humans have already warmed the planet by more than 0.5 degrees Celsius since the nineteenth century and produced enough greenhouse gases to make it a total of 2.4 degrees Celsius warmer by the end of this century. If the levels of carbon dioxide and nitrous oxide in the atmosphere continue to increase at current rates and if the climate proves more sensitive to greenhouse gases than predicted, the earth's temperature could rise by as much as five degrees before the century ends.

A temperature change of two to five degrees would have profound environmental and geopolitical effects. It would almost—certainly melt all the Arctic summer sea ice. As a result, the Arctic Ocean would absorb more sunlight, which, in turn, would further amplify the warming. Such a rise could eliminate the Himalayan and Tibetan glaciers, which feed the major water systems of some of the poorest regions of the world. It would also accelerate the melting of the Greenland and Antarctic ice sheets, raising the sea level worldwide and provoking large-scale emigration from low-lying coastal regions. Cycles of droughts and floods triggered by global warming would spell disaster for agriculture-dependent economies.

Some of global warming's environmental effects would be irreversible; some of its societal impacts, unmanageable. Given these consequences, policymakers worldwide seeking to slow climate change must weigh options beyond just reducing carbon dioxide, especially those that would produce rapid results. Cutting black carbon and ozone is one such strategy.

Powerful Pollutants

The warming effect of carbon dioxide has been known since at least the 1900s, and that of ozone since the 1970s, but the importance of black carbon was discovered only recently. During the past decade, scientists have used sophisticated instruments on drones, aircraft, ships, and satellites to track black carbon and ozone from their sources to remote locations thousands of miles away and measure and model how much atmospheric heating they cause. Black carbon, a widespread form of particulate air pollution, is what makes sooty smoke look blackish or brownish. It is a byproduct of incomplete, inefficient combustion—a sign of energy waste as much as energy use. Vehicles and ships fueled by diesel and cars with poorly maintained engines release it. So do forest fires and households and factories that use wood, dung, crop waste, or coal for cooking, heating, or other energy needs.

Black carbon alters the environment in two ways. In the sky, the suspended particles absorb sunlight, warming up the atmosphere and in turn the earth itself. On the earth's surface, deposits of black carbon on snowpacks and ice absorb sunlight, thereby heating the earth and melting glaciers. The Arctic sea ice and the Himalayan and Tibetan glaciers, for example, are melting as much as a result of black carbon as they are as a result of the global warming caused by carbon dioxide. The warming effect of black carbon is equal to about 20–50 percent of the effect of carbon dioxide, making it the second- or third-largest contributor to global warming. No one knows exactly how much warming it causes, but even the most conservative estimates indicate a nontrivial impact. And its large contribution to the melting of glaciers and sea ice, one of the most alarming near-term manifestations of climate change, is well documented.

The ozone in the lower level of the atmosphere is another major contributor to global warming that deserves attention. (This is different from the ozone in the stratosphere, which shields life on earth from the sun's ultraviolet rays.) A potent greenhouse gas, its warming effect is equal to about 20 percent of that of carbon dioxide. Unlike black carbon, which exists as particles, ozone is a gas. Ozone in the atmosphere is not emitted directly but formed from other gases, "ozone precursors," such as carbon monoxide (from the burning of fossil fuels or biomass), nitrogen oxides (from lightning, soil, and the burning of fossil fuels), methane (from agriculture, cattle, gas leaks, and the burning of wood), and other hydrocarbons (from the burning of organic materials and fossil fuels, among other sources).

Most important, black carbon and ozone stay in the atmosphere for a much shorter time than does carbon dioxide. Carbon dioxide remains in the atmosphere for centuries—maybe even millennia—before it is absorbed by oceans, plants, and algae. Even if all carbon dioxide emissions were miraculously halted today, it would take several centuries for the amount of carbon dioxide in the atmosphere to approach its preindustrial-era level. In contrast, black carbon stays in the atmosphere for only days to weeks before it is washed away by rain, and ozone (as well as some of its precursors) only stays for weeks to months before being broken down. Nonetheless, because both are widespread and continuously emitted, their atmospheric concentrations build up and cause serious damage to the environment.

Although reducing the emissions of other greenhouse gases, such as methane and halocarbons, could also produce immediate results, black carbon and ozone are the shortest-lived climate-altering pollutants, and they are relatively under-recognized in efforts to stem climate change. Reducing the emissions of these pollutants on earth would quickly lower their concentrations in the atmosphere and, in turn, reduce their impact on global warming.

An Easier Extra Step

Another promising feature of black carbon and ozone precursor emissions is that they can be significantly limited at relatively low cost with technologies that already exist. Although the sources of black carbon and ozone precursors vary worldwide, most emissions can be reduced without necessarily limiting the underlying activity that generated them. This is because, unlike carbon dioxide, black carbon and ozone precursors are not essential byproducts of energy use.

The use of fossil fuels, particularly diesel, is responsible for about 35 percent of black carbon emissions worldwide. Technologies that filter out black carbon have already been invented: diesel particulate filters on cars and trucks, for example, can reduce black carbon emissions by 90 percent or more with a negligible reduction in fuel economy. A recent study by the Clean Air Task Force, a U.S. nonprofit environmental research organization, estimated that retrofitting one million semitrailer trucks with these filters would yield the same benefits for the climate over 20 years as permanently removing over 165,000 trucks or 5.7 million cars from the road.

The remaining 65 percent of black carbon emissions are associated with the burning of biomass—through naturally occurring forest fires, man-made fires for clearing cropland, and the use of organic fuels for cooking, heating, and small-scale industry. Cleaner options for the man-made activities exist. The greenest options for households are stoves powered by the sun or by gas from organic waste, but updated designs for biomass-fueled stoves can also substantially cut the amount of black carbon and other pollutants emitted. Crop waste, dung, wood, coal, and charcoal are the cheapest, but also the least efficient and dirtiest, fuels, and so households tend to shift away from them as soon as other options become reliably available. Thus, the challenge in lowering black carbon emissions is not convincing people to sacrifice their lifestyles, as it is with convincing people to reduce their carbon dioxide emissions. The challenge is to make other options available.

Man-made ozone precursors are mostly emitted through industrial processes and fossil-fuel use, particularly in the transportation sector. These emissions can be reduced by making the combustion process more efficient (for example, through the use of fuel additives) or by removing these gases after combustion (for example, through the use of catalytic converters). Technologies that both minimize the formation of ozone precursors and filter or break down emissions are already widely used and are reducing ozone precursors in the developed world. The stricter enforcement of laws that forbid adulterating gasoline and diesel with cheaper, but dirtier, substitutes would also help.

Fully applying existing emissions-control technologies could cut black carbon emissions by about 50 percent. And that would be enough to offset the warming effects of one to two decades' worth of carbon dioxide emissions. Reducing the human-caused ozone in the lower atmosphere by about 50 percent, which could be possible through existing technologies, would offset about another decade's worth. Within weeks, the heating effect of black carbon would lessen; within months, so, too, would the greenhouse effect of ozone. Within ten years, the earth's overall warming trend would slow down, as would the retreat of sea ice and glaciers. The scientific argument for reducing emissions of black carbon and ozone precursors is clear.

A Political Possibility

Reducing emissions of black carbon and ozone precursors is also a politically promising project. It would yield significant benefits apart from slowing climate change, giving governments economic and developmental incentives to reduce them. Reducing ozone precursors, for its part, would have recognizable agricultural benefits. Ozone lowers crop yields by damaging plant cells and interfering with the production of chlorophyll, the pigment that enables plants to derive energy from sunlight. One recent study estimated that the associated economic loss (at 2000 world prices) ranged from $14 billion to $26 billion, three to five times as large as that attributed to global warming. For policymakers concerned about agricultural productivity and food security, these effects should resonate deeply.

In countries where a large portion of the population still depends on biomass fuels, reducing black carbon emissions from households would improve public health and economic productivity. Nearly 50 percent of the world's population, and up to 95 percent of the rural population in poor countries, relies on solid fuels, including biomass fuels and coal. The resulting indoor air pollution is linked to about a third of the fatal acute respiratory infections among children under five, or about seven percent of child deaths worldwide. Respiratory illnesses associated with the emissions from solid fuels are the fourth most important cause of excess mortality in developing countries (after malnutrition, unsafe sex, and waterborne diseases).

These health problems perpetuate poverty. Exposure to pollutants early in life harms children's lung development, and children who suffer from respiratory illnesses are less likely to attend school. Air pollution leaves the poor, who often earn a living from manual labor, especially worse off. Collectively, workers in India lose an estimated 1.6–2.0 billion days of work every year to the effects of indoor air pollution. Reducing black carbon emissions from households would thus promote economic growth and, particularly for rural women and children, improve public health.

Furthermore, both black carbon and ozone precursor emissions tend to have localized consequences, and governments are more likely to agree to emissions-reduction strategies that can deliver local benefits. With carbon dioxide and other long-lasting, far-spreading greenhouse gases, emissions anywhere contribute to global warming everywhere. But the effects of black carbon and ozone are more confined. When it first enters the atmosphere, black carbon spreads locally and then, within a week, dissipates more regionally before disappearing from the atmosphere entirely in the form of precipitation. Ozone precursors, too, are more regionally confined than carbon dioxide, although background levels of ozone are increasing around the globe.

Because the effects of black carbon and ozone are mostly regional, the benefits from reducing them would accrue in large part to the areas where reductions were achieved. The melting of the Himalayan and Tibetan glaciers is almost reason enough for countries in South and East Asia to take rapid action to eliminate black carbon emissions. So is the retreat of the Arctic sea ice for countries bordering the Arctic Ocean. Regional groupings are also more likely than larger collections of countries to have dense networks of the economic, cultural, and diplomatic ties that sustain difficult negotiations. Moreover, both black carbon and ozone can be contained through geographically targeted strategies because many of the sources of black carbon and ozone are largely fixed. And so even if one country in a region seeks to regulate emissions, that country's polluting activities are unlikely to move to another country with less stringent policies—a common concern with agreements to reduce carbon dioxide emissions.

Cleaning Up

So what can be done to curb black carbon and ozone precursor emissions? A logical first step is for governments, international development agencies, and philanthropists to increase financial support for reduction efforts. Although some money for this is currently available, neither pollutant has emerged as a mainstream target for public or private funding. Simply recognizing black carbon and ozone as environmental problems on par with carbon dioxide would make policymakers more inclined to spend development funds and the "green" portions of stimulus packages on initiatives to tackle them. Developed countries could put their contributions toward customizing emissions-reduction technologies for the developing world and promoting their deployment—an important gesture of goodwill that would kick-start change.

Regardless of the source of the funding, aid should support the deployment of clean-energy options for households and small industries in the developing world and of emissions-reduction technologies for transportation around the world. This could mean distributing solar lanterns and stoves that use local fuel sources more efficiently or paying for small enterprises to shift to cleaner technologies. The specific fixes for small-scale industry will vary by economic activity—making brick kilns cleaner is different from making tea and spice driers more efficient—but the number of possible customers for the new technologies offers some economies of scale. When it comes to transportation, policy options include subsidizing engine and filter upgrades, shifting to cleaner fuels, and removing the incentives, created by government subsidies that favor some fuels over others, for adulterating fuel and for using diesel.

Deploying technologies to reduce emissions from so many culturally embedded activities, from cooking to driving, will not be easy. Enforcing emissions controls on many small, mobile polluters is harder than regulating larger sources, such as power plants. And in customizing technologies, close attention will need to be paid to the varied needs of households and industry. But creating and enforcing regulations and subsidizing and disseminating energy-efficient technologies are challenges that have been met before. The "green revolution"—the remarkable growth in agricultural productivity that occurred in the second half of the twentieth century—introduced radical changes to small-scale farming. Other development initiatives have influenced fertility, gender equality, schooling, and other household decisions more sensitive than those about cooking and driving.

Moreover, the infrastructure for international financial and technological transfers already exists in the form of the World Bank, regional development banks, and UN programs that have supported development around the world for decades. The Global Environment Facility, a development and environmental fund that started as a World Bank program and is now the world's largest funder of environmental projects, is well suited to finance cleaner technologies.

Governments and international agencies should also finance technology that tracks air quality, which is generally under-monitored. In the major cities of most developing countries, the number of sensors has not kept up with the growth in population or economic activity. In rural areas, air pollution is not tracked at all. Improving the monitoring of air quality and disseminating the data would inform policymakers and environmental activists. And tracking individuals' emissions—through indoor air-pollution monitors or devices attached to cars' tailpipes—could help motivate people to curb their emissions. Experimental initiatives to measure individuals' carbon footprints and energy use have been shown to change people's behavior in some settings.

Aid alone will not be enough, however. International organizations must also help governments identify and act on opportunities that mitigate climate change and promote development. International development institutions, such as the UN Environment Program and the multilateral and regional development banks, could sponsor research, set up interministerial working groups, and establish standards for monitoring and reporting public expenditures. These initiatives would make it easier to identify possible areas of coordination among public health, agricultural, environmental, and anti-poverty programs. In most countries, domestic institutions are not designed to encourage cooperation among different authorities. Pitching the reduction of black carbon and ozone precursor emissions as public health and agricultural policies could help such efforts compete for scarce funds; enabling the clearer calculation of the environmental benefits of development policies would make policymaking more informed. Much in the same way that international development organizations currently support good governance to improve infrastructure and services, they should also promote better environmental governance.

Responding Regionally

The current piecemeal approach to climate science—in particular, the tendency to treat air pollution and climate change as separate issues—has at times led to bad policy. The decision of many countries to promote diesel as a means to encourage fuel efficiency, for example, may have had the inadvertent effect of increasing black carbon emissions. And air-pollution laws designed to reduce the use of sulfate aerosols, which cause acid rain, have ironically led to more warming because sulfates also have a cooling effect. Had policymakers instead integrated efforts to reduce air pollution with those to slow global warming, they could have ensured that the reduction of sulfates was accompanied by an equivalent reduction in greenhouse gases.

A single global framework would be the ideal way to integrate various strategies for mitigating climate change. Bilateral or multilateral agreements are more feasible for getting started on reducing black carbon and ozone precursor emissions. These can strengthen governments' incentives to act by discouraging free-riding and by motivating governments to take into account the larger-scale impacts of their own emissions. Because the sources of black carbon and ozone vary from region to region, agreements to reduce them need to be tailored to suit regional conditions. In the Northern Hemisphere, for example, ozone precursors mostly come from industrial processes and transportation, whereas in the Southern Hemisphere, especially tropical regions, they mostly come from natural emissions (soils, plants, and forest fires). The sources of black carbon vary by region, too: in Europe and North America, transportation and industrial activity play a larger role than the burning of biomass, whereas the reverse is true in developing regions.

The impact of emissions on the climate is scientifically complex, and it depends on a number of factors that have not yet been adequately taken into account when devising climate models. The challenge, then, is to quickly create agreements that consider the complex links between human activities, emissions, and climate change and that can adjust over time as the scientific understanding of the problem evolves. Regional air-pollution agreements are easier to update than global agreements with many signatories. The UN Convention on Long-Range Transboundary Air Pollution (most of whose signatories are European or Central Asian states) and its subsequent pollutant-specific protocols provide a ready model for regional agreements on short-lived climate-changing pollutants. The specific provisions of these agreements are based on the costs of reductions, scientists' knowledge of the sources and distribution of air pollution, and the ability to measure reductions—considerations that should also inform the regulation of black carbon and ozone precursor emissions. Moreover, these agreements commit countries to particular actions, not just specific outcomes. This is wise, given that emissions are difficult to monitor and quantify precisely.

Black carbon and ozone can also be built into existing bilateral discussions. The High-Level India-EU Dialogue, a working group of scientists and policymakers from Europe and India, is one such existing forum. In February 2009, it was already urging governments from Europe and India to work together to recognize and reduce the threat from black carbon. Participants proposed an interdisciplinary research project that would determine the effects of biomass-based cooking and heating on health and the climate and assess the obstacles to a large-scale deployment of cleaner stoves. Black carbon and ozone are also natural candidates for U.S.-Chinese cooperation on energy and climate change: China would reap public health and agricultural benefits from reducing emissions, and the United States would earn goodwill for helping China do so.

By building on existing air-pollution agreements, the risk of distracting climate-change negotiations from the substantial task of promoting the reduction of carbon dioxide emissions could be avoided. Putting black carbon and ozone on the table in high-level climate talks could backfire if developing nations thought that they would be tacitly admitting responsibility for global warming by committing to reducing emissions of black carbon and ozone precursors or believed that the issue was an effort by developed countries to divert attention from the need for them to reduce their carbon dioxide emissions. Therefore, efforts to reduce emissions of black carbon and ozone precursors should be presented not as substitutes for commitments to reducing carbon dioxide emissions but as ways to quickly achieve local environmental and economic benefits.

The Low-Hanging Fruit

Historically, initiatives to slow global warming have focused on reducing the emissions of carbon dioxide and other greenhouse gases and largely ignored the role played by air pollution. This strategy makes sense for the long run, since carbon dioxide emissions are, and will continue to be, the most important factor in climate change. But in the short run, it alone will not be enough. Some scientists have proposed geoengineering—manipulating the climate through the use of technology—as a potential option of last resort, but the reduction of black carbon and ozone precursor emissions offers a less risky opportunity for achieving the same end.

Such an approach would quickly lower the level of black carbon and ozone in the atmosphere, offsetting the impact of decades of greenhouse gas emissions, decelerating the rush toward a dangerously warm planet, and giving efforts to reduce carbon dioxide emissions time to get off the ground. These pollutants are also tractable policy targets: they can be reduced through the use of existing technologies, institutions, and strategies, and doing so would lead to local improvements in air quality, agricultural output, and public health. In short, reducing black carbon and ozone precursor emissions is a low-risk, high-potential addition to the current arsenal of strategies to mitigate climate change.

At the current rate of global warming, the earth's temperature stands to career out of control. Now is the time to look carefully at all the possible brakes that can be applied to slow climate change, hedge against near-term climate disasters, and buy time for technological innovations. Of the available strategies, focusing on reducing emissions of black carbon and ozone precursors is the low-hanging fruit: the costs are relatively low, the implementation is feasible, and the benefits would be numerous and immediate.

Critical Thinking

1. What other contributors to climate change are there in addition to greenhouse gases?

2. How does black carbon alter the environment?

3. Why is it less expensive to combat black carbon and ozone precursor emissions than greenhouse gases?

4. What can be done by governments and international organizations to curb these pollutants?

JESSICA SEDDON WALLACK is Director of the Center for Development Finance at the Institute for Financial Management and Research, in Chennai, India. VEERABHADRAN RAMANATHAN is Distinguished Professor of Climate and Atmospheric Sciences at the Scripps Institute of Oceanography at the University of California, San Diego; Distinguished Visiting Fellow at the Energy and Resources Institute, in New Delhi; and a recipient of the 2009 Tyler Prize for Environmental Achievement.

The Big Melt

BROOK LARMER

Glaciers in the high heart of Asia feed its greatest rivers, lifelines for two billion people. Now the ice and snow are diminishing.

The gods must be furious.

It's the only explanation that makes sense to Jia Son, a Tibetan farmer surveying the catastrophe unfolding above his village in China's mountainous Yunnan Province. "We've upset the natural order," the devout, 52-year-old Buddhist says. "And now the gods are punishing us."

On a warm summer afternoon, Jia Son has hiked a mile and a half up the gorge that Ming-yong Glacier has carved into sacred Mount Kawagebo, looming 22,113 feet high in the clouds above. There's no sign of ice, just a river roiling with silt-laden melt. For more than a century, ever since its tongue lapped at the edge of Mingyong village, the glacier has retreated like a dying serpent recoiling into its lair. Its pace has accelerated over the past decade, to more than a football field every year—a distinctly unglacial rate for an ancient ice mass.

"This all used to be ice ten years ago," Jia Son says, as he scrambles across the scree and brush. He points out a yak trail etched into the slope some 200 feet above the valley bottom. "The glacier sometimes used to cover that trail, so we had to lead our animals over the ice to get to the upper meadows."

Around a bend in the river, the glacier's snout finally comes into view: It's a deathly shade of black, permeated with pulverized rock and dirt. The water from this ice, once so pure it served in rituals as a symbol of Buddha himself, is now too loaded with sediment for the villagers to drink. For nearly a mile the glacier's once smooth surface is ragged and cratered like the skin of a leper. There are glimpses of blue-green ice within the fissures, but the cracks themselves signal trouble. "The beast is sick and wasting away," Jia Son says. "If our sacred glacier cannot survive, how can we?"

It is a question that echoes around the globe, but nowhere more urgently than across the vast swath of Asia that draws its water from the "roof of the world." This geologic colossus—the highest and largest plateau on the planet, ringed by its tallest mountains—covers an area greater than western Europe, at an average altitude of more than two miles. With nearly 37,000 glaciers on the Chinese side alone, the Tibetan Plateau and its surrounding arc of mountains contain the largest volume of ice outside the polar regions. This ice gives birth to Asia's largest and most legendary rivers, from the Yangtze and the Yellow to the Mekong and the Ganges—rivers that over the course of history have nurtured civilizations, inspired religions, and sustained ecosystems. Today they are lifelines for some of Asia's most densely settled areas, from the arid plains of Pakistan to the thirsty metropolises of northern China 3,000 miles away. All told, some two billion people in more than a dozen countries—nearly a third of the world's population—depend on rivers fed by the snow and ice of the plateau region.

But a crisis is brewing on the roof of the world, and it rests on a curious paradox: For all its seeming might and immutability, this geologic expanse is more vulnerable to climate change than almost anywhere else on Earth. The Tibetan Plateau as a whole is heating up twice as fast as the global average of 1.3°F over the past century—and in some places even faster. These warming rates, unprecedented for at least two millennia, are merciless on the glaciers, whose rare confluence of high altitudes and low latitudes make them especially sensitive to shifts in climate.

For thousands of years the glaciers have formed what Lonnie Thompson, a glaciologist at Ohio State University, calls "Asia's freshwater bank account"—an immense storehouse whose buildup of new ice and snow (deposits) has historically offset its annual runoff (withdrawals). Glacial melt plays its most vital role before and after the rainy season, when it supplies a greater portion of the flow in every river from the Yangtze (which irrigates more than half of China's rice) to the Ganges and the Indus (key to the agricultural heartlands of India and Pakistan). But over the past half century, the balance has been lost, perhaps irrevocably. Of the 680 glaciers Chinese scientists monitor closely on the Tibetan Plateau, 95 percent are shedding more ice than they're adding, with the heaviest losses on its southern and eastern edges. "These glaciers are not simply retreating," Thompson says. "They're losing mass from the surface down."

The ice cover in this portion of the plateau has shrunk more than 6 percent since the 1970s—and the damage is still greater in Tajikistan and northern India, with 35 percent and 20 percent declines respectively over the past five decades. The rate of melting is not uniform, and a number of glaciers in the Karakoram Range on the western edge of the plateau are actually advancing. This anomaly may result from increases in snowfall in the higher latitude—and therefore colder—Karakorams, where snow and ice are less vulnerable to small temperature increases. The gaps in scientific knowledge are still great, and in the Tibetan Plateau they are deepened by the region's remoteness and political sensitivity—as well as by the inherent complexities of climate science.

Though scientists argue about the rate and cause of glacial retreat, most don't deny that it's happening. And they believe the worst may be yet to come. The more dark areas that are exposed by melting, the more sunlight is absorbed than reflected, causing temperatures to rise faster. (Some climatologists believe this warming feedback loop could intensify the Asian monsoon, triggering more violent storms and flooding in places such as Bangladesh and Myanmar.) If current trends hold, Chinese scientists believe that 40 percent of the plateau's glaciers could disappear by 2050. "Full-scale glacier shrinkage is inevitable," says Yao Tandong, a glaciologist at China's Institute of Tibetan Plateau Research. "And it will lead to ecological catastrophe."

The potential impacts extend far beyond the glaciers. On the Tibetan Plateau, especially its dry northern flank, people are already affected by a warmer climate. The grasslands and wetlands are deteriorating, and the permafrost that feeds them with spring and summer melt is retreating to higher elevations. Thousands of lakes have dried up. Desert now covers about one-sixth of the plateau, and in places sand dunes lap across the highlands like waves in a yellow sea. The herders who once thrived here are running out of options.

Along the plateau's southern edge, by contrast, many communities are coping with too much water. In alpine villages like Mingyong, the glacial melt has swelled rivers, with welcome side effects: expanded croplands and longer growing seasons. But such benefits often hide deeper costs. In Mingyong, surging meltwater has carried away topsoil; elsewhere, excess runoff has been blamed for more frequent flooding and landslides. In the mountains from Pakistan to Bhutan, thousands of glacial lakes have formed, many potentially unstable. Among the more dangerous is Imja Tsho, at 16,400 feet on the trail to Nepal's Island Peak. Fifty years ago the lake didn't exist; today, swollen by melt, it is a mile long and 300 feet deep. If it ever burst through its loose wall of moraine, it would drown the Sherpa villages in the valley below.

This situation—too much water, too little water—captures, in miniature, the trajectory of the overall crisis. Even if melting glaciers provide an abundance of water in the short run, they portend a frightening endgame: the eventual depletion of Asia's greatest rivers. Nobody can predict exactly when the glacier retreat will translate into a sharp drop in runoff. Whether it happens in 10, 30, or 50 years depends on local conditions, but the collateral damage across the region could be devastating. Along with acute water and electricity shortages, experts predict a plunge in food production, widespread migration in the face of ecological changes, even conflicts between Asian powers.

The nomads' tent is a pinprick of white against a canvas of green and brown. There is no other sign of human existence on the 14,000-foot-high prairie that seems to extend to the end of the world. As a vehicle rattles toward the tent, two young men emerge, their long black hair horizontal in the wind. Ba O and his brother Tsering are part of an unbroken line of Tibetan nomads who for at least a thousand years have led their herds to summer grazing grounds near the headwaters of the Yangtze and Yellow Rivers.

Inside the tent, Ba O's wife tosses patties of dried yak dung onto the fire while her four-year-old son plays with a spool of sheep's wool. The family matriarch, Lu Ji, churns yak milk into cheese, rocking back and forth in a hypnotic rhythm. Behind her are two weathered Tibetan chests topped with a small Buddhist shrine: a red prayer wheel, a couple of smudged Tibetan texts, and several yak butter candles whose flames are never allowed to go out. "This is the way we've always done things," Ba O says. "And we don't want that to change."

But it may be too late. The grasslands are dying out, as decades of warming temperatures—exacerbated by overgrazing—turn prairie into desert. Watering holes are drying up, and now, instead of traveling a short distance to find summer grazing for their herds, Ba O and his family must trek more than 30 miles across the high plateau. Even there the grass is meager. "It used to grow so high you could lose a sheep in it," Ba O says. "Now it doesn't reach above their hooves." The family's herd has dwindled from 500 animals to 120. The next step seems inevitable: selling their remaining livestock and moving into a government resettlement camp.

Across Asia the response to climate-induced threats has mostly been slow and piecemeal, as if governments would prefer to leave it up to the industrialized countries that pumped the greenhouse gases into the atmosphere in the first place. There are exceptions. In Ladakh, a bone-dry region in northern India and Pakistan that relies entirely on melting ice and snow, a retired civil engineer named Chewang Norphel has built "artificial glaciers"—simple stone embankments that trap and freeze glacial melt in the fall for use in the early spring growing season. Nepal is developing a remote monitoring system to gauge when glacial lakes are in danger of bursting, as well as the technology to drain them. Even in places facing destructive monsoonal flooding, such as Bangladesh, "floating schools" in the delta enable kids to continue their education—on boats.

But nothing compares to the campaign in China, which has less water than Canada but 40 times more people. In the vast desert in the Xinjiang region, just north of the Tibetan Plateau, China aims to build 59 reservoirs to capture and save glacial runoff. Across Tibet, artillery batteries have been installed to launch rain-inducing silver iodide into the clouds. In Qinghai the government is blocking off degraded grasslands in hopes they can be nurtured back to health. In areas where grasslands have already turned to scrub desert, bales of wire fencing are rolled out over the last remnants of plant life to prevent them from blowing away.

Along the road near the town of Madoi are two rows of newly built houses. This is a resettlement village for Tibetan nomads, part of a massive and controversial program to relieve pressure on the grasslands near the sources of Chinas three major rivers—the Yangtze, Yellow, and Mekong—where nearly half of Qing-hai Province's 530,000 nomads have traditionally lived. Tens of thousands of nomads here have had to give up their way of life, and many more—including, perhaps, Ba O—may follow.

The subsidized housing is solid, and residents receive a small annual stipend. Even so, Jixi Lamu, a 33-year-old woman in a traditional embroidered dress, says her family is stuck in limbo, dependent on government handouts. "We've spent the $400 we had left from selling off our animals," she says. "There was no future with our herds, but there's no future here either." Her husband is away looking for menial work. Inside the one-room house, her mother sits on the bed, fingering her prayer beads. A Buddhist shrine stands on the other side of the room, but the candles have burned out.

It is not yet noon in Delhi, just 180 miles south of the Himalayan glaciers. But in the narrow corridors of Nehru Camp, a slum in this city of 16 million, the blast furnace of the north Indian summer has already sent temperatures soaring past 105 degrees Fahrenheit. Chaya, the 25-year-old wife of a fortune-teller, has spent seven hours joining the mad scramble for water that, even today, defines life in this heaving metropolis—and offers a taste of what the depletion of Tibet's water and ice portends.

Chaya's day began long before sunrise, when she and her five children fanned out in the darkness, armed with plastic jugs of every size. After daybreak, the rumor of a tap with running water sent her stumbling in a panic through the slum's narrow corridors. Now, with her containers still empty and the sun blazing overhead, she has returned home for a moment's rest. Asked if she's eaten anything today, she laughs: "We haven't even had any tea yet."

Suddenly cries erupt—a water truck has been spotted. Chaya leaps up and joins the human torrent in the street. A dozen boys swarm onto a blue tanker, jamming hoses in and siphoning the water out. Below, shouting women jostle for position with their containers. In six minutes the tanker is empty. Chaya arrived too late and must move on to chase the next rumor of water.

Delhi's water demand already exceeds supply by more than 300 million gallons a day, a shortfall worsened by inequitable distribution and a leaky infrastructure that loses an estimated 40 percent of the water. More than two-thirds of the city's water is pulled from the Yamuna and the Ganges, rivers fed by Himalayan ice. If that ice disappears, the future will almost certainly be worse. "We are facing an unsustainable situation," says Diwan Singh, a Delhi environmental activist. "Soon—not in thirty years but in five to ten—there will be an exodus because of the lack of water."

The tension already seethes. In the clogged alleyway around one of Nehru Camp's last functioning taps, which run for one hour a day, a man punches a woman who cut in line, leaving a purple welt on her face. "We wake up every morning fighting over water," says Kamal Bhate, a local astrologer watching the melee. This one dissolves into shouting and finger-pointing, but the brawls can be deadly. In a nearby slum a teenage boy was recently beaten to death for cutting in line.

As the rivers dwindle, the conflicts could spread. India, China, and Pakistan all face pressure to boost food production to keep up with their huge and growing populations. But climate change and diminishing water supplies could reduce cereal yields in South Asia by 5 percent within three decades. "We're going to see rising tensions over shared water resources, including political disputes between farmers, between farmers and cities, and between human and ecological demands for water," says Peter Gleick, a water expert and president of the Pacific Institute in Oakland, California. "And I believe more of these tensions will lead to violence."

The real challenge will be to prevent water conflicts from spilling across borders. There is already a growing sense of alarm in Central Asia over the prospect that poor but glacier-heavy nations (Tajikistan, Kyrgyzstan) may one day restrict the flow of water to their parched but oil-rich neighbors (Uzbekistan, Kazakhstan, Turkmenistan). In the future, peace between Pakistan and India may hinge as much on water as on nuclear weapons, for the two countries must share the glacier-dependent Indus.

The biggest question mark hangs over China, which controls the sources of the region's major rivers. Its damming of the Mekong has sparked anger downstream in Indochina. If Beijing follows through on tentative plans to divert the Brahmaputra, it could provoke its rival, India, in the very region where the two countries fought a war in 1962.

For the people in Nehru Camp, geopolitical concerns are lost in the frenzied pursuit of water. In the afternoon, a tap outside the slum is suddenly turned on, and Chaya, smiling triumphantly, hauls back a full, ten-gallon jug on top of her head. The water is dirty and bitter, and there are no means to boil it. But now, at last, she can give her children their first meal of the day: a piece of bread and a few spoonfuls of lentil stew. "They should be studying, but we keep shooing them away to find water," Chaya says. "We have no choice, because who knows if we'll find enough water tomorrow."

Fatalism may be a natural response to forces that seem beyond our control. But Jia Son, the Tibetan farmer watching Mingyong Glacier shrink, believes that every action counts—good or bad, large or small. Pausing on the mountain trail, he makes a guilty confession. The melting ice, he says, may be his fault.

When Jia Son first noticed the rising temperatures—an unfamiliar trickle of sweat down his back about a decade ago—he figured it was a gift from the gods. Winter soon lost some of its brutal sting. The glacier began releasing its water earlier in the summer, and for the first time in memory villagers had the luxury of two harvests a year.

Then came the Chinese tourists, a flood of city dwellers willing to pay locals to take them up to see the glacier. The Han tourists don't always respect Buddhist traditions; in their gleeful hollers to provoke an icefall, they seem unaware of the calamity that has befallen the glacier. Still, they have turned a poor village into one of the region's wealthiest. "Life is much easier now," says Jia Son, whose simple farmhouse, like all in the village, has a television and government-subsidized satellite dish. "But maybe our greed has made Kawagebo angry."

He is referring to the temperamental deity above his village. One of the holiest mountains in Tibetan Buddhism, Kawagebo has never been conquered, and locals believe its summit—and its glacier—should remain untouched. When a Sino-Japanese expedition tried to scale the peak in 1991, an avalanche near the top of the glacier killed all 17 climbers. Jia Son remains convinced the deaths were not an accident but an act of divine retribution. Could Mingyong's retreat be another sign of Kawagebo's displeasure?

Jia Son is taking no chances. Every year he embarks on a 15-day pilgrimage around Kawagebo to show his deepening Buddhist devotion. He no longer hunts animals or cuts down trees. As part of a government program, he has also given up a parcel of land to be reforested. His family still participates in the village's tourism cooperative, but Jia Son makes a point of telling visitors about the glacier's spiritual significance. "Nothing will get better," he says, "until we get rid of our materialistic thinking."

It's a simple pledge, perhaps, one that hardly seems enough to save the glaciers of the Tibetan Plateau—and stave off the water crisis that seems sure to follow. But here, in the shadow of one of the world's fastest retreating glaciers, this lone farmer has begun, in his own small way, to restore the balance.

Critical Thinking

1. What is the relationship of glacier melt to much of Asia's agricultural production and urban lifestyle?

2. How is the loss of glaciers a potential source of conflict between some of Asia's major political powers?

3. How does this article illustrate the relationship between natural resources and social structures?

4. How does this article complement or contradict articles 1, 2, and 4?

From *National Geographic*, April 2010. Copyright © 2010 by National Geographic Society. Reprinted by permission.

Troubled Waters

The sea is suffering, mostly at the hand of man, says John Grimond.

All of us have in our veins the exact same percentage of salt in our blood that exists in the ocean . . .
And when we go back to the sea . . . we are going back from whence we came.

THE ECONOMIST

Human beings no longer thrive under the water from which their ancestors emerged, but their relationship with the sea remains close. Over half the world's people live within 100 kilometres (62 miles) of the coast; a tenth are within 10km. On land at least, the sea delights the senses and excites the imagination. The sight and smell of the sea inspire courage and adventure, fear and romance. Though the waves may be rippling or mountainous, the waters angry or calm, the ocean itself is eternal. Its moods pass. Its tides keep to a rhythm. It is unchanging.

Or so it has long seemed. Appearances deceive, though. Large parts of the sea may indeed remain unchanged, but in others, especially in the surface and coastal waters where 90% of marine life is to be found, the impact of man's activities is increasingly plain. This should hardly be a surprise. Man has changed the landscape and the atmosphere. It would be odd if the seas, which he has for centuries used for food, for transport, for dumping rubbish and, more recently, for recreation, had not also been affected.

The evidence abounds. The fish that once seemed an inexhaustible source of food are now almost everywhere in decline: 90% of large predatory fish (the big ones such as tuna, swordfish and sharks) have gone, according to some scientists. In estuaries and coastal waters, 85% of the large whales have disappeared, and nearly 60% of the small ones. Many of the smaller fish are also in decline. Indeed, most familiar sea creatures, from albatrosses to walruses, from seals to oysters, have suffered huge losses.

All this has happened fairly recently. Cod have been caught off Nova Scotia for centuries, but their systematic slaughter began only after 1852; in terms of their biomass (the aggregate mass of the species), they are now 96% depleted. The killing of turtles in the Caribbean (99% down) started in the 1700s. The hunting of sharks in the Gulf of Mexico (45–99%, depending on the variety) got going only in the 1950s.

The habitats of many of these creatures have also been affected by man's activities. Cod live in the bottom layer of the ocean. Trawlermen in pursuit of these and other groundfish like pollock and haddock drag steel weights and rollers as well as nets behind their boats, devastating huge areas of the sea floor as they go. In the Gulf of Mexico, trawlers ply back and forth year in year out, hauling vast nets that scarify the seabed and allow no time for plant and animal life to recover. Off New England, off west Africa, in the Sea of Okhotsk north of Japan, off Sri Lanka, wherever fish can still be found, it is much the same story.

Coral reefs, whose profusion of life and diversity of ecosystems make them the rainforests of the sea, have suffered most of all. Once home to prolific concentrations of big fish, they have attracted human hunters prepared to use any means, even dynamite, to kill their prey. Perhaps only 5% of coral reefs can now be considered pristine, a quarter have been lost and all are vulnerable to global warming.

A hotter atmosphere has several effects on the sea. First, it means higher average temperatures for surface waters. One consequence for coral reefs is that the symbiosis between the corals and algae that constitute a living reef is breaking down. As temperatures rise, the algae leave or are expelled, the corals take on a bleached, white appearance and may then die.

Hotter Water, Slimier Slime

Warming also has consequences for ice: it melts. Melting sea ice affects ecosystems and currents. It does not affect sea levels, because floating ice is already displacing water of a weight equal to its own. But melting glaciers and ice sheets on land are bringing quantities of fresh water into the sea, whose level has been rising at an average of nearly 2 millimetres a year for over 40 years, and the pace is getting faster. Recent studies suggest that the sea level may well rise by a total of 80 centimetres this century, though the figure could plausibly be as much as 2 metres.

The burning over the past 100 years or so of fossil fuels that took half a billion years to form has suddenly, in geological terms, put an enormous amount of carbon dioxide into the atmosphere. About a third of this CO_2 is taken up by the sea, where it forms carbonic acid. The plants and animals that have evolved over time to thrive in slightly alkaline surface waters—their pH is around 8.3—are now having to adapt to a 30% increase in the acidity of their surroundings. Some will no doubt flourish, but if the trend continues, as it will for at least some decades, clams, mussels, conches and all creatures that grow shells made of calcium carbonate will struggle. So will corals, especially those whose skeletons are composed of aragonite, a particularly unstable form of calcium carbonate.

Man's interference does not stop with CO_2. Knowingly and deliberately, he throws plenty of rubbish into the sea, everything from sewage to rubber tyres and from plastic packaging to toxic waste. Inadvertently, he also lets flame retardants, bunker oil, and heavy metals seep into the mighty ocean, and often invasive species too. Much of the harm done by such pollutants is invisible to the eye: it shows up only in the analysis of dead polar bears or in tuna served in New York sushi bars.

Increasingly, though, swimmers, sailors, and even those who monitor the sea with the help of satellites are encountering highly visible algal blooms known as red tides. These have always occurred naturally, but they have increased in frequency, number and size in recent years, notably since man-made nitrogen fertilisers came into widespread use in the 1950s. When rainwater contaminated with these fertilisers and other nutrients reaches the sea, as it does where the Mississippi runs into the Gulf of Mexico, an explosion of toxic algae and bacteria takes place, killing fish, absorbing almost all the oxygen, and leaving a microbially dominated ecosystem, often based on a carpet of slime.

Each of these phenomena would be bad enough on its own, but all appear to be linked, usually synergistically. Slaughter one species in the food web and you set off a chain of alterations above or below. Thus the near extinction of sea otters in the northern Pacific led to a proliferation of sea urchins, which then laid waste an entire kelp forest that had hitherto sustained its own ecosystem. If acidification kills tiny sea snails known as pteropods, as it is likely to, the Pacific salmon that feed upon these planktonic creatures may also die. Then other fish may move in, preventing the salmon from coming back, just as other species did when cod were all but fished out in Georges Bank, off New England.

Whereas misfortunes that came singly might not prove fatal, those that come in combination often prove overwhelming. The few coral reefs that remain pristine seem able to cope with the warming and acidification that none can escape, but most of the reefs that have also suffered overfishing or pollution have succumbed to bleaching or even death. Biodiversity comes with interdependence, and the shocks administered by mankind in recent decades have been so numerous and so severe that the natural balance of marine life is everywhere disturbed.

Are these changes reversible? Most scientists believe that fisheries, for instance, could be restored to health with the right policies, properly enforced. But many of the changes are speeding up, not slowing down. Some, such as the acidification of the seas, will continue for years to come simply because of events already in train or past. And some, such as the melting of the Arctic ice cap, may be close to the point at which an abrupt, and perhaps irreversible, series of happenings is set in motion.

It is clear, in any event, that man must change his ways. Humans could afford to treat the sea as an infinite resource when they were relatively few in number, capable of only rather inefficient exploitation of the vasty deep and without as yet a taste for fossil fuels. A world of 6.7 billion souls, set to become 9 billion by 2050, can no longer do so. The possibility of widespread catastrophe is simply too great.

Critical Thinking

1. Describe some of the human activities that are damaging the world's surface and coastal waters.

2. What is meant by "synergistically linked"? Give examples to illustrate this concept. Apply the concept to other case studies in the first three units of this book.

Asian Carp, Other Invasive Species Make a Splash

David Harrison

Last month, a commercial angler netted a 19-pound Asian carp on Chicago's Lake Calumet, part of the waterway system that connects the Mississippi River to Lake Michigan. The fisherman's haul was ominous, suggesting that the carp, a prehistoric-looking behemoth, had somehow gotten past an underwater electric fence designed to keep the species from entering the Great Lakes.

Since then, officials from the Great Lakes states have been fretting about the invasive fish, which has been working its way up the Mississippi River since it was first introduced in the Southeast almost 20 years ago, crowding out native species along the way. Asian carp are just the latest alien species to threaten the lakes, following other creatures such as the zebra and quagga mussel and the sea lamprey, all of which have found homes in the lakes' waters.

But the carp have attained a degree of notoriety that has eluded the other species, owing to their size and their distressing habit of thrashing out of the water at the sound of passing motorboats. Politicians have cast the fish as a voracious invader that would annihilate the lakes' ecosystems and cause the collapse of the $7 billion fishing and tourism industry.

Scientists have disputed that claim, noting that other invasive species already have depleted food sources in the Great Lakes so much that carp could find the waters to be inhospitable. The uproar nevertheless has brought renewed attention to the problem of invasive species, which have been washing into U.S. waters for years thanks to international shipping.

Michigan Attorney General Mike Cox has been particularly vocal, calling on Illinois to close locks and gates on the Chicago River that connect the Mississippi River with the lakes. But behind his rhetoric lies the disconcerting fact that states are powerless to combat most invasive species. Fish and mollusks don't respect state sovereignty, which makes it impossible for one state to completely seal off its waters from another. The best way to effectively control the spread of invasive species, advocates say, is for the federal government to step in.

In an attempt to force Washington's hand, Michigan, Minnesota, Ohio, Pennsylvania and Wisconsin filed a lawsuit against the federal government last week to force the U.S. Army Corps of Engineers to speed up its efforts to protect the lakes from the fish. "President Obama and the Army Corps of Engineers have failed to fight Asian carp aggressively," Cox said in a statement. "Asian carp will kill jobs and ruin our way of life."

This is not the first time Cox has used the courts to combat Asian carp. Late last year, Michigan sued Illinois in the U.S. Supreme Court to try to force Illinois to close the Chicago-area locks, which are crucial to shipping. Right now, carp are massed behind an electric fence and officials fear that all it would take is a power outage for them to flood into the lakes. The court declined to take the case.

The Illinois Chamber of Commerce has criticized the latest lawsuit, calling it politically motivated — Cox is running for governor in Michigan. The state of Illinois did not join the suit. Instead, Illinois Governor Pat Quinn has suggested harvesting the fish and sending them to China, where they are considered a delicacy.

Big Eaters

Despite all the attention they've gotten recently, Asian carp are not the most dangerous invasive species to threaten the Great Lakes. Their impact pales in comparison to that of the quagga mussel which first showed up in the lakes in the late 1990s and has become ensconced there. The mussels reproduce rapidly and devour plankton, disrupting the lower levels of a food chain that native species rely upon.

"We're probably looking at one of the biggest invasions in the Great Lakes right now with the quagga mussels," says Gary Fahnenstiel, a senior ecologist at the National Oceanic and Atmospheric Administration.

Notwithstanding the dire warnings from politicians, Fahnenstiel says, should Asian carp make it to Lake Michigan they probably would have a difficult time competing with the quagga mussels for food. "They beat them to the buffet table, you might say," Fahnenstiel says.

Also, while state officials argue about sealing the lakes from the Mississippi, the biggest threat is likely to come from the north, where the Saint Lawrence Seaway connects the Great Lakes to the Atlantic Ocean. Many of the 185 invasive species in the lakes hitched rides in the cargo holds of ships sailing through the seaway.

Transatlantic cargo vessels often unload their cargo in New York or New Jersey, then take on ocean water to settle themselves. They travel through the seaway to the Great Lakes where they unload the ballast water and pick up cargo before embarking on their return trips. Over time, the mud and residual water that settles in the ships' holds becomes an ideal place for invasive species to settle before they get flushed out into the Great Lakes. That's how quagga and zebra mussels from Eastern Europe arrived on the shores of Michigan, Wisconsin and other Great Lakes states.

Heading West

Unfortunately, it now seems that the mussels' journey didn't end there. About three years ago, a recreational boater drove a mussel-encrusted boat from the Great Lakes to Lake Mead in Nevada. That introduced the species to the inland West, where it is continuing to spread as boaters move their craft from one waterway to the next. Quagga and zebra mussels have been found in Colorado, Nebraska and Utah.

They haven't come to Wyoming or Idaho yet, and those two states want to keep it that way. Recently, officials there started inspecting boats and requiring boaters to buy stickers certifying that their boats are mussel-free.

Yet officials in these states are afraid the mussels will inevitably evade their efforts. Like their Great Lakes counterparts, Western states are blaming what is widely believed to be an inadequate federal response.

"We're doing everything we can to protect our waterways here and the federal government is doing nothing," says Idaho state Representative Eric Anderson, who lives on a lake at the northern tip of the state. "To me it's an absolute crime."

One possible solution would be for the federal government to enforce strict rules on treating the ballast water of international cargo ships. Environmentalists have called on the U.S. Environmental Protection Agency, the Coast Guard or Congress to address the issue without success so far. Some also have suggested closing the Saint Lawrence Seaway to ocean ships, forcing them to transfer their cargo to lake vessels.

States have put in place a patchwork of their own ballast-water rules, which have been upheld in court challenges. But that system encourages shipping companies to find the state with the weakest regulations, putting all the other Great Lakes states at risk, says Nick Schroeck, executive director of the Great Lakes Environmental Law Center.

"Why can't we just get a national standard and be done with it?" Schroeck says. "That's what makes the most sense."

In 2008, the U.S. House of Representatives passed a bill that would have regulated treatment of ballast water, but the measure died in the Senate.

"I don't know that there's much of an appetite right now to take that up again," says Schroek. "You'd think that with the Asian carp situation there would be, but I guess they've got a lot on their plate."

Critical Thinking

1. What is an invasive species?
2. What challenges to governmental agencies does the Asian carp present?
3. What are some other examples of invasive species?

From *Stateline.org,* July 30, 2010. Copyright © 2010 by Stateline.org. Reprinted by permission. Stateline.org is a nonpartisan, nonprofit news service of the Pew Center on the States that reports and analyzes trends in state policy.

UNIT 4
Political Economy

Unit Selections

Learning Outcomes

After reading this Unit, you will be able to:

- Describe the basic structure of the contemporary global political economy.

- Describe the process of globalization and the arguments about the costs and benefits of this economic/social process.

- Describe the debate about alternative approaches to alleviating extreme poverty.

- Compare and contrast the insights into the global political economy that the various case studies offer.

- Describe the central role of fossil fuels in the global political economy.

- Identify the challenges in managing the energy transition to alternative, sustainable sources.

- Assess your ongoing effort at identifying your theory of international relations and how this unit changes/complements it.

Student Website

www.mhhe.com/cls

Internet References

Belfer Center for Science and International Affairs (BCSIA)
   http://ksgwww.harvard.edu/csia
U.S. Agency for International Development
   www.usaid.gov
The World Bank Group
   www.worldbank.org

A defining characteristic of the twentieth century was the intense struggle between proponents of two economic ideologies. At the heart of the conflict was the question of what role government should play in the management of a country's economy. For some, the dominant capitalist economic system appeared to be organized primarily for the benefit of a few wealthy people. From their perspective, the masses were trapped in poverty, supplying cheap labor to further enrich the privileged elite. These critics argued that the capitalist system could be changed only by gaining control of the political system and radically changing the ownership of the means of production. In striking contrast to this perspective, others argued that the best way to create wealth and eliminate poverty was through the profit motive, which encouraged entrepreneurs to create new products and businesses. An open and competitive marketplace, from this point of view, minimized government interference and was the best system for making decisions about production, wages, and the distribution of goods and services.

Violent conflict at times characterized the contest between capitalism and socialism/communism. The Russian and Chinese revolutions overthrew the old social order and created radical changes in the political and economic systems in these two important countries. The political structures that were created to support new systems of agricultural and industrial production (along with the centralized planning of virtually all aspects of economic activity) eliminated most private ownership of property. These two revolutions were, in short, unparalleled experiments in social engineering.

The economic collapse of the Soviet Union and the dramatic market reforms in China have recast the debate about how to best structure contemporary economic systems. Some believe that with the end of communism and the resulting participation of hundreds of millions of new consumers in the global market, an unprecedented new era has been entered. Many have noted that this process of "globalization" is being accelerated by a revolution in communication and computer technologies. Proponents of this view argue that a new global economy is emerging that will ultimately eliminate national economic systems.

Others are less optimistic about the prospects of globalization. They argue that the creation of a single economic system where there are no boundaries to impede the flow of both capital and goods and services does not mean a closing of the gap between the world's rich and poor. Rather, they argue that multinational corporations and global financial institutions will have fewer legal constraints on their behavior, and this will lead to not only increased risks of global financial crises but also greater exploitation of workers and the accelerated destruction of the environment. Further, these critics point out that the unintended globalization of drug trafficking and other criminal behaviors is developing more rapidly than appropriate remedies can be developed.

The use of the term political economy for the title of this unit recognizes that economic and political systems are not separate. All economic systems have some type of marketplace where goods

© Frederic Charpentier/Alamy

and services are bought and sold. Government (either national or international) regulates these transactions to some degree; that is, government sets the rules that regulate the marketplace.

One of the most important concepts in assessing the contemporary political economy is "development." For the purposes of this unit, the term *development* is defined as an improvement in the basic aspects of life: lower infant mortality rates, longer life expectancy, lower disease rates, higher rates of literacy, healthier diets, and improved sanitation. Judged by these standards, some countries are more developed than others. A fundamental question that a thoughtful reader must consider is whether globalization is resulting in increased development not only for a few people but also for all those participating in the global political economy.

The unit is organized into three sections. The first is a general discussion of the concept of globalization. How is it defined and what are some of the differing perspectives on this process? For example, is the idea of a global economy wishful thinking by those who sit on top of the power hierarchy, self-deluded into believing that globalization is an inexorable force that will evolve in its own way, following its own rules? Or will there continue to be the traditional tensions of nation–state power politics that transcend global economic processes, that is, conflict between the powerful and those who are either ascending or descending in power?

Following the first section are two sets of case studies. The first focuses on specific countries and/or economic sectors. The second set of case studies examines the global energy sector. All the case studies have been selected to challenge the reader to develop her or his own conclusions about the positive and negative consequences of the globalization process. Does the contemporary global political economy result in increasing the gap between economic winners and losers, or can everyone positively benefit from its system of wealth creation and distribution?

Globalization and Its Contents

Peter Marber

Ask ten different people to define the term "globalization" and you are likely to receive ten different answers. For many, the meaning of globalization has been shaped largely by media coverage of an angry opposition: from right-wing nationalist xenophobes and left-wing labor leaders who fear rampant economic competition from low-wage countries to social activists who see a conspiracy on the part of multinational corporations to seek profits no matter what the cost to local cultures and economic equality to environmentalists who believe the earth is being systematically ravaged by capitalism run amok. "Globalization"—as if it were a machine that could be turned off—has been presented as fundamentally flawed and dangerous. But "globalization" is a term that encompasses all cross-border interactions, whether economic, political, or cultural. And behind the negative headlines lies a story of human progress and promise that should make even the most pessimistic analysts view globalization in an entirely different light.

Two decades ago, globalization was hardly discussed. At the time, less than 15 percent of the world's population participated in true global trade. Pessimism colored discussions of the Third World, of "lesser developed" or "backward" countries. Pawns in the Cold War's global chess game, these countries conjured images of famine, overpopulation, military dictatorship, and general chaos. At the time, the prospect of the Soviet Union or Communist China integrating economically with the West, or of strongman regimes in Latin America or Asia abandoning central planning, seemed farfetched. The possibility of these countries making meaningful socioeconomic progress and attaining Western standards of living appeared utterly unrealistic. Yet the forces of globalization were already at work.

On average, people are living twice as long as they did a century ago. Moreover, the world's aggregate material infrastructure and productive capabilities are hundreds—if not thousands—of times greater than they were a hundred years ago.[1] Much of this acceleration has occurred since 1950, with a powerful upsurge in the last 25 years. No matter how one measures wealth—whether by means of economic, bio-social, or financial indicators—there have been gains in virtually every meaningful aspect of life in the last two generations, and the trend should continue upward at least through the middle of the twenty-first century.

Most people are living longer, healthier, fuller lives. This is most evident in poor parts of the world. For example, since 1950, life expectancy in emerging markets (countries with less than one-third the per capita income of the United States, or nearly 85 percent of the world's population) has increased by more than 50 percent, reaching levels the West enjoyed only two generations ago. These longevity gains are linked to lower infant mortality, better nutrition (including an 85 percent increase in daily caloric intake), improved sanitation, immunizations, and other public health advances.

Literacy rates in developing countries have also risen dramatically in the last 50 years. In 1950, only a third of the people in Eastern Europe and in parts of Latin [America] living in these countries (roughly 800 million) could read or write; today nearly two-thirds—more than 3.2 billion people—are literate. And while it took the United States and Great Britain more than 120 years to increase average formal education from 2 years in the early nineteenth century to 12 years by the mid-twentieth century, some fast-growing developing countries, like South Korea, have accomplished this feat in fewer than 40 years.

The world now has a far more educated population with greater intellectual capacity than at any other time in history. This is particularly clear in much of Asia, where mass public education has allowed billions of people to increase their productivity and integrate in the global economy as workers and consumers. Similar trends can be seen in Eastern Europe and in parts of Latin America. This increase in human capital has led to historic highs in economic output and financial assets per capita.

During the twentieth century, economic output in the United States and other West European countries often doubled in less than 30 years, and Japan's postwar economy doubled in less than 16 years. In recent decades, developing country economies have surged so quickly that some—like South Korea in the 1960s and 1970s, or China in recent years—have often doubled productive output in just 7 to 10 years.

We often forget that poverty was the human living standard for most of recorded history. Until approximately two hundred years ago, virtually everyone lived at a subsistence level. As the economist John Maynard Keynes wrote in 1931 in *Essays in Persuasion*: "From the earliest times of which we have record—back, say, to two thousand years before Christ—down to the beginning of the eighteenth century, there was no very great change in the standard life of the average man living in civilized centers of the earth. Ups and downs certainly. Visitation

	1950	2000	2050
Global Output, Per Capita ($)	586	6,666	15,155
Global Financial Market			
Capitalization, Per Capita ($)	158	13,333	75,000
Percent of Global GDP			
Emerging Markets	5	50	55
Industrial Countries	95	75	45
Life Expectancy (years)			
Emerging Markets	41	64	76
Industrial Countries	65	77	82
Daily Caloric Intake			
Emerging Markets	1200	2600	3000
Industrial Countries	2200	3100	3200
Infant Mortality (per 1000)			
Emerging Markets	140	65	10
Industrial Countries	30	8	4
Literacy Rate (per 100)			
Emerging Markets	33	64	90
Industrial Countries	95	98	99

Sources: Bloomberg, World Bank, United Nations, and author's estimates.
Output and financial market capitalization figures are inflation-adjusted.

Figure 1   Measured Global Progress, 1950–2050E.

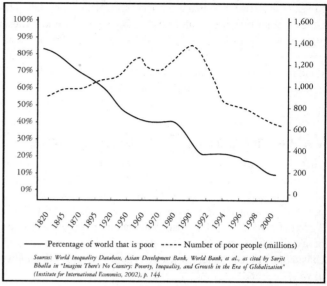

Sources: World Inequality Database, Asian Development Bank, World Bank, et al., as cited by Surjit Bhalla in "Imagine There's No Country: Poverty, Inequality, and Growth in the Era of Globalization" (Institute for International Economics, 2002), p. 144.

Figure 2   Historic World Poverty Levels, 1820–2000.

of plague, famine, and war. Golden intervals. But no progressive violent change. This slow rate of progress was due to two reasons—to the remarkable absence of technical improvements and the failure of capital to accumulate." Beginning in the early nineteenth century, this picture began to change. The proportion of the world's population living in poverty declined from over 80 percent in 1820 to under 15 percent in 2000; moreover, the actual number of people living in poverty over that period declined, even as the world's population exploded from something over 1 billion to more than 6 billion.

The application of mass production technology, together with excess capital (or "profit") and a free market technologies—is at the root of our modern prosperity. Upon further examination, one can see the virtuous cycle that connects human progress, technology, and globalization. Let's take two countries, one being richer than the other. The richer country has a more educated workforce, with nearly 99 percent literacy, while the poor one has only 50 percent literacy. Due to its less educated workforce and lack of infrastructure, the poor country might only be able to participate in global trade through exporting commodities—let's say fruits and vegetables. The rich country grows fruits and vegetables as well, but it also produces clothing and light manufactured goods such as radios. In the classic Ricardo/Smith models of comparative advantage and free trade, the wealthy country should utilize its skilled workforce to produce more clothing and radios for domestic consumption and export, and it should import more fruits and vegetables from the poorer country. This would, in turn, provide the poorer country with capital to improve education and infrastructure.

As this trade pattern creates profits for both countries, human capital can be mutually developed. Eventually, the poorer

country (by boosting literacy and education) should develop its own ability to produce clothes and radios. Over time, the wealthier country—having reinvested profits in higher education, research and development, etc.—will begin to produce higher-tech goods rather than clothes and radios, perhaps televisions and cars. At this stage, the wealthy country would export its cars and televisions, and import clothes and radios. In turn, the poorer country begins to import agricultural products from an even poorer third country while exporting clothing and radios to both countries. As participating countries make progress through crossborder trade and the continuous upgrading of their workforces, it follows naturally that patterns of labor and employment will evolve over time.

It is sometimes argued that free trade harms economic growth and the poor by causing job losses, particularly in wealthier countries. But trade liberalization works by encouraging a shift of labor and capital from import-competitive sectors to more dynamic export industries where comparative advantages lie. Therefore, the unemployment caused by open trade can be expected to be temporary, being offset by job creation in other export sectors (which often requires some transition time). Output losses due to this transitional unemployment should also be small relative to long-term gains in national income (and lower prices) due to production increases elsewhere. In other words, these short-term labor adjustments should be seen as lesser evils when compared to the costs of continued economic stagnation and isolation that occur without open trade.

The shifting U.S. labor pattern from low-wage agricultural labor to manufacturing to higher-paid office and service employment during the nineteenth and twentieth centuries resulted largely from trade. Similar shifts are now seen all over the globe. In the 1950 and 1960s, the United States imported electronics from Japan, and exported cars and other heavy goods. In the 1970s, we began importing small cars from Japan. In the last 30-odd years, Japan has seen its dominance in electronics and economy cars wither amid competition from China and South

Korea. But Japan has made a successful push upmarket into larger, pricier luxury cars and sport utility vehicles. While these markets were shifting over the last three decades, jobs were lost, gained, and relocated in the United States and abroad. But living standards in America, Japan, South Korea, and China have all improved dramatically over that same time.

Working Less, Producing More

There is a growing consensus that international trade has a positive effect on per capita income. A 1999 World Bank study estimates that increasing the ratio of trade to national output by one percentage point raises per capita income by between 0.5 and 2 percent.[2] But the most dramatic illustration of how greater prosperity is spread through globalization is by our increased purchasing power. Ultimately, what determines wealth is the ability to work less and consume more. The time needed for an average American worker to earn the purchase price of various goods and services decreased dramatically during the twentieth century.

In 1919, it took an American worker 30 minutes of labor to earn enough to buy a pound of ground beef. This number dropped to 23 minutes in 1950, 11 minutes in 1975, and 6 minutes in 1997.[3] But this downward trend is even more impressive with respect to manufactured goods and services. For example, in 1895 the list price for an American-made bicycle in the Montgomery Ward catalog was $65. Today an American can buy a Chinese-manufactured 21-speed bike at any mass retailer for the same amount. But an average American needed to work some 260 hours in 1895 to earn the purchase price of the old bicycle, whereas it would take the average worker less than 5 hours to earn enough to buy today's bicycle.[4] In our own lifetimes, the costs of goods and services, everything from televisions to household appliances to telephone calls, computers, and airplane travel have plummeted relative to income—and not just in the United States.

Around the world, both basic commodities and items once considered luxury items now fill store shelves and pantries as increasing output and income have lifted most people above the subsistence level. The 50 most populous countries average more than 95 televisions per 100 households. In the 25 wealthiest countries, there are approximately 450 automobiles per 1,000 people, and China is now among the fastest-growing markets for cars, clothes, computers, cellular phones, and hundreds of household items.

This deflationary effect has also led to a radically improved quality of life. In 1870, the average American worker labored 3,069 hours per year—or six 10-hour days a week. By 1950, the average hours worked had fallen to 2,075.[5] Today, that number is closer to 1,730.[6] This pattern has been repeated around the world. In 1960, the average Japanese worker toiled 2,432 hours a year over a six-day work week; by 1988, this figure had dropped to 2,111 hours a year, and by 2000 it was down to 1,878 hours. There were even more dramatic reductions in European countries like France, Germany, and Sweden.[7] The Nobel Prize–winning economist Robert William Fogel estimates that the average American's lifetime working hours will have declined from 182,100 in 1880 to a projected 75,900 by 2040, with similar trends in other wealthy industrial countries. Fogel notes that while work took up 60 percent of an American's life in 1870, by 1990 it only took up about 30 percent. Between 1880 and 1990, the average American's cumulative lifetime leisure time swelled from 48,300 hours to a remarkable 246,000 hours, or 22 years.[8] This is a pattern of improvement in the human condition that we first saw in the industrialized West and then in Japan, and which is now spreading to dozens of developing countries that are integrating into the global economy.

A Thriving Middle Class

The recent surge in progress is certainly tied to technological advances, but it is also due to the adoption of free-market practices. Cross-border trade has ballooned by a factor of 20 over the past 50 years and now accounts for more than 20 percent of global output, according to the World Bank. Indeed, trade—which grew twice as fast as global output in the 1990s—will continue to drive economic specialization and growth. The global economy is becoming more sophisticated, segmented, and diversified.

The adoption of free-market practices has gone hand-in-hand with greater political freedoms. At the beginning of the twentieth century, less than 10 percent of the world's population had the right to vote, according to Freedom House. By 1950, approximately 35 percent of the global population in less than a quarter of the world's countries enjoyed this right. By 2000, more than two-thirds of the world's countries had implemented universal suffrage.

These symbiotic developments have helped completely recompose the world's "middle class"—those with a per capita income of roughly $10–40 per day, adjusted for inflation and purchasing power parity (PPP). According to the United Nations, in 1960 two-thirds of the world's middle-class citizens lived in the industrialized world—that is, in the United States, Canada, Western Europe, Japan, and Australia. By 1980, over 60 percent of the global middle class lived in developing countries, and by 2000 this number had reached a remarkable 83 percent. It is anticipated that India and China combined could easily produce middle classes of 400–800 million people over the next two generations—roughly the size of the current middle-class populations of the United States, Western Europe, and Japan combined.

A thriving middle class is an important component of economic, political, and social stability that comes with globalization. According to the World Bank, a higher share of income for the middle class is associated with increased national income and growth, improved health, better infrastructure, sounder economic policies, less instability and civil war, and more social modernization and democracy. There are numerous studies that also suggest that increasing wealth promotes gender equality, greater voter participation, income equality, greater concern for the environment, and more transparency in the business and political arenas, all of the quality-of-life issues that concern globalization skeptics.[9]

Measuring Inequality

Even if they concede that the world is wealthier overall, many critics of globalization cite the dangers of growing income inequality. Although the science of analyzing such long-term trends is far from perfect, there are indicators that point toward measurable progress even on this front.[10] The preoccupation with income or gross national product (GNP) as the sole measure of progress is unfortunate. Income is one measure of wealth, but not the only one. And income comparisons do not always reflect informal or unreported economic activity, which tends to be more prevalent in poor countries.

Many social scientists use Gini coefficients (a measure of income dispersion between and within countries) to bolster their arguments about inequality. The lower the Gini figure (between one and zero), the more equal income distribution tends to be. Unfortunately, the Gini index does not take into consideration purchasing power parity, the age dispersion of a population, and other variables that affect the overall picture. When adjusted for PPP, the Gini index for world income distribution decreased from 0.59 to 0.52 between 1965 and 1997, an improvement of nearly 12 percent.[11] Poverty rate trends are also cited by condemners of globalization, but this approach is problematic as well. The impoverished are often defined as those who earn 50 percent less than the median income in a country. But because 50 percent of median American income is very different than 50 percent of median income in Bangladesh, poverty rates may not tell us as much about human progress as we might think.

We can better gauge human progress by examining broader trends in bio-social development than income-centered analyses. A yardstick like the United Nations Development Program's human development index (HDI), for example, which looks at not only income but also life expectancy and education (including literacy and school enrollment), with the higher numbers denoting greater development, provides a clearer picture of global well-being:

	1960	1993	2002
OECD Countries	.80	.91	.91
Developing Countries	.26	.56	.70
Least Developed Countries	.16	.33	.44

What these numbers show is not only that human development has improved overall but that differentials between rich and poor countries are closing. While the HDI figure for wealthy OECD countries in 1960 was five times greater than that for the least developed countries (and three times higher than that for developing countries), those gaps were nearly halved by 1993. And in the most intense period of recent globalization, from 1993 to 2002, these gaps closed even further.

This by no means negates the reality of poverty in many parts of the world. There are still an estimated 1 billion people living in "abject" poverty today, but the World Bank estimates that this number should decline by 50 percent by 2015, if current growth trends hold.

Potholes on the Road to Globalization

The great gains and momentum of the last 25 years should not be seen as sufficient or irreversible. There are still formidable impediments to continued progress, the four most serious being protectionism, armed conflict, environmental stress, and demographic imbalances.

- *Protectionism.* One of the responses to globalization has been the attempt to pull inward, to save traditional industries and cultures, and to expel foreigners and foreign ideas. In India, consumers have protested against McDonald's restaurants for violating Hindu dietary laws. In France, angry farmers have uprooted genetically engineered crops, saying they threatened domestic control over food production.

  Possibly the most harmful protectionism today relates to global agricultural policy. Farming subsidies in wealthy countries now total approximately $350 billion a year, or seven times the $50 billion that such countries provide annually in foreign aid to the developing world.[12] Global trade policies may exclude developing countries from $700 billion in commerce annually, denying them not only needed foreign currency but also the commercial and social interaction necessary to bio-social progress.[13]

  Protectionism in the form of tariffs, rigid labor and immigration laws, capital controls, and regressive tax structures also should be resisted. Wealthy countries should not cling to old industries like apparel or agriculture; it is far more profitable, economically and socially, to look forward and outward, to focus on growing higher-skill industries—like aviation, pharmaceuticals, and entertainment—and to embrace new markets. In turn, poorer countries have generally grown richer through economic interaction with foreign countries, by refocusing nationalistic energies and policies toward future-oriented, internationally engaged commercial activity. The late-twentieth-century march away from closed economies has improved the lives of billions of people. To bow to nationalistic calls for protectionist policies could slow and even reverse this momentum.

- *Armed Conflict.* Countries cannot compete economically, cultivate human capital, or develop financial markets in the midst of armed conflict. According to the Stockholm International Peace Research Institute, there were 57 major armed conflicts in 45 different locations between 1990 and 2001; all but 3 of these were civil wars, which inflict deep economic damage and stunt development. In addition to ongoing civil wars, there are a number of potential cross-border powder kegs (beyond the recent U.S. invasions of Afghanistan and Iraq): Kashmir, over which nuclearized India and Pakistan have been at odds for decades; Taiwan, over which China claims sovereignty; Israel and its Arab neighbors; and the Korean peninsula. The economic, political, and cultural uncertainty surrounding these areas of potential conflict restricts the flow of capital, and paralyzes businesses, investors, and consumers.

To the extent that defense budgets continue to grow in tandem with global tensions and economic resources are used for military purposes, there will be fewer resources devoted to the development of human capital and economic competitiveness.

- *Environmental Stress.* There is no getting around the fact that the success of globalization is underscored by dramatic increases in consumption. With increased consumption comes environmental degradation. Damage to the environment, current or projected, can impede economic progress in many ways. Climatic changes attributed to greenhouse gas emissions and pressure on natural resources are serious problems. Resource scarcity is only one issue we will have to confront as 2–3 billion more people consume like middle-class Americans over the next 50 years. In the face of these environmental dangers, a host of new regulations may be enacted locally or globally. Increased environmental awareness among wealthier populations may lead to domestic policies that will raise costs to businesses and consumers, which in turn could curb economic expansion.

One step in the right direction would be increased public spending on alternative and renewable energy sources in the wealthier countries. The world is clearly underpowered, and the need for diversified energy grows as we speak. The benefits of a burgeoning alternative energy sector could be multiplicative. First, it might spur new economic growth areas for employment in rich countries, supplying them with potential technologies for export while reducing their reliance on foreign oil. Second, it might encourage developing countries that are over-reliant on oil exports to develop and modernize their economies and societies. Third, it would allow developing countries to build their infrastructures with a more diversified, sustainable energy approach than the first wave of industrializing countries.

- *Demographic Imbalances.* There are sharply contrasting population trends around the globe: developing nations are experiencing a youth bulge while industrialized countries are aging rapidly. This divergence may present a variety of challenges to globalization. In poorer developing countries, the youth bulge equals economic opportunity but is also potentially disruptive. In more than 50 of these countries, 50 percent of the population is under the age of 25. In some cases, half the population is under 20, and in extreme cases, even younger. These developing nations are also among the poorest, the fastest urbanizing, and the least politically or institutionally developed, making them susceptible to violence and instability. The large number of unemployed, disenfranchised young men in these countries may explain the growth of Islamic fundamentalism and the existence of pillaging bands of armed warriors in sub-Saharan Africa. Large young

populations may also lead to unregulated, unlawful migration that can create long-lasting instability.[14]

While the youth bulge can cause problems that derail global progress, the richest countries may fall victim to their past success. Prosperity, while providing more lifestyle choices and wellness, also results in lower birth rates and increasing longevity which could dampen long-term economic demand. The aging of wealthier populations also stresses public pension schemes that were conceived under different demographic circumstances—eras of robust population and consumption growth. In economies where populations are stagnant or shrinking, the specter of lengthy "aging recessions"—characterized by vicious cycles of falling demand for consumer goods (and deflation), collapsing asset values (including real estate), shrinking corporate profits, deteriorating household and financial institution balance sheets, weakening currencies, and soaring budget pressures—looms large.

Preparing for the Best, Not the Worst

Globalization and its major engines—burgeoning human capital, freer markets, increasing cross-border interaction—have created a new world order that has incited passionate debate, pro and con. However, both sides have more in common than one might imagine.

First, if human capital is a key component of improved living standards, it is arguable that increased spending on education should become a priority in rich and poor countries alike. Wealthier nations continually need to boost productivity and comparative advantage, while poorer countries need to develop skills to compete in the global economy. By adding to the numbers of the educated, there will be a wider base of workers and consumers to contribute to the virtuous cycle of prosperity we have witnessed in the last 50 years.

Second, boosting human capital in poor countries through increased financial and technical aid should also help broaden the marketplace in terms of workers and consumers. Appropriating an extra $100 billion in aid each year—a drop in the bucket for the 20 richest countries—could help some 2 billion people overcome their daily struggles with malnutrition, HIV/AIDS, malaria, and dirty drinking water, thereby increasing the number of healthy, productive workers and consumers.

Third, reorienting wealthy country subsidies away from low-tech areas like agriculture and mining toward higher-tech industries (including alternative energy development) would accelerate comparative advantage and stimulate greater trade. With wealthy countries focusing on higher-value-added industries for domestic consumption and export, poorer countries could pick up the slack in lower-skilled sectors where they can begin to engage the global economy. Over time, the poorer countries would become larger markets for goods and services. This, along with the two attitudinal and policy shifts mentioned above, could have a positive effect on the well-being of the world's population.

Even with its positive trends, globalization is not a perfect process. It is not a panacea for every problem for every person at every moment in time. It is a messy, complicated web of inter-dependent relationships, some long-term, some fleeting. But globalization is too often cited as creating a variety of human miseries such as sweatshop labor, civil war, and corruption—as if such ills never existed before 1980. Poverty is more at the root of such miseries. That is why the wholesale rejection of globalization—without acknowledging its tremendously positive record in alleviating poverty—is shortsighted. Indeed, one could see how simply embracing globalization as inevitable—rather than debating its definition and purported shortcomings—could potentially foster more cross-border coordination on a variety of issues such as drug trafficking, ethnic cleansing, illegal immigration, famine, epidemic disease, environmental stress, and terrorism.

Emotion and confusion have unfortunately tainted the globalization debate both in the United States and abroad, and the focus is often on anecdotal successes or failures. Anxieties and economies may ebb and flow in the short run, but the responsibility to manage these progressive evolutions and revolutions—with worldwide human prosperity as the goal—should be our consistent aim in both government and the marketplace.

Notes

Many of the issues and arguments presented here in abbreviated form are examined at greater length in my book, *Money Changes Everything: How Global Prosperity Is Reshaping Our Needs, Values, and Lifestyles* (Upper Saddle River, NJ: FT Prentice Hall, 2003).

1. See Angus Maddison, *Monitoring the World Economy: 1820–1992* (Paris: OECD, 1995).
2. Jeffrey A. Frankel and David Romer, "Does Trade Growth Cause Growth?" *American Economic Review*, vol. 89 (June 1999), pp. 379–99.
3. W. Michael Cox and Richard Alm, *Time Well Spent: The Declining Real Cost of Living in America*, annual report (Dallas: Federal Reserve Bank, 1997), p. 4.
4. Based on average U.S. industrial wages of approximately $15 per hour in 2000.
5. W. Michael Cox and Richard Alm, *These Are the Good Old Days: A Report on US Living Standards*, annual report (Dallas: Federal Reserve Bank, 1994), p. 7.
6. Robert William Fogel, *The Fourth Great Awakening and the Future of Egalitarianism* (Chicago: University of Chicago Press, 2000), p. 185.
7. Ibid., p. 186.
8. Ibid., pp. 184–90.
9. See Marber, *Money Changes Everything*. For more on specific shifts in attitudes and values relative to economic development, the University of Michigan's Ron Inglehart's seminal Human Values Surveys are an invaluable resource.
10. For a balanced study of this subject, see Arne Mechoir, Kjetil Telle, and Henrik Wiig, *Globalisation and Inequality: World Income and Living Standards, 1960–1998*, Norwegian Ministry of Foreign Affairs, Report 6B:2000, October 2000, available at http://odin.dep.no/archive/udvedlegg/01/01/rev_016.pdf.
11. Ibid., p. 14.
12. James Wolfensohn, "How Rich Countries Keep the Rest of the World in Poverty," *Irish Independent*, September 30, 2002.
13. Ibid.
14. See Michael Teitelbaum, "Are North/South Population Growth Differentials a Prelude to Conflict?" at http://csis.org/gai/Graying/speeches/teitelbaum.html.

Critical Thinking

1. What is Peter Marber's point of view?
2. What reasons does he offer to support his point of view?
3. Identify some of the "potholes" to the continuation of globalization.
4. How is this article related to articles 1 and 4?

PETER MARBER is an author, professional money manager, and faculty member at the School of International and Public Affairs at Columbia University.

It's a Flat World, After All

Thomas L. Friedman

In 1492 Christopher Columbus set sail for India, going west. He had the Nina, the Pinta and the Santa Maria. He never did find India, but he called the people he met "Indians" and came home and reported to his king and queen: "The world is round." I set off for India 512 years later. I knew just which direction I was going. I went east. I had Lufthansa business class, and I came home and reported only to my wife and only in a whisper: "The world is flat."

And therein lies a tale of technology and geoeconomics that is fundamentally reshaping our lives—much, much more quickly than many people realize. It all happened while we were sleeping, or rather while we were focused on 9/11, the dot-com bust and Enron—which even prompted some to wonder whether globalization was over. Actually, just the opposite was true, which is why it's time to wake up and prepare ourselves for this flat world, because others already are, and there is no time to waste.

I wish I could say I saw it all coming. Alas, I encountered the flattening of the world quite by accident. It was in late February [2004], and I was visiting the Indian high-tech capital, Bangalore, working on a documentary for the Discovery Times channel about outsourcing. In short order, I interviewed Indian entrepreneurs who wanted to prepare my taxes from Bangalore, read my X-rays from Bangalore, trace my lost luggage from Bangalore and write my new software from Bangalore. The longer I was there, the more upset I became—upset at the realization that while I had been off covering the 9/11 wars, globalization had entered a whole new phase, and I had missed it. I guess the eureka moment came on a visit to the campus of Infosys Technologies, one of the crown jewels of the Indian outsourcing and software industry. Nandan Nilekani, the Infosys C.E.O., was showing me his global video-conference room, pointing with pride to a wall-size flat-screen TV, which he said was the biggest in Asia. Infosys, he explained, could hold a virtual meeting of the key players from its entire global supply chain for any project at any time on that supersize screen. So its American designers could be on the screen speaking with their Indian software writers and their Asian manufacturers all at once. That's what globalization is all about today, Nilekani said. Above the screen there were eight clocks that pretty well summed up the Infosys workday: 24/7/365. The clocks were labeled U.S. West, U.S. East, G.M.T., India, Singapore, Hong Kong, Japan, Australia.

"Outsourcing is just one dimension of a much more fundamental thing happening today in the world," Nilekani explained. "What happened over the last years is that there was a massive investment in technology, especially in the bubble era, when hundreds of millions of dollars were invested in putting broadband connectivity around the world, undersea cables, all those things." At the same time, he added, computers became cheaper and dispersed all over the world, and there was an explosion of e-mail software, search engines like Google and proprietary software that can chop up any piece of work and send one part to Boston, one part to Bangalore and one part to Beijing, making it easy for anyone to do remote development. When all of these things suddenly came together around 2000, Nilekani said, they "created a platform where intellectual work, intellectual capital, could be delivered from anywhere. It could be disaggregated, delivered, distributed, produced and put back together again—and this gave a whole new degree of freedom to the way we do work, especially work of an intellectual nature. And what you are seeing in Bangalore today is really the culmination of all these things coming together."

At one point, summing up the implications of all this, Nilekani uttered a phrase that rang in my ear. He said to me, "Tom, the playing field is being leveled." He meant that countries like India were now able to compete equally for global knowledge work as never before—and that America had better get ready for this. As I left the Infosys campus that evening and bounced along the potholed road back to Bangalore, I kept chewing on that phrase: "The playing field is being leveled."

"What Nandan is saying," I thought, "is that the playing field is being flattened. Flattened? Flattened? My God, he's telling me the world is flat!"

Here I was in Bangalore—more than 500 years after Columbus sailed over the horizon, looking for a shorter route to India using the rudimentary navigational technologies of his day, and returned safely to prove definitively that the world was round—and one of India's smartest engineers, trained at his country's top technical institute and backed by the most modern technologies of his day, was telling me that the world was flat, as flat as that screen on which he can host a meeting of his whole global supply chain. Even more interesting, he was citing this development as a new milestone in human progress and a great opportunity for India and the world—the fact that we had made our world flat!

This has been building for a long time. Globalization 1.0 (1492 to 1800) shrank the world from a size large to a size medium, and the dynamic force in that era was countries globalizing for resources and imperial conquest. Globalization 2.0 (1800 to 2000) shrank the world from a size medium to a size small, and it was spearheaded by companies globalizing for markets and labor. Globalization 3.0 (which started around 2000) is shrinking the world from a size small to a size tiny and flattening the playing field at the same time. And while the dynamic force in Globalization 1.0 was countries globalizing and the dynamic force in Globalization 2.0 was companies globalizing, the dynamic force in Globalization 3.0—the thing that gives it its unique character—is individuals and small groups globalizing. Individuals must, and can, now ask: where do I fit into the global competition and opportunities of the day, and how can I, on my own, collaborate with others globally? But Globalization 3.0 not only differs from the previous eras in how it is shrinking and flattening the world and in how it is empowering individuals. It is also different in that Globalization 1.0 and 2.0 were driven primarily by European and American companies and countries. But going forward, this will be less and less true. Globalization 3.0 is not only going to be driven more by individuals but also by a much more diverse—non-Western, nonwhite—group of individuals. In Globalization 3.0, you are going to see every color of the human rainbow take part.

"Today, the most profound thing to me is the fact that a 14-year-old in Romania or Bangalore or the Soviet Union or Vietnam has all the information, all the tools, all the software easily available to apply knowledge however they want," said Marc Andreessen, a co-founder of Netscape and creator of the first commercial Internet browser. "That is why I am sure the next Napster is going to come out of left field. As bioscience becomes more computational and less about wet labs and as all the genomic data becomes easily available on the Internet, at some point you will be able to design vaccines on your laptop."

Andreessen is touching on the most exciting part of Globalization 3.0 and the flattening of the world: the fact that we are now in the process of connecting all the knowledge pools in the world together. We've tasted some of the downsides of that in the way that Osama bin Laden has connected terrorist knowledge pools together through his Qaeda network, not to mention the work of teenage hackers spinning off more and more lethal computer viruses that affect us all. But the upside is that by connecting all these knowledge pools we are on the cusp of an incredible new era of innovation, an era that will be driven from left field and right field, from West and East and from North and South. Only 30 years ago, if you had a choice of being born a B student in Boston or a genius in Bangalore or Beijing, you probably would have chosen Boston, because a genius in Beijing or Bangalore could not really take advantage of his or her talent. They could not plug and play globally. Not anymore. Not when the world is flat, and anyone with smarts, access to Google and a cheap wireless laptop can join the innovation fray.

When the world is flat, you can innovate without having to emigrate. This is going to get interesting. We are about to see creative destruction on steroids.

How did the world get flattened, and how did it happen so fast?

It was a result of 10 events and forces that all came together during the 1990s and converged right around the year 2000. Let me go through them briefly. The first event was 11/9. That's right—not 9/11, but 11/9. Nov. 9, 1989, is the day the Berlin Wall came down, which was critically important because it allowed us to think of the world as a single space. "The Berlin Wall was not only a symbol of keeping people inside Germany; it was a way of preventing a kind of global view of our future," the Nobel Prize-winning economist Amartya Sen said. And the wall went down just as the windows went up—the breakthrough Microsoft Windows 3.0 operating system, which helped to flatten the playing field even more by creating a global computer interface, shipped six months after the wall fell.

The second key date was 8/9. Aug. 9, 1995, is the day Netscape went public, which did two important things. First, it brought the Internet alive by giving us the browser to display images and data stored on websites. Second, the Netscape stock offering triggered the dot-com boom, which triggered the dot-com bubble, which triggered the massive overinvestment of billions of dollars in fiber-optic telecommunications cable. That overinvestment, by companies like Global Crossing, resulted in the willy-nilly creation of a global undersea-underground fiber network, which in turn drove down the cost of transmitting voices, data and images to practically zero, which in turn accidentally made Boston, Bangalore and Beijing next-door neighbors overnight. In sum, what the Netscape revolution did was bring people-to-people connectivity to a whole new level. Suddenly more people could connect with more other people from more different places in more different ways than ever before.

No country accidentally benefited more from the Netscape moment than India. "India had no resources and no infrastructure," said Dinakar Singh, one of the most respected hedge-fund managers on Wall Street, whose parents earned doctoral degrees in biochemistry from the University of Delhi before emigrating to America. "It produced people with quality and by quantity. But many of them rotted on the docks of India like vegetables. Only a relative few could get on ships and get out. Not anymore, because we built this ocean crosser, called fiber-optic cable. For decades you had to leave India to be a professional. Now you can plug into the world from India. You don't have to go to Yale and go to work for Goldman Sachs." India could never have afforded to pay for the bandwidth to connect brainy India with high-tech America, so American shareholders paid for it. Yes, crazy overinvestment can be good. The overinvestment in railroads turned out to be a great boon for the American economy. "But the railroad overinvestment was confined to your own country and so, too, were the benefits," Singh said. In the case of the digital railroads, "it was the foreigners who benefited." India got a free ride.

The first time this became apparent was when thousands of Indian engineers were enlisted to fix the Y2K—the year 2000—computer bugs for companies from all over the world. (Y2K should be a national holiday in India. Call it "Indian Interdependence Day," says Michael Mandelbaum, a foreign-policy analyst at Johns Hopkins.) The fact that the Y2K work could be outsourced to Indians was made possible by the first two flat-teners, along with a third, which I call "workflow." Workflow is shorthand for all the software applications, standards and elec-tronic transmission pipes, like middleware, that connected all those computers and fiber-optic cable. To put it another way, if the Netscape moment connected people to people like never before, what the workflow revolution did was connect appli-cations to applications so that people all over the world could work together in manipulating and shaping words, data and images on computers like never before.

Indeed, this breakthrough in people-to-people and application-to-application connectivity produced, in short order, six more flatteners—six new ways in which individuals and compa-nies could collaborate on work and share knowledge. One was "outsourcing." When my software applications could connect seamlessly with all of your applications, it meant that all kinds of work—from accounting to software-writing—could be digi-tized, disaggregated and shifted to any place in the world where it could be done better and cheaper. The second was "offshor-ing." I send my whole factory from Canton, Ohio, to Canton, China. The third was "open-sourcing." I write the next oper-ating system, Linux, using engineers collaborating together online and working for free. The fourth was "insourcing." I let a company like UPS come inside my company and take over my whole logistics operation—everything from filling my orders online to delivering my goods to repairing them for customers when they break. (People have no idea what UPS really does today. You'd be amazed!). The fifth was "supply-chaining." This is Wal-Mart's specialty. I create a global supply chain down to the last atom of efficiency so that if I sell an item in Arkansas, another is immediately made in China. (If Wal-Mart were a coun-try, it would be China's eighth-largest trading partner.) The last new form of collaboration I call "informing"—this is Google, Yahoo and MSN Search, which now allow anyone to collaborate with, and mine, unlimited data all by themselves.

So the first three flatteners created the new platform for col-laboration, and the next six are the new forms of collaboration that flattened the world even more. The 10th flattener I call "the steroids," and these are wireless access and voice over Internet protocol (VoIP). What the steroids do is turbocharge all these new forms of collaboration, so you can now do any one of them, from anywhere, with any device.

The world got flat when all 10 of these flatteners converged around the year 2000. This created a global, Web-enabled play-ing field that allows for multiple forms of collaboration on research and work in real time, without regard to geography, distance or, in the near future, even language. "It is the creation of this platform, with these unique attributes, that is the truly important sustainable breakthrough that made what you call the flattening of the world possible," said Craig Mundie, the chief technical officer of Microsoft.

No, not everyone has access yet to this platform, but it is open now to more people in more places on more days in more ways than anything like it in history. Wherever you look today—whether it is the world of journalism, with blog-gers bringing down Dan Rather; the world of software, with the Linux code writers working in online forums for free to

challenge Microsoft; or the world of business, where Indian and Chinese innovators are competing against and working with some of the most advanced Western multinationals—hierarchies are being flattened and value is being created less and less within vertical silos and more and more through horizontal collaboration within companies, between companies and among individuals.

Do you recall "the IT revolution" that the business press has been pushing for the last 20 years? Sorry to tell you this, but that was just the prologue. The last 20 years were about forging, sharpening and distributing all the new tools to collaborate and connect. Now the real information revolution is about to begin as all the complementarities among these collaborative tools start to converge. One of those who first called this moment by its real name was Carly Fiorina, the former Hewlett-Packard C.E.O., who in 2004 began to declare in her public speeches that the dot-com boom and bust were just "the end of the begin-ning." The last 25 years in technology, Fiorina said, have just been "the warm-up act." Now we are going into the main event, she said, "and by the main event, I mean an era in which tech-nology will truly transform every aspect of business, of govern-ment, of society, of life."

As if this flattening wasn't enough, another convergence coincidentally occurred during the 1990s that was equally important. Some three billion people who were out of the game walked, and often ran, onto the playing field. I am talking about the people of China, India, Russia, Eastern Europe, Latin America and Central Asia. Their economies and political systems all opened up during the course of the 1990s so that their people were increasingly free to join the free market. And when did these three billion people converge with the new playing field and the new business processes? Right when it was being flattened, right when millions of them could compete and collaborate more equally, more horizontally and with cheaper and more readily available tools. Indeed, thanks to the flatten-ing of the world, many of these new entrants didn't even have to leave home to participate. Thanks to the 10 flatteners, the playing field came to them!

It is this convergence—of new players, on a new playing field, developing new processes for horizontal collaboration—that I believe is the most important force shaping global economics and politics in the early 21st century. Sure, not all three billion can collaborate and compete. In fact, for most people the world is not yet flat at all. But even if we're talking about only 10 percent, that's 300 million people—about twice the size of the American work force. And be advised: the Indians and Chinese are not rac-ing us to the bottom. They are racing us to the top. What China's leaders really want is that the next generation of underwear and airplane wings not just be "made in China" but also be "designed in China." And that is where things are heading. So in 30 years we will have gone from "sold in China" to "made in China" to "designed in China" to "dreamed up in China"—or from China as collaborator with the worldwide manufacturers on nothing to China as a low-cost, high-quality, hyperefficient collaborator with worldwide manufacturers on everything. Ditto India. Said

Craig Barrett, the C.E.O. of Intel, "You don't bring three billion people into the world economy overnight without huge consequences, especially from three societies"—like India, China and Russia—"with rich educational heritages."

That is why there is nothing that guarantees that Americans or Western Europeans will continue leading the way. These new players are stepping onto the playing field legacy free, meaning that many of them were so far behind that they can leap right into the new technologies without having to worry about all the sunken costs of old systems. It means that they can move very fast to adopt new, state-of-the-art technologies, which is why there are already more cellphones in use in China today than there are people in America.

If you want to appreciate the sort of challenge we are facing, let me share with you two conversations. One was with some of the Microsoft officials who were involved in setting up Microsoft's research center in Beijing, Microsoft Research Asia, which opened in 1998—after Microsoft sent teams to Chinese universities to administer I.Q. tests in order to recruit the best brains from China's 1.3 billion people. Out of the 2,000 top Chinese engineering and science students tested, Microsoft hired 20. They have a saying at Microsoft about their Asia center, which captures the intensity of competition it takes to win a job there and explains why it is already the most productive research team at Microsoft: "Remember, in China, when you are one in a million, there are 1,300 other people just like you."

The other is a conversation I had with Rajesh Rao, a young Indian entrepreneur who started an electronic-game company from Bangalore, which today owns the rights to Charlie Chaplin's image for mobile computer games. "We can't relax," Rao said. "I think in the case of the United States that is what happened a bit. Please look at me: I am from India. We have been at a very different level before in terms of technology and business. But once we saw we had an infrastructure that made the world a small place, we promptly tried to make the best use of it. We saw there were so many things we could do. We went ahead, and today what we are seeing is a result of that. There is no time to rest. That is gone. There are dozens of people who are doing the same thing you are doing, and they are trying to do it better. It is like water in a tray: you shake it, and it will find the path of least resistance. That is what is going to happen to so many jobs—they will go to that corner of the world where there is the least resistance and the most opportunity. If there is a skilled person in Timbuktu, he will get work if he knows how to access the rest of the world, which is quite easy today. You can make a website and have an e-mail address and you are up and running. And if you are able to demonstrate your work, using the same infrastructure, and if people are comfortable giving work to you and if you are diligent and clean in your transactions, then you are in business."

Instead of complaining about outsourcing, Rao said, Americans and Western Europeans would "be better off thinking about how you can raise your bar and raise yourselves into doing something better. Americans have consistently led in innovation over the last century. Americans whining—we have never seen that before."

Rao is right. And it is time we got focused. As a person who grew up during the cold war, I'll always remember driving down the highway and listening to the radio, when suddenly the music would stop and a grim-voiced announcer would come on the air and say: "This is a test. This station is conducting a test of the Emergency Broadcast System." And then there would be a 20-second high-pitched siren sound. Fortunately, we never had to live through a moment in the cold war when the announcer came on and said, "This is a not a test."

That, however, is exactly what I want to say here: "This is not a test."

The long-term opportunities and challenges that the flattening of the world puts before the United States are profound. Therefore, our ability to get by doing things the way we've been doing them—which is to say not always enriching our secret sauce—will not suffice any more. "For a country as wealthy as we are, it is amazing how little we are doing to enhance our natural competitiveness," says Dinakar Singh, the Indian-American hedge-fund manager. "We are in a world that has a system that now allows convergence among many billions of people, and we had better step back and figure out what it means. It would be a nice coincidence if all the things that were true before were still true now, but there are quite a few things you actually need to do differently. You need to have a much more thoughtful national discussion."

If this moment has any parallel in recent American history, it is the height of the cold war, around 1957, when the Soviet Union leapt ahead of America in the space race by putting up the Sputnik satellite. The main challenge then came from those who wanted to put up walls; the main challenge to America today comes from the fact that all the walls are being taken down and many other people can now compete and collaborate with us much more directly. The main challenge in that world was from those practicing extreme Communism, namely Russia, China and North Korea. The main challenge to America today is from those practicing extreme capitalism, namely China, India and South Korea. The main objective in that era was building a strong state, and the main objective in this era is building strong individuals.

Meeting the challenges of flatism requires as comprehensive, energetic and focused a response as did meeting the challenge of Communism. It requires a president who can summon the nation to work harder, get smarter, attract more young women and men to science and engineering and build the broadband infrastructure, portable pensions and health care that will help every American become more employable in an age in which no one can guarantee you lifetime employment.

We have been slow to rise to the challenge of flatism, in contrast to Communism, maybe because flatism doesn't involve ICBM missiles aimed at our cities. Indeed, the hot line, which used to connect the Kremlin with the White House, has been replaced by the help line, which connects everyone in America to call centers in Bangalore. While the other end of the hot line might have had Leonid Brezhnev threatening nuclear war, the other end of the help line just has a soft voice eager to help you sort out your AOL bill or collaborate with you on a new piece of software. No, that voice has none of the menace of Nikita Khrushchev pounding a shoe on the table at the United Nations, and it has none of the sinister snarl of the bad guys in "From Russia with Love." No, that voice on the help line just has a friendly Indian lilt that masks any sense of threat or challenge. It simply says: "Hello, my name is Rajiv. Can I help you?"

No, Rajiv, actually you can't. When it comes to responding to the challenges of the flat world, there is no help line we can call. We have to dig into ourselves. We in America have all the basic economic and educational tools to do that. But we have not been improving those tools as much as we should. That is why we are in what Shirley Ann Jackson, the 2004 president of the American Association for the Advancement of Science and president of Rensselaer Polytechnic Institute, calls a "quiet crisis"—one that is slowly eating away at America's scientific and engineering base.

"If left unchecked," said Jackson, the first African-American woman to earn a Ph.D. in physics from M.I.T., "this could challenge our pre-eminence and capacity to innovate." And it is our ability to constantly innovate new products, services and companies that has been the source of America's horn of plenty and steadily widening middle class for the last two centuries. This quiet crisis is a product of three gaps now plaguing American society. The first is an "ambition gap." Compared with the young, energetic Indians and Chinese, too many Americans have gotten too lazy. As David Rothkopf, a former official in the Clinton Commerce Department, puts it, "The real entitlement we need to get rid of is our sense of entitlement." Second, we have a serious numbers gap building. We are not producing enough engineers and scientists. We used to make up for that by importing them from India and China, but in a flat world, where people can now stay home and compete with us, and in a post-9/11 world, where we are insanely keeping out many of the first-round intellectual draft choices in the world for exaggerated security reasons, we can no longer cover the gap. That's a key reason companies are looking abroad. The numbers are not here. And finally we are developing an education gap. Here is the dirty little secret that no C.E.O. wants to tell you: they are not just outsourcing to save on salary. They are doing it because they can often get better-skilled and more productive people than their American workers.

These are some of the reasons that Bill Gates, the Micro-soft chairman, warned the governors' conference in a Feb. 26 speech that American high-school education is "obsolete." As Gates put it: "When I compare our high schools to what I see when I'm traveling abroad, I am terrified for our work force of tomorrow. In math and science, our fourth graders are among the top students in the world. By eighth grade, they're in the middle of the pack. By 12th grade, U.S. students are scoring near the bottom of all industrialized nations. . . . The percentage of a population with a college degree is important, but so are sheer numbers. In 2001, India graduated almost a million more students from college than the United States did. China graduates twice as many students with bachelor's degrees as the U.S., and they have six times as many graduates majoring in engineering. In the international competition to have the biggest and best supply of knowledge workers, America is falling behind."

We need to get going immediately. It takes 15 years to train a good engineer, because, ladies and gentlemen, this really is rocket science. So parents, throw away the Game Boy, turn off the television and get your kids to work. There is no sugar-coating this: in a flat world, every individual is going to have to run a little faster if he or she wants to advance his or her standard of living. When I was growing up, my parents used to say to me, "Tom, finish your dinner—people in China are starving." But after sailing to the edges of the flat world for a year, I am now telling my own daughters, "Girls, finish your homework—people in China and India are starving for your jobs."

I repeat, this is not a test. This is the beginning of a crisis that won't remain quiet for long. And as the Stanford economist Paul Romer so rightly says, "A crisis is a terrible thing to waste."

Critical Thinking

1. What does Thomas Friedman mean by a "flat" world?
2. What are some of the primary reasons for this so-called flattening?

THOMAS L. FRIEDMAN is the author of *"The World Is Flat: A Brief History of the Twenty-First Century,"* to be published this week by Farrar, Straus & Giroux and from which this article is adapted. His column appears on the Op-Ed page of *The Times,* and his television documentary "Does Europe Hate Us?" was shown on the Discovery Channel on April 7, 2005.

Why the World Isn't Flat

Globalization has bound people, countries, and markets closer than ever, rendering national borders relics of a bygone era—or so we're told. But a close look at the data reveals a world that's just a fraction as integrated as the one we thought we knew. In fact, more than 90 percent of all phone calls, Web traffic, and investment is local. What's more, even this small level of globalization could still slip away.

PANKAJ GHEMAWAT

Ideas will spread faster, leaping borders. Poor countries will have immediate access to information that was once restricted to the industrial world and traveled only slowly, if at all, beyond it. Entire electorates will learn things that once only a few bureaucrats knew. Small companies will offer services that previously only giants could provide. In all these ways, the communications revolution is profoundly democratic and liberating, leveling the imbalance between large and small, rich and poor. The global vision that Frances Cairncross predicted in her *Death of Distance* appears to be upon us. We seem to live in a world that is no longer a collection of isolated, "local" nations, effectively separated by high tariff walls, poor communications networks, and mutual suspicion. It's a world that, if you believe the most prominent proponents of globalization, is increasingly wired, informed, and, well, "flat."

It's an attractive idea. And if publishing trends are any indication, globalization is more than just a powerful economic and political transformation; it's a booming cottage industry. According to the U.S. Library of Congress's catalog, in the 1990s, about 500 books were published on globalization. Between 2000 and 2004, there were more than 4,000. In fact, between the mid-1990s and 2003, the rate of increase in globalization-related titles more than doubled every 18 months.

Amid all this clutter, several books on the subject have managed to attract significant attention. During a recent TV interview, the first question I was asked—quite earnestly—was why I still thought the world was round. The interviewer was referring of course to the thesis of *New York Times* columnist Thomas L. Friedman's bestselling book *The World Is Flat*. Friedman asserts that 10 forces—most of which enable connectivity and collaboration at a distance—are "flattening" the Earth and leveling a playing field of global competitiveness, the likes of which the world has never before seen.

It sounds compelling enough. But Friedman's assertions are simply the latest in a series of exaggerated visions that also include the "end of history" and the "convergence of tastes." Some writers in this vein view globalization as a good thing—an escape from the ancient tribal rifts that have divided humans, or an opportunity to sell the same thing to everyone on Earth. Others lament its cancerous spread, a process at the end of which everyone will be eating the same fast food. Their arguments are mostly characterized by emotional rather than cerebral appeals, a reliance on prophecy, semiotic arousal (that is, treating everything as a sign), a focus on technology as the driver of change, an emphasis on education that creates "new" people, and perhaps above all, a clamor for attention. But they all have one thing in common: They're wrong.

In truth, the world is not nearly as connected as these writers would have us believe. Despite talk of a new, wired world where information, ideas, money, and people can move around the planet faster than ever before, just a fraction of what we consider globalization actually exists. The portrait that emerges from a hard look at the way companies, people, and states interact is a world that's only beginning to realize the potential of true global integration. And what these trend's backers won't tell you is that globalization's future is more fragile than you know.

The 10 Percent Presumption

The few cities that dominate international financial activity—Frankfurt, Hong Kong, London, New York—are at the height of modern global integration; which is to say, they are all relatively well connected with one another. But when you examine the numbers, the picture is one of extreme connectivity at the local level, not a flat world. What do such statistics reveal? Most types of economic activity that could be conducted either within or across borders turn out to still be quite domestically concentrated.

One favorite mantra from globalization champions is how "investment knows no boundaries." But how much of all the capital being invested around the world is conducted by companies outside of their home countries? The fact is, the total amount of the world's capital formation that is generated from foreign direct investment

(FDI) has been less than 10 percent for the last three years for which data are available (2003–05). In other words, more than 90 percent of the fixed investment around the world is still domestic. And though merger waves can push the ratio higher, it has never reached 20 percent. In a thoroughly globalized environment, one would expect this number to be much higher—about 90 percent, by my calculation. And FDI isn't an odd or unrepresentative example.

The levels of internationalization associated with cross-border migration, telephone calls, management research and education, private charitable giving, patenting, stock investment, and trade, as a fraction of gross domestic product (GDP), all stand much closer to 10 percent than 100 percent. The biggest exception in absolute terms—the trade-to-GDP—recedes most of the way back down toward 20 percent if you adjust for certain kinds of double-counting. So if someone asked me to guess the internationalization level of some activity about which I had no particular information, I would guess it to be much closer to 10 percent—than to 100 percent. I call this the "10 Percent Presumption."

More broadly, these and other data on cross-border integration suggest a semiglobalized world, in which neither the bridges nor the barriers between countries can be ignored. From this perspective, the most astonishing aspect of various writings on globalization is the extent of exaggeration involved. In short, the levels of internationalization in the world today are roughly an order of magnitude lower than those implied by globalization proponents.

A Strong National Defense

If you buy into the more extreme views of the globalization triumphalists, you would expect to see a world where national borders are irrelevant, and where citizens increasingly view themselves as members of ever broader political entities. True, communications technologies have improved dramatically during the past 100 years. The cost of a three-minute telephone call from New York to London fell from $350 in 1930 to about 40 cents in 1999, and it is now approaching zero for voice-over-Internet telephony. And the Internet itself is just one of many newer forms of connectivity that have progressed several times faster than plain old telephone service. This pace of improvement has inspired excited proclamations about the pace of global integration. But it's a huge leap to go from predicting such changes to asserting that declining communication costs will obliterate the effects of distance. Although the barriers at borders have declined significantly, they haven't disappeared.

To see why, consider the Indian software industry—a favorite of Friedman and others. Friedman cites Nandan Nilekani, the CEO of the second-largest such firm, Infosys, as his muse for the notion of a flat world. But what Nilekani has pointed out privately is that while Indian software programmers can now serve the United States from India, access is assured, in part, by U.S. capital being invested—quite literally—in that outcome. In other words, the success of the Indian IT industry is not exempt from political and geographic constraints. The country of origin matters—even for capital, which is often considered stateless.

Or consider the largest Indian software firm, Tata Consultancy Services (TCS). Friedman has written at least two columns in the *New York Times* on TCS's Latin American operations: "[I]n today's world, having an Indian company led by a Hungarian-Uruguayan servicing American banks with Montevidean engineers managed by Indian technologists who have learned to eat Uruguayan veggie is

just the new normal," Friedman writes. Perhaps. But the real question is why the company established those operations in the first place. Having worked as a strategy advisor to TCS since 2000, I can testify that reasons related to the tyranny of time zones, languages, and the need for proximity to clients' local operations loomed large in that decision. This is a far cry from globalization proponents' oft-cited world in which geography, language, and distance don't matter.

Trade flows certainly bear that theory out. Consider Canadian-U.S. trade, the largest bilateral relationship of its kind in the world. In 1988, before the North American Free Trade Agreement (NAFTA) took effect, merchandise trade levels between Canadian provinces—that is, within the country—were estimated to be 20 times as large as their trade with similarly sized and similarly distant U.S. states. In other words, there was a built-in "home bias." Although NAFTA helped reduce this ratio of domestic to international trade—the home bias—to 10 to 1 by the mid-1990s, it still exceeds 5 to 1 today. And these ratios are just for merchandise; for services, the ratio is still several times larger. Clearly, the borders in our seemingly "borderless world" still matter to most people.

Geographical boundaries are so pervasive, they even extend to cyberspace. If there were one realm in which borders should be rendered meaningless and the globalization proponents should be correct in their overly optimistic models, it should be the Internet. Yet Web traffic within countries and regions has increased far faster than traffic between them. Just as in the real world, Internet links decay with distance. People across the world may be getting more connected, but they aren't connecting with each other. The average South Korean Web user may be spending several hours a day online—connected to the rest of the world in theory—but he is probably chatting with friends across town and e-mailing family across the country rather than meeting a fellow surfer in Los Angeles. We're more wired, but no more "global."

Just look at Google, which boasts of supporting more than 100 languages and, partly as a result, has recently been rated the most globalized website. But Google's operation in Russia (cofounder Sergey Brin's native country) reaches only 28 percent of the market there, versus 64 percent for the Russian market leader in search services, Yandex, and 53 percent for Rambler.

Indeed, these two local competitors account for 91 percent of the Russian market for online ads linked to Web searches. What has stymied Google's expansion into the Russian market? The biggest reason is the difficulty of designing a search engine to handle the linguistic complexities of the Russian language. In addition, these local competitors are more in tune with the Russian market, for example, developing payment methods through traditional banks to compensate for the dearth of credit cards. And, though Google has doubled its reach since 2003, it's had to set up a Moscow office in Russia and hire Russian software engineers, underlining the continued importance of physical location. Even now, borders between countries define—and constrain—our movements more than globalization breaks them down.

Turning Back the Clock

If globalization is an inadequate term for the current state of integration, there's an obvious rejoinder: Even if the world isn't quite flat today, it will be tomorrow. To respond, we have to look at trends, rather than levels of integration at one point in time. The results are telling. Along a few dimensions, integration reached its all-time high many years ago. For example, rough calculations suggest that the number of long-term international migrants amounted to 3 percent of the world's population in 1900—the high-water mark of an earlier era of migration—versus 2.9 percent in 2005.

Along other dimensions, it's true that new records are being set. But this growth has happened only relatively recently, and only after long periods of stagnation and reversal. For example, FDI stocks divided by GDP peaked before World War I and didn't return to that level until the 1990s. Several economists have argued that the most remarkable development over the long term was the declining level of internationalization between the two World Wars. And despite the records being set, the current level of trade intensity falls far short of completeness, as the Canadian-U.S. trade data suggest. In fact, when trade economists look at these figures, they are amazed not at how much trade there is, but how little.

It's also useful to examine the considerable momentum that globalization proponents attribute to the constellation of policy changes that led many countries—particularly China, India, and the former Soviet Union—to engage more extensively with the international economy. One of the better-researched descriptions of these policy changes and their implications is provided by economists Jeffrey Sachs and Andrew Warner:

"The years between 1970 and 1995, and especially the last decade, have witnessed the most remarkable institutional harmonization and economic integration among nations in world history. While economic integration was increasing throughout the 1970s and 1980s, the extent of integration has come sharply into focus only since the collapse of communism in 1989. In 1995, one dominant global economic system is emerging."

Yes, such policy openings are important. But to paint them as a sea change is inaccurate at best. Remember the 10 Percent Presumption, and that integration is only beginning. The policies that we fickle humans enact are surprisingly reversible. Thus, Francis Fukuyama's *The End of History,* in which liberal democracy and technologically driven capitalism were supposed to have triumphed over other ideologies, seems quite quaint today. In the wake of Sept. 11, 2001, Samuel Huntington's *Clash of Civilizations* looks at least a bit more prescient. But even if you stay on the economic plane, as Sachs and Warner mostly do, you quickly see counterevidence to the supposed decisiveness of policy openings. The so-called Washington Consensus around market-friendly policies ran up against the 1997 Asian currency crisis and has since frayed substantially—for example, in the swing toward neopopulism across much of Latin America. In terms of economic outcomes, the number of countries—in Latin America, coastal Africa, and the former Soviet Union—that have dropped out of the "convergence club" (defined in terms of narrowing productivity and structural gaps vis-à-vis the advanced industrialized countries) is at least as impressive as the number of countries that have joined the club. At a multilateral level, the suspension of

the Doha round of trade talks in the summer of 2006—prompting *The Economist* to run a cover titled "The Future of Globalization" and depicting a beached wreck—is no promising omen. In addition, the recent wave of cross-border mergers and acquisitions seems to be encountering more protectionism, in a broader range of countries, than did the previous wave in the late 1990s.

Of course, given that sentiments in these respects have shifted in the past 10 years or so, there is a fair chance that they may shift yet again in the next decade. The point is, it's not only possible to turn back the clock on globalization-friendly policies, it's relatively easy to imagine it happening. Specifically, we have to entertain the possibility that deep international economic integration may be inherently incompatible with national sovereignty—especially given the tendency of voters in many countries, including advanced ones, to support more protectionism, rather than less. As Jeff Immelt, CEO of GE, put it in late 2006, "If you put globalization to a popular vote in the U.S., it would lose." And even if cross-border integration continues on its upward path, the road from here to there is unlikely to be either smooth or straight. There will be shocks and cycles, in all likelihood, and maybe even another period of stagnation or reversal that will endure for decades. It wouldn't be unprecedented.

The champions of globalization are describing a world that doesn't exist. It's a fine strategy to sell books and even describe a potential environment that may someday exist. Because such episodes of mass delusion tend to be relatively short-lived even when they do achieve broad currency, one might simply be tempted to wait this one out as well. But the stakes are far too high for that. Governments that buy into the flat world are likely to pay too much attention to the "golden straitjacket" that Friedman emphasized in his earlier book, *The Lexus and the Olive Tree,* which is supposed to ensure that economics matters more and more and politics less and less. Buying into this version of an integrated world—or worse, using it as a basis for policymaking—is not only unproductive; It is dangerous.

Critical Thinking

1. What is Pankaj Ghemawat's point of view?
2. What is the "10 percent presumption?"
3. How do Ghemawat's arguments against a "flat" world differ from Friedman's?
4. How does the point of view of this article fit into the discussion of alternative futures presented in Article 1?

PANKAJ GHEMAWAT is the Anselmo Rubiralta professor of global strategy at IESE Business School and the Jaime and Josefina Chua Tiampo professor of business administration at Harvard Business School. His new book is *Redefining Global Strategy* (Boston: Harvard Business School Press, September 2007).

Can Extreme Poverty Be Eliminated?

**Market economics and globalization are lifting the bulk
of humanity out of extreme poverty, but special measures
are needed to help the poorest of the poor.**

Jeffrey D. Sachs

Almost everyone who ever lived was wretchedly poor. Famine, death from childbirth, infectious disease and countless other hazards were the norm for most of history. Humanity's sad plight started to change with the Industrial Revolution, beginning around 1750. New scientific insights and technological innovations enabled a growing proportion of the global population to break free of extreme poverty.

Two and a half centuries later more than five billion of the world's 6.5 billion people can reliably meet their basic living needs and thus can be said to have escaped from the precarious conditions that once governed everyday life. One out of six inhabitants of this planet, however, still struggles daily to meet some or all of such critical requirements as adequate nutrition, uncontaminated drinking water, safe shelter and sanitation as well as access to basic health care. These people get by on $1 a day or less and are overlooked by public services for health, education and infrastructure. Every day more than 20,000 die of dire poverty, for want of food, safe drinking water, medicine or other essential needs.

For the first time in history, global economic prosperity, brought on by continuing scientific and technological progress and the self-reinforcing accumulation of wealth, has placed the world within reach of eliminating extreme poverty altogether. This prospect will seem fanciful to some, but the dramatic economic progress made by China, India and other low-income parts of Asia over the past 25 years demonstrates that it is realistic. Moreover, the predicted stabilization of the world's population toward the middle of this century will help by easing pressures on Earth's climate, ecosystems and natural resources—pressures that might otherwise undo economic gains.

**Extreme poverty could become a thing
of the past in a few decades if the affluent
countries of the world pony up a small
percentage of their wealth to help the
planet's 1.1 billion indigent populations
out of conditions of dire poverty.**

Although economic growth has shown a remarkable capacity to lift vast numbers of people out of extreme poverty, progress is neither automatic nor inevitable. Market forces and free trade are not enough. Many of the poorest regions are ensnared in a poverty trap: they lack the financial means to make the necessary investments in infrastructure, education, health care systems and other vital needs. Yet the end of such poverty is feasible if a concerted global effort is undertaken, as the nations of the world promised when they adopted the Millennium Development Goals at the United Nations Millennium Summit in 2000. A dedicated cadre of development agencies, international financial institutions, nongovernmental organizations and communities throughout the developing world already constitute a global network of expertise and goodwill to help achieve this objective.

This past January my colleagues and I on the U.N. Millennium Project published a plan to halve the rate of extreme poverty by 2015 (compared with 1990) and to achieve other quantitative targets for reducing hunger, disease and environmental degradation. In my recent book, *The End of Poverty,* I argue that a large-scale and targeted public investment effort could in fact eliminate this problem by 2025, much as smallpox was eradicated globally. This hypothesis is controversial, so I am pleased to have the opportunity to clarify its main arguments and to respond to various concerns that have been raised about it.

Beyond Business as Usual

Economists have learned a great deal during the past few years about how countries develop and what roadblocks can stand in their way. A new kind of development economics needs to emerge, one that is better grounded in science—a "clinical economics" akin to modern medicine. Today's medical professionals understand that disease results from a vast array of interacting factors and conditions: pathogens, nutrition, environment, aging, individual and population genetics, and lifestyle. They also know that one key to proper treatment is the

Crossroads for Poverty

The Problem

- Much of humankind has succeeded in dragging itself out of severe poverty since the onset of the Industrial Revolution in the mid-18th century, but about 1.1 billion out of today's 6.5 billion global inhabitants are utterly destitute in a world of plenty.
- These unfortunates, who get by on less than $1 a day, have little access to adequate nutrition, safe drinking water and shelter, as well as basic sanitation and health care services. What can the developed world do to lift this huge segment of the human population out of extreme poverty?

The Plan

- Doubling affluent nations' international poverty assistance to about $160 billion a year would go a long way toward ameliorating the terrible predicament faced by one in six humans. This figure would constitute about 0.5 percent of the gross national product (GNP) of the planet's rich countries. Because these investments do not include other categories of aid, such as spending on major infrastructure projects, climate change mitigation or post conflict reconstruction, donors should commit to reaching the long stand target of 0.7 percent of GNP by 2015.
- These donations, often provided to local groups, would need to be closely monitored and audited to ensure that they are correctly targeted toward those truly in need.

ability to make an individualized diagnosis of the source of illness. Likewise, development economists need better diagnostic skills to recognize that economic pathologies have a wide variety of causes, including many outside the traditional ken of economic practice.

Public opinion in affluent countries often attributes extreme poverty to faults with the poor themselves—or at least with their governments. Race was once thought the deciding factor. Then it was culture: religious divisions and taboos, caste systems, a lack of entrepreneurship, gender inequities. Such theories have waned as societies of an ever widening range of religions and cultures have achieved relative prosperity. Moreover, certain supposedly immutable aspects of culture (such as fertility choices and gender and caste roles) in fact change, often dramatically, as societies become urban and develop economically.

Most recently, commentators have zeroed in on "poor governance," often code words for corruption. They argue that extreme poverty persists because governments fail to open up their markets, provide public services and clamp down on bribe taking. It is said that if these regimes cleaned up their acts, they, too, would flourish. Development assistance efforts have become largely a series of good governance lectures.

The availability of cross-country and time-series data now allows experts to make much more systematic analyses. Although debate continues, the weight of the evidence indicates that governance makes a difference but is not the sole determinant of economic growth. According to surveys conducted by Transparency International, business leaders actually perceive many fast-growing Asian countries to be more corrupt than some slow-growing African ones.

Geography—including natural resources, climate, topography, and proximity to trade routes and major markets—is at least as important as good governance. As early as 1776, Adam Smith argued that high transport costs inhibited development in the inland areas of Africa and Asia. Other geographic features, such as the heavy disease burden of the tropics, also interfere. One recent study by my Columbia University colleague Xavier Sala-i-Martin demonstrated once again that tropical countries saddled with malaria have experienced slower growth than those free from the disease. The good news is that geographic factors shape, but do not decide, a country's economic fate. Technology can offset them: drought can be fought with irrigation systems, isolation with roads and mobile telephones, diseases with preventive and therapeutic measures.

The other major insight is that although the most powerful mechanism for reducing extreme poverty is to encourage overall economic growth, a rising tide does not necessarily lift all boats. Average income can rise, but if the income is distributed unevenly the poor may benefit little, and pockets of extreme poverty may persist (especially in geographically disadvantaged regions). Moreover, growth is not simply a free-market phenomenon. It requires basic government services: infrastructure, health, education, and scientific and technological innovation. Thus, many of the recommendations of the past two decades emanating from Washington—that governments in low-income countries should cut back on their spending to make room for the private sector—miss the point. Government spending, directed at investment in critical areas, is itself a vital spur to growth, especially if its effects are to reach the poorest of the poor.

The Poverty Trap

So what do these insights tell us about the region most afflicted by poverty today, Africa? Fifty years ago tropical Africa was roughly as rich as subtropical and tropical Asia. As Asia boomed, Africa stagnated. Special geographic factors have played a crucial role.

Foremost among these is the existence of the Himalaya Mountains, which produce southern Asia's monsoon climate and vast river systems. Well-watered farmlands served as the starting points for Asia's rapid escape from extreme poverty during the past five decades. The Green Revolution of the 1960s and 1970s introduced high-yield grains, irrigation and fertilizers, which ended the cycle of famine, disease and despair.

It also freed a significant proportion of the labor force to seek manufacturing jobs in the cities. Urbanization, in turn, spurred growth, not only by providing a home for industry and innovation but also by prompting greater investment in a healthy and skilled labor force. Urban residents cut their fertility rates and

Globalization, Poverty and Foreign Aid

Average citizens in affluent nations often have many questions about the effects of economic globalization on rich and poor nations and about how developing countries spend the aid they receive. Here are a few brief answers:

Is Globalization Making the Rich Richer and the Poor Poorer?

Generally, the answer is no. Economic globalization is supporting very rapid advances of many impoverished economies, notably in Asia. International trade and foreign investment inflows have been major factors in China's remarkable economic growth during the past quarter century and in India's fast economic growth since the early 1990s. The poorest of the poor, notably in sub-Saharan Africa, are not held back by globalization; they are largely bypassed by it.

Is Poverty the Result of Exploitation of the Poor by the Rich?

Affluent nations have repeatedly plundered and exploited poor countries through slavery, colonial rule and unfair trade practices. Yet it is perhaps more accurate to say that exploitation is the result of poverty (which leaves impoverished countries vulnerable to abuse) rather than the cause of it. Poverty is generally the result of low productivity per worker, which reflects poor health, lack of job-market skills, patchiness of infrastructure (roads, power plants, utility lines, shipping ports), chronic malnutrition and the like. Exploitation has played a role in producing some of these conditions, but deeper factors [geographic isolation, endemic disease, ecological destruction, challenging conditions for food production] have tended to be more important and difficult to overcome without external help.

Will Higher Incomes in Poor Countries Mean Lower Incomes in Rich Countries?

By and large, economic development is a positive-sum process, meaning that all can partake in it without causing some to suffer. In the past 200 years, the world as a whole has achieved a massive increase in economic output rather than a shift in economic output to one region at the expense of another. To be sure, global environmental constraints are already starting to impose themselves. As today's poor countries develop, the climate, fisheries and forests are coming under increased strain. Overall global economic growth is compatible with sustainable management of the ecosystems on which all humans depend—indeed, wealth can be good for the environment—but only if public policy and technologies encourage sound practices and the necessary investments are made in environmental sustainability.

Do U.S. Private Contributions Make Up for the Low Levels of U.S. Official Aid?

Some have claimed that while the U.S. government budget provides relatively little assistance to the poorest countries, the private sector makes up the gap. In fact, the Organization for Economic Cooperation and Development has estimated that private foundations and nongovernmental organizations give roughly $6 billion a year in international assistance, or 0.05 percent of U.S. gross national product (GNP). In that case, total U.S. international aid is around 0.21 percent of GNP—still among the lowest ratios of all donor nations.

—J.D.S.

thus were able to spend more for the health, nutrition and education of each child. City kids went to school at a higher rate than their rural cousins. And with the emergence of urban infrastructure and public health systems, city populations became less disease-prone than their counterparts in the countryside, where people typically lack safe drinking water, modern sanitation, professional health care and protection from vector-borne ailments such as malaria.

Africa did not experience a green revolution. Tropical Africa lacks the massive floodplains that facilitate the large-scale and low-cost irrigation found in Asia. Also, its rainfall is highly variable, and impoverished farmers have been unable to purchase fertilizer. The initial Green Revolution research featured crops, especially paddy rice and wheat, not widely grown in Africa (high-yield varieties suitable for it have been developed in recent years, but they have not yet been disseminated sufficiently). The continent's food production per person has actually been falling, and Africans' caloric intake is the lowest in the world; food insecurity is rampant. Its labor force has remained tethered to subsistence agriculture.

Compounding its agricultural woes, Africa bears an overwhelming burden of tropical diseases. Because of climate and the endemic mosquito species, malaria is more intensively transmitted in Africa than anywhere else. And high transport costs isolate Africa economically. In East Africa, for example, the rainfall is greatest in the interior of the continent, so most people live there, far from ports and international trade routes.

Much the same situation applies to other impoverished parts of the world, notably the Andean and Central American highlands and the landlocked countries of Central Asia. Being economically isolated, they are unable to attract much foreign investment (other than for the extraction of oil, gas and precious minerals). Investors tend to be dissuaded by the high transport costs associated with the interior regions. Rural areas therefore remain stuck in a vicious cycle of poverty, hunger, illness and illiteracy. Impoverished areas lack adequate internal savings to make the needed investments because most households live hand to mouth. The few high-income families, who do accumulate savings, park them overseas rather than at home. This capital flight includes not only financial capital but also the human variety, in the form of skilled workers—doctors, nurses, scientists and engineers, who frequently leave in search of improved economic opportunities abroad. The poorest countries are often, perversely, net exporters of capital.

Put Money Where Mouths Are

The technology to overcome these handicaps and jump-start economic development exists. Malaria can be controlled using bed nets, indoor pesticide spraying and improved medicines. Drought-prone countries in Africa with nutrient depleted soils can benefit enormously from drip irrigation and greater use of fertilizers. Landlocked countries can be connected by paved highway networks, airports and fiber-optic cables. All these projects cost money, of course.

Many larger countries, such as China, have prosperous regions that can help support their own lagging areas. Coastal eastern China, for instance, is now financing massive public investments in western China. Most of today's successfully developing countries, especially smaller ones, received at least some backing from external donors at crucial times. The critical scientific innovations that formed the underpinnings of the Green Revolution were bankrolled by the Rockefeller Foundation, and the spread of these technologies in India and elsewhere in Asia was funded by the U.S. and other donor governments and international development institutions.

We in the U.N. Millennium Project have listed the investments required to help today's impoverished regions cover basic needs in health, education, water, sanitation, food production, roads and other key areas. We have put an approximate price tag on that assistance and estimated how much could be financed by poor households themselves and by domestic institutions. The remaining cost is the "financing gap" that international donors need to make up.

For tropical Africa, the total investment comes to $110 per person a year. To place this into context, the average income in this part of the world is $350 per annum, most or all of which is required just to stay alive. The full cost of the total investment is clearly beyond the funding reach of these countries. Of the $110, perhaps $40 could be financed domestically, so that $70 per capita would be required in the form of international aid.

Adding it all up, the total requirement for assistance across the globe is around $160 billion a year, double the current rich-country aid budget of $80 billion. This figure amounts to approximately 0.5 percent of the combined gross national product (GNP) of the affluent donor nations. It does not include other humanitarian projects such as postwar Iraqi reconstruction or Indian Ocean tsunami relief. To meet these needs as well, a reasonable figure would be 0.7 percent of GNP, which is what all donor countries have long promised but few have fulfilled. Other organizations, including the International Monetary Fund, the World Bank and the British government, have reached much the same conclusion.

When polled, Americans greatly overestimate how much foreign aid the U.S. gives—by as much as 30 times.

Foreign Aid: How Should the Money Be Spent?

Here is a breakdown of the needed investment for three typical low-income African countries to help them achieve the Millennium Development Goals. For all nations given aid, the average total annual assistance per person would come to around $110 a year. These investments would be financed by both foreign aid and the countries themselves.

Investment Area	Average per Year between 2005–2015 ($ per capita)		
	Ghana	Tanzania	Uganda
Hunger	7	8	6
Education	19	14	5
Gender equality	3	3	3
Health	25	35	34
Water supply and sanitation	8	7	5
Improving slum conditions	2	3	2
Energy	15	16	12
Roads	10	22	20
Other	10	10	10
Total	100	117	106

Calculated from data from Investing in Development [U.N. Millennium Project, Earth Scan Publications, 2005]. Numbers do not sum to totals because of rounding.

We believe these investments would enable the poorest countries to cut poverty by half by 2015 and, if continued, to eliminate it altogether by 2025. They would not be "welfare payments" from rich to poor but instead something far more important and durable. People living above mere subsistence levels would be able to save for their futures; they could join the virtuous cycle of rising incomes, savings and technological inflows. We would be giving a billion people a hand up instead of a handout.

If rich nations fail to make these investments, they will be called on to provide emergency assistance more or less indefinitely. They will face famine, epidemics, regional conflicts and the spread of terrorist havens. And they will condemn not only the impoverished countries but themselves as well to chronic political instability, humanitarian emergencies and security risks.

The debate is now shifting from the basic diagnosis of extreme poverty and the calculations of financing needs to the practical matter of how assistance can best be delivered. Many people believe that aid efforts failed in the past and that care is needed to avoid the repetition of failure. Some of these concerns are well grounded, but others are fueled by misunderstandings.

When pollsters ask Americans how much foreign aid they think the U.S. gives, they greatly overestimate the amount by as much as 30 times. Believing that so much money has been donated and so little has been done with it, the public concludes that these programs have "failed." The reality is rather different.

U.S. official assistance to sub-Saharan Africa has been running at $2 billion to $4 billion a year, or roughly $3 to $6 for every African. Most of this aid has come in the form of "technical cooperation" (which goes into the pockets of consultants), food contributions for famine victims and the cancellation of unpaid debts. Little of this support has come in a form that can be invested in systems that improve health, nutrition, food production and transport. We should give foreign aid a fair chance before deciding whether it works or not.

A second common misunderstanding concerns the extent to which corruption is likely to eat up the donated money. Some foreign aid in the past has indeed ended up in the equivalent of Swiss bank accounts. That happened when the funds were provided for geopolitical reasons rather than development; a good example was U.S. support for the corrupt regime of Mobutu Sese Seko of Zaire (now the Democratic Republic of the Congo) during part of the cold war. When assistance has been targeted at development rather than political goals, the outcomes have been favorable, ranging from the Green Revolution to the eradication of smallpox and the recent near-eradication of polio.

The aid package we advocate would be directed toward those countries with a reasonable degree of good governance and operational transparency. In Africa, these countries include Ethiopia, Ghana, Mali, Mozambique, Senegal and Tanzania. The money would not be merely thrown at them. It would be provided according to a detailed and monitored plan, and new rounds of financing would be delivered only as the work actually got done. Much of the funds would be given directly to villages and towns to minimize the chances of their getting diverted by central governments. All these programs should be closely audited.

Western society tends to think of foreign aid as money lost. But if supplied properly, it is an investment that will one day yield huge returns, much as U.S. assistance to Western Europe and East Asia after World War II did. By prospering, today's impoverished countries will wean themselves from endless charity. They will contribute to the international advance of science, technology and trade. They will escape political instability, which leaves many of them vulnerable to violence, narcotics trafficking, civil war and even terrorist takeover. Our own security will be bolstered as well. As U.N. Secretary-General Kofi Annan wrote earlier this year: "There will be no development without security, and no security without development."

Critical Thinking

1. How does Jeffery Sachs propose that extreme poverty be eliminated?
2. According to Sachs, what are the key economic and public policy issues that need to be addressed?

The author, **JEFFREY D. SACHS,** directs the Earth Institute at Columbia University and the United Nations Millennium Project. An economist, Sachs is well known for advising governments in Latin America, Eastern Europe, the former Soviet Union, Asia and Africa on economic reforms and for his work with international agencies to promote poverty reduction, disease control and debt reduction in poor countries. A native of Detroit, he received his BA, MA and PhD degrees from Harvard University.

Gazing across the Divides

Lucien Crowder

I hold in my hand two envelopes. The first, addressed to the world's developing economies, contains a coveted invitation to the Age of Steady Economic Progress. Enjoy yourselves, people. The second envelope, which I regretfully deliver to the world's advanced economies, holds an invitation—a summons, really—to the Age of Difficult Choices. This invitation ensures that rich countries' mid-term futures will be characterized by lousy alternatives, ticklish dilemmas, and widely reduced expectations. So sorry about that, folks. Best of luck to you.

This is what history might say if it could talk (and fancied itself a wry wit). History might also observe, regarding the rich-world quandary that involves economic stagnation and fiscal imbalance, that governments are not very good at engaging dilemmas. They excel instead at crisis response. Witness the 2008 financial debacle, when rich-world governments did much, in coordination with multilateral institutions, to prevent a global depression. But when crises abate governments struggle anew, once again privileging parochial concerns over long-term thinking and reverting to their characteristic mediocrity.

Two thousand and ten was a year when crisis management was slowly superseded by dilemma confrontation. The year economically speaking, while not an outright disaster like 2008 or 2009, offered little evidence that the world's affluent countries would any time soon return to vigorous growth and full employment or that, in general, advanced economies could successfully address their long-term fiscal problems—insofar as "success" means forestalling yet more crises.

The International Monetary Fund estimates that advanced-world growth in 2010 was a mere 2.7 percent—quite a poor performance considering the terribly low baseline provided by 2009. Yet prospects for the year to come look less inspiring still. Businesses have finished restocking their inventories after letting them run down at the depths of the recession. Real estate markets remain critically weak. Many government stimulus programs are expiring or have expired. Central banks have expended their traditional options for sparking growth. The euro is forever on the verge of or in the midst of a crisis. Fiscal retrenchment is under way in several large economies and is inevitable in others. For all these reasons, advanced-world growth is projected in 2011 to decelerate to 2.2 percent.

Thus governments still must promote growth—though their tools for doing so are now hard to identify. At the same time they must reduce spending and increase taxes—though doing so will suppress the very growth they mean to encourage. Governments must also, for the sake of their countries' long-term prosperity, increase expenditures in areas such as education and green-energy innovation. Alleviating a little human suffering might also be a nice gesture.

On the question of how to pursue these contradictory aims, reasonable people can disagree. (Unreasonable people certainly do.) If austerity is enacted now, is it just in time, somewhat too soon, or far too late? Germany thinks that now is the time, though many economists argue it is somewhat too soon; perhaps the country is rushing into fiscal retrenchment at the expense of growth. Japan, never in a rush to do anything, seems determined through means of political indecision and behemoth national debt to turn a lost decade into a forfeited future. The United States, so proud of its separation of powers and deliberative legislative process, cannot achieve even the vaguest consensus on how to pare its deficit, and now pursues short-term growth almost exclusively through budget-busting tax cuts. Each of these economies—three of the world's four largest—faces a different variety of the growth-and-retrenchment dilemma. Has each identified a unique path to failure?

Nice Developments

It is depressing to linger in the lands where difficult choices rule, so let us move on to the land of steady economic progress, whose capital is China. That country, due both to its underlying strengths and to an enormous stimulus package announced in 2008, proved itself nearly impervious to the global economic crisis; it has fully emerged as the most powerful engine of global growth. For the boundless masses of poor Chinese who have ascended to the middle class, and for those who still can expect to do so, this is excellent news. It is also good news, generally speaking, for the country's trading partners.

To be sure, China faces stiff challenges. These include long-term problems like negative demographic trends and profound environmental degradation; medium-term economic concerns such as how to invigorate moribund domestic consumption and reduce reliance on low-wage manufacturing; systemic issues such as official corruption and excessive government interference in the private sector; and appalling deficits in democracy, transparency, and individual rights. Still, now and for the foreseeable future, the Chinese production line hums.

In the rest of the developing world, economic trends likewise appear encouraging. This is partly because trade, with China supplying considerable demand, has substantially recovered from the collapse precipitated by the financial crisis. India, booming, achieved an estimated GDP growth of 9.7 percent in 2010. Latin America, not booming but doing nicely, evidently grew at a rate of 5.7 percent on the year. Even sub-Saharan Africa, a region that so often in the past has contracted deadly illnesses at the daintiest rich-world sneeze, looks to have grown by 5.7 percent in 2010. These numbers indicate that the developing world has quite substantially decoupled itself from the advanced economies, and this is a positive trend.

The developing world's causes for good cheer extend beyond topline economic growth. According to the United Nations' most recent report on progress toward the Millennium Development Goals (MDGs), the world is on track by 2015 to halve from 1990 levels the proportion of people living in extreme poverty—this despite the negative effects of the financial crisis. The UN also notes, regarding the AIDS epidemic, that the world has "halted and begun to reverse the spread of HIV." Still, the MDG report states that "improvements in the lives of the poor have been unacceptably slow," and the IMF meanwhile observes that much of Africa remains dangerously exposed to fluctuations in international resource prices.

If 2010 was a reasonably good year for progress against poverty and other ills of the developing world, it was a minimally acceptable one for the earth's climate. Until December, 2010 was shaping up as the time when the world gave up on global warming. That perception changed somewhat at a late-year forum in Cancún. The conference, which began amid appallingly low expectations, yielded no binding treaty on reducing greenhouse emissions. But it did generate some progress on green-energy research, emissions verification procedures, and funding for remediation of climate-induced problems in poor countries. It also produced a sense that the multilateral climate process might not be dead after all. This welcome result was miserably inadequate nonetheless. Humankind has defied many Malthusian predictions of civilizational collapse, but a workable mechanism for ensuring global cataclysm may finally have been discovered in the incorrigible combustion of coal and oil.

Climate change represented for international institutions a qualified failure in 2010; regarding other issues, institutions did virtually nothing. November's Group of 20 meeting in Seoul achieved so little that journalists covering the event struggled to fill their dispatches with content. Negotiations to further liberalize the world trading system remained moribund. As conflict raged in central Africa, the world seemed helpless to arrest people's suffering. Aside from the UN's imposition of additional sanctions against Iran in what will prove a futile effort to prevent that country from becoming a nuclear weapons state, and aside from Europe's bailout of Greece and Ireland—which Brussels could not very well have avoided—the year for international institutions was notably unproductive.

Rolling Displacement

All this talk of governments and multilateral institutions can sometimes obscure the ordinary people whose life courses are in significant measure determined by policy choices and historical forces. In years past, many workers in advanced economies performed jobs—difficult jobs and repetitive ones, but dignified and tolerably remunerative—that have vanished and will never return. Economists and policy experts have advanced many proposals for how to improve the lot of those displaced. Typical ideas include improving education, fostering innovation, establishing a society-wide emphasis on science and technology, providing targeted training for positions in growth industries, and so on. Worthy ideas, every one.

They all tend to hinge on meritocracy—a virtuous ideal that combats the old corruptions of nepotism and patronage, but that by definition is ruthless and exclusionary. Not everyone can pioneer a new technology, earn an advanced degree in organic chemistry, or master several languages. And what if they did? Advanced nations now face the danger that something beyond mere income inequality is developing in their societies—that a permanent cleft is developing instead, such that on one side of a divide stand the smart, talented, motivated, or lucky, while the frankly ordinary or merely luckless huddle sullenly on the other. If the ordinary and luckless begin justifiably to feel that the cleft is a chasm and can never be bridged, and their numbers grow great enough, what becomes of the advanced world's most cherished accomplishments, those of representative government and liberal social norms?

Such questions, today the burden and privilege of the world's advanced economies, will in time bedevil an increasing number of nations. China's industrialization has been unprecedentedly rapid; its confrontation with the problems of maturity likewise figures to begin in record time. Thus, although human beings have benefited fantastically from the broadening miracle of capitalism, mature economies must someday, somehow learn to structure themselves so that meaningful vocations are available not just to the special and the clever but also to the overwhelming masses of people. Otherwise, nations that achieve freedom and prosperity after such difficult struggle may not endure in freedom and prosperity.

Critical Thinking

1. What is Crowder's point of view?
2. What reasons and examples does he offer to support his point of view?
3. What difficult policy choices do the world's advanced economies face?
4. Does his point of view complement or contradict Friedman's concept of a "flat" world?
5. How does this article relate to articles 4 and 21?

From *Current History*, January 2011, pp. 6–8. Copyright © 2011 by Current History, Inc. Reprinted by permission.

Of the 1%, by the 1%, for the 1%

Americans have been watching protests against oppressive regimes that concentrate massive wealth in the hands of an elite few. Yet in our own democracy, 1 percent of the people take nearly a quarter of the nation's income—an inequality even the wealthy will come to regret.

JOSEPH E. STIGLITZ

It's no use pretending that what has obviously happened has not in fact happened. The upper 1 percent of Americans are now taking in nearly a quarter of the nation's income every year. In terms of wealth rather than income, the top 1 percent control 40 percent. Their lot in life has improved considerably. Twenty-five years ago, the corresponding figures were 12 percent and 33 percent. One response might be to celebrate the ingenuity and drive that brought good fortune to these people, and to contend that a rising tide lifts all boats. That response would be misguided. While the top 1 percent have seen their incomes rise 18 percent over the past decade, those in the middle have actually seen their incomes fall. For men with only high-school degrees, the decline has been precipitous—12 percent in the last quarter-century alone. All the growth in recent decades—and more—has gone to those at the top. In terms of income equality, America lags behind any country in the old, ossified Europe that President George W. Bush used to deride. Among our closest counterparts are Russia with its oligarchs and Iran. While many of the old centers of inequality in Latin America, such as Brazil, have been striving in recent years, rather successfully, to improve the plight of the poor and reduce gaps in income, America has allowed inequality to grow.

Economists long ago tried to justify the vast inequalities that seemed so troubling in the mid-19th century—inequalities that are but a pale shadow of what we are seeing in America today. The justification they came up with was called "marginal-productivity theory." In a nutshell, this theory associated higher incomes with higher productivity and a greater contribution to society. It is a theory that has always been cherished by the rich. Evidence for its validity, however, remains thin. The corporate executives who helped bring on the recession of the past three years—whose contribution to our society, and to their own companies, has been massively negative—went on to receive large bonuses. In some cases, companies were so embarrassed about calling such rewards "performance bonuses" that they felt compelled to change the name to "retention bonuses" (even if the only thing being retained was bad performance). Those who have contributed great positive innovations to our society, from the pioneers of genetic understanding to the pioneers of the Information Age, have received a pittance compared with those responsible for the financial innovations that brought our global economy to the brink of ruin.

Some people look at income inequality and shrug their shoulders. So what if this person gains and that person loses? What matters, they argue, is not how the pie is divided but the size of the pie. That argument is fundamentally wrong. An economy in which *most* citizens are doing worse year after year—an economy like America's—is not likely to do well over the long haul. There are several reasons for this.

First, growing inequality is the flip side of something else: shrinking opportunity. Whenever we diminish equality of opportunity, it means that we are not using some of our most valuable assets—our people—in the most productive way possible. Second, many of the distortions that lead to inequality—such as those associated with monopoly power and preferential tax treatment for special interests—undermine the efficiency of the economy. This new inequality goes on to create new distortions, undermining efficiency even further. To give just one example, far too many of our most talented young people, seeing the astronomical rewards, have gone into finance rather than into fields that would lead to a more productive and healthy economy.

Third, and perhaps most important, a modern economy requires "collective action"—it needs government to invest in infrastructure, education, and technology. The United States and the world have benefited greatly from government-sponsored research that led to the Internet, to advances in public health, and so on. But America has long suffered from an under-investment in infrastructure (look at the condition of our highways and bridges, our railroads and airports), in basic research, and in education at all levels. Further cutbacks in these areas lie ahead.

None of this should come as a surprise—it is simply what happens when a society's wealth distribution becomes lopsided. The more divided a society becomes in terms of wealth, the more reluctant the wealthy become to spend money on common needs. The rich don't need to rely on government for parks or education or medical care or personal security—they can buy all these things for themselves. In the process, they become more distant from ordinary people, losing whatever empathy they may once have had. They also worry about strong government—one that could use its powers to adjust the balance, take some of their wealth, and invest it for the common good. The top 1 percent may complain about the kind of government we have in America, but in truth they like it just fine: too gridlocked to re-distribute, too divided to do anything but lower taxes.

Economists are not sure how to fully explain the growing inequality in America. The ordinary dynamics of supply and demand have certainly played a role: labor-saving technologies have reduced the demand for many "good" middle-class, blue-collar jobs. Globalization has created a worldwide marketplace, pitting expensive unskilled workers in America against cheap unskilled workers overseas. Social changes have also played a role—for instance, the decline of unions, which once represented a third of American workers and now represent about 12 percent.

But one big part of the reason we have so much inequality is that the top 1 percent want it that way. The most obvious example involves tax policy. Lowering tax rates on capital gains, which is how the rich receive a large portion of their income, has given the wealthiest Americans close to a free ride. Monopolies and near monopolies have always been a source of economic power—from John D. Rockefeller at the beginning of the last century to Bill Gates at the end. Lax enforcement of anti-trust laws, especially during Republican administrations, has been a godsend to the top 1 percent. Much of today's inequality is due to manipulation of the financial system, enabled by changes in the rules that have been bought and paid for by the financial industry itself—one of its best investments ever. The government lent money to financial institutions at close to 0 percent interest and provided generous bailouts on favorable terms when all else failed. Regulators turned a blind eye to a lack of transparency and to conflicts of interest.

When you look at the sheer volume of wealth controlled by the top 1 percent in this country, it's tempting to see our growing inequality as a quintessentially American achievement—we started way behind the pack, but now we're doing inequality on a world-class level. And it looks as if we'll be building on this achievement for years to come, because what made it possible is self-reinforcing. Wealth begets power, which begets more wealth. During the savings-and-loan scandal of the 1980s—a scandal whose dimensions, by today's standards, seem almost quaint—the banker Charles Keating was asked by a congressional committee whether the $1.5 million he had spread among a few key elected officials could actually buy influence. "I certainly hope so," he replied. The Supreme Court, in its recent *Citizens United* case, has enshrined the right of corporations to buy government, by removing limitations on campaign spending. The personal and the political are today in perfect alignment. Virtually all U.S. senators, and most of the representatives in the House, are members of the top 1 percent when they arrive, are kept in office by money from the top 1 percent, and know that if they serve the top 1 percent well they will be rewarded by the top 1 percent when

they leave office. By and large, the key executive-branch policy-makers on trade and economic policy also come from the top 1 percent. When pharmaceutical companies receive a trillion-dollar gift—through legislation prohibiting the government, the largest buyer of drugs, from bargaining over price—it should not come as cause for wonder. It should not make jaws drop that a tax bill cannot emerge from Congress unless big tax cuts are put in place for the wealthy. Given the power of the top 1 percent, this is the way you would *expect* the system to work.

America's inequality distorts our society in every conceivable way. There is, for one thing, a well-documented lifestyle effect—people outside the top 1 percent increasingly live beyond their means. Trickle-down economics may be a chimera, but trickle-down behaviorism is very real. Inequality massively distorts our foreign policy. The top 1 percent rarely serve in the military—the reality is that the "all-volunteer" army does not pay enough to attract their sons and daughters, and patriotism goes only so far. Plus, the wealthiest class feels no pinch from higher taxes when the nation goes to war: borrowed money will pay for all that. Foreign policy, by definition, is about the balancing of national interests and national resources. With the top 1 percent in charge, and paying no price, the notion of balance and restraint goes out the window. There is no limit to the adventures we can undertake; corporations and contractors stand only to gain. The rules of economic globalization are likewise designed to benefit the rich: they encourage competition among countries for *business,* which drives down taxes on corporations, weakens health and environmental protections, and undermines what used to be viewed as the "core" labor rights, which include the right to collective bargaining. Imagine what the world might look like if the rules were designed instead to encourage competition among countries for *workers.* Governments would compete in providing economic security, low taxes on ordinary wage earners, good education, and a clean environment—things workers care about. But the top 1 percent don't need to care.

Or, more accurately, they think they don't. Of all the costs imposed on our society by the top 1 percent, perhaps the greatest is this: the erosion of our sense of identity, in which fair play, equality of opportunity, and a sense of community are so important. America has long prided itself on being a fair society, where everyone has an equal chance of getting ahead, but the statistics suggest otherwise: the chances of a poor citizen, or even a middle-class citizen, making it to the top in America are smaller than in many countries of Europe. The cards are stacked against them. It is this sense of an unjust system without opportunity that has given rise to the conflagrations in the Middle East: rising food prices and growing and persistent youth unemployment simply served as kindling. With youth unemployment in America at around 20 percent (and in some locations, and among some socio-demographic groups, at twice that); with one out of six Americans desiring a full-time job not able to get one; with one out of seven Americans on food stamps (and about the same number suffering from "food insecurity")—given all this, there is ample evidence that something has blocked the vaunted "trickling down" from the top 1 percent to everyone else. All of this is having the predictable effect of creating alienation—voter turnout among those in their 20s in the last election stood at 21 percent, comparable to the unemployment rate.

In recent weeks we have watched people taking to the streets by the millions to protest political, economic, and social conditions in the oppressive societies they inhabit. Governments have been toppled in Egypt and Tunisia. Protests have erupted in Libya, Yemen, and Bahrain. The ruling families elsewhere in the region look on nervously from their air-conditioned penthouses—will they be next? They are right to worry. These are societies where a minuscule fraction of the population—less than 1 percent—controls the lion's share of the wealth; where wealth is a main determinant of power; where entrenched corruption of one sort or another is a way of life; and where the wealthiest often stand actively in the way of policies that would improve life for people in general.

As we gaze out at the popular fervor in the streets, one question to ask ourselves is this: When will it come to America? In important ways, our own country has become like one of these distant, troubled places.

Alexis de Tocqueville once described what he saw as a chief part of the peculiar genius of American society—something he called "self-interest properly understood." The last two words were the key. Everyone possesses self-interest in a narrow sense: I want what's good for me right now! Self-interest "properly understood" is different. It means appreciating that paying attention to everyone else's self-interest—in other words, the common welfare—is in fact a precondition for one's own ultimate well-being. Tocqueville was not suggesting that there was anything noble or idealistic about this outlook—in fact, he was suggesting the opposite. It was a mark of American pragmatism. Those canny Americans understood a basic fact: looking out for the other guy isn't just good for the soul—it's good for business.

The top 1 percent have the best houses, the best educations, the best doctors, and the best lifestyles, but there is one thing that money doesn't seem to have bought: an understanding that their fate is bound up with how the other 99 percent live. Throughout history, this is something that the top 1 percent eventually do learn. Too late.

Critical Thinking

1. What is Stiglitz's point of view?
2. What reasons does he offer to support his point of view?
3. What are the economic consequences of the growing inequality of wealth in the United Sates?
4. What are the political consequences of this inequality?
5. Does Stiglitz's argument support or contradict other articles in this unit?

The Case against the West
America and Europe in the Asian Century

Kishore Mahbubani

There is a fundamental flaw in the West's strategic thinking. In all its analyses of global challenges, the West assumes that it is the source of the solutions to the world's key problems. In fact, however, the West is also a major source of these problems. Unless key Western policymakers learn to understand and deal with this reality, the world is headed for an even more troubled phase.

The West is understandably reluctant to accept that the era of its domination is ending and that the Asian century has come. No civilization cedes power easily, and the West's resistance to giving up control of key global institutions and processes is natural. Yet the West is engaging in an extraordinary act of self-deception by believing that it is open to change. In fact, the West has become the most powerful force preventing the emergence of a new wave of history, clinging to its privileged position in key global forums, such as the UN Security Council, the International Monetary Fund, the World Bank, and the G-8 (the group of highly industrialized states), and refusing to contemplate how the West will have to adjust to the Asian century.

Partly as a result of its growing insecurity, the West has also become increasingly incompetent in its handling of key global problems. Many Western commentators can readily identify specific failures, such as the Bush administration's botched invasion and occupation of Iraq. But few can see that this reflects a deeper structural problem: the West's inability to see that the world has entered a new era.

Apart from representing a specific failure of policy execution, the war in Iraq has also highlighted the gap between the reality and what the West had expected would happen after the invasion. Arguably, the United States and the United Kingdom intended only to free the Iraqi people from a despotic ruler and to rid the world of a dangerous man, Saddam Hussein. Even if George W. Bush and Tony Blair had no malevolent intentions, however, their approaches were trapped in the Western mindset of believing that their interventions could lead only to good, not harm or disaster. This led them to believe that the invading U.S. troops would be welcomed with roses thrown at their feet by happy Iraqis. But the twentieth century showed that no country welcomes foreign invaders. The notion that any Islamic nation would approve of Western military boots on its soil was ridiculous. Even in the early twentieth century, the British invasion and occupation of Iraq was met with armed resistance. In 1920, Winston Churchill, then British secretary for war and air, quelled the rebellion of Kurds and Arabs in British-occupied Iraq by authorizing his troops to use chemical weapons. "I am strongly in favor of using poisoned gas against uncivilized tribes," Churchill said. The world has moved on from this era, but many Western officials have not abandoned the old assumption that an army of Christian soldiers can successfully invade, occupy, and transform an Islamic society.

Many Western leaders often begin their speeches by remarking on how perilous the world is becoming. Speaking after the August 2006 discovery of a plot to blow up transatlantic flights originating from London, President Bush said, "The American people need to know we live in a dangerous world." But even as Western leaders speak of such threats, they seem incapable of conceding that the West itself could be the fundamental source of these dangers. After all, the West includes the best-managed states in the world, the most economically developed, those with the strongest democratic institutions. But one cannot assume that a government that rules competently at home will be equally good at addressing challenges abroad. In fact, the converse is more likely to be true. Although the Western mind is obsessed with the Islamist terrorist threat, the West is mishandling the two immediate and pressing challenges of Afghanistan and Iraq. And despite the grave threat of nuclear terrorism, the Western custodians of the nonproliferation regime have allowed that regime to weaken significantly. The challenge posed by Iran's efforts to enrich uranium has been aggravated by the incompetence of the United States and the European Union. On the economic front, for the first time since World War II, the demise of a round of global trade negotiations, the Doha Round, seems imminent. Finally, the danger of global warming, too, is being mismanaged.

Yet Westerners seldom look inward to understand the deeper reasons these global problems are being mismanaged. Are there domestic structural reasons that explain this? Have Western democracies been hijacked by competitive populism and structural short-termism, preventing them from addressing long-term challenges from a broader global perspective?

Fortunately, some Asian states may now be capable of taking on more responsibilities, as they have been strengthened by implementing Western principles. In September 2005, Robert Zoellick, then U.S. deputy secretary of state, called on China to become a "responsible stakeholder" in the international system. China has responded positively, as have other Asian states. In recent decades, Asians have been among the greatest beneficiaries of the open multilateral order created by the United States and the other victors of World War II, and few today want to destabilize it. The number of Asians seeking a comfortable middle-class existence has never been higher. For centuries, the Chinese and the Indians could only dream of such an accomplishment; now it is within the reach of around half a billion people in China and India. Their ideal is to achieve what the United States and Europe did. They want to replicate, not dominate, the West. The universalization of the Western dream represents a moment of triumph for the West. And so the West should welcome the fact that the Asian states are becoming competent at handling regional and global challenges.

The Middle East Mess

Western Policies have been most harmful in the Middle East. The Middle East is also the most dangerous region in the world. Trouble there affects not just seven million Israelis, around four million Palestinians, and 200 million Arabs; it also affects more than a billion Muslims worldwide. Every time there is a major flare-up in the Middle East, such as the U.S. invasion of Iraq or the Israeli bombing of Lebanon, Islamic communities around the world become concerned, distressed, and angered. And few of them doubt the problems origin: the West.

The invasion and occupation of Iraq, for example, was a multi-dimensional error. The theory and practice of international law legitimizes the use of force only when it is an act of self-defense or is authorized by the UN Security Council. The U.S.-led invasion of Iraq could not be justified on either count. The United States and the United Kingdom sought the Security Council's authorization to invade Iraq, but the council denied it. It was therefore clear to the international community that the subsequent war was illegal and that it would do huge damage to international law.

This has created an enormous problem, partly because until this point both the United States and the United Kingdom had been among the primary custodians of international law. American and British minds, such as James Brierly,

Philip Jessup, Hersch Lauterpacht, and Hans Morgenthau, developed the conceptual infrastructure underlying international law, and American and British leaders provided the political will to have it accepted in practice. But neither the United States nor the United Kingdom will admit that the invasion and the occupation of Iraq were illegal or give up their historical roles as the chief caretakers of international law. Since 2003, both nations have frequently called for Iran and North Korea to implement UN Security Council resolutions. But how can the violators of UN principles also be their enforcers?

One rare benefit of the Iraq war may be that it has awakened a new fear of Iran among the Sunni Arab states. Egypt, Jordan, and Saudi Arabia, among others, do not want to deal with two adversaries and so are inclined to make peace with Israel. Saudi Arabia's King Abdullah used the opportunity of the special Arab League summit meeting in March 2007 to relaunch his long-standing proposal for a two-state solution to the Israeli-Palestinian conflict. Unfortunately, the Bush administration did not seize the opportunity—or revive the Taba accords that President Bill Clinton had worked out in January 2001, even though they could provide a basis for a lasting settlement and the Saudis were prepared to back them. In its early days, the Bush administration appeared ready to support a two-state solution. It was the first U.S. administration to vote in favor of a UN Security Council resolution calling for the creation of a Palestinian state, and it announced in March 2002 that it would try to achieve such a result by 2005. But here it is 2008, and little progress has been made.

The United States has made the already complicated Israeli-Palestinian conflict even more of a mess. Many extremist voices in Tel Aviv and Washington believe that time will always be on Israel's side. The pro-Israel lobby's stranglehold on the U.S. Congress, the political cowardice of U.S. politicians when it comes to creating a Palestinian state, and the sustained track record of U.S. aid to Israel support this view. But no great power forever sacrifices its larger national interests in favor of the interests of a small state. If Israel fails to accept the Taba accords, it will inevitably come to grief. If and when it does, Western incompetence will be seen as a major cause.

Never Say Never

Nuclear nonproliferation is another area in which the West, especially the United States, has made matters worse. The West has long been obsessed with the danger of the proliferation of weapons of mass destruction, particularly nuclear weapons. It pushed successfully for the near-universal ratification of the Biological and Toxin Weapons Convention, the Chemical Weapons Convention, and the Nuclear Nonproliferation Treaty (NPT).

But the West has squandered many of those gains. Today, the NPT is legally alive but spiritually dead. The NPT was inherently problematic since it divided the world into nuclear haves (the states that had tested a nuclear device by 1967) and nuclear have-nots (those that had not). But for two decades it was reasonably effective in preventing horizontal proliferation (the spread of nuclear weapons to other states). Unfortunately, the NPT has done nothing to prevent vertical proliferation, namely, the increase in the numbers and sophistication of nuclear weapons among the existing nuclear weapons states. During the Cold War, the United States and the Soviet Union agreed to work together to limit proliferation. The governments of several countries that could have developed nuclear weapons, such as Argentina, Brazil, Germany, Japan, and South Korea, restrained themselves because they believed the NPT reflected a fair bargain between China, France, the Soviet Union, the United Kingdom, and the United States (the five official nuclear weapons states and five permanent members of the UN Security Council) and the rest of the world. Both sides agreed that the world would be safer if the five nuclear states took steps to reduce their arsenals and worked toward the eventual goal of universal disarmament and the other states refrained from acquiring nuclear weapons at all.

So what went wrong? The first problem was that the NPT's principal progenitor, the United States, decided to walk away from the postwar rule-based order it had created, thus eroding the infrastructure on which the NPT's enforcement depends. During the time I was Singapore's ambassador to the UN, between 1984 and 1989, Jeane Kirkpatrick, the U.S. ambassador to the UN, treated the organization with contempt. She infamously said, "What takes place in the Security Council more closely resembles a mugging than either a political debate or an effort at problem-solving." She saw the postwar order as a set of constraints, not as a set of rules that the world should follow and the United States should help preserve. This undermined the NPT, because with no teeth of its own, no self-regulating or sanctioning mechanisms, and a clause allowing signatories to ignore obligations in the name of "supreme national interest," the treaty could only really be enforced by the UN Security Council. And once the United States began tearing holes in the fabric of the overall system, it created openings for violations of the NPT and its principles. Finally, by going to war with Iraq without UN authorization, the United States lost its moral authority to ask, for example, Iran to abide by Security Council resolutions.

Another problem has been the United States'—and other nuclear weapons states'—direct assault on the treaty. The NPT is fundamentally a social contract between the five nuclear weapons states and the rest of the world, based partly on the understanding that the nuclear powers will eventually give up their weapons. Instead, during the Cold War, the United States and the Soviet Union increased both the quantity and the sophistication of their nuclear weapons: the United States' nuclear stockpile peaked in 1966 at 31,700 warheads, and the Soviet Union's peaked in 1986 at 40,723. In fact, the United States and the Soviet Union developed their nuclear stockpiles so much that they actually ran out of militarily or economically significant targets. The numbers have declined dramatically since then, but even the current number of nuclear weapons held by the United States and Russia can wreak enormous damage on human civilization.

The nuclear states' decision to ignore Israel's nuclear weapons program was especially damaging to their authority. No nuclear weapons state has ever publicly acknowledged Israel's possession of nuclear weapons. Their silence has created a loophole in the NPT and delegitimized it in the eyes of Muslim nations. The consequences have been profound. When the West sermonizes that the world will become a more dangerous place when Iran acquires nuclear weapons, the Muslim world now shrugs.

India and Pakistan were already shrugging by 1998, when they tested their first nuclear weapons. When the international community responded by condemning the tests and applying sanctions on India, virtually all Indians saw through the hypocrisy and double standards of their critics. By not respecting their own obligations under the NPT, the five nuclear states had robbed their condemnations of any moral legitimacy; criticisms from Australia and Canada, which have also remained silent about Israel's bomb, similarly had no moral authority. The near-unanimous rejection of the NPT by the Indian establishment, which is otherwise very conscious of international opinion, showed how dead the treaty already was.

The world has lost its trust in the five nuclear weapons states and now sees them as the NPT's primary violators.

From time to time, common sense has entered discussions on nuclear weapons. President Ronald Reagan said more categorically than any U.S. president that the world would be better off without nuclear weapons. Last year, with the NPT in its death throes and the growing threat of loose nuclear weapons falling into the hands of terrorists forefront in everyone's mind, former Secretary of State George Shultz, former Defense Secretary William Perry, former Secretary of State Henry Kissinger, and former Senator Sam Nunn warned in *The Wall Street Journal* that the world was "now on the precipice of a new and dangerous nuclear era." They argued, "Unless urgent new actions are taken, the U.S. soon will be compelled to enter a new nuclear era that will be more precarious, psychologically disorienting, and economically even more costly than was Cold War deterrence." But these calls may have come too late. The world has lost its trust in the five nuclear weapons states and now sees them as the NPT's primary violators rather than its custodians. Those states' private cynicism about their obligations to the NPT has become public knowledge.

Contrary to what the West wants the rest of the world to believe, the nuclear weapons states, especially the United States and Russia, which continue to maintain thousands of nuclear weapons, are the biggest source of nuclear proliferation. Mohamed ElBaradei, the director general of the International Atomic Energy Agency, warned in *The Economist* in 2003, "The very existence of nuclear weapons gives rise to the pursuit of them. They are seen as a source of global influence, and are valued for their perceived deterrent effect. And as long as some countries possess them (or are protected by them in alliances) and others do not, this asymmetry breeds chronic global insecurity." Despite the Cold War, the second half of the twentieth century seemed to be moving the world toward a more civilized order. As the twenty-first century unfurls, the world seems to be sliding backward.

Irresponsible Stakeholders

After leading the world toward a period of spectacular economic growth in the second half of the twentieth century by promoting global free trade, the West has recently been faltering in its global economic leadership. Believing that low trade barriers and increasing trade interdependence would result in higher standards of living for all, European and U.S. economists and policymakers pushed for global economic liberalization. As a result, global trade grew from seven percent of the world's GDP in 1940 to 30 percent in 2005.

But a seismic shift has taken place in Western attitudes since the end of the Cold War. Suddenly, the United States and Europe no longer have a vested interest in the success of the East Asian economies, which they see less as allies and more as competitors. That change in Western interests was reflected in the fact that the West provided little real help to East Asia during the Asian financial crisis of 1997–98. The entry of China into the global marketplace, especially after its admission to the World Trade Organization, has made a huge difference in both economic and psychological terms. Many Europeans have lost confidence in their ability to compete with the Asians. And many Americans have lost confidence in the virtues of competition.

There are some knotty issues that need to be resolved in the current global trade talks, but fundamentally the negotiations are stalled because the conviction of the Western "champions" of free trade that free trade is good has begun to waver. When Americans and Europeans start to perceive themselves as losers in international trade, they also lose their drive to push for further trade liberalization. Unfortunately, on this front at least, neither China nor India (nor Brazil nor South Africa nor any other major developing country) is ready to take over the West's mantle. China, for example, is afraid that any effort to seek leadership in this area will stoke U.S. fears that it is striving for global hegemony. Hence, China is lying low. So, too, are the United States and Europe. Hence, the trade talks are stalled. The end of the West's promotion of global trade liberalization could well mean the end of the most spectacular

economic growth the world has ever seen. Few in the West seem to be reflecting on the consequences of walking away from one of the West's most successful policies, which is what it will be doing if it allows the Doha Round to fail.

At the same time that the Western governments are relinquishing their stewardship of the global economy, they are also failing to take the lead on battling global warming. The awarding of the Nobel Peace Prize to former U.S. Vice President Al Gore, a longtime environmentalist, and the UN's Intergovernmental Panel on Climate Change confirms there is international consensus that global warning is a real threat. The most assertive advocates for tackling this problem come from the U.S. and European scientific communities, but the greatest resistance to any effective action is coming from the U.S. government. This has left the rest of the world confused and puzzled. Most people believe that the greenhouse effect is caused mostly by the flow of current emissions. Current emissions do aggravate the problem, but the fundamental cause is the stock of emissions that has accumulated since the Industrial Revolution. Finding a just and equitable solution to the problem of greenhouse gas emissions must begin with assigning responsibility both for the current flow and for the stock of greenhouse gases already accumulated. And on both counts the Western nations should bear a greater burden.

The West has to learn to share power and responsibility for the management of global issues with the rest of the world.

When it comes to addressing any problem pertaining to the global commons, such as the environment, it seems only fair that the wealthier members of the international community should shoulder more responsibility. This is a natural principle of justice. It is also fair in this particular case given the developed countries' primary role in releasing harmful gases into the atmosphere. R. K. Pachauri, chair of the Intergovernmental Panel on Climate Change, argued last year, "China and India are certainly increasing their share, but they are not increasing their per capita emissions anywhere close to the levels that you have in the developed world." Since 1850, China has contributed less than 8 percent of the world's total emissions of carbon dioxide, whereas the United States is responsible for 29 percent and western Europe is responsible for 27 percent. Today, India's per capita greenhouse gas emissions are equivalent to only 4 percent of those of the United States and 12 percent of those of the European Union. Still, the Western governments are not clearly acknowledging their responsibilities and are allowing many of their citizens to believe that China and India are the fundamental obstacles to any solution to global warming.

Washington might become more responsible on this front if a Democratic president replaces Bush in 2009. But people in the West will have to make some real concessions if they are to reduce significantly their per capita share of global emissions. A cap-and-trade program may do the trick. Western countries will probably have to make economic sacrifices. One option might be, as the journalist Thomas Friedman has suggested, to impose a dollar-per-gallon tax on Americans' gasoline consumption. Gore has proposed a carbon tax. So far, however, few U.S. politicians have dared to make such suggestions publicly.

Temptations of the East

The Middle East, nuclear proliferation, stalled trade liberalization, and global warming are all challenges that the West is essentially failing to address. And this failure suggests that a systemic problem is emerging in the West's stewardship of the international order—one that Western minds are reluctant to analyze or confront openly. After having enjoyed centuries of global domination, the West has to learn to share power and responsibility for the management of global issues with the rest of the world. It has to forgo outdated organizations, such as the Organization for Economic Cooperation and Development, and outdated processes, such as the G-8, and deal with organizations and processes with a broader scope and broader representation. It was always unnatural for the 12 percent of the world population that lived in the West to enjoy so much global power. Understandably, the other 88 percent of the world population increasingly wants also to drive the bus of world history.

First and foremost, the West needs to acknowledge that sharing the power it has accumulated in global forums would serve its interests. Restructuring international institutions to reflect the current world order will be complicated by the absence of natural leaders to do the job. The West has become part of the problem, and the Asian countries are not yet ready to step in. On the other hand, the world does not need to invent any new principles to improve global governance; the concepts of domestic good governance can and should be applied to the international community. The Western principles of democracy, the rule of law, and social justice are among the world's best bets. The ancient virtues of partnership and pragmatism can complement them.

Democracy, the foundation of government in the West, is based on the premise that each human being in a society is an equal stakeholder in the domestic order. Thus, governments are selected on the basis of "one person, one vote." This has produced long-term stability and order in Western societies. In order to produce long-term stability and order worldwide, democracy should be the cornerstone of global society, and the planet's 6.6 billion inhabitants should become equal stakeholders. To inject the spirit of democracy into global governance and global decision-making, one must turn to institutions with universal representation, especially the UN. UN institutions such as the World Health Organization and the World Meteorological Organization enjoy widespread legitimacy because of their universal membership, which means their decisions are generally accepted by all the countries of the world.

The problem today is that although many Western actors are willing to work with specialized UN agencies, they are reluctant to strengthen the UN's core institution, the UN General Assembly, from which all these specialized agencies come. The UN General Assembly is the most representative body on the planet, and yet many Western countries are deeply skeptical of it. They are right to point out its imperfections. But they overlook the fact that this imperfect assembly enjoys legitimacy in the eyes of the people of this imperfect world. Moreover, the General Assembly has at times shown more common sense and prudence than some of the most sophisticated Western democracies. Of course, it takes time to persuade all of the UN's members to march in the same direction, but consensus building is precisely what gives legitimacy to the result. Most countries in the world respect and abide by most UN decisions because they believe in the authority of the UN. Used well, the body can be a powerful vehicle for making critical decisions on global governance.

The world today is run not through the General Assembly but through the Security Council, which is effectively run by the five permanent member states. If this model were adopted in the United States, the U.S. Congress would be replaced by a selective council comprised of only the representatives from the country's five most powerful states. Would the populations of the other 45 states not deem any such proposal absurd? The West must cease its efforts to prolong its undemocratic management of the global order and find ways to effectively engage the majority of the world's population in global decision-making.

Another fundamental principle that should underpin the global order is the rule of law. This hallowed Western principle insists that no person, regardless of his or her status, is above the law. Ironically, while being exemplary in implementing the rule of law at home, the United States is a leading international outlaw in its refusal to recognize the constraints of international law. Many Americans live comfortably with this contradiction while expecting other countries to abide by widely accepted treaties. Americans react with horror when Iran tries to walk away from the NPT. Yet they are surprised that the world is equally shocked when Washington abandons a universally accepted treaty such as the Comprehensive Test Ban Treaty.

The Bush administration's decision to exempt the United States from the provisions of international law on human rights is even more damaging. For over half a century, since Eleanor Roosevelt led the fight for the adoption of the Universal Declaration of Human Rights, the United States was the global champion of human rights. This was the result of a strong ideological conviction that it was the United States' God-given duty to create a more civilized world. It also made for a good ideological weapon during the Cold War: the free United States was fighting the unfree Soviet Union. But the Bush administration has stunned the world by walking away from universally accepted human rights conventions, especially those on torture. And much as the U.S. electorate could not be expected to tolerate an attorney general who broke his own laws from time to time, how can the global body politic be expected to respect a custodian of international law that violates these very rules?

Finally, on social justice, Western nations have slackened. Social justice is the cornerstone of order and stability in modern Western societies and the rest of the world. People accept inequality as long as some kind of social safety net exists to help the dispossessed. Most western European governments took this principle to heart after World War II and introduced welfare provisions as a way to ward off Marxist revolutions seeking to create socialist societies. Today, many Westerners believe that they are spreading social justice globally with their massive foreign aid to the developing world. Indeed, each year, the members of the Organization for Economic Cooperation and Development, according to the organization's own estimates, give approximately $104 billion to the developing world. But the story of Western aid to the developing world is essentially a myth. Western countries have put significant amounts of money into their overseas development assistance budgets, but these funds' primary purpose is to serve the immediate and short-term security and national interests of the donors rather than the long-term interests of the recipients.

Some Asian countries are now ready to join the West in becoming responsible custodians of the global order.

The experience of Asia shows that where Western aid has failed to do the job, domestic good governance can succeed. This is likely to be Asia's greatest contribution to world history. The success of Asia will inspire other societies on different continents to emulate it. In addition, Asia's march to modernity can help produce a more stable world order. Some Asian countries are now ready to join the West in becoming responsible custodians of the global order; as the biggest beneficiaries of the current system, they have powerful incentives to do so. The West is not welcoming Asia's progress, and its short-term interests in preserving its privileged position in various global institutions are trumping its long-term interests in creating a more just and stable world order. Unfortunately, the West has gone from being the world's primary problem solver to being its single biggest liability.

Critical Thinking

1. According to Kishore Mahbubani, what is the fundamental flaw in the West's strategic thinking?

2. What are the reasons, according to Mahbubani, for the West's declining influence?

3. Does Mahbubani's argument support or contradict the central arguments of articles 1 and 4?

Kɪsʜᴏʀᴇ Mᴀʜʙᴜʙᴀɴɪ is Dean of the Lee Kuan Yew School of Public Policy at the National University of Singapore. This essay is adapted from his latest book, *The New Asian Hemisphere: The Irresistible Shift of Global Power to the East* (Public Affairs, 2008).

Bolivia and Its Lithium

Can the "Gold of the 21st Century" help lift a nation out of poverty?

REBECCA HOLLENDER AND JIM SHULTZ

Executive Summary

The resource curse refers to the paradox that countries and regions with an abundance of natural resources, especially minerals and fuels, tend to have less economic growth and worse development outcomes than countries with fewer natural resources.

Bolivia has a long history with that curse, dating back to the theft of its silver at the hands of the Spanish during the colonial era. Today Bolivia seeks to break that curse with what some call "the gold of the 21st century": lithium. This report examines Bolivia's prospects for doing so.

I. Lithium—The Super Hero of Metals

Every time we pick up a cell phone or iPod, look at our watch, or plug-in a laptop we are relying on batteries that contain lithium. It is also used in ceramics and glass production, bi-polar medication, air conditioners, lubricants, nuclear weaponry, and other products. The lightest metal on Earth, lithium is mined from many sources, but most cheaply from underground brines like those found in abundance under Bolivia's vast Salar de Uyuni.

Today the global focus on lithium is about its potential as a key ingredient in a new generation of electric car batteries. Powerful global players are investing billions of dollars in lithium's future. Some predictions speculate that lithium car battery sales could jump from $100 million per year to $103 billion per year in the next 2 decades. If so, the countries that possess lithium are poised to become much bigger players in the global economy.

Despite the growing enthusiasm about lithium's future, there are also real doubts as well. The process for transforming lithium into its commercially valuable form, lithium carbonate, is complex and expensive. The electric vehicle batteries currently being developed with lithium are still too large and heavy, and too slow to charge. The batteries are so expensive that they put the cost of electric cars beyond the reach of most consumers. Lithium batteries also have a record of catching fire. So while lithium car batteries might become a massive global market, they could also turn out to be the energy equivalent of the 8-track tape.

II. The Race for Bolivia's Lithium

Based even on conservative estimates, Bolivia's lithium reserves are the largest in the world. The Salar de Uyuni, a 10,000 square kilometer (3,860 square miles) expanse of salt-embedded minerals, located in Bolivia's department of Southwest Potosí, is ground zero for Bolivia's lithium dreams.

Foreign corporations and governments alike are lining up to court a Bolivian government intent on getting the best deal possible for its people. Among the major players are two Japanese giants, Mitsubishi and Sumitomo, the latter of which already has a stake in the controversial San Cristobal Mine known for contaminating the same region. The French electric vehicle manufacturer, Bolloré, is also courting the Morales government, as are the governments of South Korea, Brazil, and Iran.

The Bolivian government has sketched out a general plan for the various phases of its lithium ambitions, but many of the details of how all this will be done have yet to be defined. To get its feet wet in the technical and economic waters of lithium, the government of Bolivia has invested $5.7 million in the development of a "pilot plant" at the edge of the Salar de Uyuni. The plant is intended to test drive the steps in getting the lithium-rich brine out from under the Salar's crust and separating it into its distinct (and marketable) parts. Based on the experience of this pilot plant, the government aims to then construct a much larger industrial-scale plant, capable of producing up to 30,000 to 40,000 metric tons of lithium carbonate per year. This will be followed by a third phase to produce marketable lithium compounds, which the government plans to undertake in partnership with foreign investors.

To get help in meeting the formidable challenges it faces, the government has assembled a Scientific Advisory Committee (Scientific Research Committee for the Industrialization of the Evaporitic Resources of Bolivia) comprised of experts from universities, private companies, and governments, to give free, and mutually beneficial, advice.

III. The Challenges Ahead on Bolivia's Lithium Highway

At heart, Bolivia's lithium ambitions are simple: to lift a people out of poverty by squeezing the maximum benefit possible from a natural resource on the cutting edge of global markets. But between where Bolivia sits today and where it aims to go on its lithium highway there are major challenges that it will need to face:

Getting the Economics Right

Bolivia's dreams of lithium wealth involve hitting a complicated moving target. The electric car battery market looks like the most lucrative for lithium development, and is the one the Morales government says it's aiming for (Morales also claims that Bolivia will produce electric vehicles), but how big that market will be, and when it will peak, is still just a guessing game. Bolivia could aim for more traditional lithium markets, such as glass and ceramics, but they aren't nearly so potentially profitable. A middle option would be established types of lithium batteries for products such as watches, cell phones, iPods, laptops and other electronic gadgets.

How much will it cost to build a lithium battery industry in Bolivia? That number is one of the most elusive pieces of information in the picture. If Bolivia kicks into full industrial mode the budget would be $200 million or higher just for the main plant. But that still doesn't include massive additional investments in supporting chemical industries and huge infrastructure development in a region where today even keeping the lights on is a technological challenge. One Bolivian official has placed the potential cost at as high as $1 billion. Because of this, Bolivia is looking for serious partnerships with investors, an approach that some local community groups do not support.

The fact that the government might suddenly have substantial new revenues from lithium is also no guarantee that the Bolivian people will end up any better off. Those revenues could easily become a magnet for corruption, waste and favoritism and there will be a constant tension between the demand to use the funds for public goods and reinvesting them into state-controlled lithium production.

Environmental Impacts

Lost in the great Bolivian lithium race is a set of very deep and real environmental concerns. In the name of providing cleaner cars to the wealthy countries of the north, Bolivia's beautiful and rare Salar could end up an environmental wasteland. The adequacy of Bolivia's environmental strategy for lithium development in Southwest Potosí is doubted by several well-regarded Bolivian environmental organizations.

One major problem that lithium development could cause is a major water crisis. The region already suffers from a serious water shortage, impacting quinoa farmers, llama herders, the region's vital tourism industry, and drinking water sources. While Bolivian officials contend that the lithium project's water requirements will be minimal, their estimates are based on very limited and incomplete information.

Contamination of the air, water and soil is also a major concern. Large quantities of toxic chemicals will be needed to process the predicted 30,000 to 40,000 tons of lithium per year that the project expects to mine. The escape of such chemicals via leaching, spills, or air emissions is a danger that threatens the communities and the ecosystem as a whole. Reports from Chile's Salar de Atacama describe a landscape scarred by mountains of discarded salt and huge canals filled with blue chemically contaminated water.

Bolivian officials have dismissed those risks, and the government system in place to protect the environment is inadequate at best. Public institutions, such as Bolivia's Ministry of the Environment and Water, which are responsible for ensuring compliance with environmental requirements, clearly lack the capacity or authority to intervene in an effective way.

The Threat to Communities

How do the people and communities who live in Southwest Potosí feel about their homeland becoming the site of what could soon become one of the biggest industrial projects their nation has ever built? To be sure, many groups in the region have long supported lithium development, seeing it as a vital opportunity for increased income and development. But there are deep concerns as well.

Quinoa producers and tourism operators have expressed concern about supposed benefits that the Bolivian government has promised from lithium, saying that the benefits are irrelevant to local needs and could easily damage the two industries that are thriving in the region—agriculture and tourism. But Bolivia's laws that guarantee community involvement in planning are as weak as its environmental protections. While some local organizations—especially ones that actively support Evo Morales' political party (MAS)—have been engaged, others say they have not.

The Capacity of the Bolivian Government to Manage the Program

Finally, there are concerns about the chronic problems faced by the Bolivian government to manage such an ambitious program—problems that pre-date President Morales. To pull off its lithium ambitions, Bolivia will need highly trained and qualified experts, in the technical and scientific aspects of lithium, in business management and economics, and in social and environmental impacts. And these experts need to be solely accountable to the Bolivian people, not to foreign governments or corporations.

IV. Conclusion—Can Bolivia Beat the Resource Curse?

Whether these challenges are surmountable for the people of Bolivia and their leaders is an open debate. To be certain, there is real potential here. The demand for lithium is clearly on the rise, and with the possibility in the future of a very big rise. Bolivia is indeed sitting on the world's largest supply of lithium and it is being courted by some serious players. And importantly, all this is happening just as Bolivia has a government that has committed itself to a different way of doing resource business.

In practical terms, the government is also doing some important things right, such as beginning with a pilot effort to test the technological and economic waters. But there are many things that can go badly wrong on the lithium road ahead. In the uphill battle to make Bolivia's lithium dreams a reality, clearly the first step is to acknowledge and understand the economic, environmental, social, and capacity challenges.

What Bolivia is trying to do is hard—very hard. It is trying to break a curse—the paradox of plenty—that few impoverished nations escape. Its effort to escape that curse is extremely important, which is why so much of the world is watching. It is an experiment that is economic, social, political, technological and practical all at the same time. The fate of its success lies in the hands of the Bolivian people and in their ability to hold their leaders accountable, both for their own benefit and the planet's.

Critical Thinking

1. Why has lithium become an important raw material?
2. What do the authors mean by a "development paradox"?
3. Is Bolivia's approach to the development of its lithium reserves similar to Sachs's development approach?

Supply and Demand
Human Trafficking in the Global Economy

SIDDHARTH KARA

On New Year's Day 2011, I flew to Lagos to research human trafficking in Nigeria. Towards the end of my trip, I visited a small town called Badagry, about a two-hour drive west of Lagos. In 1502, Portuguese colonists built one of the first slave-trading posts along the coast of West Africa in this city. The non-descript, two-story building still stands today as a museum, but for more than 300 years, it was one of the most active slave-trading outposts in West Africa. Estimates are that almost 600,000 West Africans were shipped from Badagry to the Americas to be agricultural slaves. That figure represents approximately one in twenty of all slaves transported from West Africa to the Americas during the entire time of the North Atlantic Slave Trade.

It was a haunting experience walking through the old slave-holding pens, gazing at the iron shackles, imagining the fear and terror that must have coursed through the veins of slaves as they awaited their fates. Like so many millions today, those 600,000 individuals transported from Badagry to the Americas were victims of human trafficking. In fact, all 12 to 13 million of the West African slaves transported across the Atlantic to the Americas were victims of human trafficking. While their lengthy journeys at sea are very different from the journeys of most human trafficking victims today, the purpose of those journeys remains the same: the callous exploitation of the labor of vulnerable people in order to maximize profit.

The Nature of Slavery Today

However, unlike the agricultural and domestic slaves of the past, today's victims of modern-day slave trading are exploited in countless industries, and they are vastly more profitable. Whether for commercial sex, construction, domestic work, carpet weaving, agriculture, tea and coffee, shrimp, fish, minerals, dimensional stones, gems, or numerous other industries that I have investigated, human trafficking touches almost every sector of the globalized economy in a way it never has before. Understanding the reasons for this shift in the fundamental nature of human trafficking is vital if more effective efforts to combat it are to be deployed. The key thesis to understand is that the slave exploiter's ability to generate immense profits at almost no real risk directly catalyzed the pervasiveness of all forms of contemporary slave labor exploitation.

One point is crucial to establish from the start—slavery still exists. But what exactly is "modern slavery"? There is still considerable debate regarding the definition of terms such as "slavery," "forced labor," "bonded labor," "child labor," and "human trafficking." With "slavery," we can go as far back as the League of Nations Slavery Convention of 1926 and the International Labor Organization's Forced Labor Convention of 1930. These early definitions focused on the exercise of power attaching to a right of ownership over another human being.

Over the decades, international conventions and jurisprudence relating to slavery shifted away from targeting actual rights of ownership toward the nature of the exploitation, particularly as it involves coercion (physical or other), nominal or no compensation, and the absence of freedom of employment or movement. The term "forced labor" has generally come to replace the term "slavery," given the powerful historical and emotional connotations of the latter term. Similarly, "human trafficking" has come to replace the term "slave trade."

It is open to debate whether these terminological substitutions are helpful, but when it comes to "human trafficking," I believe the use of this term has done considerable disservice to the tactical prioritization required to combat these crimes more effectively. Definitions of the term "human trafficking," such as that found in the United Nations Protocol to Prevent, Suppress, and Punish Trafficking in Persons (the Palermo Protocol of 2000) or the US Trafficking Victims Protection Act (TVPA, of the same year), have historically suffered from a greater focus on the movement connotation of the term "trafficking" rather than the exploitation involved. The result has been a prioritization of efforts to stop cross-border migration instead of slave-like exploitation, the real purpose of trafficking; this approach has met with limited success.

Terminological debates aside, within the broad context of modern-day slavery, I estimate the number of slaves at the end of 2010 to have been between 30 and 36 million. Depending on how one specifies terms such as "coercion" and "held captive," the number of people considered slaves could be slightly lower or considerably higher. There are many modes by which slaves are exploited, and these can be aggregated into various categories. I have chosen three: bonded labor, forced labor, and trafficked slaves.

Bonded, Forced Labor, and Trafficked Slaves

The economic model of bonded labor dates back centuries. In essence, individuals borrow money or assets and are bound in servitude until the debts are repaid, and often they never are. Forced laborers are similar to bonded laborers but without the intermingling of credit and labor relationships. However, the line between bonded labor and forced labor is easily blurred. The more farcical a debt becomes, the more the bonded laborer is actually a forced laborer.

Human trafficking is essentially modern-day slave trading, which ensnares millions of people in debt bondage or forced labor conditions in a plethora of industries. Regardless of the industry of exploitation, there are three common steps to the business model of most human trafficking networks: acquisition, movement, and exploitation, which often results in one or more counts of re-trafficking. Acquisition of trafficked slaves primarily occurs in one of five ways: deceit, sale by family, abduction, seduction or romance (with sex trafficking), or recruitment by former slaves. Poor or marginally subsistent individuals are the ones most vulnerable to exploitation because of their economic desperation.

Trafficked slaves are moved from countries of origin through transit countries into destination countries, except in the case of internal trafficking, during which the same country acts as origin, transit, and destination. However, trafficking victims often undergo multiple stops in several countries, where they are repeatedly resold and exploited. At each destination, victims are threatened, abused, and tortured. They may be told they must work off the "debt" of trafficking them between jobs. The accounting of these debts is invariably exploitive, involving deductions for living expenses and exorbitant interest rates. For others,

no farce of debt repayment is provided—they are simply kept in a state of perpetual forced labor.

Slave exploiters often re-sell trafficked slaves to new exploiters. If the slaves do not escape, their cycle of exploitation may never end. Even if they do escape, they often return to the same conditions of poverty or vulnerability that led to their initial enslavement, resulting in one or more instances of re-trafficking.

Most importantly, slave exploiters and traffickers take advantage of the fact that movement in the globalized world is exceedingly difficult to disrupt. Borders are porous, documents can be forged, and it can be difficult to identify a potential victim of human trafficking before the forced labor has taken place. Movement is also inexpensive. Whereas ships from Badagry to the Americas had to spend weeks at sea at great expense to transport slaves to the point of exploitation, today's victims of human trafficking can be transported from one side of the planet to the other in a few days or less, at a nominal cost of doing business even when airfare is involved. For these and other reasons, any efforts to combat human trafficking by thwarting movement will prove highly challenging.

> "Whereas ships from Badagry to the Americas had to spend weeks at sea . . . to transport slaves to the point of exploitation, today's victims of human trafficking can be transported from one side of the planet to the other in a few days or less . . ."

The final step in the human trafficking business model is exploitation. Exploitation of trafficked slaves primarily involves the coercion of some form of labor or services with little or no compensation. The location and nature of the coercion is industry-specific. In cases of commercial sex, exploitation involves multiple counts of coerced sex acts every day in physical confinement and under threats of harm to the slave or their loved ones back home. The brutality of this form of human trafficking cannot be overstated. It involves rape, torture, forced drug use, and the wholesale destruction of a human body, mind, and spirit.

Another common sector is construction, which may involve exploitation of human trafficking victims under strict confinement at construction sites, with little or no payment for months at a time. In agriculture, trafficked slaves are confined to the area of harvest and are coerced to work under threats of violence or eviction from tenant homes, and with minimal or no wages. When it comes to carpets, trafficked child slaves are locked inside shacks where they are drugged and beaten to work for eighteen hours a day, suffering spinal deformation and respiratory ailments.

For these and other products that are tainted by exploitative labor, I have traced the complete supply chains from the point of production to the retailers that sell the tainted products in the United States. This is an important step toward catalyzing the kind of corporate and consumer awareness campaigns required to strike back against the use of trafficked, slave, or child labor in products consumed in Western markets. However, in order to truly combat human trafficking, we must understand exactly why it has become so prevalent throughout the global economy. What compels those involved in this type of exploitation to engage in it?

Incentives Underlying Trafficking

Just like most law-abiding citizens, criminals are rational economic agents, and when a near risk-free opportunity to generate immense profits emerges, they will flock to it. Modern-day slavery is immensely more profitable than past forms of slavery. This is the key factor driving the tremendous demand for new slaves through human trafficking networks. Whereas slaves in 1850 could be purchased for a global weighted average of between US$9,500 and US$11,000 (adjusted for inflation) and generate roughly 15 to 20 percent in annual return on investment, today's slaves sell for a global weighted average of US$420 and can generate 300 to 500 percent or more in annual return on investment, depending on the industry. In terms of risk, the laws against human trafficking and forced labor in most countries involve relatively anemic prison sentences and little or no economic penalties. Even where there are stiff financial penalties stipulated in the law, such as in the United States, the levels of prosecution and conviction of slave exploiters remain paltry.

As a result, the real risk of exploiting trafficked slaves is almost nonexistent. That is to say, the costs of exploiting a slave are miniscule as weighed against the immense profits that criminals can reap. This basic economic reality gives us a clear sense of some of the powerful forces of demand that promote the trafficking and slave-like exploitation of men, women, and children around the world. I believe these forces are also the ones we can most effectively disrupt in the near term.

However, there is also a supply-side to human trafficking, meaning those forces that promote the supply of potential human trafficking victims. We must also mitigate these forces, though it will prove difficult to effect a near-term impact on the human trafficking industry through supply-side efforts alone. The supply of contemporary trafficked

slaves is promoted by longstanding factors such as poverty, lawlessness, social instability, military conflict, environmental disaster, corruption, and acute bias against female gender and minority ethnicities.

The policies and governance of economic globalization sharply exacerbated these and other forces during the 1990s. The deepening of rural poverty, the net extraction of wealth and resources from poor economies into richer ones, the evaporation of social safety nets under structural adjustment programs, the overall destabilization of transition economies, and the broad-based erosion of real human freedoms across the developing world all increased the vulnerability of rural, poor, and otherwise disenfranchised populations. These forces unleashed mass-migration trends that shrewd criminals and slave traders could easily exploit. While these global economic and sociocultural supply-side drivers of the contemporary human trafficking industry will require considerable, long-term efforts to redress, we do not have to rely on supply-side measures alone to severely mitigate, if not virtually abolish, human trafficking.

In fact, the demand-side of most human trafficking industries is highly vulnerable to disruption. The specific forces of demand that drive any industry will vary. For example, in commercial sex, male demand to purchase commercial sex is a key factor of demand that would not be present with construction or tea. However, there are always two forces of demand that are common to any human trafficking industry and they are both economic: slave exploiter demand for maximum profit and consumer demand for lower retail prices (the price elasticity of demand).

For almost any business in the world, labor is typically the highest cost component to overall operating expenses. Thus, throughout history, producers have tried to find ways to minimize labor costs. Slavery is the extreme of this. Slaves afford a virtually nil cost of labor. With a drastically reduced cost of labor, total operating costs are substantially reduced, allowing the slave owner to maximize profit. However, drastically lower labor costs also allow producers to become more competitive by lowering retail prices. The retail price of any product or service is largely based on the costs of producing, distributing, and marketing that product or service, along with the available supply of the product or alternatives, and whatever brand premium the market will bear. If a major component of cost is stripped out of the production model, then producers can finely balance their desire to maximize profit and lower retail price.

Depending on the product, the lower it costs, the more people will tend to purchase it. Conversely, the more expensive a product is, the less people will tend to purchase it. This concept is called the price elasticity of demand,

and depending on the specific product or service, the "elasticity" can be high or low, implying changes in price can have large or small impacts on consumer demand. Because consumers in general almost always prefer the lower priced version of the same product or service (if all other variables such as quality are the same), producers often try to compete by minimizing price, and one of the most effective ways to do this while retaining profitability is to exploit labor.

In a globalized economy, where products are available in our nearby shops from all over the world, the need to be price competitive is greater than ever. A seller of t-shirts or rice no longer just competes with producers nearby, but with producers on the other side of the world. As an example, I was conducting research into bonded labor in South Asia during the summer of 2010, and an exporter of precious stones in Chennai told me quite candidly that he was forced to exploit low-wage labor (actually bonded and child labor) in order to compete with the Chinese, who he believed to be doing the same. Because transportation costs are 90 percent less than they were in 1920, and since all types of exploited labor can be used to minimize production expenses, the entire world is in competition, and human trafficking has evolved from the old world into the globalized world as a key way in which unscrupulous producers can minimize labor costs to advance profits and remain price competitive.

Combating Trafficking

Understanding the twin economic forces of demand that have helped catalyze the accretion in levels of human trafficking throughout the global economy suggests two tactical priorities in efforts to combat these crimes. First, attack the profitability human traffickers enjoy. An attack on profitability will reduce aggregate demand for slave labor because slave owners will be forced to accept a lower-profit (hence less desirable) business, or they will pass the increased costs to the consumer by elevating retail price, which will in turn reduce consumer demand.

The most effective way to attack profitability is to elevate real risk. Depending on the type of industry, the tactics will vary, but such efforts will assuredly involve the following: elevated efforts by law enforcement to proactively investigate and intervene in human trafficking crimes; the expansion of community-based antislavery efforts; elevated funding for anti-trafficking police, prosecutors, and judges, especially in developing nations; fast-track courts to prosecute trafficking crimes quickly so as to minimize risks to the survivor-witness; and a massive increase in the financial penalties associated with human trafficking crimes, including enterprise corruption, asset forfeiture, and victim compensation, to help former slaves get their lives back on track.

An increase in penalties, along with increased prosecution and conviction levels achieved through the kinds of tactics described above, should elevate the real risk and cost of human trafficking to an economically detrimental level. Put in criminal law terms, we are trying to elevate the deterrent and retributive value of the real penalty associated with the commission of slave-related crimes to a far more effective level. In turn, criminals will likely diversify their operations to other, less toxic opportunities, just as quickly as they originally flocked to trafficking and labor exploitation.

The other main force of demand relates to consumers. While we typically prefer to buy our products at the best price, we are also far removed from the complex supply chains that may be tainted by trafficked or slave labor at the bottom end of the production process. However, we are also in control of our consumer force of demand, so it is up to us to demand that lawmakers enact provisions whereby corporations must investigate and certify that their supply chains are free of trafficked, slave, or child labor of any kind. Consumers must also demand that companies whose products they purchase take a leadership role in conducting the kind of investigation and certification required, and that such activities should be a regular aspect of their internal controls and operating model. By attacking the fundamental motivation behind the exploitation of trafficking slaves—profits—and by leveraging consumer power to shift the market away from the "cheap at all costs" product to the product that is morally and socially responsible, a powerful near-term impact can be achieved on the business of human trafficking.

The ugliness of human trafficking dates back centuries, and even though we agreed 150 years ago as a human civilization that slavery is unacceptable, it is more pervasive and expansive today than it was centuries ago when the slave port at Badagry was in its prime. The forces of globalization have made human trafficking a highly profitable and virtually risk-free enterprise. As a matter of ensuring basic human dignity and freedom, the global community must utilize every resource available to combat traffickers and slave exploiters by elevating the real risk and cost of the crime, while eliminating the immense profitability that human traffickers and slave exploiters currently enjoy.

The persistence of human trafficking is an affront to human dignity and a denial of any claims of moral legitimacy by contemporary capitalist civilization. The time is long overdue for the world to come together to deploy the kinds of sustained interventions required to eliminate this evil forever.

Critical Thinking

1. What are the causes of human trafficking and slave labor?

2. How does globalization contribute to human trafficking?

3. What does Kara propose to discourage this practice?

SIDDHARTH KARA is an Affiliate of the Human Rights and Social Movements Program, and a Fellow with the Carr Center Program on Human Trafficking and Modern-Day Slavery at the Harvard Kennedy School of Government.

From *Harvard International Review,* Summer 2011, pp. 66–71. Copyright © 2011 by the President of Harvard College. Reprinted by permission via Sheridan Reprints.

More Aid Is Not the Answer

"Most analysts on the continent do not share donor nations' optimism that a big push in aid will make a big difference in the lives of poor Africans."

JONATHAN GLENNIE

Africa needs help—of this there should be no doubt. Some African countries in the past decade saw encouragingly strong growth in gross domestic product (GDP), and this can be an important part of poverty reduction. Yet hopes that the region would be somewhat immune to the recent global financial crisis have proved unfounded, and the continent remains by far the world's poorest.

In the past two years, not only has global demand for African commodity exports shrunk (except in China), but the region's financial architecture has turned out to be not as independent from the rest of the world as had been supposed. And while Africa receives relatively little foreign investment compared to other parts of the world, even that has fallen significantly.

So Africa does need aid. The question is, what kind of aid? The simple (and simplistic) calculation at the heart of the developed world's present attitude toward Africa is this: Sub-Saharan Africa is poor; if rich countries send it more money, it will be less poor, and people living in poverty will be better off.

The theory seems both logical and fair. More aid should mean less poverty, more schools and hospitals, fewer children dying of preventable diseases, and more roads and infrastructure to support developing economies. But, unfortunately, it is not that simple. Official aid to Africa (as distinct from private charity) has often meant more poverty, more hungry people, worse basic services for poor people, and increased damage to already precarious democratic institutions.

For African nations, along with other developing countries, the recent financial crisis and the ongoing global downturn present an opportunity to emerge from a vicious cycle of aid dependency and lack of accountability, and to move toward a virtuous circle of accountability and independence. The many options and decisions regarding aid currently on the international community's and African nations' table should be judged in this light. And they should be assessed with the understanding that what matters are not just economic consequences, but also shifts in power and accountability.

The New Aid Era

According to the World Bank, developing countries in 2010 face a financing shortfall of up to $700 billion, as a consequence of falling export receipts, remittances, and foreign investment. Aid has been the standard response to cash shortages in the past and, predictably, it is again one of the central issues under debate. Pressure has mounted both to reduce aid (as donor governments seek to balance their budgets and focus on national priorities) and to increase aid (to help poor countries that, according to the accepted wisdom, are not responsible for the global crisis yet are suffering its consequences).

As donor governments look for ways to cut expenditures on non-priority activities, some aid campaigners are shifting away from calling for a doubling of aid to Africa, instead trying to ensure that assistance at least does not tail off. But to continue to focus attention on the amount of aid provided would be both to ignore mistakes of the past and to miss opportunities that the present offers.

Aid to Africa has risen year on year since the turn of the millennium, though ambitious targets set by donors have not been reached. Official data show development aid to Africa, depending on which figures you use, either doubling or almost tripling since 2000, with predictions of more increases in years to come. As Angel Gurría, the secretary general of the Organization for Economic Cooperation and Development, has observed, "We are talking here about an increase in official development assistance of a magnitude and in a time frame that has never been attempted before in the history of the aid effort."

Underpinning the impressive numbers are influential studies published in the past few years (such as a 2005 report on the United Nations' Millennium Project, directed by the globe-trotting American economist Jeffrey Sachs, and a 2005 report by the Commission for Africa, chaired by then–Prime Minister Tony Blair of Britain) that provide the theoretical and evidentiary basis for this new era of aid. These reports buttress the aid optimism that is now the political consensus in donor countries, and they seek to turn back a tide of literature that, beginning in the 1990s, has questioned the impact of aid on poverty reduction.

But most analysts on the continent do not share donor nations' optimism that a big push in aid will make a big difference in the lives of poor Africans. It is hard to find a single African, nongovernmental organization that is actively campaigning for aid increases, while many explicitly reject the idea that huge increases in assistance are the way to achieve growth and development.

It is hard to find a single African, nongovernmental organization that is actively campaigning for aid increases.

In a 2005 literature review, Moses Isooba of Uganda's Community Development Resource Network found that "a majority of civil society actors in Africa see aid as a fundamental cause of Africa's deepening poverty." He went on to acknowledge that foreign assistance can make "a lasting difference in helping people to lift themselves out of poverty," but he called for a radical rethinking regarding the purpose and nature of aid giving. Charles Lwanga-Ntale of Development Research and Training, another Ugandan NGO, has observed "almost unanimous pessimism among African civil society and academia about the unworkable nature of aid, given the way in which it is structured and delivered."

According to Siapha Kamara of the Social Enterprise Development Foundation of West Africa: "Official Africa tends to be more enthusiastic about the anticipated increase in international aid than civil society. . . . The more African governments are dependent on international aid, the less ordinary citizens such as farmers, workers, teachers, or nurses have a meaningful say in politics and economic policies."

Good, Bad, Ugly

Why should so many experts in Africa question the good that aid is doing their countries? Because, while most people in rich countries consider aid to be a simple act of generosity, Africans understand it is far more complex.

To get a clearer picture of what is happening, it helps to distinguish among the various effects of foreign aid in Africa. One category is direct impacts. These are easiest to measure, and they are the ones about which we hear the most in the media—how many people have been vaccinated, how many schools have been built, and so on. Direct impacts also include less publicized and often harmful side effects such as, for example, the displacement of people by large projects like dams or mines.

A second type of impact is indirect macroeconomic consequences. Large inflows of foreign money affect prices and incentives, and the effects can be damaging to poor people if the inflows are not managed well. For example, increases in aid to Tanzania in the late 1990s led to inflation, which in turn led authorities to tighten credit, which meant private firms found it harder to expand. The syndrome that economists call Dutch Disease is a potentially serious problem for African aid recipients. When a country's exchange rate is allowed to fluctuate, large aid inflows strengthen the national currency, which makes exports less competitive and imports cheaper. As a result, people depending on export industries suffer, as do domestic producers that compete with imports.

Constituting a third and highly controversial category are the impacts of aid conditionality. Official development assistance provided by multilateral institutions and foreign governments often comes with conditions attached, and these in effect dictate policy making. These policy prescriptions have not always been helpful. For example, international demands during economic downturns for reduced deficits and increased interest rates have reflected the policies that many developed countries, with the sovereignty to make their own decisions, typically avoid.

But even more problematic than the policies promoted by donors is a fourth impact of aid—its effect on the relationship between governments and the governed. It is generally agreed that African governments' shortcomings in accountability and effectiveness over recent decades have been a major factor in the region's low growth and insignificant poverty reduction. What is less discussed, but is becoming increasingly clear, is that dependency on aid from foreign donors has undermined development of the basic institutions needed to govern and the vital link of accountability between state and citizen.

In Mali, a recent study by Isaline Bergamaschi found that, as donors' influence over policy has grown, the government's will and capacity to take the lead and manage the aid relationship has declined. "If the current political situation seems characterized by a certain degree of inertia, a lack of development strategy, weak capacities, and compliance with donors," wrote Bergamaschi, "it can only be understood as the result of the weakening of the state and donor entanglement in national institutions and politics, and several decades of aid dependence." Likewise, observers have described Ghana's federal budget as a façade, aimed at satisfying aid donors rather than serving as a genuine and thought-through spending plan.

The effect of such dependency has been to retard African civic development in fundamental and long-lasting ways. It is what Kamara was referring to when he talked about ordinary people not having a meaningful say in decisions about how their countries are run.

Optimists and Pessimists

In response to gradually building pressure around the globe for more aid, the Group of Eight industrial nations in July 2005 met in Scotland and released a communiqué promising substantially more assistance, though not all that was being demanded. On top of an agreement to forgive large amounts of debt, the G-8 members pledged $50 billion (some of it previously announced) in aid to developing nations by 2010, of which half would go to Africa.

A spokesman for Oxfam International, a leading British NGO, commented at the time that "The G-8's aid increase could save the lives of 5 million children by 2010—but 50 million children's lives will still be lost because the G-8 didn't go as far as they should have done. If the $50 billion increase had kicked in immediately, it could have lifted 300 million people out of poverty in the next five years."

This kind of claim is common on the aid campaigning circuit. Campaigners need to make clear statements about the impacts of policies. But even allowing for the fact that mega-calculations will always be more than slightly arbitrary, yet are still important to convey the magnitude of what is at stake, this statement was highly misleading. Why? Because it was made on the basis of a very lopsided analysis, which looks only at the most direct and beneficial outcomes of aid.

If one considers only the positive column on the balance sheet, ignoring all the damaging consequences of aid, it is certainly possible that, if spent well, aid money could have the kinds of benefits alluded to. Aid spent well can put children through school, build infrastructure, and save lives.

But what about all the other impacts? What about the possibly harmful effects on exchange rates and prices, with the serious consequences these might have on workers and consumers? What about the long-term consequences of consistently immature and unaccountable state institutions? Where are these impacts taken into account when we calculate millions of lives saved per billions of aid dollars spent?

At the other extreme in debates about aid to Africa are the aid pessimists. The economist Dambisa Moyo is currently the most notable of these, having attracted wide attention with her 2009 book *Dead Aid: Why Aid Is Not Working and How There Is Another Way for Africa*. Moyo's critique of aid dependency is valid. She is right about the harm done to the development of effective and accountable governance in Africa by high levels of government-to-government aid. But hers is not a serious analytical study. It is an anti-aid polemic of a sort common in the conservative media of the United States, where the only facts cited are ones that bolster a case, and where exaggeration is considered par for the course.

Rather than accepting simplistic notions—that more aid equals less poverty, or that aid only and always increases poverty—we need to look at the evidence. All the evidence. In contrast to aid optimists and aid pessimists, who selectively use evidence either to support or to dismiss aid, we need to recognize that the impacts of aid are complex. Only when we assess these effects dispassionately and systematically can we have any real expectation of making a positive and sustained impact on human rights, development, and poverty reduction in Africa.

Aid Realism

This approach can be termed aid realism. Aid realism means not getting swept away by the ethical clamor to "do something" when a proper analysis shows that what is being done is ineffective or harmful. And it means not bowing to an ideological anti-aid position in the face of the rights and urgent needs of millions of people. It means carefully analyzing the overall impact of foreign aid in African nations—first, to see how aid in itself can be improved, and, second, to question its importance in relation to other policies and factors that influence development and poverty reduction in the region.

Such an analysis emphatically does not lead to the conclusion that the West should leave Africa alone. African civil society, while heavily critical of foreign assistance, is not sitting on its haunches in despair, and neither should anyone else. There are many positive measures that rich countries should take right now to help Africans reduce poverty and improve human rights.

For example, far more money flows out of the continent each year than arrives there in aid, but where are the campaign to stem illegal capital flows via tax havens? Likewise, rich countries need to overhaul rules on international property rights and foreign investment. They should act on climate change, and invest more in transferable technology. They should better regulate an arms trade that causes turmoil in Africa. They should do many things they are not doing now.

In fact, it will be almost impossible for African states to reduce their reliance on aid without the international community's adopting a range of supporting measures. If the first reason to stop campaigning for aid increases is that aid may be doing more harm than good in some countries, the second is that all the emphasis on aid is obscuring more important policies that the West should be adopting to help Africans escape poverty.

The dominance of aid in the West's thinking about Africa is one of the reasons that other, more important, actions are not taken. Rich-country leaders are not feeling enough political pressure to make the important changes. Aid is easier—never mind all the problems it brings with it—and it benefits donors.

After all, geopolitical considerations, not analyses of poverty, have governed most donor choices about aid spending. Assistance to Africa swelled during the cold war and then declined in the 1990s, when poverty on the continent was increasing sharply. Now, in the context of a global war on terrorism, donor nations—including particularly the United States—again want to use aid to influence the politics of other countries. But aid is not always good for the recipient nations' citizens and institutions.

Decades of Dependency

Dependency is the one issue that, more than any other, separates the current period from previous episodes of aid enthusiasm. Aid dependency can be measured by looking at aid as a percentage of a recipient country's GDP, and seeing how that ratio changes over time. When official development assistance started in the 1960s, it accounted for 2.3 percent of African GDP, similar to the proportion in South Asia (home to large aid recipients like India and Bangladesh).

What has happened since is instructive. While aid to South Asia has steadily declined, and now makes up around 1 per cent of GDP, aid to Africa has trended the other way, skyrocketing in the 1980s and hardly falling since. It now averages around 9 percent of GDP across Africa (excluding South Africa and Nigeria), with many countries receiving much more than that.

Since the turn of the millennium, when this new era of aid began, aid increases have been directed not to countries hoping for a boost to help them out of short-term trouble, but to countries now severely dependent on aid. When we look at aid levels in the rest of the developing world, the contrast is stark. Only a handful of countries scattered elsewhere across the globe, such as Nicaragua and Haiti and the small islands of Oceania, come close to the type of aid dependence seen in Africa. Vietnam, which has seen aid rise significantly since the 1980s, still relies on it for only 4 percent or less of its GDP. Aid to poor countries in the Americas has progressively shrunk from 0.7 percent of GDP in the 1960s to under 0.3 percent today.

It is not that no other countries have ever received large amounts of aid before. The key factor is that, in Africa, very high aid receipts have now lasted for decades and have become the norm. Never has any group of countries been so dependent on foreign aid for their basic functioning, for so long. There is a big difference between receiving aid as a welcome support and needing it as a fundamental part of the national budget.

> ## Very high aid receipts have now lasted for decades and have become the norm.

Dependence on foreign governments for financial assistance has undermined development efforts in Africa, and it will continue to do so despite the modern (and laudable) emphasis on "good governance" and "country ownership." Although aid dependency has drawn considerable comment both in Africa and among the rich nations, the fretting has had virtually no impact on donor policy. Instead, the trend continues—and it will get worse if promised aid increases actually do kick in. While the rest of the world (with some exceptions) appears to be moving on from aid, Africa is getting more and more aid-dependent.

Government-to-government aid will always have an important supporting role, a role it has played with occasional success over the years. In some countries, depending on their economic and political contexts, aid increases may be appropriate and helpful. But most countries in Africa, rather than seeking more aid, should be reducing the amount they accept. Why? Because when the whole range of aid's impacts are taken into account, it becomes clear that aid at present levels is hindering rather than helping many countries' development prospects.

Less Aid, More Help

The biggest headline from the London Group of 20 Summit in 2009 was, as usual, a huge pledge of aid (over $1 trillion, much of it double-counted) to help poor countries. And yet, for all the efforts put into "aid effectiveness," the undermining of institutions continues to be endemic in the aid relationship. A course needs to be set to reduce, rather than entrench, aid dependency. In this regard, in response to the recent global crisis, an overhaul of the global financial system would provide a unique opportunity to undo measures that until now have prevented developing countries from maximizing their development resources.

One issue coming under increasing scrutiny, for example, is the complex global web of tax havens that serves no serious purpose for rich nations or poor, but is responsible for allowing dodgy deals, theft, and other crimes to abound. Poor African countries lose far more every year through capital flight to tax havens than they receive in aid. Plugging this leak, cracking down on corruption, and building better national financial systems could make more credit available to small and medium-sized businesses—and would also open an avenue toward reduced dependence on aid. The likelihood of such reforms has grown since the global financial crisis erupted.

Other measures that have been considered or adopted at a range of global meetings in 2009 and 2010 could have repercussions for decades to come, as the financial architecture is redrawn, and crucial issues that were previously considered off the table are suddenly on it. Reform of financial institutions such as the International Monetary Fund has been discussed for decades, but the political will to do something may finally emerge as a result of the crisis.

Aid will certainly continue to play a role in this new context, and some African countries could benefit from aid increases. Botswana is one example. It received high levels of assistance in the 1960s and 1970s (averaging 17 percent of GDP), and during that period its growth performance exceeded the growth rates of Hong Kong, Taiwan, Malaysia, and Thailand. In contrast to almost all other African countries, aid to Botswana has steadily declined over the decades. Today it receives negligible levels of assistance. Yet its economic boom has been brought to a tragic end by an AIDS pandemic that slashed life expectancy from 56 years to 35 in a decade. Botswana could use more aid again as it seeks to recover.

Other countries, however, should ideally receive less. Rwanda already funds half its government spending with aid. Rather than seeking to increase this proportion, Rwanda should set itself the goal of reducing it over time. So should other nations. Developing countries have reduced poverty when they have implemented the right policies, and when foreign governments have taken supportive measures. Aid has been at best marginal to this effort, and at worst has undermined it.

On the other hand, while government-to-government aid can have adverse effects, support for civil society and provision of global public goods, such as climate change measures and health technologies, would be a constructive use of increased aid resources. Politicians promise more aid when they do not want to make changes that are more fundamental. Now is the time for substantial reform, not for counting aid dollars.

Critical Thinking

1. What is Glennie's point of view?
2. What reasons does Glennie offer to support his point of view?
3. How does this article differ from Jeffery Sachs's point of view (article 18)?

JONATHAN GLENNIE, a country representative for Christian Aid, is the author of *The Trouble with Aid: Why Less Could Mean More for Africa* (Zed Books, 2008).

From *Current History*, May 2010, pp. 205–209. Copyright © 2010 by Current History, Inc. Reprinted by permission.

It's Still the One

Oil's very future is now being seriously questioned, debated, and challenged. The author of an acclaimed history explains why, just as we need more oil than ever, it is changing faster than we can keep up with.

DANIEL YERGIN

On a still afternoon under a hot Oklahoma sun, neither a cloud nor an ounce of "volatility" was in sight. Anything but. All one saw were the somnolent tanks filled with oil, hundreds of them, spread over the rolling hills, some brand-new, some more than 70 years old, and some holding, inside their silver or rust-orange skins, more than half a million barrels of oil each.

This is Cushing, Oklahoma, the gathering point for the light, sweet crude oil known as West Texas Intermediate—or just WTI. It is the oil whose price you hear announced every day, as in "WTI closed today at. . . ." Cushing proclaims itself, as the sign says when you ride into town, the "pipeline crossroads of the world." Through it passes the network of pipes that carry oil from Texas and Oklahoma and New Mexico, from Louisiana and the Gulf Coast, and from Canada too, into Cushing's tanks, where buyers take title before moving the oil onward to refineries where it is turned into gasoline, jet fuel, diesel, home heating oil, and all the other products that people actually use.

But that is not what makes Cushing so significant. After all, there are other places in the world through which much more oil flows. Cushing plays a unique role in the new global oil industry because WTI is the preeminent benchmark against which other oils are priced. Every day, billions of "paper barrels" of light, sweet crude are traded on the floor of the New York Mercantile Exchange in lower Manhattan and, in ever increasing volumes, at electron speed around the world, an astonishing virtual commerce that no matter how massive in scale, still connects back somehow to a barrel of oil in Cushing changing owners.

That frenetic daily trading has helped turn oil into something new—not only a physical commodity critical to the security and economic viability of nations but also a financial asset, part of that great instantaneous exchange of stocks, bonds, currencies, and everything else that makes up the world's financial portfolio. Today, the daily trade in those "paper barrels"—crude oil futures—is more than 10 times the world's daily consumption of physical barrels of oil. Add in the trades that take place on other exchanges or outside them entirely, and the ratio may be as much as 30 times greater. And though the oil may flow steadily in and out of Cushing at a stately 4 miles per hour, the global oil market is anything but stable.

That's why, as I sat down to work on a new edition of *The Prize* and considered what had changed since the early 1990s, when I wrote this history of the world's most valuable, and misunderstood, commodity, the word "volatility" kept springing to mind. How could it not? Indeed, when people are talking about volatility, they are often thinking oil. On July 11, 2008, WTI hit $147.27. Exactly a year later, it was $59.87. In between, in December, it fell as low as $32.40. (And don't forget a little more than a decade ago, when it was as low as $10 a barrel and consumers were supposedly going to swim forever in a sea of cheap oil.)

These wild swings don't just affect the "hedgers" (oil producers, airlines, heating oil dealers, etc.) and the "speculators," the financial players. They show up in the changing prices at the gasoline station. They stir political passions and feed consumers' suspicions. Volatility also makes it more difficult to plan future energy investments, whether in oil and gas or in renewable and alternative fuels. And it can have a cataclysmic impact on the world economy. After all, Detroit was knocked flat on its back by what happened at the gasoline pump in 2007 and 2008 even before the credit crisis. The enormous impact of these swings is why British Prime Minister Gordon Brown and French President Nicolas Sarkozy were recently moved to call for a global solution to "destructive volatility." But, they were forced to add, "There are no easy solutions."

This volatility is part of the new age of oil. For though Cushing looks pretty much the same as it did when *The Prize* came out, the world of oil looks very different. Some talk today about "the end of oil." If so, others reply, we are entering its very long goodbye. One characteristic of this new age is that oil has developed a split personality—as a physical commodity but also now as a financial asset. Three other defining characteristics of this new age are the globalization of the demand for oil, a vast shift from even a decade ago; the rise of climate change as a political factor shaping decisions on how we will use oil, and how much of it, in the future; and the drive for new technologies that could dramatically affect oil along with the rest of the energy portfolio.

The cast of characters in the oil business has also grown and changed. Some oil companies have become "supermajors," such as ExxonMobil and Chevron, while others, such as Amoco and ARCO, have just disappeared. "Big oil" no longer means the traditional international oil companies, their logos instantly recognizable from corner gas stations, but rather much larger state-owned companies, which, along with governments, today control more than 80 percent of the world's oil reserves. Fifteen of the world's 20 largest oil companies are now state-owned.

The cast of oil traders has also much expanded. Today's global oil game now includes pension funds, institutional money managers, endowments, and hedge funds, as well as individual investors and day traders. The managers at the pension funds and the university endowments see themselves as engaged in "asset allocation," hedging risks and diversifying to protect retirees' incomes and faculty salaries. But, technically, they too are part of the massive growth in the ranks of the new oil speculators.

With all these changes, the very future of this most vital commodity is now being seriously questioned, debated, and challenged, even as the world will need more of it than ever before. Both the U.S. Department of Energy and the International Energy Agency project that, even accounting for gains in efficiency, global energy use will increase almost 50 percent from 2006 to 2030—and that oil will continue to provide 30 percent or more of the world's energy in 2030.

But will it?

$147.27-Closing price per barrel of oil on July 11, 2008. Exactly one year later, it had fallen to $59.87.

From the beginning, oil has been a global industry, going back to 1861 when the first cargo of kerosene was sent from Pennsylvania—the Saudi Arabia of 19th-century oil—to Britain. (The potential crew was so fearful that the kerosene would catch fire that they had to be gotten drunk to shanghai them on board.) But that is globalization of supply, a familiar story. What is decisively new is the globalization of demand.

For decades, most of the market—and the markets that mattered the most—were in North America, Western Europe, and Japan. That's also where the growth was. At the time of the first Gulf War in 1991, China was still an oil exporter.

But now, the growth is in China, India, other emerging markets, and the Middle East. Between 2000 and 2007, the world's daily oil demand increased by 9.4 million barrels. Almost 85 percent of that growth was in emerging markets. There were many reasons that prices soared all the way to $147.27 last year, ranging from geopolitics to a weak dollar to the impact of financial markets and speculation (in all its manifold meanings). But the starting point was the fundamentals—the surge in oil demand driven by powerful economic growth in emerging markets. This shift may be even more powerful than people recognize: So far this year, more new cars have been sold in China than in the United States. When economic recovery

The Capital of Oil

Within three years of its discovery in 1912, the Cushing field in Oklahoma was producing almost 20 percent of U.S. oil. Two years later, it was supplying a substantial part of the fuel used by the U.S. Army in Europe during World War I. The Cushing area was so prolific that it became known as "the Queen of the Oil Fields," and Cushing became one of those classic wild oil boom-towns of the early 20th century. "Any man with red blood gets oil fever" was the diagnosis of one reporter who visited the area during those days. Production grew so fast around Cushing that pipelines had to be hurriedly built and storage tanks quickly thrown up to hold surplus supplies. By the time production began to decline, a great deal of infrastructure was in place, and Cushing turned into a key oil hub, its network of pipelines used to bring in supplies from elsewhere in Oklahoma and West Texas. Those supplies were stored in the tanks at Cushing before being put into other pipelines and shipped to refineries. When the New York Mercantile Exchange—the NYMEX—started to trade oil futures in 1983, it needed a physical delivery point. Cushing, its boom days long gone, but with its network of pipelines and tank farms and its central location, was the obvious answer. As much as 1.1 million barrels per day pass in and out of Cushing—equivalent to about 6 percent of U.S. oil consumption. But prices for much of the world's crude oil are set against the benchmark of the West Texas Intermediate crude oil—also known as "domestic sweet"—sitting in those 300 or so tanks in Cushing, making this sedate Oklahoma town not only an oil hub but one of the hubs of the world economy.

—Daniel Yergin

takes hold again, what happens to oil demand in such emerging countries will be crucial.

The math is clear: More consumers mean more demand, which means more supplies are needed. But what about the politics? There the forecasts are murkier, feeding a new scenario for international tension—a competition, even a clash, between China and the United States over "scarce" oil resources. This scenario even comes with a well-known historical model—the rivalry between Britain and "rising" Germany that ended in the disaster of World War I.

This scenario, though compelling reading, does not really accord with the way that the world oil market works. The Chinese are definitely new players, willing and able to pay top dollar to gain access to existing and new oil sources and, lately, also making loans to oil-producing countries to ensure future supplies. With more than $2 trillion in foreign reserves, China certainly has the wherewithal to be in the lending business.

But the global petroleum industry is not a go-it-alone business. Because of the risk and costs of large-scale development, companies tend to work in consortia with other companies.

Oil-exporting countries seek to diversify the countries and companies they work with. Inevitably, any country in China's position—whose demand had grown from 2.5 million barrels per day to 8 million in a decade and a half—would be worrying about supplies. Such an increase, however, is not a forecast of inevitable strife; it is a message about economic growth and rising standards of living. It would be much more worrying if, in the face of rising demand, Chinese companies were not investing in production both inside China (the source of half of its supply) and outside its borders.

There are potential flash points in this new world of oil. But they will not come from standard commercial competition. Rather, they arise when oil (along with natural gas) gets caught up in larger foreign-policy issues—most notably today, the potentially explosive crisis over the nuclear ambitions of oil- and gas-rich Iran.

Yet, despite all the talk of an "oil clash" scenario, there seems to be less overall concern than a few years ago and much more discussion about "energy dialogue." The Chinese themselves appear more confident about their increasingly important place in this globalized oil market. Although the risks are still there, the Chinese—and the Indians right alongside them—have the same stake as other consumers in an adequately supplied world market that is part of the larger global economy. Disruption of that economy, as the last year has so vividly demonstrated, does not serve their purposes. Why would the Chinese want to get into a confrontation over oil with the United States when the U.S. export market is so central to their economic growth and when the two countries are so financially interdependent?

Oil is not even the most important energy issue between China and the United States. It is coal. The two countries have the world's largest coal resources, and they are the world's biggest consumers of it. In a carbon-constrained world, they share a strong common interest in finding technological solutions for the emissions released when coal is burned.

And that leads directly to the second defining feature of the new age of oil: climate change. Global warming was already on the agenda when *The Prize* came out. It was back in 1992 that 154 countries signed the Rio Convention, pledging to dramatically reduce CO_2 concentrations in the atmosphere. But only in recent years has climate change really gained traction as a political issue—in Europe early in this decade, in the United States around 2005. Whatever the outcome of December's U.N. climate change conference in Copenhagen, carbon regulation is now part of the future of oil. And that means a continuing drive to reduce oil demand.

How does that get done? How does the world at once meet both the challenge of climate change and the challenge of economic growth—steady expansion in the industrial countries and more dramatic growth in China, India, and other emerging markets as tens of millions of their citizens rise from poverty and buy appliances and cars?

The answer has to be in another defining change—an emphasis on technology to a degree never before seen. The energy business has always been a technology business. After all, the men who figured out in 1859, exactly 150 years ago, how to drill that first oil well—Colonel Drake and his New Haven, Conn., investors—would, in today's lingo, be described as a group of disruptive technology entrepreneurs and venture capitalists. Again and again, in researching oil's history, I was struck by how seemingly insurmountable barriers and obstacles were overcome by technological progress, often unanticipated.

9.4 million-Number of barrels by which the world's daily oil demand rose from 2000 to 2007, with 85 percent coming from the developing world.

But the focus today on technology—all across the energy spectrum—is of unprecedented intensity. In the mid-1990s, I chaired a task force for the U.S. Department of Energy on "strategic energy R&D." Our panel worked very hard for a year and a half and produced what many considered a very worthy report. But there was not all that much follow-through. The Gulf War was over, and the energy problem looked like it had been "solved."

Today, by contrast, the interest in energy technology is enormous. And it will only be further stoked by the substantial increases that are ahead in government support for energy R&D. Much of that spending and effort is aimed at finding alternatives to oil. Yet the challenge is not merely to find alternatives; it is to find alternatives that can be competitive at the massive scale required.

What will those alternatives be? The electric car, which is the hottest energy topic today? Advanced biofuels? Solar systems? New building designs? Massive investment in wind? The evolving smart grid, which can integrate electric cars with the electricity industry? Something else that is hardly on the radar screen yet? Or perhaps a revolution in the internal combustion engine, making it two to three times as efficient as the ones in cars today?

We can make educated guesses. But, in truth, we don't know, and we won't know until we do know. For now, it is clear that the much higher levels of support for innovation—along with considerable government incentives and subsidies—will inevitably drive technological change and thus redraw the curve in the future demand for oil.

Indeed, the biggest surprises might come on the demand side, through conservation and improved energy efficiency. The United States is twice as energy efficient as it was in the 1970s. Perhaps we will see a doubling once again. Certainly, energy efficiency has never before received the intense focus and support that it does today.

Just because we have entered this new age of high-velocity change does not mean this story is about the imminent end of oil. Consider the "peak oil" thesis—shorthand for the presumption that the world has reached the high point of production and is headed for a downward slope. Historically, peak-oil thinking gains attention during times when markets are tight and prices are rising, stoking fears of a permanent shortage. In 2007 and 2008, the belief system built around peak oil helped drive prices to $147.27. (It was actually the fifth time that the world had supposedly "run out" of oil. The first such episode was in the 1880s; the last instance before this most recent time was in the 1970s.)

However, careful examination of the world's resource base— including my own firm's analysis of more than 800 of the largest oil fields—indicates that the resource endowment of the planet is sufficient to keep up with demand for decades to come. That, of course, does not mean that the oil will actually make it to consumers. Any number of "aboveground" risks and obstacles can stand in the way, from government policies that restrict access to tax systems to civil conflict to geopolitics to rising costs of exploration and production to uncertainties about demand. As has been the case for decades and decades, the shifting relations between producing and consuming countries, between traditional oil companies and state-owned oil companies, will do much to determine what resources are developed, and when, and thus to define the future of the industry.

There are two further caveats. Many of the new projects will be bigger, more complex, and more expensive. In the 1990s, a "megaproject" might have cost $500 million to $1 billion. Today, the price tag is more like $5 billion to $10 billion. And an increasing part of the new petroleum will come in the form of so-called "unconventional oil"—from ultradeep waters, Canadian oil sands, and the liquids that are produced with natural gas.

But through all these changes, one constant of the oil market is that it is not constant. The changing balance of supply and demand—shaped by economics, politics, technologies, consumer tastes, and accidents of all sorts—will continue to move prices. Economic recovery, expectations thereof, the pent-up demand for "demand," a shift into oil as a "financial asset"— some combination of these could certainly send oil prices up again, even with the current surplus in the market. Yet, the quest for stability is also a constant for oil, whether in reaction to the boom-and-bust world of northwest Pennsylvania in the late 19th century, the 10-cents-a-barrel world of Texas oil in the 1930s, or the $147.27 barrel of West Texas Intermediate in July 2008.

Certainly, the roller-coaster ride of oil prices over the last couple of years, as oil markets and financial markets have become more integrated, has made volatility a central pre-occupation for policymakers who do not want to see their economies whipsawed by huge price swings. Yet without the flexibility and liquidity of markets, there is no effective way to balance supply and demand, no way for consumers and producers to hedge their risks. Nor is there a way to send signals to these consumers and producers about how much oil to use and how much money to invest—or signals to would-be innovators about tomorrow's opportunities.

One part of the solution is not only enhancement of the already considerable regulation of the financial markets where oil is traded, but also greater transparency and better understanding of who the players are in the rapidly expanding financial oil markets. But regulatory changes cannot eliminate market cycles or repeal the laws of supply and demand in the world's largest organized commodity market. Those cycles may not be much in evidence amid the quiet tanks and rolling hills at Cushing. But they are inescapably part of the global landscape of the new world of oil.

Critical Thinking

1. How is the "age for oil" changing?
2. Specifically, how is the demand of oil changing?
3. How do these general and specific changes affect the U.S.-China relationship?
4. Does Yergin's analysis complement or contradict Klare's point of view in Article 3?

DANIEL YERGIN received a Pulitzer Prize for *The Prize: The Epic Quest for Oil, Money and Power,* published in an updated edition this year. He is chairman of IHS Cambridge Energy Research Associates.

Seven Myths about Alternative Energy

As the world looks around anxiously for an alternative to oil, energy sources such as biofuels, solar, and nuclear seem like they could be the magic ticket. They're not."

MICHAEL GRUNWALD

What Comes Next?
Imagining the Post-Oil World

Nothing is as fraught with myths, misperceptions, and outright flights of fancy as the conversation about oil's successors. We asked two authors—award-winning environmental journalist Michael Grunwald and energy consultant David J. Rothkopf—to take aim at some of these myths, and look over the horizon to see which technologies might win the day and which ones could cause unexpected new problems. If fossil fuels are indeed saying their very long goodbye, then their would-be replacements still have a lot to prove.

1. "We Need to Do Everything Possible to Promote Alternative Energy"

Not exactly. It's certainly clear that fossil fuels are mangling the climate and that the status quo is unsustainable. There is now a broad scientific consensus that the world needs to reduce greenhouse gas emissions more than 25 percent by 2020—and more than 80 percent by 2050. Even if the planet didn't depend on it, breaking our addictions to oil and coal would also reduce global reliance on petrothugs and vulnerability to energy-price spikes.

But though the world should do everything sensible to promote alternative energy, there's no point trying to do everything possible. There are financial, political, and technical pressures as well as time constraints that will force tough choices; solutions will need to achieve the biggest emissions reductions for the least money in the shortest time. Hydrogen cars, cold fusion, and other speculative technologies might sound cool, but they could divert valuable resources from ideas that are already achievable and cost-effective. It's nice that someone managed to run his car on liposuction leftovers, but that doesn't mean he needs to be subsidized.

Reasonable people can disagree whether governments should try to pick energy winners and losers. But why not at least agree that governments shouldn't pick losers to be winners? Unfortunately,

that's exactly what is happening. The world is rushing to promote alternative fuel sources that will actually accelerate global warming, not to mention an alternative power source that could cripple efforts to stop global warming.

We can still choose a truly alternative path. But we'd better hurry.

2. "Renewable Fuels Are the Cure for Our Addiction to Oil"

Unfortunately not. "Renewable fuels" sound great in theory, and agricultural lobbyists have persuaded European countries and the United States to enact remarkably ambitious biofuels mandates to promote farm-grown alternatives to gasoline. But so far in the real world, the cures—mostly ethanol derived from corn in the United States or biodiesel derived from palm oil, soybeans, and rapeseed in Europe—have been significantly worse than the disease.

Researchers used to agree that farm-grown fuels would cut emissions because they all made a shockingly basic error. They gave fuel crops credit for soaking up carbon while growing, but it never occurred to them that fuel crops might displace vegetation that soaked up even more carbon. It was as if they assumed that biofuels would only be grown in parking lots. Needless to say, that hasn't been the case; Indonesia, for example, destroyed so many of its lush forests and peat lands to grow palm oil for the European biodiesel market that it ranks third rather than 21st among the world's top carbon emitters.

In 2007, researchers finally began accounting for deforestation and other land-use changes created by biofuels. One study found that it would take more than 400 years of biodiesel use to "pay back" the carbon emitted by directly clearing peat for palm oil. Indirect damage can be equally devastating because on a hungry planet, food crops that get diverted to fuel usually end up getting replaced somewhere. For example, ethanol profits are prompting U.S. soybean farmers to switch to corn, so Brazilian soybean farmers are expanding into cattle pastures to pick up the slack and Brazilian ranchers are invading the Amazon rain forest, which is why another study pegged corn ethanol's payback period at 167 years. It's simple economics: The mandates increase demand for grain, which boosts prices, which makes it lucrative to ravage the wilderness.

Deforestation accounts for 20 percent of global emissions, so unless the world can eliminate emissions from all other sources—cars, coal, factories, cows—it needs to back off forests. That means limiting agriculture's footprint, a daunting task as the world's population grows—and an impossible task if vast expanses of cropland are converted to grow middling amounts of fuel. Even if the United States switched its entire grain crop to ethanol, it would only replace one fifth of U.S. gasoline consumption.

This is not just a climate disaster. The grain it takes to fill an SUV tank with ethanol could feed a hungry person for a year; biofuel mandates are exerting constant upward pressure on global food prices and have contributed to food riots in dozens of poorer countries. Still, the United States has quintupled its ethanol production in a decade and plans to quintuple its biofuel production again in the next decade. This will mean more money for well-subsidized grain farmers, but also more malnutrition, more deforestation, and more emissions. European leaders have paid a bit more attention to the alarming critiques of biofuels—including one by a British agency that was originally established to promote biofuels—but they have shown no more inclination to throw cold water on this $100 billion global industry.

3. "If Today's Biofuels Aren't the Answer, Tomorrow's Biofuels Will Be"

Doubtful. The latest U.S. rules, while continuing lavish support for corn ethanol, include enormous new mandates to jump-start "second-generation" biofuels such as cellulosic ethanol derived from switchgrass. In theory, they would be less destructive than corn ethanol, which relies on tractors, petroleum-based fertilizers, and distilleries that emit way too much carbon. Even first-generation ethanol derived from sugar cane—which already provides half of Brazil's transportation fuel—is considerably greener than corn ethanol. But recent studies suggest that any biofuels requiring good agricultural land would still be worse than gasoline for global warming. Less of a disaster than corn ethanol is still a disaster.

Back in the theoretical world, biofuels derived from algae, trash, agricultural waste, or other sources could help because they require no land or at least unspecific "degraded lands," but they always seem to be "several" years away from large-scale commercial development. And some scientists remain hopeful that fast-growing perennial grasses such as miscanthus can convert sunlight into energy efficiently enough to overcome the land-use dilemmas—someday. But for today, farmland happens to be very good at producing the food we need to feed us and storing the carbon we need to save us, and not so good at generating fuel. In fact, new studies suggest that if we really want to convert biomass into energy, we're better off turning it into electricity.

Then what should we use in our cars and trucks? In the short term . . . gasoline. We just need to use less of it.

Instead of counterproductive biofuel mandates and ethanol subsidies, governments need fuel-efficiency mandates to help the world's 1 billion drivers guzzle less gas, plus subsidies for mass transit, bike paths, rail lines, telecommuting, carpooling, and other activities to get those drivers out of their cars. Policymakers also need to eliminate subsidies for roads to nowhere, mandates that require excess parking and limit dense development in urban areas, and other sprawl-inducing policies. None of this is as enticing as inventing a magical new fuel, but it's doable, and it would cut emissions.

In the medium term, the world needs plug-in electric cars, the only plausible answer to humanity's oil addiction that isn't decades away. But electricity is already the source of even more emissions than oil. So we'll need an answer to humanity's coal addiction, too.

4. "Nuclear Power Is the Cure for Our Addiction to Coal"

Nope. Atomic energy is emissions free, so a slew of politicians and even some environmentalists have embraced it as a clean alternative to coal and natural gas that can generate power when there's no sun or wind. In the United States, which already gets nearly 20 percent of its electricity from nuclear plants, utilities are thinking about new reactors for the first time since the Three Mile Island meltdown three decades ago—despite global concerns about nuclear proliferation, local concerns about accidents or terrorist attacks, and the lack of a disposal site for the radioactive waste. France gets nearly 80 percent of its electricity from nukes, and Russia, China, and India are now gearing up for nuclear renaissances of their own.

But nuclear power cannot fix the climate crisis. The first reason is timing: The West needs major cuts in emissions within a decade, and the first new U.S. reactor is only scheduled for 2017—unless it gets delayed, like every U.S. reactor before it. Elsewhere in the developed world, most of the talk about a nuclear revival has remained just talk; there is no Western country with more than one nuclear plant under construction, and scores of existing plants will be scheduled for decommissioning in the coming decades, so there's no way nuclear could make even a tiny dent in electricity emissions before 2020.

The bigger problem is cost. Nuke plants are supposed to be expensive to build but cheap to operate. Unfortunately, they're turning out to be really, really expensive to build; their cost estimates have quadrupled in less than a decade. Energy guru Amory Lovins has calculated that new nukes will cost nearly three times as much as wind—and that was before their construction costs exploded for a variety of reasons, including the global credit crunch, the atrophying of the nuclear labor force, and a supplier squeeze symbolized by a Japanese company's worldwide monopoly on steel-forging for reactors. A new reactor in Finland that was supposed to showcase the global renaissance is already way behind schedule and way, way over budget. This is why plans for new plants were recently shelved in Canada and several U.S. states, why Moody's just warned utilities they'll risk ratings downgrades if they seek new reactors, and why renewables attracted $71 billion in worldwide private capital in 2007—while nukes attracted zero.

It's also why U.S. nuclear utilities are turning to politicians to supplement their existing loan guarantees, tax breaks, direct subsidies, and other cradle-to-grave government goodies with new public largesse. Reactors don't make much sense to build unless someone else is paying; that's why the strongest push for nukes is coming from countries where power is publicly funded. For all the talk of sanctions, if the world really wants to cripple the Iranian economy, maybe the mullahs should just be allowed to pursue nuclear energy.

Unlike biofuels, nukes don't worsen warming. But a nuclear expansion—like the recent plan by U.S. Republicans who want 100 new plants by 2030—would cost trillions of dollars for relatively modest gains in the relatively distant future.

Nuclear lobbyists do have one powerful argument: If coal is too dirty and nukes are too costly, how are we going to produce our juice? Wind is terrific, and it's on the rise, adding nearly half of new U.S. power last year and expanding its global capacity by a third in 2007. But after increasing its worldwide wattage tenfold in a decade—China is now the leading producer, and Europe is embracing wind as well—it still produces less than 2 percent of the world's electricity. Solar and geothermal are similarly wonderful and inexhaustible technologies, but they're still global rounding errors. The average U.S. household now has 26 plug-in devices, and the rest of the world is racing to catch up; the U.S. Department of Energy expects global electricity consumption to rise 77 percent by 2030. How can we meet that demand without a massive nuclear revival?

Wind is terrific, but it produces less than 2 percent of the world's electricity.

We can't. So we're going to have to prove the Department of Energy wrong.

5. "There Is No Silver Bullet to the Energy Crisis"

Probably not. But some bullets are a lot better than others; we ought to give them our best shot before we commit to evidently inferior bullets. And one renewable energy resource is the cleanest, cheapest, and most abundant of them all. It doesn't induce deforestation or require elaborate security. It doesn't depend on the weather. And it won't take years to build or bring to market; it's already universally available.

It's called "efficiency." It means wasting less energy—or more precisely, using less energy to get your beer just as cold, your shower just as hot, and your factory just as productive. It's not about some austerity scold harassing you to take cooler showers, turn off lights, turn down thermostats, drive less, fly less, buy less stuff, eat less meat, ditch your McMansion, and otherwise change your behavior to save energy. Doing less with less is called conservation. Efficiency is about doing more or

the same with less; it doesn't require much effort or sacrifice. Yet more efficient appliances, lighting, factories, and buildings, as well as vehicles, could wipe out one fifth to one third of the world's energy consumption without any real deprivation.

Efficiency isn't sexy, and the idea that we could use less energy without much trouble hangs uneasily with today's more-is-better culture. But the best way to ensure new power plants don't bankrupt us, empower petrodictators, or imperil the planet is not to build them in the first place. "Negawatts" saved by efficiency initiatives generally cost 1 to 5 cents per kilowatt-hour versus projections ranging from 12 to 30 cents per kilowatt-hour from new nukes. That's because Americans in particular and human beings in general waste amazing amounts of energy. U.S. electricity plants fritter away enough to power Japan, and American water heaters, industrial motors, and buildings are as ridiculously inefficient as American cars. Only 4 percent of the energy used to power a typical incandescent bulb produces light; the rest is wasted. China is expected to build more square feet of real estate in the next 15 years than the United States has built in its entire history, and it has no green building codes or green building experience.

But we already know that efficiency mandates can work wonders because they've already reduced U.S. energy consumption levels from astronomical to merely high. For example, thanks to federal rules, modern American refrigerators use three times less energy than 1970s models, even though they're larger and more high-tech.

The biggest obstacles to efficiency are the perverse incentives that face most utilities; they make more money when they sell more power and have to build new generating plants. But in California and the Pacific Northwest, utility profits have been decoupled from electricity sales, so utilities can help customers save energy without harming shareholders. As a result, in that part of the country, per capita power use has been flat for three decades—while skyrocketing 50 percent in the rest of the United States. If utilities around the world could make money by helping their customers use less power, the U.S. Department of Energy wouldn't be releasing such scary numbers.

6. "We Need a Technological Revolution to Save the World"

Maybe. In the long term, it's hard to imagine how (without major advances) we can reduce emissions 80 percent by 2050 while the global population increases and the developing world develops. So a clean-tech Apollo program modeled on the Manhattan Project makes sense. And we do need carbon pricing to send a message to market makers and innovators to promote low-carbon activities; Europe's cap-and-trade scheme seems to be working well after a rocky start. The private capital already pouring into renewables might someday produce a cheap solar panel or a synthetic fuel or a superpowerful battery or a truly clean coal plant. At some point, after we've milked efficiency for all the negawatts and negabarrels we can, we might need something new.

But we already have all the technology we need to start reducing emissions by reducing consumption. Even if we only hold electricity demand flat, we can subtract a coal-fired megawatt every time we add a wind-powered megawatt. And with a smarter grid, green building codes, and strict efficiency standards for everything from light bulbs to plasma TVs to server farms, we can do better than flat. Al Gore has a reasonably plausible plan for zero-emissions power by 2020; he envisions an ambitious 28 percent decrease in demand through efficiency, plus some ambitious increases in supply from wind, solar, and geothermal energy. But we don't even have to reduce our fossil fuel use to zero to reach our 2020 targets. We just have to use less.

If somebody comes up with a better idea by 2020, great! For now, we should focus on the solutions that get the best emissions bang for the buck.

7. "Ultimately, We'll Need to Change Our Behaviors to Save the World"

Probably. These days, it's politically incorrect to suggest that going green will require even the slightest adjustment to our way of life, but let's face it: Jimmy Carter was right. It wouldn't kill you to turn down the heat and put on a sweater. Efficiency is a miracle drug, but conservation is even better; a Prius saves gas, but a Prius sitting in the driveway while you ride your bike uses no gas. Even energy-efficient dryers use more power than clotheslines.

More with less will be a great start, but to get to 80 percent less emissions, the developed world might occasionally have to do less with less. We might have to unplug a few digital picture frames, substitute teleconferencing for some business travel, and take it easy on the air conditioner. If that's an inconvenient truth, well, it's less inconvenient than trillions of dollars' worth of new reactors, perpetual dependence on hostile petrostates, or a fricasseed planet.

After all, the developing world is entitled to develop. Its people are understandably eager to eat more meat, drive more cars, and live in nicer houses. It doesn't seem fair for the developed world to say: Do as we say, not as we did. But if the developing world follows the developed world's wasteful path to prosperity, the Earth we all share won't be able to accommodate us. So we're going to have to change our ways. Then we can at least say: Do as we're doing, not as we did.

Critical Thinking

1. What is Grunwald's point of view?
2. How does this article complement or contradict the point of views in articles 3, 10, 11 and 22?

MICHAEL GRUNWALD, a senior correspondent at *Time* magazine, is an award-winning environmental journalist and author of *The Swamp: The Everglades, Florida, and the Politics of Paradise.*

Reprinted in entirety by McGraw-Hill with permission from *Foreign Policy,* September/October 2009, pp. 130–133. www.foreignpolicy.com. © 2009 Washingtonpost.Newsweek Interactive, LLC.

The End of Easy Oil

MONICA HEGER

Canada's tar sands will soon be our top source of imported oil. But will that energy be worth the costs?

"We have the energy," declares a road sign that welcomes visitors to Fort McMurray in Alberta, Canada. It is no idle boast: This city of 70,000 lies in the heart of Canada's oil sands, geologic formations that collectively contain 13 percent of the world's proven oil reserves. During the early 2000s, a massive oil-extraction industry boomed here, rapidly transforming vast stretches of boreal forest into strip mines. But when oil prices tumbled with the global recession, Alberta's energy industry took a big hit. In mid-2008 the Norwegian company Statoil-Hydro withdrew its application to build a $4 billion upgrading plant; Royal Dutch Shell decided to shelve a mining construction project that fall. An estimated $90 billion in development contracts were canceled or put on hold, bringing the oil sands industry to a crossroads.

To many environmentalists—and, less predictably, to many energy developers as well—the slowdown in oil sands extraction may prove to be an unexpected blessing. The United States has become deeply reliant on extreme extraction from Canada's tar sands, which this year are expected to become this country's top source of imported crude, surpassing our purchases from the vast oil fields of Saudi Arabia. The recession "has given the oil sands industry a chance to step back and breathe," says David McColl, head of oil sands studies at the Canadian Energy Research Institute, a nonprofit whose membership includes government departments, the University of Calgary, and energy companies. With the slowdown, developers must improve efficiency to stay profitable, making changes that will both help the bottom line and begin to address some of the tough environmental problems associated with tar sands oil.

Worldwide, mostly in Canada and Venezuela, oil sand reserves total a stunning 2 trillion barrels of oil. That is equivalent to 280 years of America's current consumption, although only around a tenth of that total appears to be recoverable with current technology. Unfortunately, the process of extracting, upgrading, and refining the fuel is dirty and resource-intensive. In Canada, relatively shallow oil sand deposits lie beneath a 1,500-square-mile region just north of Fort McMurray. Developers access the sands by literally scraping away the earth's surface, along with anything that happens to be living there. The raw material extracted—a thick, black goo called bitumen— makes up 10 percent of the harvested material by weight. The rest is sand and small amounts of water. Two tons of sand must be processed to yield a single barrel of oil, producing twice as much greenhouse-gas emissions as the processing of conventional crude. (Deeper reserves must be forced to the surface by an injection of pressurized steam, with even greater emissions; about 40 percent of Canadian oil from the sands is produced this way.) Each barrel of bitumen also generates more than 500 gallons of tailings, a liquid by-product laced with traces of bitumen and other pollutants. Operators hold the tailings in giant ponds, many located adjacent to the Athabasca River, which runs through eastern Alberta. Those ponds already cover an estimated 50 square miles, and an analysis of the industry's seepage records by the Canadian environmental advocacy group Environmental Defense suggests that every day around 3 million gallons of contaminated fluid leaks into the surrounding area.

Even more unnerving are the findings of a recent study by ecologist David Schindler at the University of Alberta. He and his colleagues found that over the course of four months, 11,400 tons of particulate matter—including bitumen and cancer-causing polycyclic aromatic compounds—were deposited within 30 miles of oil sands upgrading facilities belonging to two of Canada's major oil sands development companies, Suncor and Syncrude. Sampling of the Athabasca River revealed that pollutants appeared in greater concentrations downstream from the facilities and were not Hotected in comparable sites farther away, the researchers say. "The concentrations there are in the range where deformities and mortalities would be expected in fish," Schindler says, "and the compounds that we found are known carcinogens in humans."

Environmental concerns that were brushed aside when oil prices spiked a few years back have gained traction since the economy cooled. In February the Whole Foods grocery chain threw its weight behind a campaign to boycott companies that use fuel generated from the oil sands. And in June Syncrude was found guilty of violating provincial and federal law when 1,600 waterbirds died in one of its tailings ponds near Fort McMurray (the company may appeal the decision). Regulators have also started to assert themselves more forcefully. Last year Canada's Energy Resources Conservation Board issued new rules requiring at least 20 percent of the fine particles from new tailings to be captured starting in 2011, and 50 percent by 2013. Suncor has since begun developing a new technology that would mix some refining by-products with a polymer, creating a dry solid that can be more easily contained and reducing the amount of liquid that ends up in the toxic ponds.

Such changes will become increasingly important as the world economy recovers. Oil sands development has begun to pick up, with a projected $13 billion in new investment in

2010, a $2 billion increase from 2009. A recent industry report estimates that oil sands production, which currently stands at around 1.5 million barrels a day, could jump 46 percent by 2015. The United States now imports 22 percent of its oil from our northern neighbor, and China has also shown interest in Canada's sands, taking a $1.7 billion, 60 percent stake in two new projects in northern Alberta. In short, the tar sands—like deep oil—will probably remain an important part of the energy picture for the foreseeable future.

"Oil sands and offshore drilling are both symptoms of the same problem: We're running out of easy oil," says Simon Dyer, oil sands director at the Pembina Institute, a nonprofit sustainable energy research organization. But with ingenuity, smart regulation, and better enforcement, government and industry may be able to find a path that meets our needs until clean—or at least cleaner—energy sources can step up to the task.

Critical Thinking

1. What is meant by "extreme extraction"?
2. How do Canadian tar sands fit into the changing supply and demand equation for oil?
3. How does this case study illustrate the relationship between natural resources and social structures?

Coming Soon to a Terminal Near You

Shale gas should make the world a cleaner, safer place.

THE ECONOMIST

Along the coast of China, six vast liquefied natural gas (LNG) terminals are under construction; by the end of 2015 they should have more than doubled the amount of LNG that the country can import. At the other end of the country, gas is flowing in along a new pipeline from Turkmenistan. In between the two, geologists and engineers are looking at all sorts of new wells that might boost the country's already fast-growing domestic production. China will consume 260 billion cubic metres (260bcm, which is 9.2 trillion cubic feet) of gas a year by 2015, according to the country's 12th five-year plan, more than tripling 2008's 81bcm. The roots of this rapid growth, though, do not lie in China's centralised planning. They are to be found in a piece of deregulation enacted decades ago on the other side of the world: America's Natural Gas Policy Act of 1978.

America's deregulation of its natural-gas market encouraged entrepreneurial energy companies to gamble on new technologies allowing them to extract the gas conventional drilling could not reach. Geologists had long known there was gas trapped in the country's shale beds. Now the incentives for trying new ways of recovering it were greater, not least because, if it could be recovered, it could be got to market through pipelines newly obliged to offer "open access" to all comers.

Decades of development later, the independent companies which embraced horizontal drilling and the use of high-pressure fluids to crack open the otherwise impermeable shales—a process known as "fracking"—have brought about a revolution. Shale now provides 23% of America's natural gas, up from 4% in 2005. That upheaval in American gas markets has gone on to change the way gas is traded globally. A lot of LNG export capacity created with American markets in mind—global supply increased 58% over the past five years—is looking for new outlets.

To the extent that the shale-gas success is repeated elsewhere, a vital source of energy will become available from an ever more diverse and numerous set of suppliers in increasingly free markets. This means that, unlike the boom in oil in the decades following the second world war, this growth in gas may not hand a powerful political weapon to those countries with the biggest reserves. Shale gas could significantly diminish the political clout that Russia, Venezuela and Iran once saw as part and parcel of their gas revenues.

Tanked Up

"The power of the shale-gas revolution has surprised everyone," says Christof Rühl, chief economist at BP. In 2003 America's National Petroleum Council estimated that North America (including Canada and Mexico) might have 1.1 trillion cubic metres (tcm) of recoverable shale gas. This year America's Advanced Resources International reckoned there might be 50 times as much.

The shale-gas bounty is not confined to America. The country's Energy Information Administration released a report in April that looked at 48 shale-gas basins in 32 countries. It puts recoverable reserves at 190tcm, and that excludes possible finds in the former Soviet Union and the Middle East, where huge reserves of conventional gas will make investment in shale gas unlikely for years to come. In short order estimates of the Earth's bounty of recoverable gas have expanded by about 40%. Improving extraction technologies and geological inquisitiveness are sure to raise that figure in the years to come.

Nor is shale gas the only new sort of reserve: "tight gas" in sandstones and coal-bed methane (the sort of gas that used to kill canaries down mines) are also promising. Farther in the future, and more speculatively, there's the gas frozen into hydrates on the planet's continental shelves, which might offer more than 1,000tcm if a way can be found to exploit it. The cornucopian belief that human ingenuity will always find ways to increase the availability of resources is not a sure bet. With gas, though, the odds look pretty good for decades to come.

A scenario developed for the International Energy Agency's forthcoming "World Energy Outlook" offers a sense of what may unfold. Called the "Golden age of gas", it sees annual world production rising by 1.8tcm between now and 2035, when it reaches 5.1tcm. A fair bit of that is provided by unconventional sources. The growth is about 50% stronger than in the scenario used as a baseline; trade in gas between the world's major regions doubles. Coal use declines from the late 2010s onwards, and by 2030 gas has surpassed it, providing a quarter of all the world's energy.

The development of shale-gas reserves beyond North America is still at an early stage. Although widespread pollution of groundwater by fracking seems unlikely (shales that hold gas typically lie far deeper than groundwater supplies), such risks have raised a great deal of environmental concern about the technology. Coupled with a sensitivity to the rural charms of *la France profonde,* this has led to a moratorium on shale-gas exploration in France. But in Poland, which may have Europe's largest reserves, companies are busily sinking test wells to see what is there.

In South Africa, which may have the largest shale-gas reserves on the continent, the shales in the Karoo basin have attracted the attention of Shell, which is increasingly billing itself as a gas-focused company. Shell is also one of the companies looking at shale-gas reserves in China, which may be the largest on the planet. Chinese interest in shale gas is strong, with state companies buying up American expertise as they take stakes in established shale-gas producers. The country might be producing its first shale gas at scale before the current five-year plan is over.

The Great Decoupling

Gas is currently bought and sold in three distinct global markets—North America, Europe and Asia—and prices differ widely between the three. In deregulated North America, with a competitive market and plenty of shale gas to augment conventional supplies, prices are low. In Asia, where gas is largely traded using a system of long-term contracts tied to the price of oil, prices are high. Europe sits in between: prices at the moment are around $4 per million btu in America, $8 in continental Europe and $11 in Asia (1m btu is about 300 kilowatt-hours).

The origins of long-term contracts and oil-linked pricing go back a long way. When gas first began to be used a lot in the 1960s it was a substitute for home heating oil, and so it made sense to tie its price to that of oil. Because big exploration, extraction and infrastructure investments required pots of capital, long-term contracts became an industry norm.

Today oil is generally no substitute for gas. Gas is used not to fill up cars and lorries—though there are gas-fired transport enthusiasts who would like to do something about that—but to fuel power stations and heat homes. Still, many gas producers are happy enough with the archaic pricing structure, particularly when oil prices are high. Customers with limited choices have had to put up with it. According to a recent study from the Massachusetts Institute of Technology, pipelines carry 80% of all gas traded between regions. The firms at the upstream end of those pipelines, such as Russia's Gazprom, which supplies a quarter of all western Europe's gas, thus have a strong hand in negotiations. Control of the pipelines meant that when Gazprom turned off the gas (as it did in 2009 in a dispute over trans-shipments through Ukraine), buyers had nowhere to turn for alternatives.

In the past couple of years, though, three factors—LNG from Qatar that was no longer needed in shale-gas-rich America, a little energy-market deregulation by the European Union and a drop in overall demand—have helped to loosen the grip of Gazprom. Power-sector reforms allowed smaller European utilities to compete more vigorously, buying LNG on the spot market at a price sometimes as low as half that of long-term contracts from Russia. Bigger utilities that were losing market share

approached Gazprom, not known for sympathetic customer relations, for better terms. The normally intractable Russian company renegotiated contracts with European customers for a three-year "crisis period" to allow up to 15% of gas to be priced on cheaper spot terms. (Norway, also a big supplier to EU countries, had begun to sell gas on contracts that tied an even larger fraction to spot prices.)

Since then the European market has recovered. Prices rose after Libyan gas was cut off as a result of the country's uprising and a lot of Qatari LNG has found a new destination in Japan, deprived of much of its nuclear power since the disaster at its Fukushima plant.

Unsurprisingly, further attempts to pressure Gazprom into revising its terms have faltered. In February it rebuffed appeals by Germany's e.ON, one of its most important customers, to link its gas to spot prices. Gazprom's boss, Alexei Miller, told shareholders at the end of June that oil-indexed long-term gas contracts were here to stay. In private the company is still talking to customers about changing the shape of future contracts, and appears more inclined nowadays to regard European utilities as potential partners rather than spineless adversaries.

Looking reasonable, say cynics, is a ruse to discourage investment in shale reserves and alternative pipelines. If an agreeable-seeming Gazprom, along with increased bullishness about LNG and shale gas, were to dampen European enthusiasm for Nabucco, a long-planned pipeline which might bring 30bcm of gas a year to Europe from the Caspian and the Middle East, that would suit Russia pretty well. But Russia's new attitude could also spring from a realisation that the world really is changing. A study from the James Baker Institute at Rice University, published in July, reckons that, if shale-gas reserves are fully exploited, Gazprom's share of the west European market might fall from 27% in 2009 to 13% by 2040.

And Gazprom is finding that China, with which it has been negotiating pipeline deals since 2005, is not interested in the sort of long-term locked contracts that have previously typified Asian markets; indeed it is not even willing to pay European prices. Its immense shale-gas potential might make it even less willing to pay up, inclining it to depend less on pipeline gas and to take the risk that it can smooth out ebbs and flows through spot markets. If the proportion of imported pipeline gas falls, so does the pricing power of conventional suppliers, even if the overall volume they supply goes up.

Increasingly, it looks as if today's significant regional price differences will be arbitraged away, and that gas could become as fungible and as widely traded as oil. LNG's growth (23% by volume in 2010) shows no sign of slowing. European LNG import capacity has more than doubled since 2000; the costs of building an import terminal have plunged. So far this year twice as many LNG vessels have been ordered from the world's shipyards as in the whole of 2010. Qatar, which along with Iran and Russia holds the world's most impressive conventional gas reserves, is adding new liquefaction plants. Other countries are also busily constructing export terminals; while Australia leads the way, Indonesia, Papua New Guinea and others are all set to bring more LNG to the world markets. There's even work on liquefaction plants in America.

One consequence of a global gas market supplied from widely distributed conventional and unconventional sources is that this diversity will reduce the power of big suppliers to set prices and bully buyers. There has been occasional talk of a "gas OPEC", most audibly when, just before the end of 2008, a dozen or so gas producers met in Moscow under the chairmanship of Russia's prime minister, Vladimir Putin. Despite the rattling of sabres on pipelines, though, something analogous to OPEC looks near impossible under current conditions. For one thing, utilities mostly have spare capacity and can thus adjust their fuel mix in a way that car drivers confronted with an oil shortage cannot. What is more, managing the supply of gas month by month, as the oil cartel seeks to do, would be near impossible when most gas continues to be supplied on long-term contracts that are difficult to break.

The Great Declouting

And the new technologies are widening the production base all the time, weakening the strategic importance of conventional reserves and the power of those who hold them. Before shale gas, it was thought that Venezuela might soon become an important gas source for America, and that Iran's vast gas reserves would motivate potential customers to break the sanctions imposed on it as a result of its nuclear programme. Both things are now less likely; the Baker Institute study suggests that while both countries will grow in importance—it foresees 26% of the world's LNG coming from Venezuela, Iran and Nigeria by 2040—they will do so much more slowly than they would have in a world of constrained supplies.

The growth of the gas market will not be untroubled. Large projects will be delayed sometimes, leading to periods of tight supply; there may also be overcapacity at times, as there has been recently. America's shale-gas success—a matter not just of helpful geology and Yankee ingenuity, but also of various legal and regulatory positions such as those of the 1978 act—may prove hard to replicate in some other countries. Environmental worries could stop shale gas dead in places. But although the pace may slow and the road may have bumps, for the moment the revolution looks set to roll on.

Critical Thinking

1. What are the reasons for a so-called revolution in U.S. natural gas markets?

2. What is fracking?

3. What are the three distinct global markets for natural gas, and how and why do they differ?

4. How is this revolution likely to weaken the strategic importance of some energy producing countries?

Nuclear Power after Fukushima

It is, still, the energy of the future.

Rod Adams

Does nuclear energy have a future, in light of the events at Fukushima? Fukushima Daiichi is the six-unit nuclear-power station on the northeast coast of Japan that was hit by a powerful tsunami, preceded by one of the strongest earthquakes on record. The extent of the damage is considerable: The three reactors that were operating at the time of the earthquake were destroyed by the high-pressure steam produced by heat from radioactive decay and the explosive reaction of hydrogen inside the structures. The hydrogen was produced by chemical reactions between water and the protective, corrosion-resistant layer of zirconium alloy that normally seals radioactive material in a controlled location.

Those who design, build, and operate nuclear-energy facilities know that bad things can happen. They understand energy, shock absorption, chemistry, physics, and radiation, and they invest a great deal of time and effort to build facilities with layers of defense that can undergo a number of failures while still succeeding in protecting against public harm.

In a nuclear plant, the core contains the fuel materials that generate the heat that produces the steam that turns the turbines and creates massive quantities of electricity from tiny quantities of uranium. A single fuel pellet the size of the tip of my pinkie produces as much heat, when it fissions in a conventional nuclear-energy facility, as a ton of high-quality coal does when it is burned in a modern plant. When things are going right, nuclear-fuel pellets do not produce any atmospheric pollution at all, while burning a ton of coal releases between two and four tons of waste into the environment. In the U.S., we consume about a billion tons of coal each year to produce about 45 percent of our electricity.

Nuclear facilities have occasionally suffered core damage. Sometimes core damage is a result of design mistakes, sometimes it is due to actions taken or not taken by human operators, and sometimes it is caused by external forces that were not considered sufficiently probable to be factored into the design requirements. The Fukushima disaster resulted from that last risk. The facility experienced a natural disaster that was considered too improbable to require specific protective measures, but it has happened and may happen again.

The contractor teams that are bidding to clean up the facility estimate that it will require between 10 and 30 years to do the job right, depending on how "right" is defined. The recovery effort will cost tens of billions of dollars. Replacing the power capacity of Fukushima will require Japan to import an average of roughly 700 million additional cubic feet of natural gas per day. After evaluating the other nuclear plants in the country in light of the early lessons learned from the accident, the Japanese government decided to shut down the three-unit Hamaoka nuclear station located in an especially active seismic region. That decision brings the power deficit caused by the tsunami and earthquake to the equivalent of about 1.1 to 1.3 billion cubic feet of natural gas per day. Some of that deficit can be made up by the reduction in power demand that is a result of a damaged industrial infrastructure and concerted conservation efforts.

There are additional costly effects. A plume of radioactive isotopes that are either gaseous or water-soluble left the facility and spread in a northwesterly direction, contaminating areas as far as 30 miles from the plant. Everyone living within a twelve-mile radius of the plant was evacuated in the first few hours after the event, but there have been additional evacuations as radiation surveys have shown that the material moved out farther in some areas. Tens of thousands of people are still living in temporary shelters and are not sure whether they will ever be allowed to return home.

Based on the announced results of the surveys, at least part of the area that has been evacuated could safely be repopulated today, although officials are understandably cautious. Even in areas where measured radiation levels are still higher than allowable under currently accepted international standards, the levels are steadily dropping as a result of an inherent characteristic of radioactive material: It loses strength over time. A major component of the radiation level immediately after the accident was iodine-131, an isotope that loses half of its intensity every eight days and is virtually undetectable after 80 days. By the time you read this article, that period will already have passed. But for the people who have been living in gymnasiums and have had no access to personal possessions for many months, the accident has already imposed a high cost. If you add in the inevitable deterioration of unoccupied structures, there is no way to ignore the widespread nature of the effects. Some individuals or even towns may never recover from the impact of this disaster.

Given the extensiveness of the damage and the expectation of still-uncounted costs, it is legitimate to wonder whether nuclear energy is worth the risk. There are plenty of other ways to generate power, and people flourished for several thousand years before nuclear fission was even discovered. As some who are opposed to nuclear energy remind us, there are only about 435 reactors producing commercial energy today. In many places around the world, nuclear-energy-plant construction stopped several decades ago, as costs seemed to go out of control and people were repeatedly told that nuclear power involved a high level of risk.

On the other hand, it remains almost unbelievable that a few obscure minerals contain so much densely packed, emission-free energy. Every kilogram of uranium or thorium contains as much potential energy as 2 million kilograms of oil. And that relatively small number of facilities does produce the energy equivalent of about 12 million barrels of oil per day. (That is as much energy as the daily output of Saudi Arabia and Kuwait combined; the total world petroleum output is about 80 million barrels of oil per day.)

So far, our economy has focused on only a narrow selection of the available options for harnessing this energy. The majority of the nuclear reactors in operation today are large, central-station electrical-power plants that produce a steady output and use ordinary water to cool the cores, transfer the heat, and turn the turbines. Though this approach works well and has proven its safety and reliability, there are other options, which offer improvements in fuel-use rates, thermal efficiency, and power-output flexibility. Uranium dioxide pellets are not the only fuel form available; advantages might be obtained if some reactors used metal-alloy fuels, and different advantages might result from using thorium or uranium dissolved in fluoride salts.

Society will not likely turn its back on a fuel source with so much potential, although the path will not be smooth, and there will be strong opposition from competitors and from the people who seem to dislike all forms of reliable power. Whatever happens in the U.S., nuclear-energy development will not be suppressed everywhere; China announced a program to review its planned nuclear expansion in light of Fukushima, but has already concluded that there is no reason to stop or even slow down its building of nuclear plants. And developers in the U.S. are working to incorporate the lessons of Fukushima into their designs. One possibility that seems to be particularly advantageous is to build larger numbers of smaller units that have an easier time getting rid of excess heat, even when the power goes out.

Any decision to slow down nuclear-energy development needs to be taken in full understanding that nuclear fission competes almost directly with fossil fuels, not with some idealized power source that carries no risk and causes no harm to the environment. The electricity that Germany has refused to accept from seven large nuclear plants that the government ordered closed after Fukushima has not been replaced by the output of magically spinning offshore wind turbines or highly efficient solar panels. It has been replaced by burning more gas from Russia, by burning more dirty lignite in German coal plants, and by purchasing electricity generated by nuclear-energy plants in France.

People have learned to accept that burning coal, oil, and natural gas carries risks of fires, explosions, and massive spills, and causes continuous emissions of harmful fine particulates and possibly deadly gases that are altering the atmospheric chemical balance. We accept those risks because we are acutely aware of the benefits of heat and mobility.

With nuclear energy, the benefits are substantial and the risks, relative to all other reliable energy sources, are minor. Since Fukushima, there has been a remarkable void of pro-nuclear-energy advertising, which has been filled by efforts by the natural-gas industry to convince Americans that it has recently discovered a 100-year supply.

In my opinion, something close to the worst-case scenario for nuclear power happened at Fukushima. By some calculations, the earthquake and tsunami together hit Japan with a force that was equivalent to several thousand nuclear weapons. Looking at the photos of the area around the Fukushima nuclear station makes me, a career military officer, whistle with wonder at the incredibly successful attack that nature launched.

In the midst of all of the destruction, an important fact frequently gets lost: Not a single member of the plant staff or a single member of the general public has been exposed to a sufficient dose of radiation to cause any harm. The highest dose to any of the workers involved in the recovery effort has been less than 250 millisieverts (25 rem), which is beneath the internationally accepted limit for people responding to a life-threatening accident.

The doses received by the celebrated "Fukushima Fifty" recovery workers are roughly the same as the dose that the young Lt. Jimmy Carter and several hundred other people received when responding to a December 1952 accident at an experimental reactor in Chalk River, Canada. President Carter, like many others involved in that effort, is alive and apparently healthy today.

Even after the Fukushima disaster—affecting six 30-to-40-year-old plants that had primitive control systems, inadequate backup-power supplies, and insufficient protection against the potential effects of earthquakes and tsunamis—nuclear energy has compiled a remarkable safety record. It will be an important, reliable, affordable, and clean energy source for the foreseeable future.

Critical Thinking

1. What is Adams's point of view?

2. What reasons does he offer to support his point of view?

3. Does the point of view of this article complement or contradict Article 26?

MR. ADAMS BLOGS at Atomic Insights and produces the podcast The Atomic Show. He received his nuclear training as a submarine officer in the U.S. Navy and recently retired after 29 years of service.

From *The National Review,* June 20, 2011, pp. 41–43. Copyright © 2011 by National Review, Inc, 215 Lexington Avenue, New York, NY 10016. Reprinted by permission.

UNIT 5
Conflict

Unit Selections

Learning Outcomes

After reading this Unit, you will be able to:

- Identify the dynamics of different types of international conflicts.

- Make some predictions on future hot spots where war might break out.

- Speculate about the future of armed conflict.

- Offer insights into additional international relations theories that are summarized in some of the articles.

- Assess your ongoing effort at identifying your theory of international relations and how this unit changes/complements it.

Student Website
www.mhhe.com/cls

Internet References

DefenseLINK
   www.defenselink.mil
Federation of American Scientists (FAS)
   www.fas.org
ISN International Relations and Security Network
   www.isn.ethz.ch
The NATO Integrated Data Service (NIDS)
   www.nato.int/structur/nids/nids.htm

Do you lock your doors at night? Do you secure your personal property to avoid theft? These are basic questions that have to do with your sense of personal security. Most individuals take steps to protect what they have, including their lives. The same is true for groups of people, including countries.

In the international arena, governments frequently pursue their national interest by entering into mutually agreeable "deals" with other governments. Social scientists call these types of arrangements "exchanges" (i.e., each side gives up something it values to gain something in return that it values even more). On an economic level, it functions like this: "I have the oil that you need and am willing to sell it. In return I want to buy from you the agricultural products that I lack." Whether on the governmental level or the personal level ("If you help me with my homework, then I will drive you home this weekend."), exchanges are the process used by most individuals and groups to obtain and protect what is of value. The exchange process, however, can break down. When threats and punishments replace mutual exchanges, conflict ensues. Neither side benefits, and there are costs to both. Further, each may use threats with the expectation that the other will capitulate. But if efforts at intimidation and coercion fail, the conflict may escalate into violent confrontation.

With the end of the Cold War, issues of national security and the nature of international conflict have changed. In the late 1980s agreements between the former Soviet Union and the United States led to the elimination of superpower support for participants in low-intensity conflicts in Central America, Africa, and Southeast Asia. Fighting the Cold War by proxy is now a thing of the past. In addition, Cold War military alliances have either collapsed or have been significantly redefined. Despite these historic changes, there is no shortage of conflicts in the world today.

Many experts initially predicted that the collapse of the Soviet Union would decrease the arms race and diminish the threat of nuclear war. However, some analysts now believe that the threat of nuclear war has, in fact, increased as control of nuclear weapons has become less centralized and the command structure less reliable. In addition, the proliferation of nuclear weapons into North Korea and South Asia (India and Pakistan) is a growing security issue. Further, there are concerns about both dictatorial governments and terrorist organizations obtaining weapons of mass destruction. What these changing circumstances mean for U.S. policy is a topic of considerable debate.

The unit begins with a unique perspective on the sources of international conflict. It is followed by a series of case studies that provide insights into the roots of the drug war in Mexico, political unrest in the Middle East, and the foreign policy objectives of emerging regional and global powers. The unit concludes with an article on a new domain of warfare, cyberspace.

As in the case of the other global issues described in this anthology, international conflict is a dynamic problem. It is important to understand that conflicts are not random events, but follow patterns and trends. Forty-five years of Cold War established discernable patterns of international conflict as the superpowers deterred each other with vast expenditures of money and technological

know-how. The consequence of this stalemate was often a shift to the developing world for conflict by superpower proxy.

The changing circumstances of the post-Cold War era generate a series of important new policy questions: Will there be more nuclear proliferation? Is there an increased danger of so-called rogue states destabilizing the international arena? Is the threat of terror a temporary or permanent feature of world affairs? Will there be a growing emphasis on low-intensity conflicts related to the interdiction of drugs, or will some other unforeseen issue determine the world's hot spots? Will the United States and its European allies lose interest in security issues that do not directly involve their economic interests and simply look the other way, for example, as age-old ethnic conflicts become brutally violent? Can the international community develop viable institutions to mediate and resolve disputes before they become violent? The answers to these and related questions will determine the patterns of conflict in the twenty-first century.

The Revenge of Geography

People and ideas influence events, but geography largely determines them, now more than ever. To understand the coming struggles, it's time to dust off the Victorian thinkers who knew the physical world best. A journalist who has covered the ends of the Earth offers a guide to the relief map—and a primer on the next phase of conflict.

ROBERT D. KAPLAN

When rapturous Germans tore down the Berlin Wall 20 years ago it symbolized far more than the overcoming of an arbitrary boundary. It began an intellectual cycle that saw all divisions, geographic and otherwise, as surmountable; that referred to "realism" and "pragmatism" only as pejoratives; and that invoked the humanism of Isaiah Berlin or the appeasement of Hitler at Munich to launch one international intervention after the next. In this way, the armed liberalism and the democracy-promoting neoconservatism of the 1990s shared the same universalist aspirations. But alas, when a fear of Munich leads to overreach the result is Vietnam—or in the current case, Iraq.

And thus began the rehabilitation of realism, and with it another intellectual cycle. "Realist" is now a mark of respect, "neocon" a term of derision. The Vietnam analogy has vanquished that of Munich. Thomas Hobbes, who extolled the moral benefits of fear and saw anarchy as the chief threat to society, has elbowed out Isaiah Berlin as the philosopher of the present cycle. The focus now is less on universal ideals than particular distinctions, from ethnicity to culture to religion. Those who pointed this out a decade ago were sneered at for being "fatalists" or "determinists." Now they are applauded as "pragmatists." And this is the key insight of the past two decades—that there are worse things in the world than extreme tyranny, and in Iraq we brought them about ourselves. I say this having supported the war.

So now, chastened, we have all become realists. Or so we believe. But realism is about more than merely opposing a war in Iraq that we know from hindsight turned out badly. Realism means recognizing that international relations are ruled by a sadder, more limited reality than the one governing domestic affairs. It means valuing order above freedom, for the latter becomes important only after the former has been established. It means focusing on what divides humanity rather than on what unites it, as the high priests of globalization would have it. In short, realism is about recognizing and embracing those forces beyond our control that constrain human action—culture, tradition, history, the bleaker tides of passion that lie just beneath the veneer of civilization. This poses what, for realists, is the central question in foreign affairs: Who can do what to whom? And of all the unsavory truths in which realism is rooted, the bluntest, most uncomfortable, and most deterministic of all is geography.

Indeed, what is at work in the recent return of realism is the revenge of geography in the most old-fashioned sense. In the 18th and 19th centuries, before the arrival of political science as an academic specialty, geography was an honored, if not always formalized, discipline in which politics, culture, and economics were often conceived of in reference to the relief map. Thus, in the Victorian and Edwardian eras, mountains and the men who grow out of them were the first order of reality; ideas, however uplifting, were only the second.

And yet, to embrace geography is not to accept it as an implacable force against which humankind is powerless. Rather, it serves to qualify human freedom and choice with a modest acceptance of fate. This is all the more important today, because rather than eliminating the relevance of geography, globalization is reinforcing it. Mass communications and economic integration are weakening many states, exposing a Hobbesian world of small, fractious regions. Within them, local, ethnic, and religious sources of identity are reasserting themselves, and because they are anchored to specific terrains, they are best explained by reference to geography. Like the faults that determine earthquakes, the political future will be defined by conflict and instability with a similar geographic logic. The upheaval spawned by the ongoing economic crisis is increasing the relevance of geography even further, by weakening social orders and other creations of humankind, leaving the natural frontiers of the globe as the only restraint.

So we, too, need to return to the map, and particularly to what I call the "shatter zones" of Eurasia. We need to reclaim those thinkers who knew the landscape best. And we need to update their theories for the revenge of geography in our time.

If you want to understand the insights of geography, you need to seek out those thinkers who make liberal humanists profoundly uneasy—those authors who thought the map determined nearly everything, leaving little room for human agency.

One such person is the French historian Fernand Braudel, who in 1949 published *The Mediterranean and the Mediterranean World in the Age of Philip II*. By bringing demography and nature itself into history, Braudel helped restore geography to its proper place. In his narrative, permanent environmental forces lead to enduring historical trends that preordain political events and regional wars. To Braudel, for example, the poor, precarious soils along the Mediterranean, combined with an uncertain, drought-afflicted climate, spurred ancient Greek and Roman conquest. In other words, we delude ourselves by thinking that we control our own destinies. To understand the present challenges of climate change, warming Arctic seas, and the scarcity of resources such as oil and water, we must reclaim Braudel's environmental interpretation of events.

So, too, must we reexamine the blue-water strategizing of Alfred Thayer Mahan, a U.S. naval captain and author of *The Influence of Sea Power Upon History, 1660–1783*. Viewing the sea as the great "commons" of civilization, Mahan thought that naval power had always been the decisive factor in global political struggles. It was Mahan who, in 1902, coined the term "Middle East" to denote the area between Arabia and India that held particular importance for naval strategy. Indeed, Mahan saw the Indian and Pacific oceans as the hinges of geopolitical destiny, for they would allow a maritime nation to project power all around the Eurasian rim and thereby affect political developments deep into Central Asia. Mahan's thinking helps to explain why the Indian Ocean will be the heart of geopolitical competition in the 21st century—and why his books are now all the rage among Chinese and Indian strategists.

Similarly, the Dutch-American strategist Nicholas Spykman saw the seaboards of the Indian and Pacific oceans as the keys to dominance in Eurasia and the natural means to check the land power of Russia. Before he died in 1943, while the United States was fighting Japan, Spykman predicted the rise of China and the consequent need for the United States to defend Japan. And even as the United States was fighting to liberate Europe, Spykman warned that the postwar emergence of an integrated European power would eventually become inconvenient for the United States. Such is the foresight of geographical determinism.

But perhaps the most significant guide to the revenge of geography is the father of modern geopolitics himself—Sir Halford J. Mackinder—who is famous not for a book but a single article, "The Geographical Pivot of History," which began as a 1904 lecture to the Royal Geographical Society in London. Mackinder's work is the archetype of the geographical discipline, and he summarizes its theme nicely: "Man and not nature initiates, but nature in large measure controls."

His thesis is that Russia, Eastern Europe, and Central Asia are the "pivot" around which the fate of world empire revolves. He would refer to this area of Eurasia as the "heartland" in a later book. Surrounding it are four "marginal" regions of the Eurasian landmass that correspond, not coincidentally, to the four great religions, because faith, too, is merely a function of geography for Mackinder. There are two "monsoon lands": one in the east generally facing the Pacific Ocean, the home of Buddhism; the other in the south facing the Indian Ocean, the home of Hinduism. The third marginal region is Europe, watered by the Atlantic to the west and the home of Christianity. But the most fragile of the four marginal regions is the Middle East, home of Islam, "deprived of moisture by the proximity of Africa" and for the most part "thinly peopled" (in 1904, that is).

Realism is about recognizing and embracing those forces beyond our control that constrain human action. And of all the unsavory truths in which realism is rooted, the bluntest, most uncomfortable, and most deterministic of all is geography.

This Eurasian relief map, and the events playing out on it at the dawn of the 20th century, are Mackinder's subject, and the opening sentence presages its grand sweep:

> When historians in the remote future come to look back on the group of centuries through which we are now passing, and see them fore-shortened, as we to-day see the Egyptian dynasties, it may well be that they will describe the last 400 years as the Columbian epoch, and will say that it ended soon after the year 1900.

Mackinder explains that, while medieval Christendom was "pent into a narrow region and threatened by external barbarism," the Columbian age—the Age of Discovery—saw Europe expand across the oceans to new lands. Thus at the turn of the 20th century, "we shall again have to deal with a closed political system," and this time one of "world-wide scope."

> Every explosion of social forces, instead of being dissipated in a surrounding circuit of unknown space and barbaric chaos, will [henceforth] be sharply re-echoed from the far side of the globe, and weak elements in the political and economic organism of the world will be shattered in consequence.

By perceiving that European empires had no more room to expand, thereby making their conflicts global, Mackinder foresaw, however vaguely, the scope of both world wars.

Mackinder looked at European history as "subordinate" to that of Asia, for he saw European civilization as merely the outcome of the struggle against Asiatic invasion. Europe, he writes, became the cultural phenomenon it is only because of its geography: an intricate array of mountains, valleys, and peninsulas; bounded by northern ice and a western ocean; blocked by seas and the Sahara to the south; and set against the immense, threatening flatland of Russia to the east. Into this confined landscape poured a succession of nomadic, Asian invaders from the naked steppe. The union of Franks, Goths, and Roman provincials against these invaders produced the basis for modern France. Likewise, other European powers originated, or at least matured, through their encounters with Asian nomads. Indeed, it was the Seljuk Turks' supposed ill treatment of Christian pilgrims in Jerusalem that ostensibly led to the Crusades, which Mackinder considers the beginning of Europe's collective modern history.

Russia, meanwhile, though protected by forest glades against many a rampaging host, nevertheless fell prey in the 13th century to the Golden Horde of the Mongols. These invaders decimated and subsequently changed Russia. But because most of Europe knew no such level of destruction, it was able to emerge as the world's political cockpit, while Russia was largely denied access to the European Renaissance. The ultimate land-based empire, with few natural barriers against invasion, Russia would know forevermore what it was like to be brutally conquered. As a result, it would become perennially obsessed with expanding and holding territory.

Key discoveries of the Columbian epoch, Mackinder writes, only reinforced the cruel facts of geography. In the Middle Ages, the peoples of Europe were largely confined to the land. But when the sea route to India was found around the Cape of Good Hope, Europeans suddenly had access to the entire rimland of southern Asia, to say nothing of strategic discoveries in the New World. While Western Europeans "covered the ocean with their fleets," Mackinder tells us, Russia was expanding equally impressively on land, "emerging from her northern forests" to police the steppe with her Cossacks, sweeping into Siberia, and sending peasants to sow the southwestern steppe with wheat. It was an old story: Europe versus Russia, a liberal sea power (like Athens and Venice) against a reactionary land power (like Sparta and Prussia). For the sea, beyond the cosmopolitan influences it bestows by virtue of access to distant harbors, provides the inviolate border security that democracy needs to take root.

In the 19th century, Mackinder notes, the advent of steam engines and the creation of the Suez Canal increased the mobility of European sea power around the southern rim of Eurasia, just as railways were beginning to do the same for land power in the Eurasian heartland. So the struggle was set for the mastery of Eurasia, bringing Mackinder to his thesis:

> As we consider this rapid review of the broader currents of history, does not a certain persistence of geographical relationship become evident? Is not the pivot region of the world's politics that vast area of Euro-Asia which is inaccessible to ships, but in antiquity lay open to the horse-riding nomads, and is today about to be covered with a network of railways?

Just as the Mongols banged at, and often broke down, the gates to the marginal regions surrounding Eurasia, Russia would now play the same conquering role, for as Mackinder writes, "the geographical quantities in the calculation are more measurable and more nearly constant than the human." Forget the czars and the commissars-yet-to-be in 1904; they are but trivia compared with the deeper tectonic forces of geography.

Mackinder's determinism prepared us for the rise of the Soviet Union and its vast zone of influence in the second half of the 20th century, as well as for the two world wars preceding it. After all, as historian Paul Kennedy notes, these conflicts were struggles over Mackinder's "marginal" regions, running from Eastern Europe to the Himalayas and beyond. Cold War containment strategy, moreover, depended heavily on rimland bases across the greater Middle East and the Indian Ocean. Indeed, the U.S. projection of power into Afghanistan and Iraq, and today's tensions with Russia over the political fate of Central Asia and the Caucasus have only bolstered Mackinder's thesis. In his article's last paragraph, Mackinder even raises the specter of Chinese conquests of the "pivot" area, which would make China the dominant geopolitical power. Look at how Chinese migrants are now demographically claiming parts of Siberia as Russia's political control of its eastern reaches is being strained. One can envision Mackinder's being right yet again.

The wisdom of geographical determinism endures across the chasm of a century because it recognizes that the most profound struggles of humanity are not about ideas but about control over territory, specifically the heartland and rimlands of Eurasia. Of course, ideas matter, and they span geography. And yet there is a certain geographic logic to where certain ideas take hold. Communist Eastern Europe, Mongolia, China, and North Korea were all contiguous to the great land power of the Soviet Union. Classic fascism was a predominantly European affair. And liberalism nurtured its deepest roots in the United States and Great Britain, essentially island nations and sea powers both. Such determinism is easy to hate but hard to dismiss.

To discern where the battle of ideas will lead, we must revise Mackinder for our time. After all, Mackinder could not foresee how a century's worth of change would redefine—and enhance—the importance of geography in today's world. One author who did is Yale University professor Paul Bracken, who in 1999 published *Fire in the East*. Bracken draws a conceptual map of Eurasia defined by the collapse of time and distance and the filling of empty spaces. This idea leads him to declare a "crisis of room." In the past, sparsely populated geography acted as a safety mechanism. Yet this is no longer the case, Bracken argues, for as empty space increasingly disappears, the very "finite size of the earth" becomes a force for instability. And as I learned at the U.S. Army's Command and General Staff College, "attrition of the same adds up to big change."

One force that is shrinking the map of Eurasia is technology, particularly the military applications of it and the rising power it confers on states. In the early Cold War, Asian militaries were mostly lumbering, heavy forces whose primary purpose was national consolidation. They focused inward. But as national wealth accumulated and the computer revolution took hold, Asian militaries from the oil-rich Middle East to the tiger economies of the Pacific developed full-fledged, military-civilian postindustrial complexes, with missiles and fiber optics and satellite phones. These states also became bureaucratically more cohesive, allowing their militaries to focus outward, toward other states. Geography in Eurasia, rather than a cushion, was becoming a prison from which there was no escape.

Now there is an "unbroken belt of countries," in Bracken's words, from Israel to North Korea, which are developing ballistic missiles and destructive arsenals. A map of these countries' missile ranges shows a series of overlapping circles: Not only is no one safe, but a 1914-style chain reaction leading to wider war is easily conceivable. "The spread of missiles and weapons of mass destruction in Asia is like the spread of the six-shooter in the American Old West," Bracken writes—a cheap, deadly equalizer of states.

The other force driving the revenge of geography is population growth, which makes the map of Eurasia more claustrophobic still. In the 1990s, many intellectuals viewed the 18th-century English philosopher Thomas Malthus as an overly deterministic thinker because he treated humankind as a species reacting to its physical environment, not a body of autonomous individuals. But as the years pass, and world food and energy prices fluctuate, Malthus is getting more respect. If you wander through the slums of Karachi or Gaza, which wall off multitudes of angry lumpen faithful—young men mostly—one can easily see the conflicts over scarce resources that Malthus predicted coming to pass. In three decades covering the Middle East, I have watched it evolve from a largely rural society to a realm of teeming megacities. In the next 20 years, the Arab world's population will nearly double while supplies of groundwater will diminish.

A Eurasia of vast urban areas, overlapping missile ranges, and sensational media will be one of constantly enraged crowds, fed by rumors transported at the speed of light from one Third World megalopolis to another. So in addition to Malthus, we will also hear much about Elias Canetti, the 20th-century philosopher of crowd psychology: the phenomenon of a mass of people abandoning their individuality for an intoxicating collective symbol. It is in the cities of Eurasia principally where crowd psychology will have its greatest geopolitical impact. Alas, ideas do matter. And it is the very compression of geography that will provide optimum breeding grounds for dangerous ideologies and channels for them to spread.

All of this requires major revisions to Mackinder's theories of geopolitics. For as the map of Eurasia shrinks and fills up with people, it not only obliterates the artificial regions of area studies; it also erases Mackinder's division of Eurasia into a specific "pivot" and adjacent "marginal" zones. Military assistance from China and North Korea to Iran can cause Israel to take military actions. The U.S. Air Force can attack landlocked Afghanistan from Diego Garcia, an island in the middle of the Indian Ocean. The Chinese and Indian navies can project power from the Gulf of Aden to the South China Sea—out of their own regions and along the whole rimland. In short, contra Mackinder, Eurasia has been reconfigured into an organic whole.

The map's new seamlessness can be seen in the Pakistani outpost of Gwadar. There, on the Indian Ocean, near the Iranian border, the Chinese have constructed a spanking new deep-water port. Land prices are booming, and people talk of this still sleepy fishing village as the next Dubai, which may one day link towns in Central Asia to the burgeoning middle-class fleshpots of India and China through pipelines, supertankers, and the Strait of Malacca. The Chinese also have plans for developing other

Indian Ocean ports in order to transport oil by pipelines directly into western and central China, even as a canal and land bridge are possibly built across Thailand's Isthmus of Kra. Afraid of being outflanked by the Chinese, the Indians are expanding their own naval ports and strengthening ties with both Iran and Burma, where the Indian-Chinese rivalry will be fiercest.

Much of Eurasia will eventually be as claustrophobic as the Levant, with geography controlling everything and no room to maneuver. The battle over land between Israelis and Palestinians is a case of utter geographical determinism. This is Eurasia's future as well.

These deepening connections are transforming the Middle East, Central Asia, and the Indian and Pacific oceans into a vast continuum, in which the narrow and vulnerable Strait of Malacca will be the Fulda Gap of the 21st century. The fates of the Islamic Middle East and Islamic Indonesia are therefore becoming inextricable. But it is the geographic connections, not religious ones, that matter most.

This new map of Eurasia—tighter, more integrated, and more crowded—will be even less stable than Mackinder thought. Rather than heartlands and marginal zones that imply separateness, we will have a series of inner and outer cores that are fused together through mass politics and shared paranoia. In fact, much of Eurasia will eventually be as claustrophobic as Israel and the Palestinian territories, with geography controlling everything and no room to maneuver. Although Zionism shows the power of ideas, the battle over land between Israelis and Palestinians is a case of utter geographical determinism. This is Eurasia's future as well.

The ability of states to control events will be diluted, in some cases destroyed. Artificial borders will crumble and become more fissiparous, leaving only rivers, deserts, mountains, and other enduring facts of geography. Indeed, the physical features of the landscape may be the only reliable guides left to understanding the shape of future conflict. Like rifts in the Earth's crust that produce physical instability, there are areas in Eurasia that are more prone to conflict than others. These "shatter zones" threaten to implode, explode, or maintain a fragile equilibrium. And not surprisingly, they fall within that unstable inner core of Eurasia: the greater Middle East, the vast way station between the Mediterranean world and the Indian subcontinent that registers all the primary shifts in global power politics.

This inner core, for Mackinder, was the ultimate unstable region. And yet, writing in an age before oil pipelines and ballistic missiles, he saw this region as inherently volatile, geographically speaking, but also somewhat of a secondary concern. A century's worth of technological advancement and population explosion has rendered the greater Middle East no less volatile but dramatically more relevant, and where Eurasia is most prone to fall apart now is in the greater Middle East's several shatter zones.

I'll never forget what a U.S. military expert told me in Sanaa: "Terrorism is an entrepreneurial activity, and in Yemen you've got over 20 million aggressive, commercial-minded, and well-armed people, all extremely hard-working compared with the Saudis next door. It's the future, and it terrifies the hell out of the government in Riyadh."

The Indian subcontinent is one such shatter zone. It is defined on its landward sides by the hard geographic borders of the Himalayas to the north, the Burmese jungle to the east, and the somewhat softer border of the Indus River to the west. Indeed, the border going westward comes in three stages: the Indus; the unruly crags and canyons that push upward to the shaved wastes of Central Asia, home to the Pashtun tribes; and, finally, the granite, snow-mantled massifs of the Hindu Kush, transecting Afghanistan itself. Because these geographic impediments are not contiguous with legal borders, and because barely any of India's neighbors are functional states, the current political organization of the subcontinent should not be taken for granted. You see this acutely as you walk up to and around any of these land borders, the weakest of which, in my experience, are the official ones—a mere collection of tables where cranky bureaucrats inspect your luggage. Especially in the west, the only border that lives up to the name is the Hindu Kush, making me think that in our own lifetimes the whole semblance of order in Pakistan and southeastern Afghanistan could unravel, and return, in effect, to vague elements of greater India.

In Nepal, the government barely controls the countryside where 85 percent of its people live. Despite the aura bequeathed by the Himalayas, nearly half of Nepal's population lives in the dank and humid lowlands along the barely policed border with India. Driving throughout this region, it appears in many ways indistinguishable from the Ganges plain. If the Maoists now ruling Nepal cannot increase state capacity, the state itself could dissolve.

The same holds true for Bangladesh. Even more so than Nepal, it has no geographic defense to marshal as a state. The view from my window during a recent bus journey was of the same ruler-flat, aquatic landscape of paddy fields and scrub on both sides of the line with India. The border posts are disorganized, ramshackle affairs. This artificial blotch of territory on the Indian subcontinent could metamorphose yet again, amid the gale forces of regional politics, Muslim extremism, and nature itself.

Like Pakistan, no Bangladeshi government, military or civilian, has ever functioned even remotely well. Millions of Bangladeshi refugees have already crossed the border into India illegally. With 150 million people—a population larger than Russia—crammed together at sea level, Bangladesh is vulnerable to the slightest climatic variation, never mind the changes caused by global warming. Simply because of its geography, tens of millions of people in Bangladesh could be inundated with salt water, necessitating the mother of all humanitarian relief efforts. In the process, the state itself could collapse.

Of course, the worst nightmare on the subcontinent is Pakistan, whose dysfunction is directly the result of its utter lack of geographic logic. The Indus should be a border of sorts, but Pakistan sits astride both its banks, just as the fertile and teeming Punjab plain is bisected by the India-Pakistan border. Only the Thar Desert and the swamps to its south act as natural frontiers between Pakistan and India. And though these are formidable barriers, they are insufficient to frame a state composed of disparate, geographically based, ethnic groups—Punjabis, Sindhis, Baluchis, and Pashtuns—for whom Islam has provided insufficient glue to hold them together. All the other groups in Pakistan hate the Punjabis and the army they control, just as the groups in the former Yugoslavia hated the Serbs and the army they controlled. Pakistan's raison d'être is that it supposedly provides a homeland for subcontinental Muslims, but 154 million of them, almost the same number as the entire population of Pakistan, live over the border in India.

To the west, the crags and canyons of Pakistan's North-West Frontier Province, bordering Afghanistan, are utterly porous. Of all the times I crossed the Pakistan-Afghanistan border, I never did so legally. In reality, the two countries are inseparable. On both sides live the Pashtuns. The wide belt of territory between the Hindu Kush mountains and the Indus River is really Pashtunistan, an entity that threatens to emerge were Pakistan to fall apart. That would, in turn, lead to the dissolution of Afghanistan.

The Taliban constitute merely the latest incarnation of Pashtun nationalism. Indeed, much of the fighting in Afghanistan today occurs in Pashtunistan: southern and eastern Afghanistan and the tribal areas of Pakistan. The north of Afghanistan, beyond the Hindu Kush, has seen less fighting and is in the midst of reconstruction and the forging of closer links to the former Soviet republics in Central Asia, inhabited by the same ethnic groups that populate northern Afghanistan. Here is the ultimate world of Mackinder, of mountains and men, where the facts of geography are asserted daily, to the chagrin of U.S.-led forces—and of India, whose own destiny and borders are hostage to what plays out in the vicinity of the 20,000-foot wall of the Hindu Kush.

Another shatter zone is the Arabian Peninsula. The vast tract of land controlled by the Saudi royal family is synonymous with Arabia in the way that India is synonymous with the subcontinent. But while India is heavily populated throughout, Saudi Arabia constitutes a geographically nebulous network of oases separated by massive waterless tracts. Highways and domestic air links are crucial to Saudi Arabia's cohesion. Though India is built on an idea of democracy and religious pluralism, Saudi Arabia is built on loyalty to an extended family. But while India is virtually surrounded by troubling geography and dysfunctional states, Saudi Arabia's borders disappear into harmless desert to the north and are shielded by sturdy, well-governed, self-contained sheikhdoms to the east and southeast.

Where Saudi Arabia is truly vulnerable, and where the shatter zone of Arabia is most acute, is in highly populous Yemen to the south. Although it has only a quarter of Saudi Arabia's land area, Yemen's population is almost as large, so the all-important demographic core of the Arabian Peninsula is crammed into its mountainous southwest corner, where sweeping basalt plateaus, rearing up into sandcastle formations and volcanic plugs, embrace a network of oases densely inhabited since antiquity. Because the Turks and the British never really controlled Yemen, they did not leave behind the strong bureaucratic institutions that other former colonies inherited.

When I traveled the Saudi-Yemen border some years back, it was crowded with pickup trucks filled with armed young men, loyal to this sheikh or that, while the presence of the Yemeni government was negligible. Mudbrick battlements hid the encampments of these rebellious sheikhs, some with their own artillery. Estimates of the number of firearms in Yemen vary, but any Yemeni who wants a weapon can get one easily. Meanwhile, groundwater supplies will last no more than a generation or two.

I'll never forget what a U.S. military expert told me in the capital, Sanaa: "Terrorism is an entrepreneurial activity, and in Yemen you've got over 20 million aggressive, commercial-minded, and well-armed people, all extremely hard-working compared with the Saudis next door. It's the future, and it terrifies the hell out of the government in Riyadh." The future of teeming, tribal Yemen will go a long way to determining the future of Saudi Arabia. And geography, not ideas, has everything to do with it.

The Fertile Crescent, wedged between the Mediterranean Sea and the Iranian plateau, constitutes another shatter zone. The countries of this region—Jordan, Lebanon, Syria, and Iraq—are vague geographic expressions that had little meaning before the 20th century. When the official lines on the map are removed, we find a crude finger-painting of Sunni and Shiite clusters that contradict national borders. Inside these borders, the governing authorities of Lebanon and Iraq barely exist. The one in Syria is tyrannical and fundamentally unstable; the one in Jordan is rational but under quiet siege. (Jordan's main reason for being at all is to act as a buffer for other Arab regimes that fear having a land border with Israel.) Indeed, the Levant is characterized by tired authoritarian regimes and ineffective democracies.

Of all the geographically illogical states in the Fertile Crescent, none is more so than Iraq. Saddam Hussein's tyranny, by far the worst in the Arab world, was itself geographically determined: Every Iraqi dictator going back to the first military coup in 1958 had to be more repressive than the previous one just to hold together a country with no natural borders that seethes with ethnic and sectarian consciousness. The mountains that separate Kurdistan from the rest of Iraq, and the division of the Mesopotamian plain between Sunnis in the center and Shiites in the south, may prove more pivotal to Iraq's stability than the yearning after the ideal of democracy. If democracy doesn't in fairly short order establish sturdy institutional roots, Iraq's geography will likely lead it back to tyranny or anarchy again.

But for all the recent focus on Iraq, geography and history tell us that Syria might be at the real heart of future turbulence in the Arab world. Aleppo in northern Syria is a bazaar city with greater historical links to Mosul, Baghdad, and Anatolia than to Damascus. Whenever Damascus's fortunes declined with the rise of Baghdad to the east, Aleppo recovered its greatness. Wandering through the souks of Aleppo, it is striking how distant and irrelevant Damascus seems: The bazzars are dominated by Kurds, Turks, Circassians, Arab Christians, Armenians, and others, unlike the Damascus souk, which is more a world of Sunni Arabs. As in Pakistan and the former Yugoslavia, each sect and religion in Syria has a specific location. Between Aleppo and Damascus in the increasingly Islamist Sunni heartland. Between Damascus and the Jordanian border are the Druse, and in the mountain stronghold contiguous with Lebanon are the Alawites—both remnants of a wave of Shiism from Persia and Mesopotamia that swept over Syria a thousand years ago.

Elections in Syria in 1947, 1949, and 1954 exacerbated these divisions by polarizing the vote along sectarian lines. The late Hafez al-assad came to power in 1970 after 21 changes of government in 24 years. For three decades, he was the Leonid Brezhnev of the Arab world, staving off the future by failing to build a civil society at home. His son Bashar will have to open the political system eventually, if only to keep pace with a dynamically changing society armed with satellite dishes and the Internet. But no one knows how stable a post-authoritarian Syria would be. Policymakers must fear the worst. Yet a post-Assad Syria may well do better than post-Saddam Iraq, precisely because its tyranny has been much less severe. Indeed, traveling from Saddam's Iraq to Assad's Syria was like coming up for air.

In addition to its inability to solve the problem of political legitimacy, the Arab world is unable to secure its own environment. The plateau peoples of Turkey will dominate the Arabs in the 21st century because the Turks have water and the Arabs don't. Indeed, to develop its own desperately poor southeast and thereby suppress Kurdish separatism, Turkey will need to divert increasingly large amounts of the Euphrates River from Syria and Iraq. As the Middle East becomes a realm of parched urban areas, water will grow in value relative to oil. The countries with it will retain the ability—and thus the power—to blackmail those without it. Water will be like nuclear energy, thereby making desalinization and dual-use power facilities primary targets of missile strikes in future wars. Not just in the West Bank, but everywhere there is less room to maneuver.

A final shatter zone is the Persian core, stretching from the Caspian Sea to Iran's north to the Persian Gulf to its south. Virtually all of the greater Middle East's oil and natural gas lies in this region. Just as shipping lanes radiate from the Persian Gulf, pipelines are increasingly radiating from the Caspian region to the Mediterranean, the Black Sea, China, and the Indian Ocean. The only country that straddles both energy-producing areas is Iran, as Geoffrey Kemp and

Robert E. Harkavy note in *Strategic Geography and the Changing Middle East.* The Persian Gulf possesses 55 percent of the world's crude-oil reserves, and Iran dominates the whole gulf, from the Shatt al-Arab on the Iraqi border to the Strait of Hormuz in the southeast—a coastline of 1,317 nautical miles, thanks to its many bays, inlets, coves, and islands that offer plenty of excellent places for hiding tanker-ramming speedboats.

It is not an accident that Iran was the ancient world's first superpower. There was a certain geographic logic to it. Iran is the greater Middle East's universal joint, tightly fused to all of the outer cores. Its border roughly traces and conforms to the natural contours of the landscape—plateaus to the west, mountains and seas to the north and south, and desert expanse in the east toward Afghanistan. For this reason, Iran has a far more venerable record as a nation-state and urbane civilization than most places in the Arab world and all the places in the Fertile Crescent. Unlike the geographically illogical countries of that adjacent region, there is nothing artificial about Iran. Not surprisingly, Iran is now being wooed by both India and China, whose navies will come to dominate the Eurasian sea lanes in the 21st century.

Of all the shatter zones in the greater Middle East, the Iranian core is unique: The instability Iran will cause will not come from its implosion, but from a strong, internally coherent Iranian nation that explodes outward from a natural geographic platform to shatter the region around it. The security provided to Iran by its own natural boundaries has historically been a potent force for power projection. The present is no different. Through its uncompromising ideology and nimble intelligence services, Iran runs an unconventional, postmodern empire of substate entities in the greater Middle East: Hamas in Palestine, Hezbollah in Lebanon, and the Sadrist movement in southern Iraq. If the geographic logic of Iranian expansion sounds eerily similar to that of Russian expansion in Mackinder's original telling, it is.

The geography of Iran today, like that of Russia before, determines the most realistic strategy to securing this shatter zone: containment. As with Russia, the goal of containing Iran must be to impose pressure on the contradictions of the unpopular, theocratic regime in Tehran, such that it eventually changes from within. The battle for Eurasia has many, increasingly interlocking fronts. But the primary one is for Iranian hearts and minds, just as it was for those of Eastern Europeans during the Cold War. Iran is home to one of the Muslim world's most sophisticated populations, and traveling there, one encounters less anti-Americanism and anti-Semitism than in Egypt. This is where the battle of ideas meets the dictates of geography.

In this century's fight for Eurasia, like that of the last century, Mackinder's axiom holds true: Man will initiate, but nature will control. Liberal universalism and the individualism of Isaiah Berlin aren't going away, but it is becoming clear that the success of these ideas is in large measure bound and determined by geography. This was always the case, and it is harder to deny now, as the ongoing recession will likely cause the global economy to contract for the first time in six decades. Not only wealth, but political and social order, will erode in many places, leaving only nature's frontiers and men's passions as the main arbiters of that age-old question: Who can coerce whom? We thought globalization had gotten rid of this antiquarian world of musty maps, but now it is returning with a vengeance.

We all must learn to think like Victorians. That is what must guide and inform our newly rediscovered realism. Geographical determinists must be seated at the same honored table as liberal humanists, thereby merging the analogies of Vietnam and Munich. Embracing the dictates and limitations of geography will be especially hard for Americans, who like to think that no constraint, natural or otherwise, applies to them. But denying the facts of geography only invites disasters that, in turn, make us victims of geography.

Better, instead, to look hard at the map for ingenious ways to stretch the limits it imposes, which will make any support for liberal principles in the world far more effective. Amid the revenge of geography, that is the essence of realism and the crux of wise policymaking—working near the edge of what is possible, without slipping into the precipice.

Critical Thinking

1. What does Robert Kaplan mean by "realism"?
2. According to Kaplan, what role does geography have in understanding global issues?
3. Identify Mackinder's "heartland" and what its modern implications are.
4. What are the main reasons that the "map of Eurasia is more claustrophobic"?
5. What are some of the most important "shatter zones"?
6. How does this article complement/contradict articles 1, 4, 21 and 25?

ROBERT D. KAPLAN is national correspondent for *The Atlantic* and senior fellow at the Center for a New American Security.

Reprinted in entirety by McGraw-Hill with permission from *Foreign Policy,* May/June 2009, pp. 96, 98–105. www.foreignpolicy.com. © 2009 Washingtonpost.Newsweek Interactive, LLC.

A Himalayan Rivalry

Asia's two giants are still unsure what to make of each other. But as they grow, they are coming closer—for good and bad.

Memories of a war between India and China are still vivid in the Tawang valley, a lovely, cloud-blown place high on the south-eastern flank of the Himalayas. They are nurtured first by the Indian army, humiliated in 1962 when the People's Liberation Army swept into Tawang from next-door Tibet. India now has three army corps—about 100,000 troops—in its far north-eastern state of Arunachal Pradesh, which includes Tawang.

With another corps in reserve, and a few Sukhoi fighter planes deployed last year to neighbouring Assam, they are a meaty border force, unlike their hapless predecessors. In 1962 many Indian troops were sent shivering to the front in light cotton uniforms issued for Punjab's fiery plains. In a weeklong assault the Chinese seized much of Arunachal, as well as a slab of Kashmir in the western Himalayas, and killed 3,000 Indian officers and men. Outside Tawang's district headquarters a roadside memorial, built in the local Buddhist style, commemorates these dead. At a famous battle site, below the 14,000-foot pass that leads into Tawang, army convoys go slow, and salute their ghosts.

In wayside villages of solid white houses fluttering with coloured prayer-flags, China's two-week occupation of Tawang is also remembered. Local peasants, aged 60 and more but with youthful Tibetan features, light-brown and creased by the wind, recall playing Sho (Tibetan Mahjong) with the invaders. Many say they remember them fondly: the Chinese, they note, helped get in the wheat harvest that year. "They were little men, but they were always ready to help. We had no problem with them," says Mem Nansey, an aged potato farmer. The Chinese withdrew to Tibet, their superiority established but their supply lines overstretched, barely a fortnight after they had come. "We weren't sorry to see the back of them, either," says Mr Nansey, concerned, it seems, that no one should doubt his loyalty to Delhi, 1,500km (930 miles) to the west.

His ambivalence is widely shared. China and India, repositories of 40% of the world's people, are often unsure what to make of each other. Since re-establishing diplomatic ties in 1976, after a post-war pause, they and their relationship have in many ways been transformed. The 1962 war was an act of Chinese aggression most obviously springing from China's desire for western Aksai Chin, a lofty plain linking Xinjiang to Tibet. But its deeper causes included a famine in China and economic malaise in both countries. China and India are now the world's fastest-growing big economies, however, and in a year or two, when India overtakes Japan on a purchasing-power-parity basis, they will be the world's second- and third-biggest. And as they grow, Asia's giants have come closer.

Their two-way trade is roaring: only $270m in 1990, it is expected to exceed $60 billion this year. They are also tentatively co-operating, for their mutual enrichment, in other ways: for example, by co-ordinating their bids for the African oil supplies that both rely on. Given their contrasting economic strengths—China's in manufacturing, India's in services—some see an opportunity for much deeper co-operation. There is even a word for this vision, "Chindia." On important international issues, notably climate-change policy and world trade, their alignment is already imposing.

Their leaders naturally talk up these pluses: at the summit of the BRICs (Brazil, Russia, India, China) in Brasília in April, for example, and during celebrations in Beijing earlier this year to commemorate the 60th anniversary of India's recognition of the People's Republic. "India and China are not in competition," India's sage-like prime minister, Manmohan Singh, often says. "There is enough economic space for us both."

China's president, Hu Jintao, says the same. And no doubt both want to believe it. The booms in their countries have already moved millions out of poverty, especially in China, which is far ahead on almost every such measure of progress (and also dismissive of the notion that India could ever rival it). A return to confrontation, besides hugely damaging the improved image of both countries, would plainly jeopardise this movement forward. That is why the secular trend in China-India relations is positive.

Yet China and India are in many ways rivals, not Asian brothers, and their relationship is by any standard vexed—as recent quarrelling has made abundantly plain. If you then consider that they are, despite their mutual good wishes, old enemies, bad neighbours and nuclear powers, and have two of the world's biggest armies—with almost 4m troops between them—this may seem troubling.

Forget Chindia

There are many caveats to the recent improvement in their relationship. As the world's oil wells run dry, many—including sober analysts in both countries—foresee China-India rivalry redrawn as a cut-throat contest for an increasingly scarce resource. The two oil-gluggers' recent co-operation on energy was, after all, as unusual as it was tentative. More often, Chinese state-backed energy firms compete with all-comers, for Sudanese oil and Burmese gas, and win.

Rivalry over gas supplies is a bigger concern for Indian policymakers. They fear China would be more able to "capture" gas by building massive pipelines overnight. Water is already an object of contention, given that several of the big rivers of north India, including the Brahmaputra, on which millions depend, rise in Tibet. China recently announced that it is building a dam on the Brahmaputra, which it calls the Yarlung Tsangpo, exacerbating an old Indian fear that the Beijing regime means to divert the river's waters to Chinese farmers.

As for Chindia, it can seem almost too naive to bother about. Over 70% of India's exports to China by value are raw materials, chiefly iron ore, bespeaking a colonial-style trade relationship that is hugely favourable to China. A proliferating range of Chinese non-tariff barriers to Indian companies, which India grumbles about, is a small part of this. The fault lies chiefly with India's uncompetitive manufacturing. It is currently cheaper, an Indian businessman says ruefully, to export plastic granules to China and then import them again in bucket-form, than it is to make buckets in India.

This is a source of tension. India's great priority is to create millions of jobs for its young, bulging and little-skilled population, which will be possible only if it makes huge strides in manufacturing. Similarly, if China trails India in IT services at present, its recent investments in the industry suggest it does not plan to lag for long.

Yet there is another, more obvious bone of contention, which exacerbates all these others and lies at the root of them: the 4,000km border that runs between the two countries. Nearly half a century after China's invasion, it remains largely undefined and bitterly contested.

The basic problem is twofold. In the undefined northern part of the frontier India claims an area the size of Switzerland, occupied by China, for its region of Ladakh. In the eastern part, China claims an Indian-occupied area three times bigger, including most of Arunachal. This 890km stretch of frontier was settled in 1914 by the governments of Britain and Tibet, which was then in effect independent, and named the McMahon Line after its creator, Sir Henry McMahon, foreign secretary of British-ruled India. For China—which was afforded mere observer status at the negotiations preceding the agreement—the McMahon Line represents a dire humiliation.

China also particularly resents being deprived of Tawang, which—though south of the McMahon Line—was occupied by Indian troops only in 1951, shortly after China's new Communist rulers dispatched troops to Tibet. This district of almost 40,000 people, scattered over 2,000 square kilometres of valley and high mountains, was the birthplace in the 17th century of the sixth Dalai Lama (the incumbent incarnation is the 14th). Tawang is a centre of Tibet's Buddhist culture, with one of the biggest Tibetan monasteries outside Lhasa. Traditionally, its ethnic Monpa inhabitants offered fealty to Tibet's rulers—which those aged peasants around Tawang also remember. "The Tibetans came for money and did nothing for us," said Mr Nansey, referring to the fur-cloaked Tibetan officials who until the late 1940s went from village to village extracting a share of the harvest.

Making matters worse, the McMahon Line was drawn with a fat nib, establishing a ten-kilometre margin for error, and it has never been demarcated. With more confusion in the central sector, bordering India's northern state of Uttarakhand, there are in all a dozen stretches of frontier where neither side knows where even the disputed border should be. In these "pockets," as they are called, Indian and Chinese border guards circle each other endlessly while littering the Himalayan hillsides—as dogs mark lampposts—to make their presence known. When China-India relations are strained, this gives rise to tit-for-tat and mostly bogus accusations of illegal border incursions—for which each side can offer the other's empty cigarette and noodle packets as evidence. In official Indian parlance such proof is grimly referred to as "telltale signs." It is plainly garbage. Yet this is a carefully rehearsed and mutually comprehensible ritual for which both sides deserve credit, of a sort. Despite several threatened dust-ups—including one in 1986 that saw 200,000 Indian troops rushed to northern Tawang district—there has been no confirmed exchange of fire between Indian and Chinese troops since 1967.

Hands Extended— and Withdrawn

It would be even better if the two countries would actually settle their dispute, and, until recently, that seemed imaginable. The obvious solution, whereby both sides more or less accept the status quo, exchanging just a few bits of turf to save face, was long ago advocated by China, including in the 1980s by the then prime minister, Deng Xiaoping. India's leaders long considered this politically impossible. But in 2003 a coalition government led by the Hindu-nationalist Bharatiya Janata Party—which in 1998 had cited the Chinese threat to justify its decision to test a nuclear bomb—launched an impressive bid for peace. For the first time India declared itself ready to compromise on territory, and China appeared ready to meet it halfway. Both countries appointed special envoys, who have since met 13 times, to lead the negotiations that followed. This led to an outline deal in 2005, containing the "guiding principles and political parameters" for a final settlement. Those included an agreement that it would involve no exchange of "settled populations"—which implied that China had dropped its historical demand for Tawang.

Yet the hopes this inspired have faded. In ad hoc comments from Chinese diplomats and through its state-controlled media—which often refer to Arunachal as Chinese South Tibet—China appears to have reasserted its demand for most of India's far north-eastern state. Annoying the Indians further, it started issuing special visas to Indians from Arunachal and Kashmir—after having denied a visa to an Indian official from Arunachal on the basis that he was, in fact, Chinese. It also objected to a $60m loan to India from the Asian Development Bank, on the basis that some of the money was earmarked for irrigation schemes in Arunachal. Its spokesman described a visit to Tawang by Mr Singh, ahead of a general election last year, as "provocative and dangerous." Chinese analysts warn against understanding from these hints that China has formally revised its position on the border. But that is India's suspicion. And no one, in either country, is predicting a border settlement soon.

In fact, the relationship has generally soured. Having belatedly woken up to the huge improvements China has made in its border infrastructure, enabling a far swifter mobilisation of Chinese troops there, India announced last year that it would deploy another 60,000 troops to Arunachal. It also began upgrading its airfields in Assam and deploying the Sukhois to them. India's media meanwhile reported a spate of "incursions" by Chinese troops. China's state-controlled media was more restrained, with striking exceptions. Last year an editorial in the *Global Times,* an English-language tabloid in Beijing, warned that "India needs to consider whether or not it can afford the consequences of a potential confrontation with China." Early this year India's outgoing national security adviser and special envoy to China, M.K. Narayanan, accused Chinese hackers of attacking his website, as well as those of other Indian government departments.

Recent diplomacy has brought more calm. Officials on both sides were especially pleased by their show of unity at the United Nations climate meeting in Copenhagen last December, where China and India, the world's biggest and fourth-biggest emitters of carbon gas, faced down American-led demands for them to undertake tougher anti-warming measures. A slight cooling in the America-India relationship, which President George Bush had pushed with gusto, has also helped. So, India hopes, has its appointment of a shrewd Mandarin-speaker, Shivshankar Menon, as its latest national security adviser and special envoy to China. He made his first visit to Beijing in this role last month; a 14th round of border talks is expected. And yet the China-India relationship has been bruised.

Negative Views

In China, whose Communist leaders are neither voluble nor particularly focused on India, this bruising is mostly clear from last year's quarrel itself. The Chinese, many of whom consider India a dirty, third-rate sort of place, were perhaps most obviously to blame for it. This is despite China's conspicuous recent success in settling its other land disputes, including with Russia and Vietnam—a fact Chinese commentators often cite to indicate Indian intransigence. Chinese public opinion also seems to be turning against India, a country the Chinese have been wont to remark on fondly, if at all, as the birthplace of Buddhism. According to a recent survey of global opinion released by the BBC, the Chinese show a "distinct cooling" towards India, which 47% viewed negatively.

In garrulous, democratic India, the fallout is easier to gauge. According to the BBC poll, 38% of Indians have a negative view of China. In fact, this has been more or less the case since the defeat of 1962. Lamenting the failure of Indian public opinion to move on, Patricia Uberoi, a sociologist at Delhi's Centre for the Study of Developing Societies, notes that while there have been many Indian films on the subcontinent's violent partition, including star-crossed Indo-Pakistani romances, there has been only one notable Indian movie on the 1962 war: a

propaganda film called "Haqeeqat," or "Truth," supported by the Indian defence ministry.

Hawkish Indian commentators are meanwhile up in arms. "China, in my view, does not want a rival in Asia," says Brajesh Mishra, a former national security adviser and special envoy to China, who drafted the 2005 agreement and is revered by the hawks. "Its main agenda is to keep India preoccupied with events in South Asia so it is constrained from playing a more important role in Asian and global affairs." Senior officials present a more nuanced analysis, noting, for example, that India has hardly been alone in getting heat from China: many countries, Asian and Western, have similarly been singed. Yet they admit to heightened concern over China's intentions in South Asia, and foresee no hope for a settlement of the border. Nicholas Burns, a former American diplomat who led the negotiations for an America-India nuclear co-operation deal that was concluded in 2008, and who now teaches at Harvard University, suspects that over the past year China has supplanted Pakistan as the main worry of Indian policymakers. He considers the China-India relationship "exceedingly troubled and perturbed" and thinks that it will remain "uneasy for many years to come."

Fear of Encirclement

For foreign-policy realists, who see China and India locked in a battle for Asian supremacy, this is inevitable. Even fixing the border could hardly mitigate the tension. More optimistic analysts, and there are many, even if currently hushed, consider this old-school nonsense. Though both India and China have their rabid fringe, they say, they are rational enough to know that a strategic struggle would be sapping and, given each other's vast size, unwinnable. Both are therefore committed, as they claim, to fixing the border and fostering better relations. Yet there are a few impediments to this—of which two are most often cited by analysts in Beijing and Delhi.

One is represented by the America-India nuclear deal, agreed in principle between Mr Singh and Mr Bush in 2005. Not unreasonably, China took this as a sign that America wanted to use India as a counterweight to China's rise. It also considered the pact hypocritical: America, while venting against China's ally, North Korea, going nuclear (which it did a year later), was offering India a free pass to nuclear-power status, despite its refusal to sign the Nuclear Non-Proliferation Treaty. Indian analysts believe that China, in a cautious way, tried to scupper the deal by encouraging some of its opponents, including Ireland and Sweden, to vote against it in the Nuclear Suppliers Group, a 46-member club from which it required unanimous approval.

This glitch reflects a bigger Chinese fear of encirclement by America and its allies, a fear heightened by a recent burst of American activity in Asia. The United States has sought to strengthen security ties with South-East Asian countries, including Vietnam and Indonesia. It has also called on China, in an unusually public fashion, to be more accommodating over contested areas of the South China Sea—where America and India share concerns about a Chinese naval build-up, including the construction of a nuclear-submarine base on the Chinese island of Hainan. In north-east Asia, America has launched military exercises with South Korea in response to North Korea's alleged sinking of a South Korean warship in March. Some Chinese analysts, with ties to the government, consider these a direct challenge to China.

China is deeply suspicious of America's military campaign in nearby Afghanistan (and covertly in Pakistan), which is supported from bases in Central Asian countries. It is also unimpressed by a growing closeness between India and Japan, its main Asian rival. Japanese firms are, for example, expected to invest $10 billion, and perhaps much more, in a 1,500km "industrial corridor" between Delhi and Mumbai. In 2007 Japanese warships took part in a naval exercise in the Bay of Bengal, also involving Indian, Australian and Singaporean ships and the American nuclear-powered vessels *USS Nimitz* and *USS Chicago,* which was hosted by India and was the biggest ever held in the region.

This seemed to back a proposal, put about by American think-tankers, for an "axis of democracies" to balance China. Officially, India would want no part of this. "We don't want to balance China," says a senior Indian official. But, he adds, "all the democracies do feel it is safer to be together. Is China going to be peaceful or not? We don't know. In the event that China leaves the path of peaceful rise, we would work very closely together."

India also fears encirclement, and with reason. America's Pentagon, in an annual report on China's military power released on August 16th, said China's armed forces were developing "new capabilities" that might extend their reach into the Indian Ocean. China has also made big investments in all India's neighbours. It is building deepwater ports in Pakistan and Bangladesh, roads in Nepal and oil and gas pipelines in Myanmar. Worse, it agreed in 2008 to build two nuclear-power plants for its main regional ally, Pakistan—a deal that also worried America, who saw it as a tit-for-tat response to its nuclear deal with India. (China has become Pakistan's biggest supplier of military hardware, including fighter jets and guided-missile frigates, and in the past has given it weapons-grade fissile material and a tested bomb design as part of its nuclear support.)

Muffling Tibet

Hawkish Indians consider these Chinese investments as a "string of pearls" to throttle India. Wiser ones point out that India is too big to throttle—and that China's rising influence in South Asia is an indictment of India's past inability to get on with almost any of its neighbours. Under Mr Singh, India has sought to redress this. It is boosting trade with Sri Lanka and Bangladesh, and sticking, with commendable doggedness in the face of little encouragement, to the task of making peace with Pakistan. That would be glorious for both countries; it would also remove a significant China-India bugbear.

The other great impediment to better relations is Tibet. Its fugitive Dalai Lama and his "government-in-exile" have found refuge in India since 1959—and China blames him, and by

extension his hosts, for the continued rebelliousness in his homeland. A Tibetan uprising in March 2008, the biggest in decades, was therefore a major factor in last year's China-India spat. It led to China putting huge pressure on India to stifle the anti-China Tibetan protests that erupted in India—especially one intended to disrupt the passage of the Olympic torch through Delhi en route to Beijing. It also objected to a visit to Tawang by the Dalai Lama last November, which it predictably called a "separatist action." This visit, from which leftover banners of welcome still festoon the town's main bazaar, perhaps reminded China why it is so fixated on Tawang—as a centre of the Tibetan Buddhist culture that it is struggling, all too visibly, to control.

Mindful of the huge support the Dalai Lama enjoys in India, its government says it can do little to restrict him. Yet it policed the protest tightly, and also barred foreign journalists from accompanying him to Tawang. India would perhaps rather be spared discreet balancing acts of this sort. "But we're stuck with him, he's our guest," says V.R. Raghavan, a retired Indian general and veteran of the 1962 war. Indeed, many Indian pundits consider that China will never settle the border, and so relinquish a potential source of leverage over India, while the 75-year-old lama is alive.

After his death, China will attempt to control his holy office as it has those of other senior lamas. It will "discover" the reincarnated Dalai Lama in Tibet, or at least endorse the choice of its agents, and attempt to groom him into a more biddable monk. In theory that would end a major cause of China-India discord, but only if the Chinese can convince Tibetans that their choice is the right one, which seems unlikely. The Dalai Lama has already indicated that he may choose to be "reborn" outside China. There is talk of the important role Tawang has often played in identifying incarnations of the Dalai Lama, or even that the 14th may choose to reincarnate in Tawang itself.

For the abbot of Tawang's main monastery, Guru Tulku Rinpoche, that would be a great blessing. "If his holiness chooses to be born in Tawang, we would be so happy," he says in his red-carpeted monastic office, as half a dozen skinny lads file in to be inducted into monkhood. Silently, they prostrate themselves before the abbot, while he scribbles down their new monastic names. Outside his window, the early morning sun sparkles through the white clouds that hang low over Tawang. It is hard to think that this remote and tranquil spot could have caused such a continent-sized ruckus. Yet, if the abbot has his wish, it will cause a lot more trouble yet.

Critical Thinking

1. What is the point of view of this article?
2. What reasons are offered to support this point of view?
3. How does this article complement/contradict Kaplan's geopolitical analysis in article 30?
4. How does this article complement/contradict the points of view presented in articles 1 and 4?

Living with a Nuclear Iran

Iran can be contained. The path to follow? A course laid out half a century ago by a young Henry Kissinger, who argued that American chances of checking revolutionary powers such as the Soviet Union depended on our credible willingness to engage them in limited war.

ROBERT D. KAPLAN

IN 1957, A 34-year-old Harvard faculty member, Henry Kissinger, published a book, *Nuclear Weapons and Foreign Policy,* putting forth a counterintuitive proposition: that at the height of the Cold War, with the United States and the Soviet Union amassing enough hydrogen bombs for Armageddon, a messy, limited war featuring conventional forces and a tactical nuclear exchange or two was still possible, and the United States had to be prepared for such a conflict. Fresh in Kissinger's mind was the Korean War, which had concluded with a truce only four years earlier—"a war to which," as he wrote, "an all-out strategy seemed particularly unsuited." But President Dwight D. Eisenhower believed that any armed conflict with Moscow would accelerate into a thermonuclear holocaust, and he rejected outright this notion of "limited" nuclear war.

The absence of a nuclear exchange during the Cold War makes Eisenhower and what became the doctrine of mutual assured destruction look wise in hindsight. But more than half a century after *Nuclear Weapons and Foreign Policy* was published, it still offers swift, searing insights into human nature and a deeply troubling contemporary relevance. Eurasia—from the Mediterranean Sea to the Sea of Japan—is today an almost unbroken belt of overlapping ballistic-missile ranges: those of Israel, Syria, Iran, Pakistan, India, China, and North Korea. Many of these nations have or seek to acquire nuclear arsenals; some are stirred by religious zealotry; and only a few have robust bureaucratic control mechanisms to inhibit the use of these weapons. This conjunction of circumstances increases the prospect of limited nuclear war in this century. Kissinger long ago considered this problem in full, and the current nuclear impasse with Iran gives fresh reason to bring his book back into the debate.

Kissinger begins his study by challenging the idea that peace constitutes the " 'normal' pattern of relations among states." Indeed, he describes a world that seems anything but peaceful:

On the ideological plane, the contemporary ferment is fed by the rapidity with which ideas can be communicated and by the inherent impossibility of fulfilling the expectations aroused by revolutionary slogans. On the economic and social plane, millions are rebelling against standards of living as well as against social and racial barriers which had remained unchanged for centuries.

Continuing his description of a world that matches our own, he writes, "International relationships have become truly global . . . There are no longer any isolated areas." In 2010, that sounds utterly mundane; but then again, in Eisenhower's day, the idea that North Korea would help Syria to build a nuclear plant and thereby precipitate an Israeli military raid (as happened in 2007) would have seemed wildly improbable. Kissinger foresaw an interconnected world incessantly roiled by unsettling ideologies and unmet expectations.

Out of this turbulence inevitably come revolutionary powers, whose emergence is a critical theme in Kissinger's book:

Time and again states appear which boldly proclaim that their purpose is to destroy the existing structure and to recast it completely. And time and again, the powers that are the declared victims stand by indifferent or inactive, while the balance of power is overturned.

Obviously, Kissinger was concerned here with the Soviet Union. As he told me in an interview last spring in his Manhattan office, he considered Moscow a revolutionary power because of its instigation of the 1948–49 Berlin blockade, and its encouragement of the Korean War in 1950, which were very much recent history when he wrote—Stalin had been dead for only four years. Over nearly five decades, thanks at least in part to a Western strategy of containment that resulted in no limited nuclear exchanges, the behavior of the Soviet regime evolved. The revolutionary power had been tamed, if not by us, then by its own longevity.

To insert a nuclearizing Iran in place of the mid-20th-century Soviet Union is to raise several tantalizing possibilities. In his book, Kissinger writes that, by acquiring nuclear weapons, a nation becomes able, for the first time, to change the regional or global balance of power without an invasion or a declaration of war. Let us assume that Iran develops a nuclear capability— an outcome that seems likely despite the imposition of sanctions and the threat by Israel of some kind of preemptive military strike. Would a nuclear Iran be as dangerous a revolutionary power as the old Soviet Union? More broadly, how should the United States contend with the threat posed by Iran, North Korea, and other would-be revolutionary powers that seek to use their possession of nuclear weapons to overturn the status quo?

Kissinger's 1957 analysis of how the status quo powers respond to revolutionary powers seems sadly applicable to the situation with Iran today: "All their instincts will cause them to seek to integrate the revolutionary power into the legitimate framework with which they are familiar and which to them seems 'natural'." They see negotiations as the preferred way to manage emerging differences. The problem is that for a revolutionary power, a negotiation is not "in itself a symptom of reduced tension," as the status quo powers would have us believe, but merely a tactic to gain time. Whereas for normal nations, a treaty has legal and moral weight, for the revolutionary power, treaty talks are merely a concessionary phase in the continuing struggle. Think of how North Korea has skillfully—and repeatedly—used the promise of giving up its nuclear capability as a negotiating tool to secure other benefits, from fuel oil to relief from sanctions.

"Iran," Kissinger told me, "merely by pursuing nuclear weapons, has given itself a role in the region out of proportion to its actual power, and it gains further by the psychological impact of its being able to successfully defy the United Nations Security Council." Nevertheless, he went on, he does not consider Iran a threat of the "same order of magnitude" as the 1950s' Soviet Union, even as it "ideologically and militarily challenges the Middle East order."

When I asked Kissinger whether a nuclear Iran would be containable, he suggested that he would want to take tough measures to prevent a nuclear Iran in the first place. He did tell me that the United States had "different deterrence equations" to consider: Iran versus Israel, Iran versus the Sunni Arabs, Iran versus its own dissidents, and Islam versus the West. All of these dynamics, he explained, would interact in the event of an Iran that goes nuclear, and lead to "even more-frequent crises" than we currently have in the Middle East.

But in spite of Iran's refusal thus far to avail itself of "the genuine opportunity to transform itself from a cause to a nation," Kissinger told me, the country's true strategic interests should "run parallel with our own." For example, Iran should want to limit Russia's influence in the Caucasus and Central Asia, it should want to limit the Taliban's influence in neighboring Afghanistan, it should accept stability in Iraq, and it should want to serve as a peaceful balancing power in the Sunni Arab world.

Indeed, I would argue that because Sunni Arabs from Saudi Arabia, the United Arab Emirates, Lebanon, and Egypt perpetrated the attacks of September 11, 2001, and because Sunni hostility to American and Israeli interests remains a conspicuous problem, the United States should theoretically welcome a strengthened Shiite role in the Middle East, were Iran to go through an even partial political transformation. And demographic, cultural, and other indicators all point to a positive ideological and philosophical shift in Iran in the medium to long term. Given this prognosis, and the high cost and poor

chances for success of any military effort to eliminate Iran's nuclear program, I believe that containment of a nuclear Iran is the most sensible policy for the United States.

The success of containment will depend on a host of regional factors. But its sine qua non will be the ability of the United States to underline any policy toward a nuclear-armed Iran with the credible threat of military action. As Kissinger told me, "I want America to sustain whatever measures it takes about Iran." As he writes in *Nuclear Weapons and Foreign Policy,* "Deterrence . . . is achieved when one side's readiness to run risks in relation to the other is high; it is least effective when the willingness to run risks is low, however powerful the military capability."

Kissinger well knows from personal experience that domestic politics temper U.S. willingness to run such risks. Limited wars—those conflicts when a nation chooses for political reasons not to bring to bear all the weapons at its disposal—have always been difficult for Americans. "My book" he told me, "was written after one limited war, in Korea, where the U.S. achieved some of its objectives. Since the book was published, we had a limited war in Vietnam, in which a sector of the U.S. population wanted to lose the war in order to purify America's soul. To a lesser extent, that was also the case in Iraq. That is a new experience. You can't fight a war for an exit strategy." His conclusion: "America can no longer engage in a conflict unless it knows it can win it."

The crux of Kissinger's book and, in many ways, his professional life is this ongoing tension between his belief that limited war is something that the United States must be prepared to wage and his recognition of the domestic upheavals that such wars inevitably trigger. To refuse as a matter of principle to fight limited wars is to leave America powerless, with only an inflexible and reactive policy against the subtle maneuvers of adversaries: "Our empiricism," Kissinger writes, "dooms us" to requiring all the facts of a case beforehand, by which point it is too late to act. The search for certainty, he goes on, reduces us to dealing with emergencies, not preventing them. But for a democracy that needs to mobilize an entire population through patient argument in order to deploy troops for war—and, therefore, requires a good-versus-evil cause to ensure public support—limited wars, with their nuanced objectives, are far more challenging than all-out ones.

We must be more willing, not only to accept the prospect of limited war but, as Kissinger does in his book of a half century ago, to accept the prospect of a limited nuclear war between states. For most of the 1950s, observes Lawrence Freedman, a strategic theorist and historian at King's College London, in *The Evolution of Nuclear Strategy,* "the imminence of a strategic stalemate was taken as a basic premise." Although Kissinger was not the first or only thinker to advocate that the West develop strategies for the limited use of nuclear weapons, his "challenging, confident, and assertive style" made him easily the most forceful and articulate.

Kissinger recognizes the inherent dangers of this new strategic approach. Indeed, writing in 1957 about a possible superpower confrontation, he is also describing a possible 21st-century India-Pakistan one:

A limited nuclear war which had to be improvised in the midst of military operations would be undertaken under the worst possible conditions. . . . Because of the need for rapid reaction which is imposed by the speed and power of modern weapons, a misinterpretation of the opponent's intentions . . . may well produce a cataclysm . . . And [the two adversaries'] difficulties would be compounded by the fact that they would have had no previous experience to serve as a guide.

As Kissinger argues in his book, the psychological advantage in limited war will constantly shift in favor of the side that convincingly conveys the intention of escalating, particularly if the escalation entails nuclear weapons. Armed with nuclear weapons, in other words, a cornered Pakistan in a limited war with India would be a fearsome thing to behold.

At the time of his writing *Nuclear Weapons and Foreign Policy,* some analysts took Kissinger to task for what one reviewer called "wishful thinking"—in particular, his insufficient consideration of civilian casualties in a limited nuclear exchange. Moreover, Kissinger himself later moved away from his advocacy of a NATO strategy that relied on short-range, tactical nuclear weapons to counterbalance the might of the Soviet Union's conventional forces. (The doctrinal willingness to suffer millions of West German civilian casualties to repel a Soviet attack seemed a poor way to demonstrate the American commitment to the security and freedom of its allies.) But that does not diminish the utility of Kissinger's thinking the unthinkable. Indeed, now that the nuclear club has grown, and nuclear weaponry has become more versatile and sophisticated, the questions that his book raises are even more relevant. The dreadful prospect of limited nuclear exchanges is inherent in a world no longer protected by the carapace of mutual assured destruction. Yet much as limited war has brought us to grief, our willingness to wage it may one day save us from revolutionary powers that have cleverly obscured their intentions—Iran not least among them.

Critical Thinking

1. What is the central premise of Kissinger's containment policy toward revolutionary powers?

2. How does Robert Kaplan interpret this 1950s-era doctrine in the context of contemporary Iran?

3. Robert Kaplan is the author of articles 30 and 32. How does this article complement/contradict Article 30?

ROBERT D. KAPLAN is an *Atlantic* national correspondent, a senior fellow at the Center for a New American Security, and a member of the Defense Policy Board. His newest book is *Monsoon: The Indian Ocean and the Future of American Power.*

Drug Violence Isn't Mexico's Only Problem

Francisco González

In 2010, as Mexico celebrated the bicentennial of the start of its war of independence against Spain and the centennial of its pioneering social revolution, the nation found itself in the midst of another general and bloody conflict, the "war on drugs" that President Felipe Calderón declared shortly after he took office in December 2006. Indeed, commentary about Mexico has come to be so dominated by this "war" that the country's broader political and economic challenges have receded to the background.

If one steps back to assess these structural challenges facing Mexico, the picture that emerges is fraught with hazards. The risks stem on one hand from dysfunctional democratic institutions, and on the other from low economic and employment growth.

It goes without saying that the institutional and economic problems, however important for Mexico's medium- to long-term well-being, are subsidiary right now to the climate of violence and insecurity intensified by the war on drugs. It is important to note that drug-related violence as well as common crime increased significantly in the wake of the country's 1994–95 financial and economic collapse, and that such crime and violence became a top concern for the citizenry as well as the government during the administrations of Presidents Ernesto Zedillo (1994–2000) and Vicente Fox (2000–2006).

Still, if the evolution of annual murder rates per 100,000 inhabitants is taken as a proxy (the rate rose from approximately 6 to 7 in the 1990s to 10 to 12 recently), the explosion of violence and insecurity belongs to Calderón's presidency. At this point, the president will stay the course; he will step down next year hoping that a restoration of some measure of security on the ground will soften the verdict of history. That verdict, however, could be harsh on him and his circle of collaborators for having fanned the flames of barbarism that overtook Mexico in the second half of the 2000s.

The top priority for whoever wins the presidency in 2012 will be to reduce the insecurity and violence intensified by the war on drugs. This may require secret negotiations—about which the public at large and foreign governments will know nothing, because any Mexican government, left, center, or right, will advocate continuing an uncompromising war on drug traffickers while trying to draw red lines agreed on by the combatants.

Only after, and if, the violence is tamped down will a future government generate the leadership and legitimacy necessary even to raise the likelihood of accomplishing the political and economic reforms that the country needs. Until then, Mexicans will yearn for the social peace, political stability, and solid economic performance that they now recall with a sense of morbid nostalgia. Better a respected, effective authoritarian regime than a dysfunctional democracy, some Mexicans are thinking to themselves.

For the longer term, the political dangers facing the country arise from perverse institutional incentives that have generated short-term horizons and pronounced self-serving behavior among the nation's principal leaders and their followers. The economic danger results from the country's specialization as a manufacturing assembler and re-exporter, in which capacity Mexico adds little local content value to the goods that it supplies to the US market. Opportunities for finding new sources of growth abound, but they have remained underexploited in the current climate of political and economic uncertainty, and particularly amid the generalized domestic and foreign perception that the risk of random physical harm in Mexico is high and growing.

> **Mexico adds little local content value to the goods that it supplies to the US market.**

Nonetheless, if Mexico between now and 2030 successfully meets the structural challenges that it faces, it could take its place among the leading emerging-market countries in the world.

Learning Democracy

Democracy is a relatively new game that Mexicans are still learning to play. The fight for effective political rights—in a nutshell, the fight for free and fair elections—in Mexico took the form of a long-term, highly institutionalized transition to democracy, based on successive electoral reforms enacted between 1977 and 1996.

From 1929 the country was ruled by an authoritarian regime under a hegemonic party that since 1947 has been called the Institutional Revolutionary Party (PRI). When alternation of power finally occurred in 2000 with Fox of the conservative National Action Party (PAN) winning the presidency peacefully and through the ballot box, the country achieved a remarkable feat.

However, the 2006 presidential election aroused considerable controversy. That year Calderón, the PAN candidate, defeated Andrés Manuel López Obrador of the left-wing Party of the Democratic Revolution (PRD) by less than a quarter of a million votes—out of more than 41 million votes cast. Following the election protests erupted, lasting several months, which ultimately resulted in a credibility deficit for the Federal Election Institute (IFE), one of Mexico's two most important electoral institutions. (The other electoral pillar is the judiciary's Federal Electoral Tribunal.)

The nine councilors who head the IFE are supposed to be apolitical, but their appointment is in fact a very political process. Members of the Chamber of Deputies, the lower house of the Mexican Congress, "scrutinize" prospective councilors and vote for them, which means that the IFE's composition reflects the balance of power among parties in that chamber. (The PRI and the PAN are the largest parties, followed by the PRD, and then by three or four very small parties whose votes are up for grabs.) As a result, doubts and distrust persist among the Mexican public regarding the freedom and fairness of elections. A public opinion survey conducted by the newspaper *Reforma* at the end of 2010 indicated that only about 44 percent trust the IFE and its management of elections.

This is not to say that no important steps were taken to improve elections after the turmoil of 2006. The social and political conflict ensuing from that year's election forced the PRI and the PAN—though, significantly, not the PRD—to agree in November 2007 on an electoral reform package, which was supported and signed by Calderón. The reforms changed the IFE's leadership; strengthened the institute's capacity for monitoring parties, the media, and political advertising during electoral campaigns; and also shortened the duration of campaigns. As a result, the contestation and outcomes of midterm legislative elections in 2009 and a multi-gubernatorial election in 2010 were broadly accepted.

The significance of the PRD's nonparticipation in the electoral reform negotiations of 2007 has to do with the left's accusations of foul play in presidential elections on two occasions–1988 as well as 2006. The left and its supporters believe that, unless its candidate wins in a landslide, powerful interests referred to as *los poderes fácticos* (de facto powers, including big business and its foreign partners, the mass media, the Catholic Church, and, ominously, organized criminal groups) will likely conspire with their political allies in both the PRI and the PAN to prevent a transfer of power to a popularly elected left-wing government.

Left Out

In reality, the left in Mexico has traditionally been fractious and unstable, and López Obrador's combative and uncompromising stance has contributed to infighting on the left and to weakening

electoral performance for the PRD since 2006. These developments have reduced the left's chances of winning a presidential election in 2012.

Still, a basic question remains for the consolidation of democracy in Mexico—namely, whether the country can alternate power not only on the right but also to the left. Can the left gain power without producing social and political turmoil that in turn creates authoritarian regression or a prolonged period of political instability?

Some insight into this question might be gained by examining what has happened elsewhere in Latin America when the left has gained power. Latin America's alternations of power to the left, according to conventional wisdom established by scholars, analysts, and the media, have in recent years belonged to two broad types. Chile, Brazil, and Uruguay are cited as countries where pragmatic left-wing leaders have pursued moderate policies once in power, thereby reassuring traditional economic elites and their foreign partners and strengthening democracy.

Venezuela, Ecuador, and Bolivia, on the other hand, are mentioned as countries where the left gained power in discredited democratic systems that had been captured by domestic elites and their foreign partners. In those situations, uncompromising radical leaders implemented populist policies and rewrote the rules of the constitutional game, leading to polarization and frequently to violent confrontation between the government's supporters and the opposition. This made democracy potentially less stable.

Mexico seems unlikely to fit into either type. By 2012, after 12 years of conservative rule under the PAN, a return of the PRI is likelier (given strong electoral victories in 2009 and 2010) than a victory by the PRD. Still, the PAN and the PRD fielded alliances during 2010 local and state elections that yielded significant gains for their partnerships at the level of governor (Oaxaca, Puebla, Sinaloa) and state legislatures and municipal governments (aside from Oaxaca and Puebla and other traditional PRI strongholds such as Hidalgo and Durango).

Although this sort of marriage of ideological opposites proved effective at slowing the PRI's electoral momentum, past experience from Nayarit, Chiapas, and Yucatán suggests that electoral triumphs based on such a strategy cannot be translated into a coherent coalition government. In all of these cases, one of the partners left the coalition or was relegated to a subordinate position once in power, leading to critics' characterization of PAN–PRD coalitions as unnatural or unviable.

The leaders of both the PAN and the PRD have said repeatedly that they would not contemplate running a common candidate in 2012. But if the governorship victories in 2010 tempt them into such a bargain, and if the strategy were to triumph—an unlikely but not impossible outcome—it is not difficult to see how a president supported by a coalition of ideological opposites could end up as a lame duck.

That is, if either of the main coalition partners withdrew its support for the government (which would not be unlikely, given that the prospective partners maintain widely diverging positions on social, economic, and cultural policies), severe weakness at the helm might ensue, or potentially even an interrupted presidency.

Meet the Old Boss?

For many, meanwhile, the PRI's return to power would mean the return of the authoritarian system that the country experienced during the *presidencia imperial* from 1940 to the mid-1990s. Although a restoration of authoritarianism via the return of the PRI to Los Pinos (the presidential residence) is an attractive idea to many Mexicans who benefited under PRI rule, it is highly improbable. The country has enjoyed open pluralism for a decade and a half, and this genie cannot be put back in the bottle.

A more legitimate concern regarding a PRI return to the presidency would be whether the country's system of crony capitalism would be strengthened. Throughout Mexico, economic opportunity and advantage are inextricably connected to the governing party at all three levels of government. Many Mexicans have complained that this system has simply continued over recent years despite the PAN and the PRD having held power at various levels for extended periods.

> **Throughout Mexico, economic opportunity and advantage are inextricably connected to the governing party.**

Even so, a PRI return to the presidency could further strengthen the position of dominant vested interests that grew powerful through economic concessions granted to them under PRI presidents. This would be bad news for those who have over the past 10 years denounced public and private monopolies and called for their breakup, thus far unsuccessfully.

A more worrisome concern, at least in the short term, is that a PRI president would likely resemble his immediate predecessors—Zedillo of the PRI and Fox and Calderón of the PAN; that is, he would be constitutionally and politically weak. Certainly, a new PRI president would not be quasi-omnipotent like the PRI presidents of the *presidencia imperial*.

Congress is stronger now than the presidency, which has limited constitutional powers. Yet the national assembly is split among the three largest parties and a few smaller ones. This has led to a deadlocked legislative process, which in turn has stalled the enactment of structural reforms that the country badly needs.

A central fact of the Mexican political system is a prohibition against consecutive reelection to public offices across the board. This prohibition provides popular representatives with an incentive to demonstrate total loyalty to party leaders on whose whims their next jobs in public life depend, and to exhibit no loyalty or accountability to voters. Under this system, political actors' time horizons are short-term and their motivations self-serving, and they will continue to be.

Governors, under a federal system that was adapted from the US model, have become in the words of Mexico scholar George Grayson "new feudal lords." Federal rules and standards break down to different degrees in the states and municipalities, many of which are still ruled by traditional *caciques* (political bosses) and strongmen. Policies cannot simply be decreed from the center. Implementation varies hugely across the country's territory. Standard application of rules and norms is a faraway dream.

Unsurprisingly, many have concluded that Mexico's basic political institutions have put the country and its young democracy in a bind. Mexico's main organized political voices—including Calderón's government, the principal political parties, a large and growing pundit class, and civil society groups ranging from universities to foundations—have all put forward versions of the grand constitutional reform that the nation needs to undertake to improve what is widely perceived as dysfunctional democracy.

But a grand constitutional bargain appears unlikely, given that the main parties' leaderships naturally oppose reforms that would weaken their grip on the power and privileges that they enjoy under the current system. Power in Mexico will remain divided and territorially fragmented, making it difficult for any president to do as he or she wishes. This should not surprise anyone, as exactly the same thing happens in more mature presidential democracies such as the United States.

Troubled Voters

Meanwhile, another great challenge stands in the way of democracy's becoming self-reinforcing in Mexico—construction of the rule of law. This shapes up as a medium- to long-term process that will require the youngest Mexicans to be exposed to a public culture in which rules are applied equally and fairly in open forums such as—crucially—criminal courts of justice. Improved rule of law would also force into the open the actions of public authorities so that citizens could scrutinize them and hold politicians accountable.

I spent a year carrying out research on behalf of the nonpartisan organization Freedom House for a wide-ranging report card (published in 2010) on democratic governance in Mexico. According to the evidence gathered by my colleagues and me, Mexico is, particularly in the spheres of basic civil rights and the rule of law, far from being a liberal democracy. Individual rights continue to be violated systematically at all three levels of government, but particularly at the state and municipal levels. It is not far-fetched to say that the average Mexican citizen lives in fear of both criminals and public authorities.

> **It is not far-fetched to say that the average Mexican citizen lives in fear of both criminals and public authorities.**

The past decade has proved a difficult one for Mexico's young democracy. Weak economic performance, inflated expectations about the peace and prosperity that democratic institutions would deliver, and the great rise in violence and insecurity associated with the war on drugs have contributed to public doubts about democracy. According to opinion polling by

Latinobarómetro, a declining proportion of Mexicans over the second half of the past decade has expressed strong support for democracy. In 2009–10, Mexico's support for democracy was the lowest, alongside Guatemala's, of the 18 Latin American countries annually polled by *Latinobarómetro* (though Mexico's support in 2010 was stronger than it had been in 2009).

"Weak economic performance . . . and the great rise in violence and insecurity associated with the war on drugs have contributed to public doubts about democracy."

With average Mexican citizens fearful about the most basic and immediate aspects of their well-being—their physical security as well as their socioeconomic opportunity—it is unsurprising that a diffuse sense of malaise and pessimism has begun to affect public evaluations of democracy, its prospects, and even its desirability.

To be sure, weakening support for democracy is not specific to Mexico. It has been observed in other Latin American countries when social and economic conditions have worsened, particularly after harsh financial shocks and during economic crises. The majority of Mexican citizens do not highly value democracy as an end in itself, independent of its consequences. But again, this is not unique to Mexico; it is part of the fabric of democracy everywhere.

And citizens are justified in caring about the outcomes of procedures, not just their effective implementation. Although candidates across the ideological spectrum promise growth, jobs, and general prosperity, Mexico's economic growth under PAN governments starting in 2000 has been very unsatisfactory, compared with the economic performance of countries such as Brazil, Argentina, Peru, and Chile.

Assembled in Mexico

One cannot assign all the blame to the Fox and Calderón governments, nor to the Banco de Mexico's monetary policy, criticized as too orthodox and conservative. In fact, Mexico has experienced more than a decade of fiscal discipline and under-control inflation. This has led to lower real borrowing rates, which in turn have helped create a vast consumer credit market that has helped make Mexico a society, according to some analysts, in which the middle class is now a majority.

But it is not government or central bank policies that are the key determinants of the Mexican economy's main challenges. Instead, it is the country's integration with the economies of the United States and Canada under the North American Free Trade Agreement since 1994. This project was launched by President Carlos Salinas and consolidated under Zedillo, both of the PRI; PAN representatives in the federal and state legislatures supported the agreement and governments under PAN presidents

have continued to support it. The result of the project is that about 80 percent of Mexico's external economic activity now involves the United States.

The US economy is more than 15 times larger than Mexico's, and when it registers high, sustained growth, as in the second half of the 1990s, Mexico benefits. But when the US economy undergoes crises—such as the dot-com bust and the Great Recession—Mexico suffers. In 2009, Mexico experienced by far Latin America's biggest year-on-year decline in economic activity (6.5 percent). Contractions in US economic activity are transmitted to Mexico via several channels, including manufacturing activity, tourism, oil production and exports, mining, and remittances. Some specialists estimate that for each 1 percent decrease in US GDP, Mexico's GDP drops by 3 percent.

Mexico's comparative strength—preferential access to the biggest consumer market in the world—has also become a basic structural weakness. Indeed, academics and analysts tend to prescribe offhandedly that Mexico should diversify its export markets. This is much easier said than done. Mexico's economy has become specialized as a supplier of finished manufactured goods to the United States. Many assembly plants have been relocated to Mexico, where labor is relatively cheap, and they produce goods that, to qualify for free entry into the United States, contain varying amounts of inputs from the United States, Mexico, and Canada.

In my view, these so-called rules of origin are a source of potential strength for Mexico but also a source of current weakness. The potential strength derives from the fact that finished products could qualify for free entry into the United States even if they had much higher Mexican content than they typically have. The weakness derives from the fact that most of the high–value-added manufacturing that Mexico produces, from automobiles to electronic goods to refined textiles, is made with American inputs, which are not necessarily the cheapest in world markets.

The finished products are priced competitively in the US market thanks to relatively low Mexican wages and the products' free entry into the country. But Mexico finds it difficult to sell its goods in, say, the European Union or Japan, because the international market offers cheaper alternatives to high-cost US inputs.

An example often used to illustrate this phenomenon—known among trade economists as trade diversion—involves the price of textile inputs. To enjoy free entry into the US market, a majority of textile inputs must come from US sources, but such inputs are considerably more expensive than equivalents from, say, Bangladesh or India. If Mexico were to purchase inputs from such countries, prices for its finished textile products might be internationally competitive—but such goods could not gain access to the US market free of charge.

Mexican assemblers have thus far remained linked to their US input suppliers, and have concentrated on re-exporting high-volume goods to the United States. In spite of the fact that Mexico is among the world's leaders in free trade agreements, a vast majority of its importing and exporting is conducted with the

United States and to a much lesser extent Canada. Commerce with other free trade partners has remained very modest.

Investment Potential

A chorus of voices advances a "decline and fall" narrative regarding US political and economic performance and relative power. I am of the opinion, however, that Mexico should deepen its economic relationship with the United States, and smarten it up. This does not mean that Mexico should cultivate relations only with the United States, but neither should Mexico desperately attempt to be seen in the near term as a global player—as some Mexican political leaders, from left, right, and center alike, seem to favor.

Mexico has no reason to disperse its scarce resources trying to emulate big emerging-market countries like China and Brazil. Mexico's core interests should remain its bilateral relationships with the United States, the small nations of Central America and the Caribbean, and the two large countries of northern South America: Colombia and Venezuela. In addition, basic geopolitics and the global shift of economic activity to the Far East suggest that Mexico should ramp up its relations with China, India, Japan, and South Korea.

Nonetheless, no plan for raising Mexico's long-term growth trajectory can be successful without a sequence of events that starts with raising rates of investment. Substantially higher rates of capital formation are required if Mexico is to generate the infrastructure, knowledge, networks, and labor capacities that will in turn allow it to generate locally a higher proportion of inputs for the US market.

Unfortunately, Mexico's investment potential is limited because of entrenched weakness in fiscal capacity. The federal government gathers very low revenues in proportion to GDP—around 12 to 15 percent, in contrast to an average of 30 percent in other OECD countries—and also relies significantly on steeply declining oil rents. More than one third of the annual federal budget currently comes from the revenues of the state oil monopoly PEMEX. Given long-neglected investment in upstream activity, Mexico has experienced a sharp drop in oil production and proven reserves, threatening to transform the country, according to analysts, into a net crude oil importer before the end of the 2010s if no new sources are found.

For these reasons the country's sovereign debt was downgraded toward the end of 2009. Public investment in Mexico will continue to be modest compared with levels achieved in countries like Brazil and China over the past decade, or other high-growth East Asian countries since the 1970s; in these nations, public investment has been the backbone of rapid, sustained growth.

At the same time, Mexico's private investment is highly concentrated among the top 20 Mexican corporations. Such concentration of credit access and affordability has starved the potentially vast sector of small and medium-sized enterprises of credit. These businesses are the main generator of formal employment and of finished goods that have higher local content

and higher added value. But the past two decades have been very adverse for a majority of them.

Inasmuch as competitive entry into the US market will remain a desirable objective for producers around the world, Mexico's preferential access and, crucially, its geographical proximity might make it an attractive investment location for manufacturing giants such as China. Mexico *could* benefit enormously from "near-shoring," which involves moving closer to final market destinations production that was previously off-shored to, say, China or India.

The extent to which near-shoring could become a trend depends on questions such as whether Chinese wages increase or global transportation costs rise due to increasing demand for energy resources. In any case, Mexico should not only pursue a strategy of luring the production of US firms whose manufacturing is now carried out in China. It should also encourage cash-rich investors from China, India, Japan, and South Korea to form ventures aimed at adding both Asian and Mexican value to production chains that will continue to supply the US and also a growing Mexican consumer market.

The Challenges Ahead

But before such Asian–Mexican capital ventures can be established, or grow where they already exist, Mexico's public authorities and industrial leaders have to prove that the country is a safe, cost-effective, value-adding platform for the North American economic space. Regarding these issues, investors have seemed increasingly unconvinced over the past decade.

It is understandable that so much attention has been focused over the past four years on Mexico's war on drugs and the appalling mayhem that has accompanied it. Civilized human interaction disintegrates among barbaric acts of violence and the degenerate triumphal display of such acts. Sadly, Mexicans have come to expect daily reports of such outrages in mass media that morbidly cultivate accounts of violence. But even if the state gains the ability to protect civilization against the barbarians—and that is a big *if*—Mexico is due for a hangover after its bicentennial and centennial celebrations. The hangover is likely to be head-pounding and wretched, given the magnitude of the challenges ahead.

First, Mexico's government and society must restore basic social peace in many parts of the country. Second, they must reform institutions so that political actors' time horizons are lengthened, and so politicians become more responsive to the citizenry, not just their party leaders. Third, they need to attract investment that will raise capital formation rates, allowing domestic economic actors to add more local knowledge and value to production chains.

These structural challenges—political and economic—may appear overwhelming. But I predict the 2010s will be less uncertain, less unstable, and less violent than the 1810s and the 1910s. Cold comfort? Maybe. But if events prove this prediction wrong, the future will be very cold indeed.

Critical Thinking

1. How experienced is Mexico with a democratic government?

2. According to public opinion polls, is support for democracy growing or declining in Mexico?

3. What democratic reforms does González propose?

4. What are some of the strengths and weaknesses of Mexico's economy?

5. How does the author's point of view relate to articles 1, 16, and 17?

FRANCISCO GONZÁLEZ is an associate professor of Latin American studies at Johns Hopkins University's School of Advanced International Studies. He is the author of *Dual Transitions from Authoritarian Rule: Institutionalized Regimes in Chile and Mexico, 1970–2000* (Johns Hopkins University Press, 2008) and the democratic governance analysis "Mexico" in Countries at the Crossroads (Freedom House, 2010).

From *Current History*, February 2011, pp. 68–74. Copyright © 2011 by Current History, Inc. Reprinted by permission.

Demystifying the Arab Spring

Parsing the Differences between Tunisia, Egypt, and Libya

LISA ANDERSON

I n Tunisia, protesters escalated calls for the restoration of the country's suspended constitution. Meanwhile, Egyptians rose in revolt as strikes across the country brought daily life to a halt and toppled the government. In Libya, provincial leaders worked feverishly to strengthen their newly independent republic.

It was 1919.

That year's events demonstrate that the global diffusion of information and expectations—so vividly on display in Tahrir Square this past winter—is not a result of the Internet and social media. The inspirational rhetoric of U.S. President Woodrow Wilson's Fourteen Points speech, which helped spark the 1919 upheavals, made its way around the world by telegraph. The uprisings of 1919 also suggest that the calculated spread of popular movements, seen across the Arab world last winter, is not a new phenomenon. The Egyptian Facebook campaigners are the modern incarnation of Arab nationalist networks whose broadsheets disseminated strategies for civil disobedience throughout the region in the years after World War I.

The important story about the 2011 Arab revolts in Tunisia, Egypt, and Libya is not how the globalization of the norms of civic engagement shaped the protesters' aspirations. Nor is it about how activists used technology to share ideas and tactics. Instead, the critical issue is how and why these ambitions and techniques resonated in their various local contexts. The patterns and demographics of the protests varied widely. The demonstrations in Tunisia spiraled toward the capital from the neglected rural areas, finding common cause with a once powerful but much repressed labor movement. In Egypt, by contrast, urbane and cosmopolitan young people in the major cities organized the uprisings. Meanwhile, in Libya, ragtag bands of armed rebels in the eastern provinces ignited the protests, revealing the tribal and regional cleavages that have beset the country for decades. Although they shared a common call for personal dignity and responsive government, the revolutions across these three countries reflected divergent economic grievances and social dynamics—legacies of their diverse encounters with modern Europe and decades under unique regimes.

As a result, Tunisia, Egypt, and Libya face vastly different challenges moving forward. Tunisians will need to grapple with the class divisions manifesting themselves in the country's continuing political unrest. Egyptians must redesign their institutions of government. And Libyans will need to recover from a bloody civil war. For the United States to fulfill its goals in the region, it will need to understand these distinctions and distance itself from the idea that the Tunisian, Egyptian, and Libyan uprisings constitute a cohesive Arab revolt.

Ben Ali's Tunisian Fiefdom

The profound differences between the Tunisian, Egyptian, and Libyan uprisings are not always apparent in the popular media. The timing of the popular revolts—so sudden and almost simultaneous—suggests that the similarities these autocracies shared, from their aging leaders and corrupt and ineffectual governments to their educated, unemployed, and disaffected youth, were sufficient to explain the wave of revolutions. Yet the authorities that these young protesters confronted were unique in each nation—as will be the difficulties they face in the future.

Former Tunisian President Zine el-Abidine Ben Ali—the first Arab dictator to fall to mass protests—initially seemed an unlikely victim. Tunisia has long enjoyed the Arab world's best educational system, largest middle class, and strongest organized labor movement. Yet behind those achievements, Ben Ali's government tightly restricted free expression and political parties. In an almost Orwellian way, he cultivated and manipulated the country's international image as a modern, technocratic regime and a tourist-friendly travel destination. Beyond the cosmopolitan façade frequented by tourists lay bleak, dusty roads and miserable prospects. It is small wonder that the Islamists' claim that the government was prostituting the country for foreign exchange resonated in Tunisia.

Ben Ali's family was also unusually personalist and predatory in its corruption. As the whistleblower Web site WikiLeaks recently revealed, the U.S. ambassador to Tunisia reported in 2006 that more than half of Tunisia's commercial elites were personally related to Ben Ali through his three adult children, seven siblings, and second wife's ten brothers and sisters. This network became known in Tunisia as "the Family."

That said, although the scale of corruption at the top was breathtaking, Ben Ali's administration did not depend on the kind of accumulation of small bribes that subverted bureaucracies elsewhere, including in Libya and, to a lesser extent, Egypt. This means that Tunisia's government institutions were relatively healthy, raising the prospects for a clean, efficient, and technocratic government to replace Ben Ali.

Tunisia's military also played a less significant role in the country's revolt than the armed forces in the other nations experiencing unrest. Unlike militaries elsewhere in the Arab world, such as Egypt, the Tunisian army has never experienced combat and does not dominate the domestic economy. Under Ben Ali, it existed in the shadow of the country's domestic security services, from which Ben Ali, a former military police officer, hailed. Although its refusal to support Ben Ali's regime contributed to the country's revolution, the military has not participated meaningfully in managing the transition period and is unlikely to shape the ultimate outcome in any significant way.

Since Tunisia's protests initiated the wave of unrest in the Arab world, they were more spontaneous and less well organized than subsequent campaigns in other nations. Yet they demonstrated the power of the country's labor movement, as repeated strikes fueled protests both before Ben Ali fled and as the first short-lived successor government—soon replaced by a second one more amenable to the major unions—attempted to contain the damage to what remained of his regime.

The protests also revealed a sharp generational divide among the opposition. The quick-fire demonstrations filled with angry youth made the generation of regime dissidents from the 1980s, primarily union activists and Islamist militants then led by Rachid al-Ghannouchi, appear elderly and outmoded. Images of an enfeebled Ghannouchi returning to Tunisia after 20 years in exile in the wake of Ben Ali's ouster reflected the radical changes in the agenda of Tunisia's protest movement. Tunisians may once again prove receptive to Ghannouchi's brand of political Islam, but only if his Islamists can capture the imagination of Tunisia's young people, who are principally concerned with receiving what they see as their fair share of the country's wealth and employment opportunities. Tunisia's new leadership must therefore incorporate a generation of young people with only theoretical exposure to freedom of belief, expression, and assembly into a system that fosters open political debate and contestation. And it must respond to some of the demands, especially of the labor movement, that will feature prominently in those debates.

Egypt's Army Makes Its Move

In Egypt, Hosni Mubarak's fumbling end epitomized the protracted decline of his regime's efficacy. The government's deteriorating ability to provide basic services and seeming indifference to widespread unemployment and poverty alienated tens of millions of Egyptians, a feeling that was exacerbated by growing conspicuous consumption among a business elite connected to Mubarak's son Gamal. Yet the army's carefully calibrated intervention in the uprising indicated the continuing power of a military establishment honed by equal parts patronage and patriotism. And the protesters' political and tactical sophistication

came about as a result of Mubarak's reluctant but real tolerance of a raucous and unruly press.

As it assumed control of Egypt after Mubarak's downfall, the army revealed its enormous influence in Egyptian society. The military is run by generals who earned their stripes in the 1967 and 1973 wars with Israel and who have cooperated closely with the United States since Cairo's 1979 peace treaty with Jerusalem. In contrast to the other Arab militaries that have grappled with unrest this year, the Egyptian army is widely respected by the general populace. It is also deeply interwoven into the domestic economy. As a result, the military leadership remains largely hostile to economic liberalization and private-sector growth, views that carry considerable weight within the provisional government. Thus, as in Tunisia (although for different reasons), the pace of privatization and economic reform will likely be slow, and so the emphasis of reforms will be on democratization.

Repairing decades of public-sector corrosion may also prove problematic. Everything in Egypt—from obtaining a driver's license to getting an education—is formally very cheap but in practice very expensive, since most transactions, official and unofficial, are accompanied by off-the-books payments. The government pays schoolteachers a pittance, so public education is poor and teachers supplement their salaries by providing private lessons that are essential preparation for school exams. The national police were widely reviled long before their brutal crackdowns at the inception of the January 25 revolt because they represented, in essence, a nationwide protection racket. Ordinary citizens had to bribe police officers all too ready to confiscate licenses and invent violations. The disappearance of the police during the height of the protests—considered by many Egyptians a deliberate attempt to destabilize the country—only deepened that animosity. The process of applying democratic rule of law must begin with the police themselves, meaning that the Interior Ministry will need to reestablish trust between the police and the people.

But the remarkable discipline demonstrated by Egypt's protesters and their subsequent wide-ranging debates about how to reshape their country speak to the unusually high tolerance for free expression in Egypt (by regional standards) prior to the revolution. The campaign to honor Khaled Said, the blogger killed by Egyptian police and whose death initiated the uprising, for example, would have been unimaginable in Tunisia. Egyptians were relatively well prepared to engage in serious and sustained conversations about the composition of their future government, even as they understood that, whatever the outcome, the military would not allow its institutional prerogatives to be substantially eroded.

This latent political wisdom reflects the changes that transformed Egyptian society over the last 15 years, even while the country's aging and ineffectual autocracy remained in place. As Tahrir's protesters were at pains to demonstrate, Egypt has a culture of deep communal bonds and trust, which manifested itself in the demonstrators' incredible discipline: their sustained nonviolence, their refusal to be provoked by thugs and saboteurs, their capacity to police themselves and coordinate their demands, and their ability to organize without any centralized leadership. Perhaps the finest example of this egalitarian spirit was the appearance, in communities rich and poor, of spontaneous citizen mobilizations to maintain order once the police had disengaged. All these developments should give one cause for optimism today about the new Egypt's potential to build and sustain an open society.

The Wreckage of Libya

Whereas demonstrators in Tunis and Cairo successfully ousted their former rulers, Tripoli collapsed into a protracted civil war. Its sustained fighting resulted from Libyan leader Muammar al-Qaddafi's four-decade-long effort to consolidate his power and rule by patronage to kin and clan. Years of artificially induced scarcity in everything from simple consumer goods to basic medical care generated widespread corruption. And the capricious cruelty of Qaddafi's regime produced widespread and deep-seated suspicion. Libyans' trust in their government, and in one another, eroded, and they took refuge in the solace of tribe and family. Libyan society has been fractured, and every national institution, including the military, is divided by the cleavages of kinship and region. As opposed to Tunisia and Egypt, Libya has no system of political alliances, network of economic associations, or national organizations of any kind. Thus, what seemed to begin as nonviolent protests similar to those staged in Tunisia and Egypt soon became an all-out secession—or multiple separate secessions—from a failed state.

Libya under Qaddafi has borne traces of the Italian fascism that ruled the country in its colonial days: extravagance, dogmatism, and brutality. In the name of his "permanent revolution," Qaddafi also prohibited private ownership and retail trade, banned a free press, and subverted the civil service and the military leadership. In the absence of any public-sector bureaucracy, including a reliable police force, kin networks have provided safety and security as well as access to goods and services. It was along such networks that Libyan society fractured when the regime's capacity to divide and rule began to unravel at the beginning of the protests. Meanwhile, Qaddafi had distributed his armed forces across a deliberately confusing and uncoordinated array of units. Some forces joined the opposition quickly but were prevented from organizing effectively or deploying sophisticated military equipment.

This lack of social and governmental cohesion will hamper any prospective transition to democracy. Libya must first restore security and introduce the law and order missing for decades under Qaddafi's regime. As daunting as that task may seem, further difficulties lie on the horizon: reviving trust across clans and provinces; reconstructing public administration; strengthening civil society through political parties, open media, and nongovernmental organizations. Libya's decades of international isolation have left the generation in its 30s and 40s—the one likely to assume leadership in a new Libya—poorly educated and ill equipped to manage the country. Others have been co-opted by the regime and stand to lose should Qaddafi fall. The challenge for Libya is both simpler and more vexing than those facing Tunisia and Egypt: Libya confronts the complexity not of democratization but of state formation. It will need to construct a coherent national identity and public administration out of Qaddafi's shambles.

The Challenges Ahead

The young activists in each country have been sharing ideas, tactics, and moral support, but they are confronting different opponents and operating within different contexts. The critical distinctions between Tunisia, Egypt, and Libya will shape the outcomes of their respective movements. While Tunisia and Egypt grapple in their own ways with building political institutions—constitutions, political parties, and electoral systems—Libya will need to begin by constructing the rudiments of a civil society. While Egypt struggles with the long shadow of military rule, Tunisia and Libya will need to redefine the relationship between their privileged capital cities and their sullen hinterlands. Tempting as it is to treat the Arab uprisings as a single movement, their causes and future missions demonstrate the many variations between them.

These distinctions will matter for the United States and its allies. In June 2009, little more than 90 years after Woodrow Wilson's ringing endorsement of self-determination, U.S. President Barack Obama invigorated the Muslim world with his historic speech in Cairo. There, he declared that he has

> an unyielding belief that all people yearn for certain things: the ability to speak your mind and have a say in how you are governed; confidence in the rule of law and the equal administration of justice; government that is transparent and doesn't steal from the people; the freedom to live as you choose. These are not just American ideas; they are human rights. And that is why we will support them everywhere.

His proclamation did not produce this year's democratic upheavals in the Arab world, but it set expectations for how the United States would respond to them. If Washington hopes to fulfill its promise to support these rights, it will need to acquire a nuanced understanding of the historic circumstances of the uprisings. The Obama administration must encourage and rein in various constituencies and institutions in each country, from championing the labor movement in Tunisia to curtailing the military in Egypt. In each case, the United States cannot pursue the goals so eloquently identified by Obama without discarding the notion of a singular Arab revolt and grappling with the conditions of the countries themselves.

Critical Thinking

1. What is the author's point of view?
2. Compare and contrast the uprisings in Tunisia, Egypt, and Libya.
3. What lessons can be drawn from the three case studies?

LISA ANDERSON is President of the American University in Cairo.

From *Foreign Affairs*, May/June 2011, pp. 2–7. Copyright © 2011 by Council on Foreign Relations, Inc. Reprinted by permission of Foreign Affairs. www.ForeignAffairs.com

Deliver Us from Evil

The Democratic Republic of Congo is one of the most tragic nations on earth. It has been ravaged by war for nearly two decades. The largest United Nations peacekeeping mission in history is based in the country. But now it is being asked to leave.

DAVID PATRIKARAKOS

On 30 June, the Democratic Republic of Congo celebrated the 50th anniversary of its independence from Belgium. Over the course of a pallid and humid morning, several thousand soldiers marched down the wide, balloon-covered Boulevard Triomphal in Kinshasa, the capital, while tanks, Jeeps and other military hardware rolled past as part of a triumphant military parade. After an hour or so, President Joseph Kabila stood up to give a speech but the microphone was broken, like so much else in this blighted country, and his words were unheard by the crowd.

Since independence, as many as five million people have died in Congo's wars. The curse of Congo is to have promiscuous natural wealth in the world's roughest neighbourhood. It has diamonds, gold, cassiterite, coltan, timber and rubber—as well as the largest UN peacekeeping mission in history. For more than ten years, the United Nations has had a mandate to keep the peace here—but there has been no lasting peace, least of all in the eastern Congo, where violence continues between various militia groups who scavenge off the land, killing innocent people and each other as they scramble for resources in this mineral rich country. Now, the government of President Joseph Kabila wants the UN to leave altogether.

Kinshasa is a city of 11 million people, most of them confined to scorched tenement buildings and rusting tin shacks. The average wage is 90 cents a day in a city where a meal of steak and chips can cost $18. In the city centre, the Congolese elite live in luxury apartments, with rents comparable to those in central London. The UN headquarters is in the northern part of the city. The compound looks like an embattled fort in a war zone: high walls of barbed wire and broken glass sit behind concrete breeze blocks placed strategically along the road. Outside, people beg for money, with a refrain that I heard again and again: "Un dollar, un dollar, un dollar."

General Babacar Gaye is the Senegalese commander of the 20,000-odd UN troops in Congo. "Peacekeeping is not a job for soldiers [but] it is a job only soldiers can perform," he told me when we met. "This is not classic warfare where the objective is to defeat the enemy. Occasionally you need to use force, to ensure things stay on track or to deter or convince. But you are accompanying a [political] process."

The soldiers operate under Chapter VII of the UN Charter, which allows for the use of "lethal force" to keep the peace. "Lethal force gives you more freedom of action," said General Gaye. "You can take the initiative when you feel that the population is under imminent threat." (In Rwanda during the genocide of 2004 the UN peacekeeping force, led by Lieutenant-General Roméo Dallaire, a Canadian, was not permitted to use "lethal force" against the local population, and was thus rendered helpless to prevent the slaughter of as many as 900,000 people, mostly ethnic Tutsis.)

Since independence, five million people have died in Congo's wars. After the Belgians left, Patrice Lumumba became the first indigenous prime minister, but his strident antiimperialism alarmed the western powers and he was assassinated in a Belgian–US plot only three months after coming to office. In 1965, following a period of infighting, Mobutu Sese Seko, a tough but sharp army chief of staff, seized power in bloodless coup and, in 1971, renamed the country Zaire.

His despotic regime was toppled in 1996 by Laurent Désiré Kabila, a corrupt regional governor from eastern Congo. He was supported by neighbouring Rwanda and Uganda. Kabila had learned well from his predecessor and he installed his own sprawling kleptocracy as well as changing the country's name to the Democratic Republic of the Congo. But he made a fatal mistake: in 1998 he ordered the Rwandans and Ugandans to leave. They pulled back temporarily, before launching a counter-invasion during which they seized a third of the country.

Kabila called on the support of Zimbabwe, Namibia and Angola, who entered the war on his behalf, bribed with the promise of access to Congo's vast mineral wealth. In 1999, the UN decided enough was enough and passed resolution 1279, which resulted in the creation of a permanent peacekeeping force in

Congo. It is the largest and most expensive peacekeeping mission in history. The war officially ended in 2003, but militia groups continue to operate with impunity—especially in the east, where Rwanda is fighting a proxy war against Hutu militia—and different ethnic groups from inside the country clash over land and territory.

The current president, in office since the assassination of his father in 2001, is Joseph Kabila Kabange, commonly known as Joseph Kabila. Aged 39, he is something of a mystery. Kabila has maintained close relations with the Rwandans (he fought alongside them during his father's rebellion against Mobutu) and this has aroused suspicion among political rivals and international agencies that his policies may not be entirely independent. A fear of assassination means he makes few public appearances and his intentions are opaque.

What is clear is that, from 2001 to 2006, he ruled as the head of a transitional government, one strongly influenced by the international agencies present in Congo. However, in 2006, following internationally supervised elections deemed "free and fair" by the UN, he emerged as the head of a sovereign state with a genuine democratic mandate. He then began to assert his authority, pushing back all foreign influence—including the UN.

However, there are suspicions that there may be something more sinister beyond mere grandstanding in his desire to have the UN leave Congo. Since the elections, he has displayed increasingly authoritarian behaviour. Local elections scheduled for 2010 have been postponed, and he wants to extend the presidential mandate from five to seven years. The chances of his forging a more dictatorial regime during his second presidential mandate (presidential elections are due in 2011) increase if the UN leaves, and international scrutiny with it.

One morning in Kinshasha, I visited a ramshackle government building to speak to Lambert Mende, Congo's smooth and smiling minister of information. "The UN has done a good job in Congo," he said. "But it has been ten years that it is here. No nation in the world accepts that others fulfill tasks on their behalf. They are here for a given time. And this time should end one day."

Peacekeeping is by its nature temporary; the UN is never any more than a guest in someone else's country. Whether widescale violence returns to Congo will depend on the ability of its own army, the Forces Armées de la République Démocratique du Congo (FARDC), to keep order. But what exactly is the army? Last year, 22 militia groups were invited to stop killing and join up. Absorbed into the FARDC, they retained parallel chains of command, "taxing" and terrorising the local population. Many believe the FARDC is a collection of killers and rapists who now wear one uniform instead of many. I put this to Mende. "Two and a half per cent of the army is in prison," he said, rather triumphantly. "I know very few armies in the world which, in the middle of a conflict, would immobilise 2.5 percent of its forces for disciplinary reasons. They never tell you this!

"The Congolese army is being rebuilt. In 18 months it will be sufficiently trained to defend the Congolese people, and to deal with this existing threat in the east [of the country]—which

is a residual threat, not a significant one. We will be ready and that is the truth," he added.

Ever since Belgian rule, Congo has fed the world's lust for resources. During colonial times, we wanted rubber; today we want cassiterite and coltan, minerals that are used in the manufacture of PlayStations and mobile phones.

Congo has a border with nine countries, seven of which have had armies on its soil in the past 30 years. In 1998 the Rwandans invaded, citing the need to combat Hutu rebel units that had fled into Congo; a claim somewhat undermined, as their armies headed not for the Hutu encampments but for the mineral mines in the north-east of the country, where foreign backed militia continue to loot and kill. On 24 February 2003, before the UN arrived in Congo, rebel militias entered Bogoro—a village near the small town of Bunia, the capital of Ituri province in the north-east, close to the Ugandan and Sudanese borders—and killed more than 200 people, a crime for which the militia leaders Germain Katanga and Mathieu Ngudjolo Chui are now on trial at the International Criminal court in The Hague.

One afternoon, I went out on patrol with Banbat7, the Bangladeshi peacekeeping battalion in Bunia, and there I met a woman named Banébuné; she was 13 when the militia raided her village that February day seven years ago. "They were killing with machetes," she said. "They were saying, 'Don't waste bullets—just slash them.' There was so much blood. Children, old people, even pregnant women—anyone who couldn't run was cut down."

"They were killing with machetes. Anyone who couldn't run was cut down."

How did the FARDC army respond? "They did nothing." I asked Banébuné how she felt about the people that raided her village. "I cannot forgive them," she told me. "Only God can forgive. I pray to him that justice will find those that did this."

Another villager called Mwengwe picked up the story. He used to farm cows but the militia stole them, he said. "When we heard the firing, we all fled to the school." But the militia were waiting in the classroom where we now stood. "I jumped out of the window and ran away. I wasn't alone; there were many of us running. But on the way so many were killed. I lost my mother and two of my sisters [in the slaughter]." As we were leaving, Mwengwe asked if someone from the government would put headstones on the graves as had been promised.

In July 2003, the UN passed Resolution 1493, bringing Chapter VII to the Congo. Back at base, General Hasan, the Bangladeshi commander, spoke of how effective it had been. "A peacekeeper is the most constrained man," he said. "Chapter VII enabled us to properly protect civilians."

The last rebel attack was in February this year. Militias had emerged from the bush to shoot dead three villagers before fleeing. The situation remains uneasy, but there has at least been an improvement and local people feel safer. "Guns are a last resort—to save people who don't have guns," General Hasan said. "So it is for the greater good."

It is the UN mission, bolstered by Chapter VII, that has made the difference in Bunia, not the Congolese army. But a larger conflict still smoulders. I travelled on a UN helicopter 300 miles further north to the town of Dungu, in the Haut Uélé district, where the murderous Ugandan rebel group the Lord's Resistance Army has its stronghold. Led by the notorious Joseph Kony, a high-school drop-out who believes he is God's spokesman on earth, the LRA has, since its formation in 1986, kidnapped as many as 30,000 children and displaced over a million people. In 2005 the government of President Yoweri Museveni forced Kony and his followers to flee Uganda; they settled in Congo's Garamba National Park. They have been killing and raping ever since.

In 2008, Congo, Uganda and South Sudan undertook a joint military campaign against the LRA, "Operation Lightning Thunder", but which failed to kill Kony and his lieutenants, who disappeared into the bush. They took their revenge on the local population. On 24 and 25 December, the LRA simultaneously attacked three surrounding Congolese towns, and 500 people were killed in what became known as the Christmas Massacres. The LRA remains the main threat to peace in this part of the country; the freedom it has to strike will be a test of both the UN and of FARDC's efficacy and of the possibility of lasting stability in Congo.

At Dungu airport, we were greeted by a Tunisian peace-keeper in a battered Jeep, with one door hanging from its hinge. The Jeep's tyres churned up red dust as it sped along a dirt track on the approach to the Guatemalan special forces base, a few kilometres from Garamba. A ten-foot-high barbed-wire security fence surrounded the camp, with watchtowers at each corner of the perimeter. Three white tents, with "UN" emblazoned across them, 30 feet long and ten feet wide, were home to 80 soldiers. Three UN Jeeps, with mounted machine-guns, lined the dirt courtyard, and nearby helicopters took off and landed.

The FARDC camp was located 30 metres away along the same dirt track. In place of gates there was only a makeshift barrier—a gnarled tree trunk that was raised and lowered by a bored soldier. A huge white tent was home to a group of 100 men. The front two poles of the tent had fallen down and the whole thing was close to collapse. Two rusty Soviet-era Jeeps were parked next to the tent. Someone had painted "FARDC" on a piece of cardboard and hung it by the entrance. This was the camp of the troops who will be required to protect the people once the UN peacekeepers have gone.

The Guatemalans are on the front line of the peacekeeping mission and, after much argument, I was allowed to go out on patrol with them to Dungu. The patrols, explained our guide, Private Byron Monzon, were vital because of the LRA threat in the region.

I t began to rain heavily as we set off and our vehicle was soon sluicing across the saturated, pitted road. A soldier sat at the mounted machine-gun. "As far as we know, the LRA have rocket launchers," Monzon said as we drove along Dungu's main street. Children played in pools of mud, and women—it is always women—struggled beneath improbably heavy loads.

We were meeting Rémy Sitako, a local priest. "Since the LRA arrived, things have worsened," he said, sitting in his gloomy office, lit by single splinter of light from a tiny window. "They commit massacres and burn houses. Sometimes they mutilate. They cut off people's lips and ears . . . I believe some undisciplined elements in the Congolese army are also involved."

What did he think of the UN and its peacekeeping mission? "Occasionally, they take part in joint operations to re-establish security. This is reassuring. But we would like them to intervene more." What if they were to leave? "Insecurity is still too high. If they go now, there will be a catastrophe."

The key to security is the night patrols. The LRA uses the cover of darkness to scavenge from or raid local villages. One evening, out on patrol, we travelled with two platoons for safety as our armoured personnel carrier cut its way through maize fields. On the edge of the town, we paused alongside a bridge straddling a stream. What happened next happened very quickly: without warning our vehicle surged across the bridge and swerved to the right, creating a protective shield for the three Jeeps behind it. Six soldiers jumped out and formed an armoured wall while four more soldiers fanned out across the bridge. There were guttural shouts in Spanish and another six soldiers from the Jeep behind ran into thickets of bush either side of us. Gun mounted lights crisscrossed in the gloom. Monzon whistled and two villagers emerged from the darkness. The LRA had been sighted two kilometres to the north, they said, not close enough for engagement but close enough for alarm. Monzon was relaxed enough: troops from the LRA will not attack tonight, he said. They do not like to fight those who can fight back.

Spend any time in Congo and you quickly become articulate in the language of international diplomacy—"failed state", "nation-building", "peacekeeping" and so on. On the ground, you understand the hollowness of all such talk. But on that night patrol in Dungu, I understood the importance of the UN's continuing role in the country, because it is the peacekeepers alone who have the means to protect the people.

There is a fundamental political difference in Congo today between the government and the UN: the latter wants greater transparency and democracy; President Kabila wants nothing of the kind. He wants the UN peacekeepers out; the UN fears the violence that would follow its departure. The UN mission is underfunded, overstretched and imperfect. Tens of thousands of innocents continue to suffer, as was shown by the recent mass rape of around 200 women in Luvungi, only 20 miles from a UN base.

Congo works on Darwinian arithmetic. The strong oppress the weak, as they have done for as long as Europeans have been present in this part of Africa. However, in Dungu and in many other places like it, a thin blue line of UN peacekeepers is all that separates the people from the cruelty and violence of the Lord's Resistance Army and from many other rebel groups like them. It is a bleak truth that, without the presence of United Nations peacekeepers, Congo would collapse again into a chaos of violence and destruction; and with its mineral-hungry neighbours still meddling in the country and ethnic hatreds simmering, Congo's war will once more be Africa's war.

Critical Thinking

1. Using the world map in the preface, locate the Democratic Republic of Congo and identify the countries that border on it.

2. What is the history of the war in the Democratic Republic of Congo?

3. What are the underlying reasons for the war?

4. What is the role of the United Nations in this war?

5. What are prospects of peace?

6. How does this article relate to Article 30?

From *New Statesman,* November 2010, pp. 25–27. Copyright © 2010 by New Statesman, Ltd. Reprinted by permission.

War in the Fifth Domain

Are the mouse and keyboard the new weapons of conflict?

At the height of the cold war, in June 1982, an American early-warning satellite detected a large blast in Siberia. A missile being fired? A nuclear test? It was, it seems, an explosion on a Soviet gas pipeline. The cause was a malfunction in the computer-control system that Soviet spies had stolen from a firm in Canada. They did not know that the CIA had tampered with the software so that it would "go haywire, after a decent interval, to reset pump speeds and valve settings to produce pressures far beyond those acceptable to pipeline joints and welds," according to the memoirs of Thomas Reed, a former air force secretary. The result, he said, "was the most monumental non-nuclear explosion and fire ever seen from space."

This was one of the earliest demonstrations of the power of a "logic bomb". Three decades later, with more and more vital computer systems linked up to the internet, could enemies use logic bombs to, say, turn off the electricity from the other side of the world? Could terrorists or hackers cause financial chaos by tampering with Wall Street's computerised trading systems? And given that computer chips and software are produced globally, could a foreign power infect high-tech military equipment with computer bugs? "It scares me to death," says one senior military source. "The destructive potential is so great."

After land, sea, air and space, warfare has entered the fifth domain: cyberspace. President Barack Obama has declared America's digital infrastructure to be a "strategic national asset" and appointed Howard Schmidt, the former head of security at Microsoft, as his cyber-security tsar. In May the Pentagon set up its new Cyber Command (Cybercom) headed by General Keith Alexander, director of the National Security Agency (NSA). His mandate is to conduct "full-spectrum" operations—to defend American military networks and attack other countries' systems. Precisely how, and by what rules, is secret.

Britain, too, has set up a cyber-security policy outfit, and an "operations centre" based in GCHQ, the British equivalent of the NSA. China talks of "winning informationised wars by the mid-21st century". Many other countries are organising for cyberwar, among them Russia, Israel and North Korea. Iran boasts of having the world's second-largest cyber-army.

What will cyberwar look like? In a new book Richard Clarke, a former White House staffer in charge of counter-terrorism and cyber-security, envisages a catastrophic breakdown within 15 minutes. Computer bugs bring down military e-mail systems; oil refineries and pipelines explode; air-traffic-control systems collapse; freight and metro trains derail; financial data are scrambled; the electrical grid goes down in the eastern United States; orbiting satellites spin out of control. Society soon breaks down as food becomes scarce and money runs out. Worst of all, the identity of the attacker may remain a mystery.

In the view of Mike McConnell, a former spy chief, the effects of full-blown cyberwar are much like nuclear attack. Cyberwar has already started, he says, "and we are losing it." Not so, retorts Mr Schmidt. There is no cyberwar. Bruce Schneier, an IT industry security guru, accuses securocrats like Mr Clarke of scaremongering. Cyberspace will certainly be part of any future war, he says, but an apocalyptic attack on America is both difficult to achieve technically ("movie-script stuff") and implausible except in the context of a real war, in which case the perpetrator is likely to be obvious.

For the top brass, computer technology is both a blessing and a curse. Bombs are guided by GPS satellites; drones are piloted remotely from across the world; fighter planes and warships are now huge data-processing centres; even the ordinary foot-soldier is being wired up. Yet growing connectivity over an insecure internet multiplies the avenues for e-attack; and growing dependence on computers increases the harm they can cause.

By breaking up data and sending it over multiple routes, the internet can survive the loss of large parts of the network. Yet some of the global digital infrastructure is more fragile. More than nine-tenths of internet traffic travels through undersea fibre-optic cables, and these are dangerously bunched up in a few choke-points, for instance around New York, the Red Sea or the Luzon Strait in the Philippines. Internet traffic is directed by just 13 clusters of potentially vulnerable domain-name servers. Other dangers are coming: weakly governed swathes of Africa are being connected up to fibre-optic cables, potentially creating new havens for cyber-criminals. And the spread of mobile internet will bring new means of attack.

The internet was designed for convenience and reliability, not security. Yet in wiring together the globe, it has merged the garden and the wilderness. No passport is required in cyberspace. And although police are constrained by national borders, criminals roam freely. Enemy states are no longer on the other side of the ocean, but just behind the firewall. The ill-intentioned can mask their identity and location, impersonate others and con their way into the buildings that hold the digitised wealth of the electronic age: money, personal data and intellectual property.

Mr Obama has quoted a figure of $1 trillion lost last year to cybercrime—a bigger underworld than the drugs trade, though such figures are disputed. Banks and other companies do not like to admit how much data they lose. In 2008 alone Verizon, a telecoms company, recorded the loss of 285m personal-data records, including credit-card and bank-account details, in investigations conducted for clients.

About nine-tenths of the 140 billion e-mails sent daily are spam; of these about 16% contain moneymaking scams, including "phishing" attacks that seek to dupe recipients into giving out passwords or bank details, according to Symantec, a security-software vendor. The amount of information now available online about individuals makes it ever easier to attack a computer by crafting a personalised e-mail that is more likely to be trusted and opened. This is known as "spear-phishing".

The ostentatious hackers and virus-writers who once wrecked computers for fun are all but gone, replaced by criminal gangs seeking to harvest data. "Hacking used to be about making noise. Now it's about staying silent," says Greg Day of McAfee, a vendor of IT security products. Hackers have become wholesale providers of malware—viruses, worms and Trojans that infect computers—for others to use. Websites are now the favoured means of spreading malware, partly because the unwary are directed to them through spam or links posted on social-networking sites. And poorly designed websites often provide a window into valuable databases.

Malware is typically used to steal passwords and other data, or to open a "back door" to a computer so that it can be taken over by outsiders. Such "zombie" machines can be linked up to thousands, if not millions, of others around the world to create a "botnet". Estimates for the number of infected machines range up to 100m. Botnets are used to send spam, spread malware or launch distributed denial-of-service (DDoS) attacks, which seek to bring down a targeted computer by overloading it with countless bogus requests.

The Spy Who Spammed Me

Criminals usually look for easy prey. But states can combine the criminal hacker's tricks, such as spear-phishing, with the intelligence apparatus to reconnoitre a target, the computing power to break codes and passwords, and the patience to probe a system until it finds a weakness—usually a fallible human being. Steven Chabinsky, a senior FBI official responsible for cybersecurity, recently said that "given enough time, motivation and funding, a determined adversary will always—always—be able to penetrate a targeted system."

Traditional human spies risk arrest or execution by trying to smuggle out copies of documents. But those in the cyberworld face no such risks. "A spy might once have been able to take out a few books' worth of material," says one senior American military source. "Now they take the whole library. And if you restock the shelves, they will steal it again."

China, in particular, is accused of wholesale espionage, attacking the computers of major Western defence contractors and reputedly taking classified details of the F-35 fighter, the mainstay of future American air power. At the end of 2009 it appears to have targeted Google and more than a score of other IT companies. Experts at a cyber-test-range built in Maryland

by Lockheed Martin, a defence contractor (which denies losing the F-35 data), say "advanced persistent threats" are hard to fend off amid the countless minor probing of its networks. Sometimes attackers try to slip information out slowly, hidden in ordinary internet traffic. At other times they have tried to break in by leaving infected memory-sticks in the car park, hoping somebody would plug them into the network. Even unclassified e-mails can contain a wealth of useful information about projects under development.

"Cyber-espionage is the biggest intelligence disaster since the loss of the nuclear secrets [in the late 1940s]," says Jim Lewis of the Centre for Strategic and International Studies, a think-tank in Washington, DC. Spying probably presents the most immediate danger to the West: the loss of high-tech know-how that could erode its economic lead or, if it ever came to a shooting war, blunt its military edge.

Western spooks think China deploys the most assiduous, and most shameless, cyberspies, but Russian ones are probably more skilled and subtle. Top of the league, say the spooks, are still America's NSA and Britain's GCHQ, which may explain why Western countries have until recently been reluctant to complain too loudly about computer snooping.

The next step after penetrating networks to steal data is to disrupt or manipulate them. If military targeting information could be attacked, for example, ballistic missiles would be useless. Those who play war games speak of being able to "change the red and blue dots": make friendly (blue) forces appear to be the enemy (red), and vice versa.

General Alexander says the Pentagon and NSA started co-operating on cyberwarfare in late 2008 after "a serious intrusion into our classified networks". Mr Lewis says this refers to the penetration of Central Command, which oversees the wars in Iraq and Afghanistan, through an infected thumb-drive. It took a week to winkle out the intruder. Nobody knows what, if any, damage was caused. But the thought of an enemy lurking in battle-fighting systems alarms the top brass.

That said, an attacker might prefer to go after unclassified military logistics supply systems, or even the civilian infrastructure. A loss of confidence in financial data and electronic transfers could cause economic upheaval. An even bigger worry is an attack on the power grid. Power companies tend not to keep many spares of expensive generator parts, which can take months to replace. Emergency diesel generators cannot make up for the loss of the grid, and cannot operate indefinitely. Without electricity and other critical services, communications systems and cash-dispensers cease to work. A loss of power lasting just a few days, reckon some, starts to cause a cascade of economic damage.

Experts disagree about the vulnerability of systems that run industrial plants, known as supervisory control and data acquisition (SCADA). But more and more of these are being connected to the internet, raising the risk of remote attack. "Smart" grids, which relay information about energy use to the utilities, are promoted as ways of reducing energy waste. But they also increase security worries about both crime (eg, allowing bills to be falsified) and exposing SCADA networks to attack.

General Alexander has spoken of "hints that some penetrations are targeting systems for remote sabotage". But precisely what is happening is unclear: are outsiders probing SCADA systems only for reconnaissance, or to open "back doors" for future use? One senior American military source said that if any country were found to be planting logic bombs on the grid, it would provoke the equivalent of the Cuban missile crisis.

Estonia, Georgia and WWI

Important thinking about the tactical and legal concepts of cyber-warfare is taking place in a former Soviet barracks in Estonia, now home to NATO's "centre of excellence" for cyber-defence. It was established in response to what has become known as "Web War I", a concerted denial-of-service attack on Estonian government, media and bank web servers that was precipitated by the decision to move a Soviet-era war memorial in central Tallinn in 2007. This was more a cyber-riot than a war, but it forced Estonia more or less to cut itself off from the internet.

Similar attacks during Russia's war with Georgia the next year looked more ominous, because they seemed to be coordinated with the advance of Russian military columns. Government and media websites went down and telephone lines were jammed, crippling Georgia's ability to present its case abroad. President Mikheil Saakashvili's website had to be moved to an American server better able to fight off the attack. Estonian experts were dispatched to Georgia to help out.

Many assume that both these attacks were instigated by the Kremlin. But investigations traced them only to Russian "hacktivists" and criminal botnets; many of the attacking computers were in Western countries. There are wider issues: did the cyber-attack on Estonia, a member of NATO, count as an armed attack, and should the alliance have defended it? And did Estonia's assistance to Georgia, which is not in NATO, risk drawing Estonia into the war, and NATO along with it?

Such questions permeate discussions of NATO's new "strategic concept", to be adopted later this year. A panel of experts headed by Madeleine Albright, a former American secretary of state, reported in May that cyber-attacks are among the three most likely threats to the alliance. The next significant attack, it said, "may well come down a fibre-optic cable" and may be serious enough to merit a response under the mutual-defence provisions of Article 5.

During his confirmation hearing, senators sent General Alexander several questions. Would he have "significant" offensive cyber-weapons? Might these encourage others to follow suit? How sure would he need to be about the identity of an attacker to "fire back"? Answers to these were restricted to a classified supplement. In public the general said that the president would be the judge of what constituted cyberwar; if America responded with force in cyberspace it would be in keeping with the rules of war and the "principles of military necessity, discrimination, and proportionality".

General Alexander's seven-month confirmation process is a sign of the qualms senators felt at the merging of military and espionage functions, the militarisation of cyberspace and the fear that it may undermine Americans' right to privacy. Cyber-command will protect only the military ".mil" domain. The government domain, ".gov", and the corporate infrastructure, ".com" will be the responsibility respectively of the Department of Homeland Security and private companies, with support from Cybercom.

One senior military official says General Alexander's priority will be to improve the defences of military networks. Another bigwig casts some doubt on cyber-offence. "It's hard to do it at a specific time," he says. "If a cyber-attack is used as a military weapon, you want a predictable time and effect. If you are using it for espionage it does not matter; you can wait." He implies that cyber-weapons would be used mainly as an adjunct to conventional operations in a narrow theatre.

The Chinese may be thinking the same way. A report on China's cyber-warfare doctrine, written for the congressionally mandated US-China Economic and Security Review Commission, envisages China using cyber-weapons not to defeat America, but to disrupt and slow down its forces long enough for China to seize Taiwan without having to fight a shooting war.

Apocalypse or Asymmetry?

Deterrence in cyber-warfare is more uncertain than, say, in nuclear strategy: there is no mutually assured destruction, the dividing line between criminality and war is blurred and identifying attacking computers, let alone the fingers on the keyboards, is difficult. Retaliation need not be confined to cyberspace; the one system that is certainly not linked to the public internet is America's nuclear firing chain. Still, the more likely use of cyber-weapons is probably not to bring about electronic apocalypse, but as tools of limited warfare.

Cyber-weapons are most effective in the hands of big states. But because they are cheap, they may be most useful to the comparatively weak. They may well suit terrorists. Fortunately, perhaps, the likes of al-Qaeda have mostly used the internet for propaganda and communication. It may be that jihadists lack the ability to, say, induce a refinery to blow itself up. Or it may be that they prefer the gory theatre of suicide-bombings to the anonymity of computer sabotage—for now.

Critical Thinking

1. What is meant by the term "cyberwar"?
2. In addition to hostile governments, what other types of international actors employ this tactic?
3. How serious a problem is cyberwar and what efforts are being made to address it?

UNIT 6

Cooperation

Unit Selections

Learning Outcomes

After reading this Unit, you will be able to:

- Describe the role of nongovernmental organizations in developing international cooperative processes.

- Assess the prospects for major, multilateral international agreements to address problems such as climate change and human trafficking.

- Describe challenges to existing international agreements such as the Geneva Conventions.

- Discuss the basic issues surrounding the proliferation of nuclear weapons.

- Summarize case studies where NGOs have contributed to solving serious social and environmental problems.

- Assess your ongoing effort at identifying your theory of international relations and how this unit changes/complements it.

Student Website
www.mhhe.com/cls

Internet References

Carnegie Endowment for International Peace
www.ceip.org
OECD/FDI Statistics
www.oecd.org/statistics
U.S. Institute of Peace
www.usip.org

An individual can write a letter and, assuming it is properly addressed, be relatively certain that it will be delivered to just about any location in the world. This is true even though the sender pays for postage only in the country of origin and not in the country where it is delivered. A similar pattern of international cooperation is true when a traveler boards an airplane and never gives a thought to the issue of potential language and technical barriers, even though the flight's destination is halfway around the world.

Many of the most basic activities of our lives are the direct result of governments cooperating across borders. International organizational structures, for example, have been created to eliminate barriers to trade, monitor and respond to public health threats, set standards for international telecommunications, arrest and judge war criminals, and monitor changing atmospheric conditions. Individual governments, in other words, have recognized that their self-interest directly benefits from cooperation (in most cases by giving up some of their sovereignty through the creation of international governmental organizations, or IGOs).

Transnational activities are not limited to the governmental level. There are now tens of thousands of international nongovernmental organizations (INGOs). The activities of INGOs range from staging the Olympic Games to organizing scientific meetings to actively discouraging the hunting of seals. The number of INGOs, along with their influence, has grown tremendously in the past 60 years.

During the same period in which the growth in importance of IGOs and INGOs has taken place, there also has been a parallel expansion of corporate activity across international borders. Most U.S. consumers are as familiar with Japanese or German brand-name products as they are with items made in their own country. The multinational corporation (MNC) is an important nonstate actor. The value of goods and services produced by the biggest MNCs is far greater than the gross domestic product (GDP) of many countries. The international structures that make it possible to buy a German automobile in Sacramento or a South Korean television in Buenos Aires have been developed over many years.

© U.S. Air Force photo by Tech. Sgt. James L. Harper Jr.

They are the result of governments negotiating treaties that create IGOs to implement the agreements (e.g., the World Trade Organization). As a result, corporations engaged in international trade and manufacturing have created complex transnational networks of sales, distribution, and service that employ millions of people.

To some observers these trends indicate that the era of the nation–state as the dominant player in international politics is passing. Other experts have observed these same trends and have concluded that the state system has a monopoly of power and that the diverse variety of transnational organizations depends on the state system and, in significant ways, perpetuates it.

In many of the articles that appear elsewhere in this book, the authors have concluded their analysis by calling for greater international cooperation to solve the world's most pressing problems. The articles in this section provide examples of successful cooperation. In the midst of a lot of bad news, it is easy to overlook the fact that we are surrounded by international cooperation and that basic day-to-day activities in our lives often directly benefit from it.

Climate Change after Copenhagen: Beyond Doom and Gloom

BERNICE LEE

ritics of multilateral climate action have stepped up their attacks. They argue that change is not possible; that failure in last year's Copenhagen climate summit was inevitable as the public would never accept the cost of change towards a low-carbon future; nations will never concede their immediate economic interests; and that there is no prospect of collective climate change action. In their version of reality, the lowest common denominator rules. This narrative can be persuasive in times of austerity, but overlooks two critical points. Despite the political setback, investments in clean energy and efficiency continue to rise in response to policy change in developed economies like the European Union and the United States, or in emerging countries like China and India. International cooperation—together with solid national action—best serves even narrowly defined national interests on climate change. National welfare cannot be safeguarded if the world fails to deal with climate change and its resource challenges.

The Copenhagen summit on climate change last December is often described as a game-changer in global geopolitics. The world not only saw disagreements between developed and developing countries but also in the developing world, with plenty of cloak and dagger politics as well as megaphone diplomacy.

Fights over the level of ambition ended in procedural delays in Copenhagen, culminating in a last-minute dash by frustrated world leaders to come up with an acceptable political outcome. The BASIC countries—China, Brazil, South Africa and India— became critical brokers in the final political compromise, sidelining the European Union, Japan and others.

Eight months on, the international community remains divided over how to manage climate change collectively. The capacity of the international system to deliver global action in a multipolar context has been called into question; as has the effectiveness of the United Nations negotiating process. Developments so far this year have not produced renewed optimism.

These events have strengthened those who have long been vociferous against multilateral action—or any action at all— to reduce global greenhouse gas emissions. Some hailed the end of top-down climate solutions imposed by elites. Others questioned the ability of politicians to make meaningful compromises in global negotiations in a world of Twitter and instant news. The political appetite for such action is also dampened by the protracted economic downturn and controversy over climate science.

At this critical moment, it is important to get to the heart of the political disputes that surround the Copenhagen disappointment. Beyond the doom and gloom, the practical reality is more encouraging than purely political narratives. The key to unlocking the climate deadlock will lie in the ability of politicians to align global ambition with emerging realities.

A New Global Order?

For many commentators, the wrangling over the substance of the Copenhagen Accord reflected the dawning of a new world political order in which decision-making shifts to a smaller group of emerging powerful nations and away from traditional powers. Discussions on the final Copenhagen outcome were dominated largely by the United States, China, India, Brazil and South Africa. Connie Hedegaard, who part-presided over the Copenhagen conference, said that in 'the last hours in Copenhagen—China, India, the US, Russia and Japan—each spoke with one voice while Europe spoke with many different voices. We are almost unable to negotiate'. The EU has also been portrayed by the media as a minor player in brokering and drafting the accord.

China was widely characterised by many as a villain in the negotiations. Representatives, especially those from Sweden and Britain, openly lambasted Beijing for attempting to block the inclusion of the emissions target of two degrees Celsius above pre-industrial levels in the final text, as well as its rejection of the eighty percent emissions reduction target by developed countries by 2050.

Perhaps more curious is the lack of a public and international defence of Beijing's position by China or its allies. This is surprising because its view is in line with a long-standing G77 developing countries' stance that these two targets would imply a far higher per capita emissions level for developed countries, which is regarded as unfair by poorer economies. That said, there is no doubt the Chinese miscalculated the expectations not only of developed countries but also the vulnerable economies whose survival is at stake. There will be more teething pains as China juggles its two increasingly divergent profiles: as an emerging great power and as the largest developing country.

Competing Realities

Geopolitical manoeuvring aside, at the heart of the Copenhagen discord is the failure of many nations to view a strong global climate deal as central to their national interest. Many simply did not see the benefits of acting beyond the lowest common denominator. The often technical, jargonistic nature of climate talks also alienates the general public.

Other intractable issues abound: from the historical responsibility over carbon already in the atmosphere, to a process that can ill-accommodate the increasingly blurred dividing lines between developed and emerging economies, as well as multiple alliances. Many governments ended up treating climate negotiations like zero sum games that resemble trade bargaining, rather than focusing on collective problem-solving to deliver global public benefits.

Private sector groups, including the Confederation of British Industry, describe Copenhagen as a missed opportunity. Energy companies like E.ON and Britain's Centrica suggest they are likely to wait until ageing reactors and coal plants close over the next decade before investing in clean power generation.

But the overall picture is less clear-cut. The Nex index of clean energy stocks did stumble in the immediate aftermath of Copenhagen, but shares across a range of sectors surged from December 1 to early January. The Nex rose a further 4.1 percent in the first week of this year.

Following Copenhagen, many in the cleantech community believe new investments will be driven by local and national policies, mandates and incentive programmes, rather than carbon markets. Deutsche Bank identified 270 climate policies around the world, including Renewable Portfolio Standards in various US States, feed-in tariffs in Europe and energy intensity targets in China.

Low-Carbon Leaders

In any case, the change towards a low-carbon world economy continues. According to Bloomberg New Energy Finance, investment in clean energy sources globally reached $112 billion last year, up from just $18 billion in 2004. Tougher emission standards are anticipated across major sectors. This is already visible in transport, with binding legislation or voluntary standards in the world's major vehicle markets.

As competition heats up, the race for leadership in low carbon technology will be as important as the contest for energy supply. Research and development activity in low carbon options will be an important benchmark to judge company performance. The carbon portfolio and exposure of companies and governments will continue to come under increasing public scrutiny.

At the political level, it is too early to declare that all is lost. After all the Copenhagen process did attract the largest numbers of world leaders to discuss multilateral action on climate action. It is the first time developed and developing countries both agreed to take-on carbon-related commitments to limit greenhouse gas emissions.

Also, despite the unconvincing outcome, without the political momentum in the run-up to Copenhagen, the world would not have seen such a wide variety of nations taking on new national commitments to reduce carbon. Climate diplomacy did make a difference, even if it is inadequate so far.

Grim Prospects

The short-term prospects for a comprehensive global treaty on emissions reduction are grim. The Copenhagen process itself has dampened trust between many countries—and in the negotiation process—which will take time to get back on track.

Politically, activist governments will call for 'coalitions of the willing' which are likely to result in alliances that cut across developed and developing economies; certainly something to watch. More attention will also be paid to the question of variable geometry, and the extent to which different international groups like the Major Economies Forum or the G20 developed and emerging economies have helped or complicated international decision-making.

To rebuild trust, developed countries must focus on delivering the $30 billion of 'fast-start' finance pledged at Copenhagen for the next two years. It should be used to demonstrate low-carbon development models on a larger scale, in addition to incremental efficiency improvements.

On a positive note, it is now widely accepted that strong national action is a foundation for—not a result of—any future global agreement. The global focus is likely to shift onto national policy and increasing the scale of low carbon investment.

For example, the EU is considering raising its 2020 target for reducing greenhouse gas emissions from twenty to thirty percent on 1990 levels. China has proposed reducing the carbon intensity of its economy by forty to forty-five percent by 2020, from a 2005 base line. The more bottom up approach may be less efficient, but it is delivering change, which is important to build confidence. It also demonstrates the economic and technical viability of moving towards a low carbon economy.

Technical Fixes

At the global level, technology will be a key part of any policy package on the transformation towards a low-carbon world. Many of the necessary technologies like concentrated solar power, heat pumps and offshore wind are already commercially available; others are near-to-market. The next great energy investment wave will be missed if these are not deployed globally in twenty to thirty years.

But there will be some setbacks. To hedge against this risk, greater investment in innovation and demonstrations of technology like carbon capture and storage and smart grids are needed today to create a wide portfolio of commercially available lower carbon options by 2020. This will require new public-private cooperation as well as stronger policy to provide market incentives for rapid diffusion and innovation.

Meanwhile, there must be rapid progress in finalising the process to generate and distribute climate funds, and in the design of innovative financial arrangement to enhance low carbon and efficiency investments. This will underpin the technology cooperation mechanism proposed in the Copenhagen Accord. Measurement, reporting and verification systems will also need to proceed apace. There is the challenging task too of building consensus on reforms to the UN climate process, as well as strengthening the institutional capacity for scaling-up finance beyond 2012.

Short-term political calculations must not set the terms of our future. Even though there are dangers in navigating the low carbon transition, the perception of risks of change must be balanced by a greater understanding of economic and security opportunities.

Critical Thinking

1. What are some of the reasons the Copenhagen Summit failed to reach an international agreement addressing climate change?

2. What are some of the reasons Bernice Lee identifies for the prospect of continued progress towards a low-carbon economy without a broad international agreement?

3. What are some specific examples of progress towards this low-carbon goal?

Geneva Conventions

They help protect civilians and soldiers from the atrocities of war. But these hard-won rules of battle are falling by the wayside: Terrorists ignore them, and governments increasingly find them quaint and outdated. With every violation, war only gets deadlier for everyone.

STEVEN R. RATNER

"The Geneva Conventions Are Obsolete"

Only in the minor details. The laws of armed conflict are old; they date back millennia to warrior codes used in ancient Greece. But the modern Geneva Conventions, which govern the treatment of soldiers and civilians in war, can trace their direct origin to 1859, when Swiss businessman Henri Dunant happened upon the bloody aftermath of the Battle of Solferino. His outrage at the suffering of the wounded led him to establish what would become the International Committee of the Red Cross, which later lobbied for rules improving the treatment of injured combatants. Decades later, when the devastation of World War II demonstrated that broader protections were necessary, the modern Geneva Conventions were created, producing a kind of international "bill of rights" that governs the handling of casualties, prisoners of war (POWs), and civilians in war zones. Today, the conventions have been ratified by every nation on the planet.

Of course, the drafters probably never imagined a conflict like the war on terror or combatants like al Qaeda. The conventions were always primarily concerned with wars between states. That can leave some of the protections enshrined in the laws feeling a little old-fashioned today. It seems slightly absurd to worry too much about captured terrorists' tobacco rations or the fate of a prisoner's horse, as the conventions do. So, when then White House Counsel Alberto Gonzales wrote President George W. Bush in 2002 arguing that the "new paradigm" of armed conflict rendered parts of the conventions "obsolete" and "quaint," he had a point. In very specific—and minor—details, the conventions have been superseded by time and technology.

But the core provisions and, more crucially, the spirit of the conventions remain enormously relevant for modern warfare. For one, the world is still home to dozens of wars, for which the conventions have important, unambiguous rules, such as forbidding pillaging and prohibiting the use of child soldiers.

These rules apply to both aggressor and defending nations, and, in civil wars, to governments and insurgent groups.

The conventions won't prevent wars—they were never intended to—but they can and do protect innocent bystanders, shield soldiers from unnecessary harm, limit the physical damage caused by war, and even enhance the chances for cease-fires and peace. The fundamental bedrock of the conventions is to prevent suffering in war, and that gives them a legitimacy for anyone touched by conflict, anywhere and at any time. That is hardly quaint or old-fashioned.

"The Conventions Don't Apply to Al Qaeda"

Wrong. The Bush administration's position since Sept. 11, 2001, has been that the global war on terror is a different kind of war, one in which the Geneva Conventions do not apply. It is true that the laws do not specifically mention wars against nonstate actors such as al Qaeda. But there have always been "irregular" forces that participate in warfare, and the conflicts of the 20th century were no exception. The French Resistance during World War II operated without uniforms. Vietcong guerrillas fighting in South Vietnam were not part of any formal army, but the United States nonetheless treated those they captured as POWs.

So what treatment should al Qaeda get? The conventions contain one section—Article 3—that protects all persons regardless of their status, whether spy, mercenary, or terrorist, and regardless of the type of war in which they are fighting. That same article prohibits torture, cruel treatment, and murder of all detainees, requires the wounded to be cared for, and says that any trials must be conducted by regular courts respecting due process. In a landmark 2006 opinion, the U.S. Supreme Court declared that *at a minimum* Article 3 applies to detained al Qaeda suspects. In other words, the rules apply, even if al Qaeda ignores them.

And it may be that even tougher rules should be used in such a fight. Many other governments, particularly in Europe, believe that a "war" against terror—a war without temporal or geographic limits—is complete folly, insisting instead that the fight against terrorist groups should be a law enforcement, not a military, matter. For decades, Europe has prevented and punished terrorists by treating them as criminals. Courts in Britain and Spain have tried suspects for major bombings in London and Madrid. The prosecutors and investigators there did so while largely complying with obligations enshrined in human rights treaties, which constrain them far more than do the Geneva Conventions.

"The Geneva Conventions Turn Soldiers into War Criminals"

Only if they commit war crimes. For centuries, states have punished their own soldiers for violations of the laws of war, such as the mistreatment of prisoners or murder of civilians. The Geneva Conventions identify certain violations that states must prosecute, including murder outside of battle, causing civilians great suffering, and denying POWs fair trials, and most countries have laws on the books that punish such crimes. The U.S. military, for example, has investigated hundreds of servicemembers for abuses in Iraq and Afghanistan, leading to dozens of prosecutions. Canada prosecuted a group of its peacekeepers for the murder of a young Somali in 1993.

Yet the idea that ordinary soldiers could be prosecuted in a foreign country for being, in effect, soldiers fighting a war is ridiculous. Yes, many countries, including the United States, have laws allowing foreigners to be tried for various abuses of war committed anywhere. Yet the risk of prosecution abroad, particularly of U.S. forces, is minuscule. Those foreign laws only address bona fide war crimes, and it is rarely in the interest of foreign governments to aggravate relations with the United States over spurious prosecutions.

The idea that the International Criminal Court could one day put U.S. commanders on trial is unlikely in the extreme. That court could theoretically prosecute U.S. personnel for crimes committed in, say, Afghanistan, but only if the United States failed to do so first. What's more, the court is by its charter dedicated to trying large-scale, horrendous atrocities like those in Sudan. It is virtually inconceivable that this new institution will want to pick a fight with the United States over a relatively small number of abuses.

"The Conventions Prevent Interrogations of Terrorists"

False. If you've seen a classic war movie such as *The Great Escape,* you know that prisoners of war are only obligated to provide name, rank, date of birth, and military serial number to their captors. But the Geneva Conventions do not ban interrogators from asking for more. In fact, the laws were written with the expectation that states will grill prisoners, and clear rules were created to manage the process. In interstate war, any form of coercion is forbidden, specifically threats, insults, or punish-

ments if prisoners fail to answer; for all other wars, cruel or degrading treatment and torture are prohibited. But questioning detainees is perfectly legal; it simply must be done in a manner that respects human dignity. The conventions thus hardly require rolling out the red carpet for suspected terrorists. Many interrogation tactics are clearly allowed, including good cop-bad cop scenarios, repetitive or rapid questioning, silent periods, and playing to a detainee's ego.

The Bush administration has engaged in legal gymnastics to avoid the conventions' restrictions, arguing that preventing the next attack is sufficient rationale for harsh tactics such as waterboarding, sleep deprivation, painful stress positions, deafening music, and traumatic humiliation. These severe methods have been used despite the protests of a growing chorus of intelligence officials who say that such approaches are actually counterproductive to extracting quality information. Seasoned interrogators consistently say that straightforward questioning is far more successful for getting at the truth. So, by mangling the conventions, the United States has joined the company of a host of unsavory regimes that make regular use of torture. It has abandoned a system that protects U.S. military personnel from terrible treatment for one in which the rules are made on the fly.

"The Geneva Conventions Ban Assassinations"

Actually, no. War is all about killing your enemy, and though the Geneva Conventions place limits on the "unnecessary suffering" of soldiers, they certainly don't seek to outlaw war. Assassinating one's enemy when hostilities have been declared is not only permissible; it is expected. But at the core of the conventions is the "principle of distinction," which bans all deliberate targeting of civilians. The boundless scope of the war on terror makes it difficult to decide who is and is not a civilian. The United States claims that it can target and kill terrorists at any time, just like regular soldiers; but the conventions treat these individuals like quasi-civilians who can be targeted and killed only during "such time as they take a *direct* part in hostilities" [emphasis mine]. The Israeli Supreme Court recently interpreted this phrase to give Israel limited latitude to continue targeted killings, but it insisted on a high standard of proof that the target had lost protected status and that capture was impossible. What standards the United States might be using—such as when the CIA targeted and killed several al Qaeda operatives in Yemen in 2002—are highly classified, so there's no way to know how much proof is insisted upon before the trigger is pulled or the button pushed.

For European countries and others who reject the idea of a "war" against terrorists to begin with, targeted killings are especially abhorrent, as international law prohibits states in peacetime from extrajudicial killings. There are very specific exceptions to this rule, such as when a police officer must defend himself or others against imminent harm. To that end, a suicide bomber heading for a crowd could legally be assassinated as a last resort. By contrast, suspected terrorists—whether planning a new attack or on the lam—are to be captured and tried.

"The Conventions Require Closing Guantánamo"

No, but changes must be made. The Geneva Conventions allow countries to detain POWs in camps, and, if someone in enemy hands does not fit the POW category, he or she is automatically accorded civilian status, which has its own protections. But none of the residents of Guantánamo's military prison qualifies as either, according to the Bush administration, thus depriving the roughly 275 detainees who remain there of the rights accorded by the conventions, such as adequate shelter and eventual release.

The possibility that detainees could remain in legal limbo indefinitely at Guantánamo has turned the issue into a foreign-relations disaster for the United States. But let's be clear—the Geneva Conventions don't require the United States to close up shop in Cuba. The rules simply insist that a working legal framework be put in place, instead of the legal vacuum that exists now.

There are several options worth consideration. The prison at Guantánamo could be turned into a pre-trial holding area where detainees are held before they are brought before U.S. courts on formal charges. (The hiccup here is that most of the detainees haven't clearly violated any U.S. law.) Alternatively, the U.S. Congress could pass legislation installing a system of preventive detention for dangerous individuals. The courts could occasionally review detainees' particular circumstances and judge whether continued detention is necessary and lawful. (The problem here is that such a system would run against 200 years of American jurisprudence.) In the end, closing Guantánamo is probably the only option that would realistically restore America's reputation, though it isn't required by any clause in the conventions. It's just the wisest course of action.

"No Nation Flouts the Geneva Conventions More than the United States"

That's absurd. When bullets start flying, rules get broken. The degree to which any army adheres to the Geneva Conventions is typically a product of its professionalism, training, and sense of ethics. On this score, U.S. compliance with the conventions has been admirable, far surpassing many countries and guerrilla armies that routinely ignore even the most basic provisions. The U.S. military takes great pride in teaching its soldiers

civilized rules of war: to preserve military honor and discipline, lessen tensions with civilians, and strive to make a final peace more durable. Contrast that training with Eritrea or Ethiopia, states whose ill-trained forces committed numerous war crimes during their recent border war, or Guatemala, whose army and paramilitaries made a policy of killing civilians on an enormous scale during its long civil conflict.

More importantly, the U.S. military cares passionately that other states and nonstate actors follow the same rules to which it adheres, because U.S. forces, who are deployed abroad in far greater numbers than troops from any other nation, are most likely to be harmed if the conventions are discarded. Career U.S. military commanders and lawyers have consistently opposed the various reinterpretations of the conventions by politically appointed lawyers in the Bush White House and Justice Department for precisely this reason.

It is enormously important that the United States reaffirms its commitment to the conventions, for the sake of the country's reputation and that of the conventions. Those who rely on the flawed logic that because al Qaeda does not treat the conventions seriously, neither should the United States fail to see not only the chaos the world will suffer in exchange for these rules; they also miss the fact that the United States will have traded basic rights and protections harshly learned through thousands of years of war for the nitpicking decisions of a small group of partisan lawyers huddled in secret. Rather than advancing U.S. interests by following an established standard of behavior in this new type of war, the United States—and any country that chooses to abandon these hard-won rules—risks basing its policies on narrow legalisms. In losing sight of the crucial protections of the conventions, the United States invites a world of wars in which laws disappear. And the horrors of such wars would far surpass anything the war on terror could ever deliver.

Critical Thinking

1. What reasons are given to support Steven Ratner's contention that the hard-won rules of battle are falling by the wayside?
2. Do the Geneva Conventions prevent the interrogation of terrorists?
3. Do the Geneva Conventions ban assassinations?

STEVEN R. RATNER is professor of law at the University of Michigan.

America's Nuclear Meltdown towards "Global Zero"

"The Obama Administration ought to ensure that, in making moves toward zero, the U.S. will, in fact, receive concrete, reciprocal concessions from China and India regarding their own nuclear disarmament. . . ."

Lavina Lee

CHINA'S 2008 "White Paper on National Defense"— still the most definitive statement of Beijing's strategic doctrine—asserts that "all nuclear-weapon states should make an unequivocal commitment to the thorough destruction of nuclear weapons." Consistent with this statement, China already has responded favorably to the New START (Strategic Arms Reduction Treaty) agreement between the U.S. and Russia. Although this response should be encouraging to the Obama Administration, New START likely is to be viewed in Beijing as merely a first, tentative step toward global zero, rather than a dramatic signal that alters Chinese strategic calculations and threat perceptions regarding America. In China's view, the U.S. and Russia, as "the two countries possessing the largest nuclear arsenals, bear special and primary responsibility for nuclear disarmament" and should "further drastically reduce their nuclear arsenals in a verifiable and irreversible manner, so as to create the necessary conditions for the participation of other nuclear-weapon states in the process of nuclear disarmament."

Although New START commits the U.S. and Russia to significant reductions in deployed strategic warheads, limiting them to no more than 1,550 each, it places no limits on either state's nondeployed nuclear warheads. Given that the U.S. currently has 5,113 warheads in its nuclear stockpile (not including "several thousand" warheads that are retired and awaiting dismantlement), and China's nuclear capabilities are estimated at around 240 nuclear warheads, it is unlikely that the Chinese will believe that New START has created anywhere near the "necessary conditions" to enable China to begin force reductions of its own. The Chinese have not placed a precise number on the level of force reductions they expect of the U.S. and Russia, but it almost is certain that some semblance of nuclear parity with Beijing will be required.

In any case, given Pres. Barack Obama's own admission that global zero is unlikely to be achieved in his lifetime, the Chinese have cause to question whether the U.S. and Russia voluntarily will relinquish their nuclear superiority any time soon. Under these circumstances, America will be waiting a long time for any Chinese reciprocity on nuclear force reductions. At a minimum, Beijing's posture will stiffen domestic opposition in the U.S. to further cuts in America's own arsenal.

At the April 2010 Nuclear Security Summit in Washington, D.C., Prime Minister Manmohan Singh of India welcomed New START as a "step in the right direction" toward global zero and stated that he was "encouraged" by the "U.S. Nuclear Posture Review" (NPR). That position is consistent with the stance of successive Indian governments of various political persuasions that have advocated global nuclear disarmament since India gained independence. The present Congress Party-led government has called for negotiations on a multilateral, "nondiscriminatory" and "verifiable" Nuclear Weapons Convention that would ban the "development, production, stockpiling, and use of nuclear weapons" in a "time-bound" manner.

India's development of an indigenous nuclear capacity, despite New Delhi's strong stance on nuclear disarmament, would appear at first glance to undermine the credibility of its stance on global zero. However, Indian leaders have maintained that the indefinite extension of the Nuclear Proliferation Treaty (NPT) in 1995, despite the failure of the nuclear weapons states to take concrete steps toward nuclear disarmament in a time-bound manner, left New Delhi no choice but to seek a nuclear deterrent to protect its "autonomy of decisionmaking" (*i.e.*, as a defense against nuclear blackmail). In light of its own experience, India's response to the Obama Administration's global zero agenda has emphasized the connection between comprehensive nuclear disarmament and nonproliferation as "mutually reinforcing processes."

Apart from rhetorical support for nuclear disarmament, India has not made any commitment to join the U.S. and Russia on the path to zero in the near future. Given the historical and existing defense linkages between India and the USSR/ Russia, and the developing security partnership between the U.S. and India, New Delhi has little reason to view the continuing strategic nuclear superiority of America and Russia as a security threat. However, in keeping with its moral and political stance against nuclear weapons, India will continue to insist that both states must take the lead by making even further cuts to their nuclear arsenals. For example, Singh, while welcoming the New START agreement, also called on "all states with substantial nuclear arsenals to further accelerate this process by making deeper cuts that will lead to meaningful disarmament."

India vs. China and Pakistan

The greatest influence over when India will begin nuclear force reductions remains its assessment of the security threats emanating from its nuclear armed regional competitors, China and Pakistan. India maintains a minimum credible deterrent nuclear posture aimed primarily toward these states, with which it has a history of unresolved territorial disputes that have erupted into outright conflict, including the 1962 border war with China and recurring clashes with Pakistan over Kashmir. Any commitments India is likely to make on nuclear force reductions will be linked to both of these states doing the same.

From the Chinese perspective, NPR takes some of the essential steps necessary to achieve the eventual eradication of nuclear weapons. These steps include the decisions to abstain from the development of new nuclear warheads, limit the potential targets and the circumstances under which the U.S. might use nuclear weapons, and elevate nuclear proliferation and terrorism as security threats above the possible threat posed by other nuclear weapons states. China will, however, view NPR as not going far enough in a number of areas. First, the U.S. has stopped short of committing to a "no first use" policy or unconditionally exempting non-nuclear weapons states or states within nuclear-weapon-free-zones from the threat or use of nuclear weapons," all policies that China has adopted. Regardless of whether those commitments are themselves believable or reliable, Chinese officials will use them as a reason to be skeptical of U.S. commitments toward global zero, given that the retention of offensive options will require America to maintain a much larger nuclear arsenal at a higher level of alert than China possesses.

Second, although the U.S. has stated in NPR that it only will use nuclear weapons in "extreme circumstances" where its "vital interests" are at stake, as long as those terms remain undefined—particularly where the status of Taiwan is concerned—China will argue that NPR remains strategically ambiguous and does not, therefore, reduce Beijing's threat perceptions of U.S. nuclear forces. Chinese officials will use this ambiguity within NPR to deflect U.S. calls to improve the transparency of China's own nuclear force modernization program, which has the ostensible goal of avoiding destabilization of the strategic balance between the two countries. Thus, this aspect of NPR will not reduce the incentives for China to magnify its deterrent capabilities by maintaining opacity about the nature and scope of its nuclear modernization activities. Yet, prodding China to increase transparency regarding its arsenal and doctrine is an important goal of the U.S. in getting to zero.

Third, the Chinese are likely to be concerned particularly about the greater emphasis within NPR and Washington's "2010 Ballistic Missile Review" on ballistic missile defense and the upgrade of conventional ballistic missile capabilities, both of which most directly threaten the strategic balance between the two countries. Within NPR, the U.S. specifically links the pursuit of ballistic missile defense as a means to reduce reliance on nuclear weapons for deterring an attack (nuclear, biological, or chemical) on America or its allies. However, U.S. theater missile defense cooperation with Japan, or potentially with Taiwan, provides the opposite incentive to China by raising the prospect that its smaller arsenal and delivery capabilities will be unable to penetrate U.S. missile defenses, thereby calling into question the credibility of Beijing's nuclear deterrent.

Although aware of China's concerns, the "U.S. Ballistic Missile Review Report, 2010" explicitly foresees a role for missile defense to counter China's military modernization program, including the development and deployment of advanced and anti-ship ballistic missile capabilities. The report describes Chinese advances in those systems as having created a "growing imbalance of power across the Taiwan Strait in China's favor."

Strategic arms reductions and the possibility of missile defense cooperation between the U.S. and Russia, suggested within NPR, have become possible only because the underlying conflict of strategic interests between the two countries has dissipated significantly since the end of the Cold War. These conditions do not apply in the case of China, because each side remains uncertain about the other's future intentions within the Asian theater. That especially is true in relation to Taiwan, but there is mutual wariness more generally in terms of China's regional aspirations and Washington's reaction to them.

The continued US. emphasis on—and development of—ballistic missile defense, however understandable, has the potential to undermine the Obama Administration's global zero agenda, particularly by eroding Chinese support for the Comprehensive Test Ban Treaty (CTBT) or a fissile material cutoff treaty. If improvements in U.S. ballistic missile defense capabilities undermine the credibility of China's nuclear deterrent, Beijing likely will be compelled to increase the number and quality of its nuclear warheads, which would, in turn, increase requirements for fissile material. In short, from China's perspective, NPR does not go far enough to reduce Beijing's concerns about U.S. nuclear forces and, therefore, does not provide significant additional incentives to join America on the path to global zero.

India, meanwhile, has made a number of proposals to the Conference on Disarmament regarding steps toward the elimination of nuclear weapons, including the "reduction of the salience of nuclear weapons in security doctrines," the negotiation of a treaty among nuclear weapons states on the "no first use" of nuclear weapons and the nonuse of nuclear weapons against non-nuclear weapons states. The specific steps within NPR to limit the potential targets and the circumstances in which the U.S. nuclear arsenal may be used certainly reduces the "salience" of nuclear weapons within Washington's nuclear posture. However, India is likely to argue that it is the U.S. that needs to go much further in establishing its bona fides on disarmament by emulating New Delhi's nuclear doctrine, which explicitly commits to a no-first-use policy and exempts all non-nuclear weapons states from attack.

The specific measures contained in NPR also are unlikely to influence the future development of India's own nuclear doctrine, because India is an emerging strategic partner of the U.S. and, therefore, an unlikely target of America's nuclear forces. Rather, India's nuclear posture and decisions to join arms control treaties, such as the CTBT and a fissile material cutoff treaty, will be influenced most by developments in the nuclear programs of its regional competitors, Pakistan and China.

Apart from the no-first-use posture and negative security assurance given to non-nuclear weapons states, India's nuclear doctrine centers on the maintenance of a "credible minimum deterrent." Precisely what that means in terms of the adequacy of the size and quality of India's nuclear arsenal and delivery systems is calculated primarily with China, rather than Pakistan (much less the U.S.), in mind.

China has loomed large in India's strategic calculations since Chinese forces defeated the Indian army decisively in the October–November 1962 border war. The decision to develop a nuclear capability largely was spurred by China's first nuclear weapons test in 1964. Likewise, India's 1998 nuclear tests were motivated at least as much by increasing fears about being exposed to Chinese nuclear coercion if New Delhi failed to take the next step from fission to thermo-nuclear weapons—as it was by serious and continuing conflicts with Pakistan over control of the disputed territory of Kashmir.

China's positioning of tactical nuclear weapons on the Tibetan plateau, force projection into the Indian Ocean, and willingness to supply missile and nuclear technology to Pakistan all are seen by New Delhi as indicators of a Chinese strategy to hobble Indian influence within South Asia. Further tensions between the two countries continue regarding unresolved border disputes from the 1962 war over geostrategically significant territory in Arunachal Pradesh (claimed as part of Tibet by China but controlled by India) and Aksai Chin (controlled by China but claimed by India). India particularly has been concerned about China's infrastructure-building programs within the disputed border areas, which would enable the efficient movement of land forces during a crisis.

In response, New Delhi has stationed 100,000 troops and two squadrons of advanced Sukhoi-30 MKI aircraft in the northeastern state of Assam as of June 2009. Given these continuing sources of tension between the two countries, Indian support for either the CTBT or a fissile material cutoff treaty most immediately is influenced by how adherence to either treaty will affect the balance of nuclear forces between it and China, rather than any disarmament initiatives of the Obama Administration. Indian negotiators successfully resisted the Bush Administration's pressure to sign the CTBT as a prerequisite to the successful conclusion of the U.S.–India nuclear cooperation agreement in 2008. Instead, New Delhi merely reiterated its commitment to a voluntary moratorium on nuclear testing announced after the 1998 tests.

Questioning Nuclear Testing

The political commitment of India's Congress-led government to this moratorium was tested in August 2009 after a prominent nuclear official involved in the 1998 tests, Kumitithadai Santhanam, publicly expressed doubts about the officially claimed yield of the devices tested in 1998, thereby calling into question the credibility of India's nuclear deterrent. That allegation set off a vigorous internal debate about whether India should resist pressure to sign the CTBT. Nevertheless, members of the Indian government vigorously have disputed Santhanam's claims and maintained that no new testing will be required.

The government is well aware that any resumption of nuclear testing would trigger the termination of the U.S.–India nuclear cooperation agreement, and potentially the reversal of the September 2008 Nuclear Suppliers Group waiver, which allowed its members to trade with India for the first time. Further testing therefore also would put at risk recently signed contracts for nuclear materials and reactors with countries such as Russia and France, which are essential to the success of the government's ambitious plans to expand nuclear energy capacity. In all likelihood, India will maintain a voluntary moratorium on testing to keep its options open unless—and until—the U.S. and China agree to ratify the CTBT.

In terms of a fissile material cutoff treaty, India officially supports the future development of a multilateral and verifiable treaty that will limit future production of fissile material, but has refused to commit to a voluntary moratorium in the meantime. Clearly, India does not believe it has sufficient fissile material to support a nuclear arsenal in keeping with a "credible minimum deterrent" nuclear posture. India's nuclear arsenal is similar in size to Pakistan's at around 60–70 warheads, but only about one-quarter the size of China's. Nongovernmental sources also estimate that China has sufficient enriched uranium and weapons-grade plutonium to produce between 500 and 1,500 additional warheads.

The U.S.–India nuclear deal potentially has increased India's capacity to produce fissile material by allowing domestic sources of uranium to be reserved for military purposes. The completion of a Prototype Fast Breeder Reactor, due this year, will increase that capacity as well. While there is the potential for a nuclear arms race to develop between the two countries, India so far has shown no signs of attempting to reach parity, in terms of numbers of nuclear weapons, with China. New Delhi instead seeks to maintain a credible minimum deterrent by establishing a survivable nuclear triad of bombers, land-based missiles, and missiles deployed aboard submarines.

Whereas Pakistan remains vocally opposed to a fissile material cutoff treaty that prohibits only the future production of fissile material, India has been able to keep a low profile and avoid making any commitment to a treaty either way. Should this obstacle to negotiations be removed, India still is likely to seek to avoid a firm commitment to a treaty on fissile material until it has built up greater stocks. To buy time, India will seek to link support for a fissile material agreement to additional binding disarmament commitments by the U.S. and Russia within a specific time frame. The most fruitful potential point of leverage for the U.S. on this issue is the prospect of cooperation in the field of high technology, particularly the development of ballistic missile defense systems.

Within the NPR and elsewhere, the Obama Administration clearly has elevated disarmament to the center of its nuclear agenda. The Administration hopes that credible moves toward the goal of zero nuclear weapons will lead to reciprocity in terms of disarmament by other states, as well as encourage greater cooperation on measures to limit nuclear proliferation and the threat of nuclear terrorism.

The question remains, though, how far should America move beyond symbolism in "getting to zero"? The Obama Administration ought to ensure that, in making moves toward zero, the U.S. will, in fact, receive concrete, reciprocal concessions from China and India regarding their own nuclear disarmament and their commitments to joining the CTBT. However, the prospects for both results look quite doubtful at this juncture.

Critical Thinking

1. Define "global zero."
2. What steps have Russia and the United States taken to reduce the number of deployed nuclear weapons?
3. Compare and contrast India, China, and Pakistan's nuclear weapons policies.

LAVINA LEE is a lecturer in the Department of Modern History, Politics, and International Relations at Macquarie University, Sydney, Australia, and the author of *U.S. Hegemony and Legitimacy: Norms, Power, and Followership in the War on Iraq.*

Article 40

The 30 Years War

Hard pounding is gradually bringing AIDS under control.

THE ECONOMIST

It was not quite a birthday present, but it was pretty close. On May 12th the HIV Prevention Trials Network (HPTN), an international research collaboration, announced that its most important project was being terminated—not because it had failed, but because it had succeeded. The study, led by Myron Cohen of the University of North Carolina, Chapel Hill, had looked at 1,763 couples, most straight, some gay, from Africa, Asia and North and South America, in which one partner but not the other was infected. All were counselled in safe sex, given free condoms and offered regular medical checkups. In half, the infected partner was also offered anti-retroviral drugs, even though he or she did not show actual symptoms of AIDS and would thus not normally have been treated. Over the course of six years there were 28 cross-infections. Of those, only one was in the group receiving the drugs.

On June 5th, a little over three weeks after HPTN's announcement, AIDS will be 30 years old—or, more accurately, it will be 30 years since America's Centres for Disease Control and Prevention reported a cluster of unusual infections in Los Angeles that were the first medically recognised cases. On June 8th a meeting of the United Nations' General Assembly, expected to be attended by 40 heads of state and government, will discuss progress in fighting the pandemic and wrestle with the question of what to do next. HPTN052, as the trial in question is known, points the way.

What HPTN052 shows is that the drug treatment used to prolong the lives of those infected with HIV, by stopping the virus reproducing in their bodies, can also stop the virus's transmission. It might therefore be the key to bringing the pandemic under control. The crucial word is "might". People do not like taking medicine, particularly if they have no symptoms. And drugs cost money. The war on AIDS has done well, financially, over the past decade (see Figure 1), but people are feeling the pinch and the cash is no longer increasing. That is ironic, as there are now several clear ways of attacking the problem, above and beyond the usual exhortations of chastity, fidelity and condom use. It is no time to give up the fight.

The past decade has seen real progress. Though it is true that there are two new infections for every new person put on anti-retroviral drugs, and that AIDS is killing 1.8m people a year (see Figure 2), it is also the case, according to UNAIDS, the United Nations agency responsible for monitoring and combating the disease, that 6.6m people in low- and middle-income countries are on such drugs, and that the rate of new HIV infections in 33 poor countries has fallen by a quarter or more from its peak. In 2001 the number on drugs was trivial (see Figure 3) and the peak number of deaths, in 2005, was 2.1m.

At the moment, only those showing symptoms of AIDS, or whose level of a crucial immune-system cell has fallen below

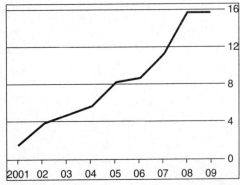

Figuer 1   Flatlining   Resources available for HIV in low- and middle-income countries, $bn
Source: UNAIDS

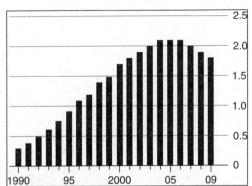

Figuer 2   A gift of life   Estimated deaths due to AIDS, m
Source: UNAIDS

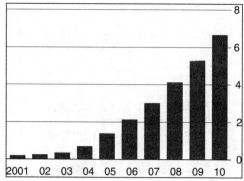

Figuer 3 Drugged up Number of people on anti-retroviral therapy in low- and middle-income countries, m

Source: UNAIDS

a certain threshold, are offered treatment. Even so, there are reckoned to be about 9m people who need treatment but are not receiving it. Add those who have no symptoms and that becomes about 27m. At $100 for a year's course of the drugs, plus around $400 for the cost of administration, they would need a lot of money. In 2010, according to UNAIDS, the world spent $16 billion on the epidemic. Treating all 34m people infected might mean almost doubling that.

New Balls, Please

Prevention by treatment is, nevertheless, a heady prospect. Indeed, Michel Sidibé, UNAIDS's boss, thinks the result of HPTN052 is "a game changer". It would be a long game. Not only would anti-AIDS drugs have to be made available to everyone infected—so-called universal access, which is a UN objective, and which the organisation hopes might be achieved by 2015—but all those people, or, at least, the vast majority of them, would have to be persuaded to take them. That is difficult enough when someone is ill. The latest report from UNAIDS[1] suggests that almost one in five of those put on the drugs stops taking them within a year. It will be even harder to persuade the asymptomatic to pop a daily pill or two for the public good.

They might do so for love, of course. More selfishly, one result of HPTN052 in those receiving drugs was less tuberculosis, a disease that is a common consequence of AIDS. So people now thought symptomless may not be quite as symptomless as they seem. Indeed, in 2010 the World Health Organisation raised the immune-system threshold below which drugs are offered by 75%. That is a step on the way to offering the drugs to all infected people anyway.

Nor is treating the infected, whether for their own good or for the good of others, the only approach being investigated. Several trials have shown that circumcision is a good way to stop men catching the virus. It can reduce the risk by about 50%, and the message has got out. The rate of circumcision in Africa is rocketing. Attempts to protect women, by developing vaginal microbicides that destroy HIV in infected semen, have been less successful. Initial trials using a seaweed derivative failed, and might even have made things worse. But a trial using a drug called tenofovir had promising results, reported last year, and

further tests are going on at the moment. Moreover, there is already one well-proven way of stopping the virus's transmission using drugs. This is between mothers and children at birth. Even a single dose of another drug, nevirapine, halves the risk of an infected mother passing the virus to her baby. More extensive courses can reduce the risk by 90%.

There are also the good-old standbys, behaviour change (a euphemism for less promiscuous sex) and condom use. Here, the data are equivocal. As might be expected, the message is getting through in some places, but not in others. In South Africa, for example, according to UNAIDS, 77% of men and 68% of women reported using a condom last time they had sex. In 14 other high-prevalence countries, though, more than 70% of both sexes reported that they had not.

The armory, in other words, is getting fuller. But war costs money, and money is in short supply at the moment. The first UN meeting on AIDS, held ten years ago near the 20th anniversary, catalysed the formation of the Global Fund (which also has tuberculosis and malaria in its remit) and that, in turn, led to the United States President's Emergency Plan for AIDS Relief (PEPFAR) created by George Bush junior. No one likes to be seen as mean and so, in a decade of rising prosperity, politicians put their hands in their taxpayers' pockets and donated generously to the cause.

This time, the atmosphere is different. It is still the case that no one wants to be seen as mean, but the game of chicken is now the other way round. Then, each act of generosity made it harder for others to refuse. Now, each withdrawal from the fray makes another's easier. Many of the biggest donors to the Global Fund, including America, Britain, Canada, France and the Scandinavians, are still committed (Japan's position, in light of the recent earthquake and tsunami, is unclear). But the Netherlands and Spain have announced cuts. Germany (and also Spain) are delaying their payments during a review of the fund's auditing procedures. (The review, ironically, is a result of those procedures being uniquely transparent for an international aid agency, and thus highlighting shenanigans in a few recipient countries that might otherwise have remained buried.) And one country, Italy, has simply stopped paying its pledged contribution without explanation.

There is also dark talk of several countries trying to water down the language of the declaration that the UN meeting is expected to issue, so that it no longer has numerical targets with specific dates. In a time of austerity, then, value for money is even more important than it might otherwise be. A group of researchers led by Bernhard Schwartländer, director of evidence, strategy and results at UNAIDS, have therefore put their minds to how to spend what is available most wisely.

Dr Schwartländer and his team looked at ten approaches to treating and preventing AIDS, ranging from drugs, via intervening in the prostitution industry, to searching for joint savings by collaborating with other areas of international development. They then devised a computer model that attempted to show how these would play out in each of 139 low- and middle-income countries. The result (see Figure 4) is that expenditure peaks at $22 billion in 2015, and drops below $20 billion in 2020. If Dr Schwartländer and his colleagues are right, therefore, the

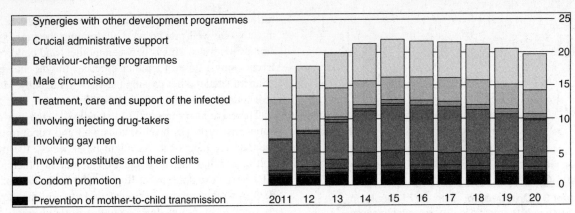

Synergies with other development programmes
Crucial administrative support
Behaviour-change programmes
Male circumcision
Treatment, care and support of the infected
Involving injecting drug-takers
Involving gay men
Involving prostitutes and their clients
Condom promotion
Prevention of mother-to-child transmission

2011 12 13 14 15 16 17 18 19 20

Figuer 4   Every dollar counts   Estimated cost of the main anti-AIDS strategies, $bn

Source: Schwartländer et al, *Lancet*

world (and this includes at least the middle-income members of the 139) needs to stump up a maximum of $6 billion more at the peak of things than it is doing now. Moreover, this extra money would, according to Dr Schwartländer's sums, largely be offset by savings on treatment avoided—for, compared with business as usual, 12.2m infections would be averted, and 7.4m deaths.

Game, Set and Match?

There are even a few ambitious scientists who talk not just of treatment, but of cure. Exactly how this would be done induces a flurry of arm-waving, but their reasons for believing it is theoretically possible—and thus worth investigating—are that about one infected person in 1,000 is now known to control the infection naturally and never develop symptoms, and that several studies have identified antibodies that appear to neutralise HIV. This suggests that boosting the immune system with an appropriate vaccine, or developing appropriate antibodies for injection as a drug, might be possible. Certainly Bertrand Audoin, the executive head of the International AIDS Society, thinks so. He, and people like him, are now talking guardedly of the idea

of a cure for AIDS—destroying the virus in people's bodies completely, rather than just stopping it reproducing.

That is a wild hope, but this is the sort of area where a single scientific breakthrough might, like the invention of AIDS-suppressing drugs and the discovery that those drugs could be used to break the chain of transmission, change everything. Scientists always say that more research is needed, for their livelihoods depend on it. In this case, though, there is little doubt they are right.

Notes

1. "AIDS at 30: Nations at the crossroads" UNAIDS, Geneva

Critical Thinking

1. What is the meaning of the United Nations' objective of "universal access"?

2. What new approaches are being taken to combat AIDS?

3. What is the level and nature of international cooperation to combat AIDS?

Is Bigger Better?

Using market incentives, Fazle Hasan Abed built the largest antipoverty group in the world and helped pull Bangladesh out of the ashes. Now he wants to take on Africa.

DAVID ARMSTRONG

From the large glass window of his modern, well-lit and spacious offices 19 floors above Dhaka, Bangladesh, Fazle Hasan Abed, a former executive for Shell Oil, can keep tabs on nearby Korail, a dense slum of 60,000 people living in single-story mud, aluminum and bamboo shacks, some built on thin stilts over the brackish water of an urban lake. Abed, 72, has more than a little interest in the slum. The organization he founded in 1972, BRAC, the largest antipoverty group in the world, with 110,000 paid employees and a $482 million annual budget, has its hands everywhere in Korail.

Down one muddy lane a teacher trained by BRAC instructs 36 students using a BRAC-designed curriculum of Bengali, math and English. Nearby a group of women in the final month of pregnancy sit shrouded in colorful saris on the floor of a BRAC-built "birthing hut," staffed with BRAC-trained health workers, getting a lesson in prenatal nutrition. Not far away, Mosammat Anwaraan, an energetic woman in her late 50s, runs a mini real estate empire, the fruits of a 3,000 taka ($44) microloan in 1997 from BRAC. She owns 25 rooms in the slum, renting out 18 for 700 to 800 taka a month, making $2,500 a year. "I think rent will go up to 1,000 taka by next year," she says proudly.

Abed has replicated all-in-one programs like these in 1,000 urban slums and 70,000 rural villages across Bangladesh (the group was originally called the Bangladesh Rural Advancement Committee). Its microfinance program has made $4.6 billion in loans versus $6.9 billion from the better-known microlender Grameen. It runs 52,000 preschools and primary schools, with 1.5 million students. Its 68,000 health care volunteers, egged on by financial incentives, cover a population of 80 million. It operates commercial dairies, silkworm-raising centers and department stores to provide markets for the goods its poor beneficiaries produce. Says Abed, "If you want to do significant work, you have to be large. Otherwise we'd be tinkering around on the periphery."

The World Bank credits BRAC in part with what it calls the "Bangladesh paradox": Despite an impotent government (leaders of the two primary political parties are currently in jail on corruption charges), this country of 145 million people has improved significantly. According to the World Bank, the fraction of the population living in poverty (defined as below $2 a day in purchasing power) dropped from 58% in 1992 to 40% in 2005; secondary school enrollment has climbed from 19% in 1990 to 43% today and childhood immunization from 1% in 1980 to 80% today.

In the 1980s a woman had, on average, seven kids. Today it's two.

Thirty years ago a woman had, on average, seven children. Today the fertility rate is two, thanks in large part to widespread delivery of contraceptives to the countryside, a practice pioneered by BRAC. The country's 5% annual average growth in GDP since 1990 (to $2,300 per capita) leads the World Bank to suggest that Bangladesh could join the list of "middle income" countries in ten years. To be sure, trade liberalization, garment exports and remittances from laborers abroad are vital, but the effectiveness of these macroeconomic advances are largely dependent on the kind of ground-level social progress BRAC has made.

"I don't know of any developing-world NGO [nongovernmental organization] that has been more successful," says Dr. Allan Rosenfield, dean of Columbia University's School of Public Health, who serves on the board of BRAC's U.S. arm. "Certainly in terms of the issues they work on, they're more like a minigovernment. If I were giving out Nobel Prizes, there is no doubt I would give it to Abed."

Born to a wealthy landowning family in the Bengal region of British India in 1936, Abed grew up in a household full of servants. His father was a government official. His mother, a religious woman, often brought poor villagers to the Abed home for food. He attended Glasgow University before going to London to study accounting and business. He stayed for 12 years, working as a corporate financial officer and enjoying the life of a professional expatriate: yearly drives through continental Europe, vacations in Italy, reading Western literature. In 1968 he returned to Dhaka with a prestigious job, managing Shell's accounting department.

On Nov. 21, 1970 a cyclone hit the Chittagong area in the southern part of the country, killing perhaps 500,000 people, still the deadliest cyclone on record. Abed and friends volunteered to help. "It really changed the way I look at things," Abed says.

At the time, Bangladesh was the eastern portion of the country of Pakistan, ruled over by an unsympathetic government in Islamabad. A crackdown on the pro-East Pakistan independence movement sent Abed back to London, where he raised funds for the millions of Bangladeshi refugees in India.

After a bloody war Bangladesh won its independence in 1971. Abed sold his London flat for $17,000 and returned to a country that lay in ruins. Hundreds of thousands had been killed and the economy was in tatters—soon after, Henry Kissinger famously called Bangladesh "an international basket case."

Abed and a small group of friends worked on aid projects, but he felt much of the work wasn't benefiting those who needed it most. "Poor people are poor because they are powerless," Abed says. He turned his attention to poverty relief, mapping villages into quartiles based on wealth and focusing his efforts on only those households at the bottom.

Using the proceeds of his London apartment sale, he formed BRAC in 1972. His biggest early success was reducing child mortality. In 1975, 25% of Bangladeshi children wouldn't live to see their fifth birthday; almost half of those deaths were caused by diarrhea. Abed trained groups of women to fan out into the countryside and teach others how to mix a solution of water, salt and sugar that would combat the potentially fatal loss of fluid and electrolytes. Monitors would grade the households based on how well family members did, and that grade would determine the pay of the instructors. This was an incentive-based "social entrepreneurship" program long before that phrase became common. The average worker made $40 a month, with most households scoring in the A or B range.

BRAC researchers estimate that the program, along with a government immunization initiative, has cut the mortality rate of Bangladeshi children ages 1 to 4 from 25% to 7%.

Abed vertically integrates many BRAC programs. A BRAC village organizer will first gather 20 to 30 women and extend microcredit. Many use the loans to set up small shops and grocery stores. If the women buy a cow, for example, BRAC will help them double the price they can get for milk

by collecting it via refrigerated truck and bringing it to one of BRAC's 67 "chilling stations," then to BRAC's commercial dairy production center, which processes 10,000 liters of milk, yogurt and ice cream an hour, and selling it in the cities. It earns BRAC $1.7 million on sales of $13.4 million, all of which goes back into the programs.

Likewise, silkworm raising is the bottom step of another commercial market. Majeda Begum, who lives in a small village a day's drive from Dhaka, used her loan to buy silkworm eggs from BRAC, paying $3 for 50 grams. She hatches them in a tin-roofed shack behind her home. Begum feeds them by spreading mulberry leaves over the top, easy enough to collect, since BRAC has planted 20 million mulberry trees around the area to support the enterprise. She'll sell the cocoons back to BRAC for $5.75 a kilo. She earns, she figures, $370 a year, and no longer needs BRAC's loans. All three of her children, including two daughters, go to school. Without the income? "I'd probably only send my son," she says.

Vertically integrated, BRAC's businesses produce $90 million in revenue.

The silk is eventually woven into clothes and sold to Aarong, a chain of upmarket department stores BRAC owns in Bangladesh's big cities. Aarong netted $4.6 million on $28 million in sales in 2006. In all, BRAC's commercial enterprises account for some $90 million in revenue; it pulls in $116 million from its interest on microloans. BRAC still relies on donor funding for 20% of its budget.

Abed uses incentives for health programs, as well. Community health workers are asked to make home visits to 15 houses a day and can resell at a small markup common medicines, balm and birth control pills that they have bought from BRAC.

Recently health volunteers have been trained to recognize the symptoms of tuberculosis, which kills 70,000 Bangladeshis a year. Volunteers collect a sample of phlegm from suspect people and send it to a BRAC health office for testing. If it's positive, the volunteer gets 200 taka (about $2.50). Patients are given medicine free of charge but must post a $3.50 bond to ensure that they continue the six-month course of medication. "There are market incentives in everything we do," Abed says. Bangladesh has upped its cure rate of known TB cases to 90%.

BRAC has recently started targeting the 14% of women too poor to take advantage of microloans. A day's drive from Dhaka, in an un-air-conditioned BRAC field office swarming with flies, Akhtar Hossain unfurls a large sheet of brown paper on which is drawn a map of a nearby village. His house-by-house survey is meant to find "beggars and those with no land." The government is supposed to give these people a card that entitles the holder to 35 kilos of rice every three months. "But they never get it," he says. "The district official in charge of disbursing the cards gives it to people he knows."

To this group BRAC distributes cows, goats or a small plot of arable land. Haliman Khatun, who once worked as a laborer in others' homes and was paid only with small amounts of rice, shares her small shack in Pakundia with her cow, proudly showing off the space where the cow sleeps next to her own bed. She sells milk from the cow at the market but has bigger ambitions: She might sell it for the end of Eid, a Muslim holiday when livestock is slaughtered; cows can fetch a premium in the marketplace, and with that she could buy a plot of land or more goats, she says.

Abed is now bringing BRAC into Africa. The Gates Foundation has given $15 million in grants and loans to replicate BRAC's microfinance, agriculture and health programs in Tanzania, and the Nike Foundation is giving $1 million to establish designated centers for teenage girls in Tanzania. BRAC has set up organizations in the U.S. and the U.K. to bring in more charitable dollars.

It remains to be seen if BRAC can repeat the success it's had in Bangladesh. But Abed is encouraged by its track record in Afghanistan, where it set up shop in 2002. Some 180,000 women have borrowed $96 million from BRAC, and 4,000 have been trained as community health workers. When Abed sets out to do something, he does it big.

Critical Thinking

1. What is a non-governmental organization (NGO)?
2. What is the mission and strategic plan of BRAC?
3. How is BRAC organized?
4. What other important NGOs can you identify?

From *Forbes Magazine,* June 2, 2008, pp. 66–70. Reprinted by permission of Forbes Magazine, © 2008 Forbes Media Inc.

Humanitarian Workers
Comprehensive Response

In February's edition of *The World Today*, Lieutenant General Louis Lillywhite argued that "humanitarian aid has been 'politicised' in the context of the current conflicts by becoming part of the Comprehensive Approach." Here, Médecins Sans Frontières (MSF) presents a different angle.

MARC DUBOIS AND VICKIE HAWKINS

Lieutenant General Louis Lillywhite argues in his article that the delivery of aid has become one component within a broader military and political strategy. Such an approach blurs the distinction between humanitarian (emergency) assistance to save lives and other forms of aid falling under the rubric of development or delivery of state services, which are designed to build the legitimacy of governments, win hearts and minds in a conflict zone, and contribute to stabilisation efforts.

Lillywhite astutely notes that it then becomes "entirely rational" for insurgents to perceive humanitarian operations as a key component of their enemy's approach, with the outcome being increased violence against humanitarian workers. This politicisation of humanitarian aid will thereby lead to a reduced ability to provide relief, hence contrary to the intended outcome of the 'Comprehensive Approach' itself. From our perspective, Lillywhite then exactly reverses the question at hand. He examines the measures that could be taken by humanitarians to protect the Comprehensive Approach. The better question is this: Why continue with the Comprehensive Approach in a place like Afghanistan if it endangers humanitarians and, ultimately, fails to deliver aid to those most in need?

Humanitarian organisations like our own often talk of three key principles: independence, neutrality and impartiality. Perhaps there is a suspicion that we use these terms in order to claim some moral high ground—but in fact they are essential to the way we must work on the ground. These operating principles act as a 'guarantee' to all civilians and warring parties alike that they can trust us, that our work does not seek to advance the political or military interests of one side, and that our aid is based on immediate need, not ideology.

Put simply, humanitarian action has to be several things in order to be humanitarian. First and foremost, it has to provide aid on the basis of immediate human needs—for medical care, food and water for example. Being humanitarian means making our own assessments of these needs, delivering the aid in a way that ensures it reaches the people who need it, and then making our own examinations of the impact.

In the case of Médecins Sans Frontierés (MSF), these principles are partly safeguarded through financial independence. This means a reliance on a majority of private funds, so that we do not have to accept funding from a belligerent party in the war. In fact, for Afghanistan, Pakistan, Somalia and Iraq we exclude all government funding and work only with private resources. Armed groups tell MSF that independence of action matters to those whom we negotiate with, and is fundamental to our access. Hence, the reality of acting in this way means that it is necessary to have relations not just with the local communities that humanitarians are trying to assist, but with all parties in a conflict area: national governments, armed opposition groups, international forces, private security forces and criminal gangs.

It is hard. The Comprehensive Approach makes aid a target to opposition groups. We do our best to build the trust of local communities and belligerents in order to work in the heart of conflict, and at times we see some success. In Afghanistan for example, MSF actually sees an opening. We are in the process of looking to expand our work in several locations including Kunduz in the north. At the same time, access to people who desperately need assistance remains severely inadequate in many of today's most difficult conflict areas. Many conflict-affected parts of north-west Pakistan remain 'off-limits' to MSF teams in the minds of government officials. In Somalia, what MSF is able to do is dwarfed by the massive needs of those war-ravaged communities. And in Iraq, we continue to struggle to have medical impact. Yet we remain present, with both international and national staff on the ground—we continue to talk to people on all sides, and to be as transparent as possible about our motives and our actions.

Is there any escape from the Comprehensive Approach; from the politicization of aid? In his article, General Lillywhite asserts that even our own organisation, while openly rejecting efforts to co-opt us into the Comprehensive Approach, is inadvertently benefiting the Comprehensive Approach in Afghanistan by working in areas of the country of lower priority to western forces. We disagree.

MSF's decision to work in these areas, namely the Ahmed Shah Baba district of Kabul—where the primary health-care system has been put under intense pressure by a quadrupling of the population yet international investment was woefully inadequate—was driven by need alone, and with no regard to counter-insurgency or stabilisation priorities. In Helmand, we provide access to quality secondary health-care for people across the province, a decision again driven solely by our assessment of medical need. By making the decision to work in an area of high-priority to western forces, because the opposition exert a significant level of control over the population, are we inadvertently contributing to the war aims of the opposition?

In both cases, MSF can recognise and accept that that is the case. However, it would be ludicrous to criticise genuine humanitarian aid for such inadvertent outcomes. Firstly, because such aid—aid given to civilians in a highly polarised, fluid and violent context that has no inadvertent benefits to warring parties—does not exist. Secondly, because the integrity of aid is best judged by its lack of direct political intentions/objectives, rather than the inescapable fact of its potential political consequences. Thirdly, because in emergency situations, where communities and sometimes whole populations struggle to survive a precarious existence, the medical impact of our activities far outweighs any arguable contribution that MSF is making to the war efforts of either party. Finally, perhaps the best indication that our activities do not significantly provide inadvertent benefit to the Comprehensive Approach comes from the Taliban themselves, with whom we have negotiated our access and who have thereby approved of our projects.

It is part of the responsibility of every humanitarian organisation to constantly monitor and question the extent to which its efforts support and promote the objectives of one party or other to the conflict. Attempts by political and military forces to co-opt humanitarian assistance into their efforts, are not a new phenomenon—we have witnessed them first hand in many contexts over the last forty years. Yet today, co-option has been achieved on a more categorically different scale than ever before. In a large part this is due to the explicit and public placement of aid at the centre of the west's war effort, and the substantial aid funds available. In turn, this co-option is facilitated by the blurring between humanitarian and development within the NGO sector itself, by accepting funding from belligerent parties, and engaging in activity that is gauged to support the ambitions of one side in the conflict.

General Lillywhite's bottom-line was that the instigators of the Comprehensive Approach may have diminished its effectiveness through politicising humanitarian aid in the process. MSF's by contrast is that much of the sector is responsible itself for the extent of this politicisation. In a war zone like Afghanistan, by not ensuring that the principles of impartiality, neutrality and independence guide decisions around project funding and project objectives, and by not ensuring a negotiated access among all parties to the conflict, many NGOs have become much more than 'inadvertent' supporters of the Comprehensive Approach.

Critical Thinking

1. What is the "comprehensive approach" that the authors argue against?
2. What is the general strategy humanitarian organizations pursue to maintain neutrality in conflict situations?

UNIT 7

Values and Visions

Unit Selections

Learning Outcomes

After reading this Unit, you will be able to:

• Identify specific examples of the "meta" component of the Allegory of the Balloon (i.e., changing values and new ideas).

• Consider how the "meta" factor impacts social structures and natural resources.

• Assess your ongoing effort at identifying your theory of international relations and how this unit changes/complements it.

• Compare your theory to the Allegory of the Balloon. How are they similar/different?

Student Website

www.mhhe.com/cls

Internet References

Human Rights Web
   www.hrweb.org
InterAction
   www.interaction.org

The final unit of this book considers how humanity's view of itself is changing. Values, like all other elements discussed in this anthology, are dynamic. Visionary people with new ideas can have a profound impact on how a society deals with problems and adapts to changing circumstances. Therefore, to understand the forces at work in the world today, values, visions, and new ideas in many ways are every bit as important as new technology or changing demographics.

Novelist Herman Wouk, in his book *War and Remembrance,* observed that many institutions have been so embedded in the social fabric of their time that people assumed that they were part of human nature; for example, human sacrifice and blood sport. However, forward-thinking people opposed these institutions. Many knew that they would never see the abolition of these social systems within their own lifetimes, but they pressed on in the hope that someday these institutions would be eliminated.

Wouk believes the same is true for warfare. He states, "Either we are finished with war or war will finish us." Aspects of society such as warfare, slavery, racism, and the secondary status of women are creations of the human mind; history suggests that they can be changed by the human spirit.

The articles of this unit have been selected with the previous six units in mind. Each explores some aspect of world affairs from the perspective of values and alternative visions of the future.

New ideas are critical to meeting these challenges. The examination of well-known issues from new perspectives can yield new insights into old problems. Feminist Susan B. Anthony once remarked that "social change is never made by the masses, only by educated minorities." The redefinition of human values (which, by necessity, will accompany the successful confrontation of important global issues) is a task that few people take on willingly. Nevertheless, to deal with the dangers of nuclear war, overpopulation, and environmental degradation, educated people must take a broad view of history. This is going to require considerable effort and much personal sacrifice.

When people first begin to consider the magnitude of contemporary global problems, many often become disheartened

© Go Go Images Corporation/Alamy

and depressed. Some ask: What can I do? What does it matter? Who cares? There are no easy answers to these questions, but people need only look around to see good news as well as bad. How individuals react to the world is not solely a function of so-called objective reality but a reflection of themselves.

As stated at the beginning of the first unit, the study of global issues is the study of people. The study of people, furthermore, is the study of both values and the level of commitment supporting these values and beliefs.

It is one of the goals of this book to stimulate you, the reader, to react intellectually and emotionally to the discussion and description of various global challenges. In the process of studying these issues, hopefully you have had some new insights into your own values and commitments. In the presentation of the Allegory of the Balloon, the fourth color added represented the "meta" component, all those qualities that make human beings unique. It is these qualities that have brought us to this unique moment in time, and it will be these same qualities that will determine the outcome of our historically unique challenges.

Humanity's Common Values

Seeking a Positive Future

Overcoming the discontents of globalization and the clashes of civilizations requires us to reexamine and reemphasize those positive values that all humans share.

WENDELL BELL

Some commentators have insisted that the terrorist attacks of September 11, 2001, and their aftermath demonstrate Samuel P. Huntington's thesis of "the clash of civilizations," articulated in a famous article published in 1993. Huntington, a professor at Harvard University and director of security planning for the National Security Council during the Carter administration, argued that "conflict between groups from differing civilizations" has become "the central and most dangerous dimension of the emerging global politics."

Huntington foresaw a future in which nation-states no longer play a decisive role in world affairs. Instead, he envisioned large alliances of states, drawn together by common culture, cooperating with each other. He warned that such collectivities are likely to be in conflict with other alliances formed of countries united around a different culture.

Cultural differences do indeed separate people between various civilizations, but they also separate groups within a single culture or state. Many countries contain militant peoples of different races, religions, languages, and cultures, and such differences do sometimes provoke incidents that lead to violent conflict—as in Bosnia, Cyprus, Northern Ireland, Rwanda, and elsewhere. Moreover, within many societies today (both Western and non-Western) and within many religions (including Islam, Judaism, and Christianity) the culture war is primarily internal, between fundamentalist orthodox believers on the one hand and universalizing moderates on the other. However, for most people most of the time, peaceful accommodation and cooperation are the norms.

Conflicts between groups often arise and continue not because of the differences between them, but because of their similarities. People everywhere, for example, share the capacities to demonize others, to be loyal to their own group (sometimes even willing to die for it), to believe that they themselves and those they identify with are virtuous while all others are wicked, and to remember past wrongs committed against their group and seek revenge. Sadly, human beings everywhere share the capacity to hate and kill each other, including their own family members and neighbors.

Discontents of Globalization

Huntington is skeptical about the implications of the McDonaldization of the world. He insists that the "essence of Western civilization is the Magna Carta not the Magna Mac." And he says further, "The fact that non-Westerners may bite into the latter has no implications for accepting the former."

His conclusion may be wrong, for if biting into a Big Mac and drinking Coca-Cola, French wine, or Jamaican coffee while watching a Hollywood film on a Japanese TV and stretched out on a Turkish rug means economic development, then demands for public liberties and some form of democratic rule may soon follow where Big Mac leads. We know from dozens of studies that economic development contributes to the conditions necessary for political democracy to flourish.

Globalization, of course, is not producing an all-Western universal culture. Although it contains many Western aspects, what is emerging is a *global* culture, with elements from many cultures of the world, Western and non-Western.

Local cultural groups sometimes do view the emerging global culture as a threat, because they fear their traditional ways will disappear or be corrupted. And they may be right. The social world, after all, is constantly in flux. But, like the clean toilets that McDonald's brought to Hong Kong restaurants, people may benefit from certain changes, even when their fears prevent them from seeing this at once.

And local traditions can still be—and are—preserved by groups participating in a global culture. Tolerance and even the celebration of many local variations, as long as they do not harm others, are hallmarks of a sustainable world community. Chinese food, Spanish art, Asian philosophies, African drumming, Egyptian history, or any major religion's version of the Golden Rule can enrich the lives of everyone. What originated locally can become universally adopted (like Arabic numbers). Most important, perhaps, the emerging global culture is a fabric woven from tens of thousands—possibly hundreds of thousands—of individual networks of communication, influence, and exchange that link people and organizations across civilizational boundaries. Aided by electronic communications systems, these networks are growing stronger and more numerous each day.

Positive shared value: Unity.

Searching for Common, *Positive* Values

Global religious resurgence is a reaction to the loss of personal identity and group stability produced by "the processes of social, economic, and cultural modernization that swept across the world in the second half of the twentieth century," according to Huntington. With traditional systems of authority disrupted, people become separated from their roots in a bewildering maze of new rules and expectations. In his view, such people need "new sources of identity, new forms of stable community, and new sets of moral precepts to provide them with a sense of meaning and purpose." Organized religious groups, both mainstream and fundamentalist, are growing today precisely to meet these needs, he believes.

Positive shared value: Love.

Although uprooted people may need new frameworks of identity and purpose, they will certainly not find them in fundamentalist religious groups, for such groups are *not* "new sources of identity." Instead, they recycle the past. Religious revival movements are reactionary, not progressive. Instead of facing the future, developing new approaches to deal with perceived threats of economic, technological, and social change, the movements attempt to retreat into the past.

Religions will likely remain among the major human belief systems for generations to come, despite—or even because of—the fact that they defy conventional logic and reason with their ultimate reliance upon otherworldly beliefs. However, it is possible that some ecumenical accommodations will be made that will allow humanity to build a generally accepted ethical system based on the many similar and overlapping moralities contained in the major religions. A person does not have to believe in supernatural beings to embrace and practice the principles of a global ethic, as exemplified in the interfaith declaration, "Towards a Global Ethic," issued by the Parliament of the World's Religions in 1993.

Positive shared value: Compassion.

Interfaith global cooperation is one way that people of different civilizations can find common cause. Another is global environmental cooperation seeking to maintain and enhance the life-sustaining capacities of the earth. Also, people everywhere have a stake in working for the freedom and welfare of future generations, not least because the future of their own children and grandchildren is at stake.

Positive shared value: Welfare of future generations.

Many more examples of cooperation among civilizations in the pursuit of common goals can be found in every area from medicine and science to moral philosophy, music, and art. A truly global commitment to the exploration, colonization, and industrialization of space offers still another way to harness the existing skills and talents of many nations, with the aim of realizing and extending worthy human capacities to their fullest. So, too, does the search for extraterrestrial intelligence. One day, many believe, contact will be made. What, then, becomes of Huntington's "clash of civilizations"? Visitors to Earth will likely find the variations among human cultures and languages insignificant compared with the many common traits all humans share.

Universal human values do exist, and many researchers, using different methodologies and data sets, have independently identified similar values. Typical of many studies into universal values is the global code of ethics compiled by Rushworth M. Kidder in *Shared Values for a Troubled World* (Wiley, 1994). Kidder's list includes love, truthfulness, fairness, freedom, unity (including cooperation, group allegiance, and oneness with others), tolerance, respect for life, and responsibility (which includes taking care of yourself, of other individuals, and showing concern for community interests). Additional values mentioned are courage, knowing right from wrong, wisdom, hospitality, obedience, and stability.

The Origins of Universal Human Values

Human values are not arbitrary or capricious. Their origins and continued existence are based in the facts of biology and in how human minds and bodies interact with their physical and social environments. These realities shape and constrain human behavior. They also shape human beliefs about the world and their evaluations of various aspects of it.

Human beings cannot exist without air, water, food, sleep, and personal security. There are also other needs that, although not absolutely necessary for the bodily survival of individuals, contribute to comfort and happiness. These include clothing, shelter, companionship, affection, and sex. The last, of course, is also necessary for reproduction and, hence, for the continued survival of the human species.

Thus, there are many constraints placed on human behavior, if individuals and groups are to continue to survive and to thrive. These are *not* matters of choice. *How* these needs are met involves some—often considerable—leeway of choice, but, obviously, these needs set limits to the possible.

Much of morality, then, derives from human biological and psychological characteristics and from our higher order capacities of choice and reasoning. If humans were invulnerable and immortal, then injunctions against murder would be unnecessary. If humans did not rely on learning from others, lying would not be a moral issue.

Some needs of human individuals, such as love, approval, and emotional support, are inherently social, because they can only be satisfied adequately by other humans. As infants, individuals are totally dependent on other people. As adults, interaction with others satisfies both emotional and survival needs. The results achieved through cooperation and division of labor within a group are nearly always superior to what can be achieved by individuals each working alone. This holds true for hunting, providing protection from beasts and hostile groups, building shelters, or carrying out large-scale community projects.

Thus, social life itself helps shape human values. As societies have evolved, they have selectively retained only some of the logically possible variations in human values as norms, rights, and obligations. These selected values function to make social life possible, to permit and encourage people to live and work together.

Socially disruptive attitudes and actions, such as greed, dishonesty, cowardice, anger, envy, promiscuity, stubbornness, and disobedience, among others, constantly threaten the survival of society. Sadly, these human traits are as universal as are societal efforts to control them. Perhaps some or all of them once had survival value for individuals. But with the growth of society, they have become obstacles to the cooperation needed to sustain large-scale, complex communities. Other actions and attitudes that individuals and societies ought to avoid are equally well-recognized: abuses of power, intolerance, theft, arrogance, brutality, terrorism, torture, fanaticism, and degradation.

Positive shared value: Honesty.

I believe the path toward a harmonious global society is well marked by widely shared human values, including patience, truthfulness, responsibility, respect for life, granting dignity to all people, empathy for others, kindliness and generosity, compassion, and forgiveness. To be comprehensive, this list must be extended to include equality between men and women, respect for human rights, nonviolence, fair treatment of all groups, encouragement of healthy and nature-friendly lifestyles, and acceptance of freedom as an ideal limited by the need to avoid harming others. These value judgments are not distinctively Islamic, Judeo-Christian, or Hindu, or Asian, Western, or African. They are *human* values that have emerged, often independently, in many different places based on the cumulative life experience of generations.

Human societies and civilizations today differ chiefly in how well they achieve these positive values and suppress negative values. No society, obviously, has fully achieved the positive values, nor fully eliminated the negative ones.

But today's shared human values do not necessarily represent the ultimate expression of human morality. Rather, they provide a current progress report, a basis for critical discourse on a global level. By building understanding and agreement across cultures, such discourse can, eventually, lead to a further evolution of global morality.

In every society, many people, groups, and institutions respect and attempt to live by these positive values, and groups such as the Institute for Global Ethics are exploring how a global ethic can be improved and implemented everywhere.

Principle for global peace: Inclusion.

The Search for Global Peace and Order

Individuals and societies are so complex that it may seem foolhardy even to attempt the ambitious task of increasing human freedom and wellbeing. Yet what alternatives do we have? In the face of violent aggressions, injustice, threats to the environment, corporate corruption, poverty, and other ills of our present world, we can find no satisfactory answers in despair, resignation, and inaction.

Rather, by viewing human society as an experiment, and monitoring the results of our efforts, we humans can gradually refine our plans and actions to bring closer an ethical future world in which every individual can realistically expect a long, peaceful, and satisfactory life.

Given the similarity in human values, I suggest three principles that might contribute to such a future: *inclusion, skepticism*, and *social control.*

1. The Principle of Inclusion

Although many moral values are common to all cultures, people too often limit their ethical treatment of others to members of their own groups. Some, for example, only show respect or concern for other people who are of their own race, religion, nationality, or social class.

Such exclusion can have disastrous effects. It can justify cheating or lying to people who are not members of one's own ingroup. At worst, it can lead to demonizing them and making them targets of aggression and violence, treating them as less than human. Those victimized by this shortsighted and counterproductive mistreatment tend to pay it back or pass it on to others, creating a nasty world in which we all must live.

Today, our individual lives and those of our descendants are so closely tied to the rest of humanity that our identities ought to include a sense of kinship with the whole human race and our circle of caring ought to embrace the welfare of people everywhere. In practical terms, this means that we should devote more effort and resources to raising the quality of life for the worst-off members of the human community; reducing disease, poverty, and illiteracy; and creating equal opportunity for all men and women. Furthermore, our circle of caring ought to include protecting natural resources, because all human life depends on preserving the planet as a livable environment.

2. The Principle of Skepticism

One of the reasons why deadly conflicts continue to occur is what has been called "the delusion of certainty." Too many people refuse to consider any view but their own. And, being sure that they are right, such people can justify doing horrendous things to others.

As I claimed in "Who Is Really Evil?" (*The Futurist,* March–April 2004), we all need a healthy dose of skepticism, especially about our own beliefs. Admitting that we might be wrong can lead to asking questions, searching for better answers, and considering alternative possibilities.

Critical realism is a theory of knowledge I recommend for everyone, because it teaches us to be skeptical. It rests on the assumption that knowledge is never fixed and final, but changes as we learn and grow. Using evidence and reason, we can evaluate our current beliefs and develop new ones in response to new information and changing conditions. Such an approach is essential to futures studies, and indeed to any planning. If your cognitive maps of reality are wrong, then using them to navigate through life will not take you where you want to go.

Critical realism also invites civility among those who disagree, encouraging peaceful resolution of controversies by investigating and discussing facts. It teaches temperance and tolerance, because it recognizes that the discovery of hitherto unsuspected facts may overturn any of our "certainties," even long-cherished and strongly held beliefs.

3. The Principle of Social Control

Obviously, there is a worldwide need for both informal and formal social controls if we hope to achieve global peace and order. For most people most of the time, informal social controls may be sufficient. By the end of childhood, for example, the norms of behavior taught and reinforced by family, peers, school, and religious and other institutions are generally internalized by individuals.

Principle for global peace: Skepticism.

Yet every society must also recognize that informal norms and even formal codes of law are not enough to guarantee ethical behavior and to protect public safety in every instance. Although the threats we most often think of are from criminals, fanatics, and the mentally ill, even "normal" individuals may occasionally lose control and behave irrationally, or choose to ignore or break the law with potentially tragic results. Thus, ideally, police and other public law enforcement, caretaking, and rehabilitation services protect us not only from "others," but also from ourselves.

Likewise, a global society needs global laws, institutions to administer them, and police/peacekeepers to enforce them. Existing international systems of social control should be strengthened and expanded to prevent killing and destruction, while peaceful negotiation and compromise to resolve disputes are encouraged. A global peacekeeping force with a monopoly on the legitimate use of force, sanctioned by democratic institutions and due process of law, and operated competently and fairly, could help prevent the illegal use of force, maintain global order, and promote a climate of civil discourse. The actions of these global peacekeepers should, of course, be bound not only by law, but also by a code of ethics. Peacekeepers should use force as a last resort and only to the degree needed, while making every effort to restrain aggressors without harming innocent people or damaging the infrastructures of society.

Expanding international law, increasing the number and variety of multinational institutions dedicated to controlling armed conflict, and strengthening efforts by the United Nations and other organizations to encourage the spread of democracy, global cooperation, and peace, will help create a win-win world.

Conclusion: Values for a Positive Global Future

The "clash of civilizations" thesis exaggerates both the degree of cultural diversity in the world and how seriously cultural differences contribute to producing violent conflicts.

In fact, many purposes, patterns, and practices are shared by all—or nearly all—peoples of the world. There is an emerging global ethic, a set of shared values that includes:

- Individual responsibility.
- Treating others as we wish them to treat us.
- Respect for life.
- Economic and social justice.
- Nature-friendly ways of life.
- Honesty.
- Moderation.
- Freedom (expressed in ways that do not harm others).
- Tolerance for diversity.

The fact that deadly human conflicts continue in many places throughout the world is due less to the differences that separate societies than to some of these common human traits and values. All humans, for example, tend to feel loyalty to their group, and

181

Toward Planetary Citizenship

A global economy that values competition over cooperation is an economy that will inevitably hurt people and destroy the environment. If the world's peoples are to get along better in the future, they need a better economic system, write peace activists Hazel Henderson and Daisaku Ikeda in *Planetary Citizenship*.

Henderson, an independent futurist, is one of the leading voices for a sustainable economic system; she is the author of many books and articles on her economic theories, including most recently *Beyond Globalization*. Ikeda is president of Soka Gakkai International, a peace and humanitarian organization based on Buddhist principles.

"Peace and nonviolence are now widely identified as fundamental to human survival," Henderson writes. "Competition must be balanced by cooperation and sharing. Even economists agree that peace, nonviolence, and human security are global public goods along with clean air and water, health and education—bedrock conditions for human well-being and development."

Along with materialistic values and competitive economics, the growing power of technology threatens a peaceful future, she warns. Humanity needs to find ways to harness these growing, "godlike" powers to lead us to genuine human development and away from destruction.

Henderson eloquently praises Ikeda's work at the United Nations to foster global cooperation on arms control, health, environmental protection, and other crucial issues. At the heart of these initiatives is the work of globally minded grass-root movements, or "planetary citizens," which have the potential to become the next global superpower, Henderson suggests.

One example of how nonmaterial values are starting to change how societies perceive their progress is the new Gross National Happiness indicators developed in Bhutan, which "[reflect] the goals of this Buddhist nation, [and] exemplify the importance of clarifying the goals and values of a society and creating indicators to measure what we treasure: health, happiness, education, human rights, family, country, harmony, peace, and environmental quality and restoration," Henderson writes.

The authors are optimistic that the grassroots movement will grow as more people look beyond their differences and seek common values and responsibilities for the future.

Source: *Planetary Citizenship: Your Values, Beliefs and Actions Can Shape a Sustainable World* by Hazel Henderson and Daisaku Ikeda. Middleway Press, 606 Wilshire Boulevard, Santa Monica, California 90401. 2004. 200 pages. $23.95. Order from the Futurist Bookshelf, www.wfs.org/bkshelf.htm.

---

may easily overreact in the group's defense, leaving excluded "outsiders" feeling marginalized and victimized. Sadly, too, all humans are capable of rage and violent acts against others.

In past eras, the killing and destruction of enemies may have helped individuals and groups to survive. But in today's interconnected world that is no longer clearly the case. Today, violence and aggression too often are blunt and imprecise instruments that fail to achieve their intended purposes, and frequently blow back on the doers of violence.

The long-term trends of history are toward an ever-widening definition of individual identity (with some people already adopting self-identities on the widest scale as "human beings"), and toward the enlargement of individual circles of caring to embrace once distant or despised "outsiders." These trends are likely to continue, because they embody values—learned from millennia of human experience—that have come to be nearly universal: from the love of life itself to the joys of belonging to a community, from the satisfaction of self-fulfillment to the excitement of pursuing knowledge, and from individual happiness to social harmony.

How long will it take for the world to become a community where every human everywhere has a good chance to live a long and satisfying life? I do not know. But people of [goodwill] can do much today to help the process along. For example, we can begin by accepting responsibility for our own life choices: the goals and actions that do much to shape our future. And we can be more generous and understanding of what we perceive as mistakes and failures in the choices and behavior of oth-

ers. We can include all people in our circle of concern, behave ethically toward everyone we deal with, recognize that every human being deserves to be treated with respect, and work to raise minimum standards of living for the least well-off people in the world.

We can also dare to question our personal views and those of the groups to which we belong, to test them and consider alternatives. Remember that knowledge is not constant, but subject to change in the light of new information and conditions. Be prepared to admit that anyone—even we ourselves—can be misinformed or reach a wrong conclusion from the limited evidence available. Because we can never have all the facts before us, let us admit to ourselves, whenever we take action, that mistakes and failure are possible. And let us be aware that certainty can become the enemy of decency.

In addition, we can control ourselves by exercising self-restraint to minimize mean or violent acts against others. Let us respond to offered friendship with honest gratitude and cooperation; but, when treated badly by another person, let us try, while defending ourselves from harm, to respond not with anger or violence but with verbal disapproval and the withdrawal of our cooperation with that person. So as not to begin a cycle of retaliation, let us not overreact. And let us always be willing to listen and to talk, to negotiate and to compromise.

Finally, we can support international law enforcement, global institutions of civil and criminal justice, international courts and global peacekeeping agencies, to build and strengthen nonviolent means for resolving disputes. Above all, we can work to ensure that global institutions are honest and fair and that they hold all countries—rich and poor, strong and weak—to the same high standards.

If the human community can learn to apply to all people the universal values that I have identified, then future terrorist acts like the events of September 11 may be minimized, because all people are more likely to be treated fairly and with dignity and because all voices will have peaceful ways to be heard, so some of the roots of discontent will be eliminated. When future terrorist acts do occur—and surely some will—they can be treated as the unethical and criminal acts that they are.

There is no clash of civilizations. Most people of the world, whatever society, culture, civilization, or religion they revere or feel a part of, simply want to live—and let others live—in peace and harmony. To achieve this, all of us must realize that the human community is inescapably bound together. More and more, as Martin Luther King Jr. reminded us, whatever affects one, sooner or later affects all.

Critical Thinking

1. How does Wendell Bell contrast his argument with Samuel Huntington's "clash of civilizations" thesis?

2. What are some of the shared values that Bell identifies?

3. What is "critical realism"? How does this concept relate to the study of global issues?

4. Describe what Bell calls an "emerging global ethic."

WENDELL BELL is professor emeritus of sociology and senior research scientist at Yale University's Center for Comparative Research. He is the author of more than 200 articles and nine books, including the two-volume *Foundations of Futures Studies* (Transaction Publishers, now available in paperback 2003, 2004). His address is Department of Sociology, Yale University, P.O. Box 208265, New Haven, Connecticut 06520. E-mail wendell.bell@yale.edu.

This article draws from an essay originally published in the *Journal of Futures Studies 6*.

Visible Man

Ethics in a World without Secrets

PETER SINGER

In 1787, the philosopher Jeremy Bentham proposed the construction of a "Panopticon," a circular building with cells along the outer walls and, at the center, a watch-tower or "inspector's lodge" from which all the cells could be seen but no one would know, at any given moment, due to a system of blinds and partitions, whether he was actually being observed. Bentham thought this design would be particularly suited to prisons but suggested it could also be applied to factories, hospitals, mental asylums, and schools. Not only would prisoners, workers, the ill, the insane, and students be subject to observation, but also—if the person in charge of the facility visited the inspector's area—the warders, supervisors, caregivers, and teachers. The gradual adoption of this "inspection principle," would, Bentham predicted, create "a new scene of things," transforming the world into a place with "morals reformed, health preserved, industry invigorated, instruction diffused, public burdens lightened."

The modern Panopticon is not a physical building, and it doesn't require the threat of an inspector's presence to be effective. Technological breakthroughs have made it easy to collect, store, and disseminate data on individuals, corporations, and even the government. With surveillance technology like closed-circuit television cameras and digital cameras now linked to the Internet, we have the means to implement Bentham's inspection principle on a much vaster scale. What's more, we have helped construct this new Panopticon, voluntarily giving up troves of personal information. We blog, tweet, and post what we are doing, thinking, and feeling. We allow friends and contacts, and even strangers, to know where we are at any time. We sign away our privacy in exchange for the conveniences of modern living, giving corporations access to information about our financial circumstances and our spending habits, which will then be used to target us for ads or to analyze our consumer habits.

Then there is the information collected without our consent. Since 2001, the number of U.S. government organizations involved in spying on our own citizens, both at home and abroad, has grown rapidly. Every day, the National Security Agency intercepts 1.7 billion emails, phone calls, instant messages, bulletin-board postings, and other communications. This system houses information on thousands of U.S. citizens, many of them not accused of any wrongdoing. Not long ago, when traffic police stopped a driver they had to radio the station and wait while someone checked records. Now, handheld devices instantly call up a person's Social Security number and license status, records of outstanding warrants, and even mug shots. The FBI can also cross-check your fingerprints against its digital archive of 96 million sets.

Yet the guarded have also struck back, in a sense, against their guardians, using organizations like WikiLeaks, which, according to its founder Julian Assange, has released more classified documents than the rest of the world's media combined, to keep tabs on governments and corporations. When Assange gave the *Guardian* 250,000 confidential cables, he did so on a USB drive the size of your little finger. Efforts to close down the WikiLeaks website have proven futile, because the files are mirrored on hundreds of other sites. And in any case, WikiLeaks isn't the only site revealing private information. An array of groups are able to release information anonymously. Governments, corporations, and other organizations interested in protecting privacy will strive to increase security, but they will also have to reckon with the likelihood that such measures are sometimes going to fail.

New technology has made greater openness possible, but has this openness made us better off? For those who think privacy is an inalienable right, the modern surveillance culture is a means of controlling behavior and stifling dissent. But perhaps the inspection principle, universally applied, could also be the perfection of democracy, the device that allows us to know what our governments are really doing, that keeps tabs on corporate abuses, and that protects our individual freedoms just as it subjects our personal lives to public scrutiny. In other words, will this technology be a form of tyranny or will it free us from tyranny? Will it upend democracy or strengthen it?

The standards of what we want to keep private and what we want to make public are constantly evolving. Over the course of Western history, we've developed a desire for more privacy, quite possibly as a status symbol, since an impoverished peasant could not afford a house with separate rooms. Today's affluent Americans display their status not only by having a bedroom for each member of the family, plus one for guests, but also by having a bathroom for every bedroom, plus one for visitors so that they do not have to see the family's personal effects. It wasn't always this way. A seventeenth-century Japanese *shunga* depicts a man making love with his wife while their daughter kneels on the floor nearby, practicing calligraphy. The people of Tikopia, a Pacific island inhabited by Polynesians, "find it good to sleep side by side crowding each other, next to their children or their parents or their brothers and sisters, mixing sexes and generations," according to the anthropologist Dorothy Lee. "[A]nd if a widow finds herself alone in her one-room house, she may adopt a child or a brother to allay her intolerable privacy." The Gebusi people in New Guinea live in communal longhouses and are said to "shun privacy," even showing reluctance to look at photos in which they are on their own.

With some social standards, the more people do something, the less risky it becomes for each individual. The first women to wear dresses that did not reach their knees were no doubt looked upon with disapproval, and may have risked unwanted sexual attention; but once many women were revealing more of their legs, the risks dissipated. So too with privacy: when millions of people are prepared to post personal information, doing so becomes less risky for everyone. And those collective, large-scale forfeitures of personal privacy have other benefits as well, as tens of thousands of Egyptians showed when they openly became fans of the Facebook page "We are all Khaled Said," named after a young man who was beaten to death by police in Alexandria. The page became the online hub for the protests that forced the ouster of President Hosni Mubarak.

Whether Facebook and similar sites are reflecting a change in social norms about privacy or are actually driving that change, that half a billion are now on Facebook suggests that people believe the benefits of connecting with others, sharing information, networking, self-promoting, flirting, and bragging outweigh breaches of privacy that accompany such behavior.

More difficult questions arise when the loss of privacy is not in any sense a choice. Bentham's Panopticon has become a symbol of totalitarian intrusion. Michel Foucault described it as "the perfection of power." We all know that the police can obtain phone records when seeking evidence of involvement in a crime, but most of us would be surprised by the frequency of such requests. Verizon alone receives 90,000 demands for information from law-enforcement agencies annually. Abuses have undoubtedly accompanied the recent increase in government surveillance. One glaring example is the case of Brandon Mayfield, an Oregon attorney and convert to Islam who was jailed on suspicion of involvement in the 2004 Madrid train bombings. After his arrest, Mayfield sued the government and persuaded a federal judge to declare the provision of the Patriot Act that the FBI used in investigating him

unconstitutional. But as with most excesses of state power, the cause is not so much the investigative authority of the state as the state's erroneous interpretation of the information it uncovers and the unwarranted detentions that come about as a result. If those same powers were used to foil another 9/11, most Americans would likely applaud.

There is always a danger that the information collected will be misused—whether by regimes seeking to silence opposition or by corporations seeking to profit from more detailed knowledge of their potential customers. The scale and technological sophistication of this data-gathering enterprise allow the government to intercept and store far more information than was possible for secret police of even the most totalitarian states of an earlier era, and the large number of people who have access to sensitive information increases the potential for misuse.[1] As with any large-scale human activity, if enough people are involved eventually someone will do something corrupt or malicious. That's a drawback to having more data gathered, but one that may well be outweighed by the benefits. We don't really know how many terrorist plots have been foiled because of all this data-gathering.[2] We have even less idea how many innocent Americans were initially suspected of terrorism but *not* arrested because the enhanced data-gathering permitted under the Patriot Act convinced law-enforcement agents of their innocence.

The degree to which a government is repressive does not turn on the methods by which it acquires information about its citizens, or the amount of data it retains. When regimes want to harass their opponents or suppress opposition, they find ways to do it, with or without electronic data. Under President Nixon, the administration used tax audits to harass those on his "enemies list." That was mild compared with how "enemies" were handled during the dirty wars in Argentina, Guatemala, and Chile, and by the Stasi in East Germany. These repressive governments "disappeared" tens of thousands of dissidents, and they targeted their political enemies with what now seem impossibly cumbersome methods of collecting, storing, and sorting data. If such forms of abuse are rare in the United States, it is not because we have prevented the state from gathering electronic data about us. The crucial step in preventing a repressive government from misusing information is to have alert and well-informed citizens with a strong sense of right and wrong who work to keep the government democratic, open, just, and under the rule of law. The technological innovations used by governments and corporations to monitor citizens must be harnessed to monitor those very governments and corporations.

One of the first victories for citizen surveillance came in 1991, when George Holliday videotaped Los Angeles police officers beating Rodney King. Without that video, yet another LAPD assault on a black man would have passed unnoticed. Instead, racism and violence in police departments became a national issue, two officers went to prison, and King received $3.8 million in civil damages. Since then, videos and photographs, many of them taken on mobile phones, have captured innumerable crimes and injustices. Inverse surveillance—what Steve Mann, professor of computer engineering and proponent of wearing imaging devices, terms "sousveillance"—has become an effective way of informing the world of abuses of power.

We have seen the usefulness of sousveillance again this year in the Middle East, where the disclosure of thousands of diplomatic cables by WikiLeaks helped encourage the Tunisian and Egyptian revolutions, as well as the protest movements that spread to neighboring countries. Yet most government officials vehemently condemned the disclosure of state secrets. Secretary of State Hillary Clinton claimed that WikiLeaks' revelations "tear at the fabric of the proper function of responsible government." In February of this year, at George Washington University, she went further, saying that WikiLeaks had endangered human rights activists who had been in contact with U.S. diplomats, and rejecting the view that governments should conduct their work in full view of their citizens. As a counterexample, she pointed to U.S. efforts to secure nuclear material in the former Soviet states. Here, she claimed, confidentiality was necessary in order to avoid making it easier for terrorists or criminals to find the materials and steal them.

Clinton is right that it is not a good idea to make public the location of insecurely stored nuclear materials, but how much of diplomacy is like that? There may be some justifiable state secrets, but they certainly are few. For nearly all other dealings between nations, openness should be the norm. In any case, Clinton's claim that WikiLeaks releases documents "without regard for the consequences" is, if not deliberately misleading, woefully ignorant. Assange and his colleagues have consistently stated that they are motivated by a belief that a more transparent government will bring better consequences for all, and that leaking information has an inherent tendency toward greater justice, a view Assange laid out on his blog in December 2006, the month in which WikiLeaks published its first document:

> The more secretive or unjust an organization is, the more leaks induce fear and paranoia in its leadership and planning coterie . . . Since unjust systems, by their nature induce opponents, and in many places barely have the upper hand, leaking leaves them exquisitely vulnerable to those who seek to replace them with more open forms of governance.[3]

Assange could now claim that WikiLeaks' disclosures have confirmed his theory. For instance, in 2007, months before a national election, WikiLeaks posted a report on corruption commissioned but not released by the Kenyan government. According to Assange, a Kenyan intelligence official found that the leaked report changed the minds of 10 percent of Kenyan voters, enough to shift the outcome of the election.

Two years later, in the aftermath of the global financial crisis, WikiLeaks released documents on dealings by Iceland's Kaupthing Bank, showing that the institution made multibillion-dollar loans, in some cases unsecured, to its major shareholders shortly before it collapsed. Kaupthing's successor, then known as New Kaupthing, obtained an injunction to prevent Iceland's national television network from reporting on the leaked documents but failed to prevent their dissemination. WikiLeaks' revelations stirred an uproar in the Icelandic parliament, which then voted unanimously to strengthen free speech and establish an international prize for freedom of expression. Senior officials of the bank are now facing criminal charges.

And of course, in April 2010, WikiLeaks released thirty-eight minutes of classified cockpit-video footage of two U.S. Army helicopters over a Baghdad suburb. The video showed the helicopter crews engaging in an attack on civilians that killed eighteen people, including two Reuters journalists, and wounded two children. Ever since the attack took place, in 2007, Reuters had unsuccessfully sought a U.S. military inquiry into the deaths of its two employees, as well as access to the cockpit video under the Freedom of Information Act. The United States had claimed that the two journalists were killed during a firefight. Although no action has been taken against the soldiers involved, if the military is ever going to exercise greater restraint when civilian lives are at risk, it will have been compelled to do so through the release of material like this.

Months before the Arab Spring began, Assange was asked whether he would release the trove of secret diplomatic cables that he was rumored to have obtained. Assange said he would, and gave this reason: "These sort of things reveal what the true state of, say, Arab governments are like, the true human rights abuses in those governments." As one young Tunisian wrote to the *Guardian,* his countrymen had known for many years that their leaders were corrupt, but that was not the same as reading the full details of particular incidents, rounded off with statements by American diplomats that corruption was keeping domestic investment low and unemployment high. The success of Tunisia's revolution undoubtedly influenced the rest of the Arab world, putting U.S. diplomats in an uncomfortable predicament. A mere three months after condemning WikiLeaks for releasing stolen documents "without regard to the consequences," Secretary Clinton found herself speaking warmly about one of those outcomes: the movement for reform in the Middle East.

WikiLeaks' revelations have had profound ramifications, but as with any event of this scale, it is not easy to judge whether those consequences are, on the whole, desirable. Assange himself admitted to the *Guardian* that as a result of the leaked corruption report in Kenya, and the violence that swept the country during its elections, 1,300 people were killed and 350,000 displaced; but, he added, 40,000 Kenyan children die every year from malaria, and these and many more are dying because of the role corruption plays in keeping Kenyans poor.[4] The Kenyan people, Assange believes, had a right to the information in the leaked report because "decision-making that is based upon lies or ignorance can't lead to a good conclusion."

In making that claim, Assange aligned himself with a widely held view in democratic theory, and a standard argument for freedom of speech: elections can express the will of the people only if the people are reasonably well informed about the issues on which they base their votes. That does not mean that decision-making based on the truth always leads to better outcomes than decision-making based on ignorance. There is no reason for Assange to be committed to that claim, any more than a supporter of democracy must be committed to the claim that democratic forms of government always reach better decisions than authoritarian regimes. Nor does a belief in the benefits of transparency imply that people must know the truth about everything; but it does suggest that more information is generally better, and so provides grounds for a presumption against withholding the truth.

What of Clinton's claims that the leaks have endangered human rights activists who gave information to American diplomats? When WikiLeaks released 70,000 documents about the war in Afghanistan, in July 2010, Admiral Mike Mullen, chairman of the Joint Chiefs of Staff, said that Assange had blood on his hands, yet no casualties resulting from the leaks have been reported—unless you count the ambassadors forced to step down due to embarrassing revelations. Four months after the documents were released, a senior NATO official told CNN that there had not been a single case of an Afghan needing protection because of the leaks. Of course, that may have been "just pure luck," as Daniel Domscheit-Berg, a WikiLeaks defector, told the *New York Times* in February. Assange himself has admitted that he cannot guarantee that the leaks will not cost lives, but in his view the likelihood that they will save lives justifies the risk.

WikiLeaks has never released the kind of information that Clinton pointed to in defending the need for secrecy. Still, there are other groups out there, such as the Russian anti-corruption site Rospil.info, the European Union site BrusselsLeaks, the Czech PirateLeaks, Anonymous, and so on, that release leaked materials with less scrupulousness. It is entirely possible that there will be leaks that everyone will regret. Yet given that the leaked materials on the wars in Afghanistan and Iraq show tens of thousands of civilian lives lost due to the needless, reckless, and even callous actions of members of the U.S. military, it is impossible to listen to U.S. leaders blame WikiLeaks for endangering innocent lives without hearing the tinkle of shattering glass houses.

In the Panopticon, of course, transparency would not be limited to governments. Animal rights advocates have long said that if slaughterhouses had glass walls, more people would become vegetarian, and seeing the factory farms in which most of the meat, eggs, and milk we consume are produced would be more shocking even than the slaughterhouses. And why should restaurant customers have to rely on occasional visits by health inspectors? Webcams in food-preparation areas could provide additional opportunities for checking on the sanitary conditions of the food we are about to eat.

Bentham may have been right when he suggested that if we all knew that we were, at any time, liable to be observed, our morals would be reformed. Melissa Bateson and her colleagues at England's Newcastle University tested this theory when they put a poster with a pair of eyes above a canteen honesty box. People taking a hot drink put almost three times as much money in the box with the eyes present as they did when the eyes were replaced by a poster of flowers. The mere suggestion that someone was watching encouraged greater honesty. (Assuming that the eyes did not lead people to overpay, the study also implies a disturbing level of routine dishonesty.)

We might also become more altruistic. Dale Miller, a professor of organizational behavior at Stanford University, has pointed out that Americans assume a "norm of self-interest" that makes acting altruistically seem odd or even irrational. Yet Americans perform altruistic acts all the time, and bringing those acts to light might break down the norm that curtails our generosity. Consistent with that hypothesis, researchers at the University of Pennsylvania found that people are likely to give more to listener-sponsored radio stations when they are told that other callers are giving above-average donations. Similarly, when utility companies send customers a comparison of their energy use with the average in their neighborhood, customers with above-average use reduce their consumption.

The world before WikiLeaks and Facebook may have seemed a more secure place, but to say whether it was a better world is much more difficult. Will fewer children ultimately die from poverty in Kenya because WikiLeaks released the report on corruption? Will life in the Middle East improve as a result of the revolutions to which WikiLeaks and social media contributed? As the Chinese communist leader Zhou Enlai responded when asked his opinion of the French Revolution of 1789, it is too soon to say. The way we answer the question will depend on whether we share Assange's belief that decision-making leads to better outcomes when based on the truth than when based on lies and ignorance.

Notes

1. Including those involved in international operations relating to homeland security and intelligence, 854,000 people currently hold top-secret security clearances, according to the *Washington Post*.

2. In 2003, FBI director Robert Mueller claimed that the number of thwarted plots was more than one hundred.

3. Robert Manne, a professor of politics at Australia's La Trobe University and the author of a detailed examination of Assange's writings that appeared recently in *The Monthly*,

comments: "There are few original ideas in politics. In the creation of WikiLeaks, Julian Assange was responsible for one."

4. The United Nations claimed that as many as 600,000 Kenyans were displaced after the election.

Critical Thinking

1. What is the author's point of view?

2. What reasons does he offer to support his point of view?

3. What are some specific examples he offers to illustrate his reasons?

4. What are the counter arguments to his point of view?

PETER SINGER is a professor of bioethics at Princeton University and Laureate Professor at the University of Melbourne. His books include *Animal Liberation, Practical Ethics,* and *The Life You Can Save.*

From *Harper's Magazine*, August 2011, pp. 31–36. Copyright © 2011 by Harper's Magazine. Reprinted by permission.

UN Women's Head Michelle Bachelet
A New Superhero?

She wants more female peacekeepers and an end to violence against women. Meet Michelle Bachelet, the former Chilean president and now head of the UN's new women's rights body.

JANE MARTINSON

Let it not be said that those wags at the United Nations don't have a sense of humour. Given the task of finding an office for its new women's rights body, the premises managers found some space in the iconic Daily News building—otherwise known as the home of Superman.

But now, instead of Clark Kent, the world has Michelle Bachelet—taking on the superhuman challenge of redressing gender inequality. Unlike the last son of Krypton, relatively little is known about Bachelet outside her native Chile and the corridors of international diplomacy. And more than 100 days after it was set up, there are still significant questions about UN Women: what exactly will it do, what are its powers, and how it will be financed?

The body takes over from four existing, underfunded and relatively powerless institutions devoted to women's rights, which the UN general council voted to replace after Kofi Annan, former UN secretary general, pointed out "study after study has taught us that there is no tool for development more effective than the empowerment of women". Bachelet, who was Chile's first female head of state, will report directly to the secretary general and should command a start-up budget of $500m (£300m) by 2013, double what was available previously—though only about 1.6% of total UN funding. But just three months in, there are already disappointing signs of foot-dragging by major donors, including the UK.

UN watchers believe Bachelet, however, may have a better chance than most to cajole and bully her way through UN diplomacy. The daughter of an army general who died after months of torture by Augusto Pinochet's forces, Bachelet was herself tortured before being exiled. She then trained as a doctor and returned to Chile. An avowed atheist, her achievements in office include a controversial decree allowing the morning-after pill to be distributed to women older than 14 years of age without parental consent, policies to abolish shanty towns, and daycare for poor children.

In person, this former paediatrician is the opposite of a dry UN bureaucrat. In her first interview to a British newspaper since taking office, she rattles off a list of priorities, ranging from political and economic empowerment to the ending of sexual violence. But first she is apologising, in her fast-paced heavily accented English, for the UN's parsimony with teabags.

"In my country, offering tea is a sign of hospitality," she begins. "In the UN, nothing. You cannot use the money from the UN for that. My God! It's not like I'm going to be offering whisky, you know. Just a cup of tea. Water. Something." Once the team is all together and not in temporary accommodation, she promises to "bring my china cups" and her own tea. Later, she laughs: "I don't mean to change the UN attitude but . . . well, a little bit."

Charming and voluble, she is credited with getting her own way while making relatively few enemies in her home country. (Her approval rating was 84% when she stood down after her presidential term in March 2010.) She will need all her skills of persuasion to convince member states to help her department, some of which place a very low national priority on women's rights.

"I am an optimist," she laughs when asked about the snail-like pace of funding. "My main issue is to have enough arguments to convince [member states] to build capacity." Given such underfunding, she will not be focusing on saving money, but increasing her budget. "We have had scarce investment in women . . . One of my tasks is that everyone spends much more on women."

A woman who took herself off to study military strategy before being elected head of state, her arguments are backed by a wealth of relevant data. In the same breath, she manages to reference a gender study by the World Economic Forum that found greater productivity in countries where women achieved senior positions, and the benefits of a $3m (£1.8m) programme in Liberia to improve conditions of women market traders.

"Just 19% of parliamentarians are women and we are more than half of humanity," she says. "There are 19 female head of states in 192 member states. And just 15 of Fortune 500 chief executives are women. You see we have a problem. Gender equality will only be reached if we are able to empower women."

Sixteen years after the Beijing assembly set a target of 30% women in national parliaments, only 28 countries meet this target. Most of these (23) did so after introducing quotas, a controversial practice that Bachelet makes no bones about supporting. "I am in favour of affirmative action when there is exclusion," she states.

Economic empowerment is high on her agenda and she lays out the huge financial benefit of ending violence against women. "In the US, violence against women costs $5.8bn (£3.5bn) a year in terms of medical costs, loss of productivity and childcare. In Australia they estimated that it cost $A13.6bn (£8.8bn) a year, more than the $10bn (£6.5bn) they spent stimulating economy."

Perhaps the easiest way to understand the five priorities of UN Women—expanding women's leadership; enhancing women's economic empowerment; ending violence against women and girls; bringing women to the centre of the peace and security agenda; focusing national plans and budgets on gender equality—is to think of all the things not necessarily covered by far larger organisations, such as health (WHO), and children (Unicef). However, the new body will also help co-ordinate gender policies at those organisations and, perhaps more importantly, improve accountability.

"We have accountability but we're not going to be the gender police," she says, perhaps hoping to squash any possible resentment felt by those better-funded organisations.

Yet there is work to be done closer to home. UN Women research last year suggested that women made up less than 8% of negotiating teams in 24 peace processes over the past two decades, and she believes women's issues are missing from peace agreements as a result. A survey of 300 peace agreements in 45 conflicts since the end of the cold war found only 18 mentioning sexual and gender violence—even though this has become a widespread violation in modern conflicts.

So Bachelet wants more female peacekeepers and policewomen, pointing out not only that female victims of sexual violence are happier speaking to other women but that "when they [the perpetrators] see women, strong, with arms, they know also that women are not weak".

Keen to start up local outposts to help on the ground, the issue comes back to whether and when donor states are going to cough up. Next month, Bachelet is due to visit London for talks with the government. The Department for International Development was expected to announce its funding commitment earlier this year, but has instead delayed any announcement until the UN Women's strategic plan is unveiled in June. The charity VSO was among those to condemn the move, calling for funding to be announced to help UN Women, "a once-in-a-generation opportunity to end the discrimination and violence that prevents many women worldwide from earning an income, holding political office or giving birth safely".

Zohra Moosa, ActionAid UK women's rights adviser, describes the situation as a catch-22—the money won't be committed until the plans are made but UN Women needs to know the plans can be paid for. So far, only Spain and Norway of the major donor countries have pledged a significant amount. "[The UN] may have a great ambition but where is the matching resource?" asks Moosa. "It may have €33m (£29m) a year from Spain but, let's get real, that's not going to cut it."

As a former head of state, Bachelet is not going to criticise any countries just a few months into the job. "The real owners [of the UN] are the member states. For me, it is easier to understand as I was head of government and I wouldn't have liked to see an agency come to my country and do what they liked."

Ever emollient, she adds: "If we succeed it should mean that the rest of the system should be doing more and better."

It has been more than 30 years since the UN first adopted the Convention on the Elimination of All Forms of Discrimination Against Women, and some would argue that inequality has got worse. Yet Bachelet, in arguing for positive discrimination, believes real change could come. "Maybe one day UN Women won't be necessary because women won't be discriminated against and will be in power. Until then, we need special measures to level the playing field."

Critical Thinking

1. Describe Bachelet's career.
2. What are the five UN priorities for women?

The End of Men

HANNA ROSIN

Earlier this year, women became the majority of the workforce for the first time in U.S. history. Most managers are now women too. And for every two men who get a college degree this year, three women will do the same. For years, women's progress has been cast as a struggle for equality. But what if equality isn't the end point? What if modern, postindustrial society is simply better suited to women? A report on the unprecedented role reversal now under way—along with its vast cultural consequences.

In the 1970s the biologist Ronald Ericsson came up with a way to separate sperm carrying the male-producing Y chromosome from those carrying the X. He sent the two kinds of sperm swimming down a glass tube through ever-thicker albumin barriers. The sperm with the X chromosome had a larger head and a longer tail, and so, he figured, they would get bogged down in the viscous liquid. The sperm with the Y chromosome were leaner and faster and could swim down to the bottom of the tube more efficiently. Ericsson had grown up on a ranch in South Dakota, where he'd developed an Old West, cowboy swagger. The process, he said, was like "cutting out cattle at the gate." The cattle left flailing behind the gate were of course the X's, which seemed to please him. He would sometimes demonstrate the process using cartilage from a bull's penis as a pointer.

In the late 1970s, Ericsson leased the method to clinics around the U.S., calling it the first scientifically proven method for choosing the sex of a child. Instead of a lab coat, he wore cowboy boots and a cowboy hat, and doled out his version of cowboy poetry. (*People* magazine once suggested a TV miniseries based on his life called Cowboy in the Lab.) The right prescription for life, he would say, was "breakfast at five-thirty, on the saddle by six, no room for Mr. Limp Wrist." In 1979, he loaned out his ranch as the backdrop for the iconic "Marlboro Country" ads because he believed in the campaign's central image—"a guy riding on his horse along the river, no bureaucrats, no lawyers," he recalled when I spoke to him this spring. "He's the boss." (The photographers took some 6,500 pictures, a pictorial record of the frontier that Ericsson still takes great pride in.)

Feminists of the era did not take kindly to Ericsson and his Marlboro Man veneer. To them, the lab cowboy and his sperminator portended a dystopia of mass-produced boys. "You have to be concerned about the future of all women," Roberta Steinbacher, a nun-turned-social-psychologist, said in a 1984 *People* profile of Ericsson. "There's no question that there

exists a universal preference for sons." Steinbacher went on to complain about women becoming locked in as "second-class citizens" while men continued to dominate positions of control and influence. "I think women have to ask themselves, 'Where does this stop?'" she said. "A lot of us wouldn't be here right now if these practices had been in effect years ago."

Ericsson, now 74, laughed when I read him these quotes from his old antagonist. Seldom has it been so easy to prove a dire prediction wrong. In the '90s, when Ericsson looked into the numbers for the two dozen or so clinics that use his process, he discovered, to his surprise, that couples were requesting more girls than boys, a gap that has persisted, even though Ericsson advertises the method as more effective for producing boys. In some clinics, Ericsson has said, the ratio is now as high as 2 to 1. Polling data on American sex preference is sparse, and does not show a clear preference for girls. But the picture from the doctor's office unambiguously does. A newer method for sperm selection, called MicroSort, is currently completing Food and Drug Administration clinical trials. The girl requests for that method run at about 75 percent.

Even more unsettling for Ericsson, it has become clear that in choosing the sex of the next generation, he is no longer the boss. "It's the women who are driving all the decisions," he says—a change the MicroSort spokespeople I met with also mentioned. At first, Ericsson says, women who called his clinics would apologize and shyly explain that they already had two boys. "Now they just call and [say] outright, 'I want a girl.'" These mothers look at their lives and think their daughters will have a bright future their mother and grandmother didn't have, brighter than their sons, even, so why wouldn't you choose a girl?"

Why wouldn't you choose a girl? That such a statement should be so casually uttered by an old cowboy like Ericsson—or by anyone, for that matter—is monumental. For nearly as long as civilization has existed, patriarchy—enforced through the rights of the firstborn son—has been the organizing principle, with few exceptions. Men in ancient Greece tied off their left testicle in an effort to produce male heirs; women have killed themselves (or been killed) for failing to bear sons. In her iconic 1949 book, *The Second Sex*, the French feminist Simone de Beauvoir suggested that women so detested their own "feminine condition" that they regarded their newborn daughters with irritation and disgust. Now the centuries-old preference for sons is eroding—or even reversing. "Women of our generation want daughters precisely because we like who we are," breezes one woman in *Cookie* magazine. Even Ericsson, the stubborn old goat, can sigh and mark the passing of an era. "Did male dominance exist? Of course it existed. But it seems to be gone now. And the era of the firstborn son is totally gone."

Ericsson's extended family is as good an illustration of the rapidly shifting landscape as any other. His 26-year-old granddaughter—"tall, slender, brighter than hell, with a take-no-prisoners personality"—is a biochemist and works on genetic sequencing. His niece studied civil engineering at the University of Southern California. His grandsons, he says, are bright and handsome, but in school "their eyes glaze over. I have to tell 'em: 'Just don't screw up and crash your pickup truck and get some girl pregnant and ruin your life.'" Recently Ericsson joked with the old boys at his elementary-school reunion that he was going to have a sex-change operation. "Women live longer than men. They do better in this economy. More of 'em graduate from college. They go into space and do everything men do, and sometimes they do it a whole lot better. I mean, hell, get out of the way—these females are going to leave us males in the dust."

Man has been the dominant sex since, well, the dawn of mankind. But for the first time in human history, that is changing—and with shocking speed. Cultural and economic changes always reinforce each other. And the global economy is evolving in a way that is eroding the historical preference for male children, worldwide. Over several centuries, South Korea, for instance, constructed one of the most rigid patriarchal societies in the world. Many wives who failed to produce male heirs were abused and treated as domestic servants; some families prayed to spirits to kill off girl children. Then, in the 1970s and '80s, the government embraced an industrial revolution and encouraged women to enter the labor force. Women moved to the city and went to college. They advanced rapidly, from industrial jobs to clerical jobs to professional work. The traditional order began to crumble soon after. In 1990, the country's laws were revised so that women could keep custody of their children after a divorce and inherit property. In 2005, the court ruled that women could register children under their own names. As recently as 1985, about half of all women in a national survey said they "must have a son." That percentage fell slowly until 1991 and then plummeted to just over 15 percent by 2003. Male preference in South Korea "is over," says Monica Das Gupta, a demographer and Asia expert at the World Bank. "It happened so fast. It's hard to believe it, but it is." The same shift is now beginning in other rapidly industrializing countries such as India and China.

Up to a point, the reasons behind this shift are obvious. As thinking and communicating have come to eclipse physical strength and stamina as the keys to economic success, those societies that take advantage of the talents of all their adults, not just half of them, have pulled away from the rest. And because geopolitics and global culture are, ultimately, Darwinian, other societies either follow suit or end up marginalized. In 2006, the Organization for Economic Cooperation and Development devised the Gender, Institutions and Development Database, which measures the economic and political power of women in 162 countries. With few exceptions, the greater the power of women, the greater the country's economic success. Aid agencies have started to recognize this relationship and have pushed to institute political quotas in about 100 countries, essentially forcing women into power in an effort to improve those countries' fortunes. In some war-torn states, women are stepping in as a sort of maternal rescue team. Liberia's president, Ellen Johnson Sirleaf, portrayed her country as a sick child in need of her care during her campaign five years ago. Postgenocide Rwanda elected to heal itself by becoming the first country with a majority of women in parliament.

In feminist circles, these social, political, and economic changes are always cast as a slow, arduous form of catch-up in a continuing struggle for female equality. But in the U.S., the world's most advanced economy, something much more remarkable seems to be happening. American parents are beginning to choose to have girls over boys. As they imagine the pride of watching a child grow and develop and succeed as an adult, it is more often a girl that they see in their mind's eye.

What if the modern, postindustrial economy is simply more congenial to women than to men? For a long time, evolutionary psychologists have claimed that we are all imprinted with adaptive imperatives from a distant past: men are faster and stronger and hardwired to fight for scarce resources, and that shows up now as a drive to win on Wall Street; women are programmed to find good providers and to care for their offspring, and that is manifested in more-nurturing and more-flexible behavior, ordaining them to domesticity. This kind of thinking frames our sense of the natural order. But what if men and women were fulfilling not biological imperatives but social roles, based on what was more efficient throughout a long era of human history? What if that era has now come to an end? More to the point, what if the economics of the new era are better suited to women?

Once you open your eyes to this possibility, the evidence is all around you. It can be found, most immediately, in the wreckage of the Great Recession, in which three-quarters of the 8 million jobs lost were lost by men. The worst-hit industries were overwhelmingly male and deeply identified with macho: construction, manufacturing, high finance. Some of these jobs will come back, but the overall pattern of dislocation is neither temporary nor random. The recession merely revealed—and accelerated—a profound economic shift that has been going on for at least 30 years, and in some respects even longer.

Earlier this year, for the first time in American history, the balance of the workforce tipped toward women, who now hold a majority of the nation's jobs. The working class, which has long defined our notions of masculinity, is slowly turning into a matriarchy, with men increasingly absent from the home and women making all the decisions. Women dominate today's colleges and professional schools—for every two men who will receive a B.A. this year, three women will do the same. Of the 15 job categories projected to grow the most in the next decade in the U.S., all but two are occupied primarily by women. Indeed, the U.S. economy is in some ways becoming a kind of traveling sisterhood: upper-class women leave home and enter the workforce, creating domestic jobs for other women to fill.

The postindustrial economy is indifferent to men's size and strength. The attributes that are most valuable today—social intelligence, open communication, the ability to sit still and focus—are, at a minimum, not predominantly male. In fact, the opposite may be true. Women in poor parts of India are learning English faster than men to meet the demands of new global call centers. Women own more than 40 percent of private businesses in China, where a red Ferrari is the new status symbol for female entrepreneurs. Last year, Iceland elected Prime Minister Johanna Sigurdardottir, the world's first openly lesbian head of state, who campaigned explicitly against the male elite she claimed had destroyed the nation's banking system, and who vowed to end the "age of testosterone."

Yes, the U.S. still has a wage gap, one that can be convincingly explained—at least in part—by discrimination. Yes, women still do most of the child care. And yes, the upper reaches of society are still dominated by men. But given the power of the forces pushing at the economy, this setup feels like the last gasp of a dying age rather than the permanent establishment. Dozens of college women I interviewed for this story assumed that they very well might be the ones working while their husbands stayed at home, either looking for work or minding the children. Guys, one senior remarked to me, "are the new ball and chain." It may be happening slowly and unevenly, but it's unmistakably happening: in the long view, the modern economy is becoming a place where women hold the cards.

Dozens of college women I interviewed assumed that they very well might be the ones working while their husbands stayed at home. Guys, one senior remarked to me, "Are the new ball and chain."

In his final book, *The Bachelors' Ball,* published in 2007, the sociologist Pierre Bourdieu describes the changing gender dynamics of Beam, the region in southwestern France where he grew up. The eldest sons once held the privileges of patrimonial loyalty and filial inheritance in Beam. But over the decades, changing economic forces turned those privileges into curses. Although the land no longer produced the impressive income it once had, the men felt obligated to tend it. Meanwhile, modern women shunned farm life, lured away by jobs and adventure in the city. They occasionally returned for the traditional balls, but the men who awaited them had lost their prestige and become unmarriageable. This is the image that keeps recurring to me, one that Bourdieu describes in his book: at the bachelors' ball, the men, self-conscious about their diminished status, stand stiffly, their hands by their sides, as the women twirl away.

Men dominate just two of the 15 job categories projected to grow the most over the next decade: janitor and computer engineer. Women have everything else—nursing, home health assistance, child care, food preparation. Many of the new jobs, says Heather Boushey of the Center for American Progress, "replace the things that women used to do in the home for free." None is especially high-paying. But the steady accumulation of these jobs adds up to an economy that, for the working class, has become more amenable to women than to men.

The list of growing jobs is heavy on nurturing professions, in which women, ironically, seem to benefit from old stereotypes and habits. Theoretically, there is no reason men should not be qualified. But they have proved remarkably unable to adapt. Over the course of the past century, feminism has pushed women to do things once considered against their nature—first enter the workforce as singles, then continue to work while married, then work even with small children at home. Many professions that started out as the province of men are now filled mostly with women—secretary and teacher come to mind. Yet I'm not aware of any that have gone the opposite way. Nursing schools have tried hard to recruit men in the past few years, with minimal success. Teaching schools, eager to recruit male role models, are having a similarly hard time. The range of acceptable masculine roles has changed comparatively little, and has perhaps even narrowed as men have shied away from some careers women have entered. As Jessica Grose wrote in *Slate,* men seem "fixed in cultural aspic." And with each passing day, they lag further behind.

As we recover from the Great Recession, some traditionally male jobs will return—men are almost always harder-hit than women in economic downturns because construction and manufacturing are more cyclical than service industries—but that won't change the long-term trend. When we look back on this period, argues Jamie Ladge, a business professor at Northeastern University, we will see it as a "turning point for women in the workforce."

When we look back at this period we will see it as a "Turning point for women in the workforce."

The economic and cultural power shift from men to women would be hugely significant even if it never extended beyond working-class America. But women are also starting to dominate middle management, and a surprising number of professional careers as well. According to the Bureau of Labor Statistics, women now hold 51.4 percent of managerial and professional jobs—up from 26.1 percent in 1980. They make up 54 percent of all accountants and hold about half of all banking and insurance jobs. About a third of America's physicians are now women, as are 45 percent of associates in law firms—and both those percentages are rising fast. A white-collar economy values raw intellectual horsepower, which men and women have in equal amounts. It also requires communication skills and social intelligence, areas in which women, according to many studies, have a slight edge. Perhaps most important—for better or worse—it increasingly requires formal education credentials, which women are more prone to acquire, particularly early in adulthood. Just about the only professions in which women still make up a relatively small minority of newly minted workers are engineering and those calling on a hard-science background, and even in those areas, women have made strong gains since the 1970s.

Near the top of the jobs pyramid, of course, the upward march of women stalls. Prominent female CEOs, past and present, are so rare that they count as minor celebrities, and most of us can tick off their names just from occasionally reading the business pages: Meg Whitman at eBay, Carly Fiorina at Hewlett-Packard, Anne Mulcahy and Ursula Burns at Xerox, Indra Nooyi at PepsiCo; the accomplishment is considered so extraordinary that Whitman and Fiorina are using it as the basis for political campaigns. Only 3 percent of Fortune 500 CEOs are women, and the number has never risen much above that.

But even the way this issue is now framed reveals that men's hold on power in elite circles may be loosening. In business circles, the lack of women at the top is described as a "brain drain" and a crisis of "talent retention." And while female CEOs may be rare in America's largest companies, they are highly prized: last year, they outearned their male counterparts by 43 percent, on average, and received bigger raises.

If you really want to see where the world is headed, of course, looking at the current workforce can get you only so far. To see the future—of the workforce, the economy, and the culture—you need to spend some time at America's colleges and professional schools, where a quiet revolution is under way. More than ever, college is the gateway to economic success, a necessary precondition for moving into the upper-middle class—and increasingly even the middle class. It's this broad, striving middle class that defines our society. And demographically, we can see with absolute clarity that in the coming decades the middle class will be dominated by women.

We've all heard about the collegiate gender gap. But the implications of that gap have not yet been fully digested. Women now earn 60 percent of master's degrees, about half of all law and medical degrees, and 42 percent of all M.B.A.s. Most important, women earn almost 60 percent of all bachelor's degrees—the minimum requirement, in most cases, for an affluent life. In a stark reversal since the 1970s, men are now more likely than women to hold only a high-school diploma. "One would think that if men were acting in a rational way, they would be getting the education they need to get along out there," says Tom Mortenson, a senior scholar at the Pell Institute for the Study of Opportunity in Higher Education. "But they are just failing to adapt."

Since the 1980s, as women have flooded colleges, male enrollment has grown far more slowly. And the disparities start before college. Throughout the '90s, various authors and researchers agonized over why boys seemed to be failing at every level of education, from elementary school on up, and identified various culprits: a misguided feminism that treated normal boys as incipient harassers (Christina Hoff Sommers); different brain chemistry (Michael Gurian); a demanding, verbally focused curriculum that ignored boys' interests (Richard Whitmire). But again, it's not all that clear that boys have become more dysfunctional—or have changed in any way. What's clear is that schools, like the economy, now value the self-control, focus, and verbal aptitude that seem to come more easily to young girls.

Researchers have suggested any number of solutions. A movement is growing for more all-boys schools and classes, and for respecting the individual learning styles of boys. Some people think that boys should be able to walk around in class, or take more time on tests, or have tests and books that cater to their interests. In their desperation to reach out to boys, some colleges have formed football teams and started engineering programs. Most of these special accommodations sound very much like the kind of affirmative action proposed for women over the years—which in itself is an alarming flip.

Whether boys have changed or not, we are well past the time to start trying some experiments. It is fabulous to see girls and young women poised for success in the coming years. But allowing generations of boys to grow up feeling rootless and obsolete is not a recipe for a peaceful future. Men have few natural support groups and little access to social welfare; the men's-rights groups that do exist in the U.S. are taking on an angry, antiwoman edge. Marriages fall apart or never happen at all, and children are raised with no fathers. Far from being celebrated, women's rising power is perceived as a threat.

In fact, the more women dominate, the more they behave, fittingly, like the dominant sex. Rates of violence committed by middle-aged women have skyrocketed since the 1980s, and no one knows why. High-profile female killers have been showing up regularly in the news: Amy Bishop, the homicidal Alabama professor; Jihad Jane and her sidekick, Jihad Jamie; the latest generation of Black Widows, responsible for suicide bombings in Russia. In Roman Polanski's *The Ghost Writer*, the traditional political wife is rewritten as a cold-blooded killer at the heart of an evil conspiracy. In her recent video *Telephone*, Lady Gaga, with her infallible radar for the cultural edge, rewrites Thelma and Louise as a story not about elusive female empowerment but about sheer, ruthless power. Instead of killing themselves, she and her girlfriend (played by Beyoncé) kill a bad boyfriend and random others in a homicidal spree and then escape in their yellow pickup truck, Gaga bragging, "We did it, Honey B."

The Marlboro Man, meanwhile, master of wild beast and wild country, seems too farfetched and preposterous even for advertising. His modern equivalents are the stunted men in the Dodge Charger ad that ran during this year's Super Bowl in February. Of all the days in the year, one might think, Super Bowl Sunday should be the one most dedicated to the cinematic celebration of macho. The men in Super Bowl ads should be throwing balls and racing motorcycles and doing whatever it is men imagine they could do all day if only women were not around to restrain them.

Instead, four men stare into the camera, unsmiling, not moving except for tiny blinks and sways. They look like they've been tranquilized, like they can barely hold themselves up against the breeze. Their lips do not move, but a voice-over explains their predicament—how they've been beaten silent by the demands of tedious employers and enviro-fascists and women. Especially women. "I will put the seat down, I will separate the recycling, I will carry your lip balm." This last one—lip balm—is expressed with the mildest spit of emotion, the only hint of the suppressed rage against the dominatrix. Then the commercial abruptly cuts to the fantasy, a Dodge Charger vrooming toward the camera punctuated by bold all caps: MAN'S LAST STAND. But the motto is unconvincing. After that display of muteness and passivity, you can only imagine a woman—one with shiny lips—steering the beast.

Critical Thinking

1. What is Hanna Rosin's point of view?
2. What is a patriarchal society?
3. Why does Rosin argue that a modern economy advantages women over men?
4. How does this article complement/contradict Article 45?
5. Do the authors of Article 1 give sufficient attention to changing gender roles in their alternative future scenarios?

HANNA ROSIN is an Atlantic contributing editor and the co-editor of DoubleX.

From *The Atlantic* by Hanna Rosin, July/August 2010, pp. 56–58, 60, 62–66, 68, 70, 72. Copyright © 2010 by Atlantic Monthly Group. Reprinted by permission of Hanna Rosin and Tribune Media Services.

Test-Your-Knowledge Form

We encourage you to photocopy and use this page as a tool to assess how the articles in *Annual Editions* expand on the information in your textbook. By reflecting on the articles you will gain enhanced text information. You can also access this useful form on a product's book support website at www.mhhe.com/cls.

NAME:

DATE:

TITLE AND NUMBER OF ARTICLE:

BRIEFLY STATE THE MAIN IDEA OF THIS ARTICLE:

LIST THREE IMPORTANT FACTS THAT THE AUTHOR USES TO SUPPORT THE MAIN IDEA:

WHAT INFORMATION OR IDEAS DISCUSSED IN THIS ARTICLE ARE ALSO DISCUSSED IN YOUR TEXTBOOK OR OTHER READINGS THAT YOU HAVE DONE? LIST THE TEXTBOOK CHAPTERS AND PAGE NUMBERS:

LIST ANY EXAMPLES OF BIAS OR FAULTY REASONING THAT YOU FOUND IN THE ARTICLE:

LIST ANY NEW TERMS/CONCEPTS THAT WERE DISCUSSED IN THE ARTICLE, AND WRITE A SHORT DEFINITION:

NOTES

NOTES

NOTES

NOTES

NOTES

NOTES